In Step with the Times

# NEW AFRICAN HISTORIES

SERIES EDITORS: JEAN ALLMAN, ALLEN ISAACMAN, AND DEREK R. PETERSON

*Books in this series are published with support from the
Ohio University National Resource Center for African Studies.*

# In Step with the Times

## Mapiko Masquerades of Mozambique

∽

Paolo Israel

OHIO UNIVERSITY PRESS ∽ ATHENS, OHIO

Ohio UniversityPress, Athens, Ohio 45701
ohioswallow.com
© 2014 by Ohio University Press

To obtain permission to quote, reprint, or otherwise reproduce or distribute
material from Ohio University Press publications, please contact our rights
and permissions department at (740) 593-1154 or (740) 593-4536 (fax).

Printed in the United States of America
Ohio University Press books are printed on acid-free paper ⊗ ™

24 23 22 21 20 19 18 17 16 15 14   5 4 3 2 1

*Library of Congress Cataloging-in-Publication Data*
Israel, Paolo, author.
In step with the times : mapiko masquerades of Mozambique / Paolo Israel.
    pages cm. — (New African histories)
Includes bibliographical references and index.
ISBN 978-0-8214-2088-1 (pb : alk. paper) — ISBN 978-0-8214-4486-3 (pdf)
1. Mapiko (Dance drama)—History—20th century. 2. Masks, Makonde—
History—20th century. 3. Makonde (African people)—Rites and
ceremonies. 4. Makonde (African people)—Social life and customs. 5.
Mozambique—Social life and customs. I. Title. II. Series: New African
histories series.
PN3000.M85I87 2014
394'.3—dc23

                    2014009787

Time is invention or it is nothing at all

—Henri Bergson, *L'évolution créatrice*

# Contents

# Illustrations

# Acknowledgments

| | |
|---|---|
| Madyoko | You, kids |
| Amunapikiti' ingangoshi | Don't play with the cashew tree |
| Au mwitu ukumene | That is a mighty bush |
| Aulima bila ukave' na tupa | You won't farm it without a file |
| Vana vawme mama | The mothers' sons |
| Nelo vandikoma Uhuru | Today struck their Independence |
| Vanguvalenge mushu mwangu | They told me my future |
| Lidengo vandishukuru | They thanked for the work |

—Mpambe, "Amunapikiti' ingangoshi," Atata, 2011

This project grew in a tangle of places and tongues: across four countries, three continents, and five languages. It began as a doctorate at the Ecole des Hautes Etudes en Sciences Sociales in Paris, where I was attracted to the anthropology of art through the conjoined influence of Jean-Loup Amselle, Brigitte Derlon, Bogumil Jewsiewicki, and Johannes Fabian. A doctoral research grant from the Ecole (2001–4) and a welfare unemployment subsidy (2005–6) allowed me respectively to carry out research and write it up. Throughout this period I enjoyed a head-spinning freedom—my supervisor Amselle always reminded me, "Vous faîtes ce que vous voulez"—that allowed me to stay almost three years on the field. The Doctoral Workshop of the Center for African Studies provided a friendly and engaging platform to connect back with academia after the time spent under the mango trees. Sofie Manus enlightened me about tones and Simakonde; from nearby London, Harry West provided steady support and stimulation.

In Mozambique, Vicente Muanga made me dream of the Makonde Plateau and its masks; Atanásio Cosme Nhussi brought me there, taught me how to live and do research, and set my intellectual agenda by remarking that "they call it traditional dance, but this is our contemporary." I was drawn to the district of Muidumbe on account of its renown for masking creativity; I was kept there by Pedro Justino Seguro and *mama* Josina Ntambudyange, who opened the doors of their house and memories and let me build my improved hut on the lands of the Vanang'alolo. I shared the joys of the road with Mario Malyamungu Matias and Evaristo Angelina Januário—only the angels know how far we went. Fidel Suka Mbalale joined us when he could, busy as he was with studying, but has been ever since present with his linguistics. Too many are the people to be thanked in Muidumbe—elders and youths who shared a story, a song, an *igoli*, a smile. Let me mention specifically Antonio Baccarelli, who lent me his lions; Sandra Lourenço, who gave meaning to the hut; and Gerónimo Mussa Katembe, my favorite district director of culture. In Pemba, Sonja Cappello and Beto Massinga provided comfort and conversation; Estevão Jaime Mpalume and Marcelino Ding'ano oriented me in the mazes of national culture. In Maputo, Gianfranco Gandolfo shared his knowledge of Makonde art; Valério Mwale made me feel at home in the military neighborhood; and Pascoal Mbundi kept my spirits up. The Companhia Nacional de Canto e Dança, the Arquivo do Patrimonio Cultural, and the Cabo Delgado Provincial Directorate of Culture provided invaluable institutional support.

My dissertation over, I ended up in Cape Town. Love brought me there, but the University of the Western Cape turned out to be the best intellectual environment, both near and far from what I had to think and write. Premesh Lalu put me back on track; the Centre for Humanities Research offered me generous Ford and Mellon postdoctoral fellowships (2008–10) and an electric environment of intellectual stupefaction. Ciraj Rassool and Leslie Witz taught me how to masquerade as a historian. Patricia Hayes made me think about War and the Everyday and Love and Revolution; she also explained that "you need to learn to say no if you want to finish a book." Colleagues at the History Department and CHR fellows provided stimulation, support, and friendship; Ruth Lowenthal was the least-intrusive editor; Rui Assubuji shared the Muidumbe fever; Zukiswa Mona made it possible for me to write on the leather couch of the living room, in a house blessed with the presence of a growing baby.

While I never set foot in the United States in the past twenty years, established networks of solidarity and intellectual exchange made my manuscript land on that side of the Atlantic; I found in Allen Isaacman, Gill Berchowitz, and Jean Allman most supportive editors.

The seed of this project, however, lies back in Italy where I was born. It was my mother who brought me to Mozambique, Anna Maria Gentili and Enrico Luzzati who instilled the desire to work there. Pietro Clemente showed me early on the importance of Bateson. My father taught me determination and the need for intellectual distance. My in-laws offered peaceful hours of reading and writing in their country house.

Throughout these spaces and tongues, my wife, Annachiara, was there with love, patience, and innumerable insights. Without her, I would have ended up a slave pasturing goats in the hamlet of Yangua.

The following persons provided important commentary on draft chapters: Jimi Adesina, Edward Alpers, Kelly Askew, Andrew Bank, Liazzat Bonate, Cesare Casarino, Ruchi Chaturvedi, Jean Comaroff, David Coplan, Colin Darch, Jacques Depelchin, Uma Duphelia-Mesthrie, Carlos Fernandes, Jung Ran Forte, Josephine Frater, Rebecca Gearhart, Euclides Gonçalves, Liz Gunner, Pamila Gupta, Patricia Hayes, Allen Isaacman, Qadri Ismail, Ivan Karp, Zachary Kingdon, Corinne Kratz, Sanjay Krishnan, Premesh Lalu, Riedwaan Moosage, Olusegun Morakinyo, Neo Muyanga, Michael Neocosmos, Okechuku Nwafor, Steve Ouma, Tanja Petrovic, Brian Raftopolous, Ciraj Rassool, Steven Robbins, Fernando Rosa Ribeiro, Jane Taylor, Joel Das Neves Tembe, Drew Thompson, Kaingu Kalume Tinga, Daria Trentini, Harry West, Leslie Witz, Valdemir Zamparoni, and the two anonymous readers.

As the formula goes, all mistakes are mine. If I have forgotten you, *pole.*

# Note on Language

In transcribing the Shimakonde texts that punctuate this book I have respected the orthographic convention laid out by the NELIMO (Núcleo de Estudo das Linguas Moçambicanas). I have thus agreed to the principle—questionable, if justified by prosody and tonology—of aggregating to the noun the connexive prefix of adjectival constructions, instead of separating it (as it occurs in Kiswahili). Thus, I write *shinu shakukamadyanga* ("thing of being-complex," a complex thing) instead of *shinu sha kukamadyanga*. I also "Makondize" Kiswahili words when the users mix the two languages (for instance, conjugating a Swahili root with Makonde verbal prefixes).

Makonde orthography is not completely stabilized, and I sometimes had to decide on the spelling of individual words on shaky grounds. For instance, the word for *ghost* can be spelled as *lioka* or *liyoka*, and it is mistakenly spelled as *lihoka* in colonial-era texts; both *shitengamato* and *shitengamatu* are used in the literature to refer to women's clay masks; and *neijale, nijale,* and *naijale* could all have been used to refer to the large-eared mask-character. Seeking advice from speakers was often inconclusive: for instance, three Makonde persons, all knowledgeable on cultural matters, could not agree on whether it should be *shitengamato* or *shitengamatu*; I finally chose the latter on account of etymological considerations.

I have introduced one alteration of my own: I hyphenate names of places, in order to capitalize the name itself and not the prefix, which might be variable. So, I write *kuna-Ntumbati* and *pana-Ntumbati* and not *Kunantumbati* and *Panantumbati*, as well as *ku-Mweda* and *pa-Mweda* and not *Kumweda* and *Pamweda*. Following common usage, however, in case of proper names I put the capital on the class prefix rather than on the name itself, that is, *Vanantumbati* (the Ntumbati people) and not *vana-Ntumbati*, *Vamweda* and not *va-Mweda*, *Shimakonde* and not *shi-Makonde* or *shiMakonde*.

The transcription and translation of Makonde texts was carried out with the help of various persons—especially Evaristo "Angelina" Januário, Fidel Suka Mbalale, Vicente Muanga, Atanásio Nhussi, Pascoal Mbundi, and Mateo Kajanja. While each translation was checked with at least two persons, who sometimes suggested different turns of phrase, I bear the final responsibility for stylistic choices. All translations from Portuguese are my own.

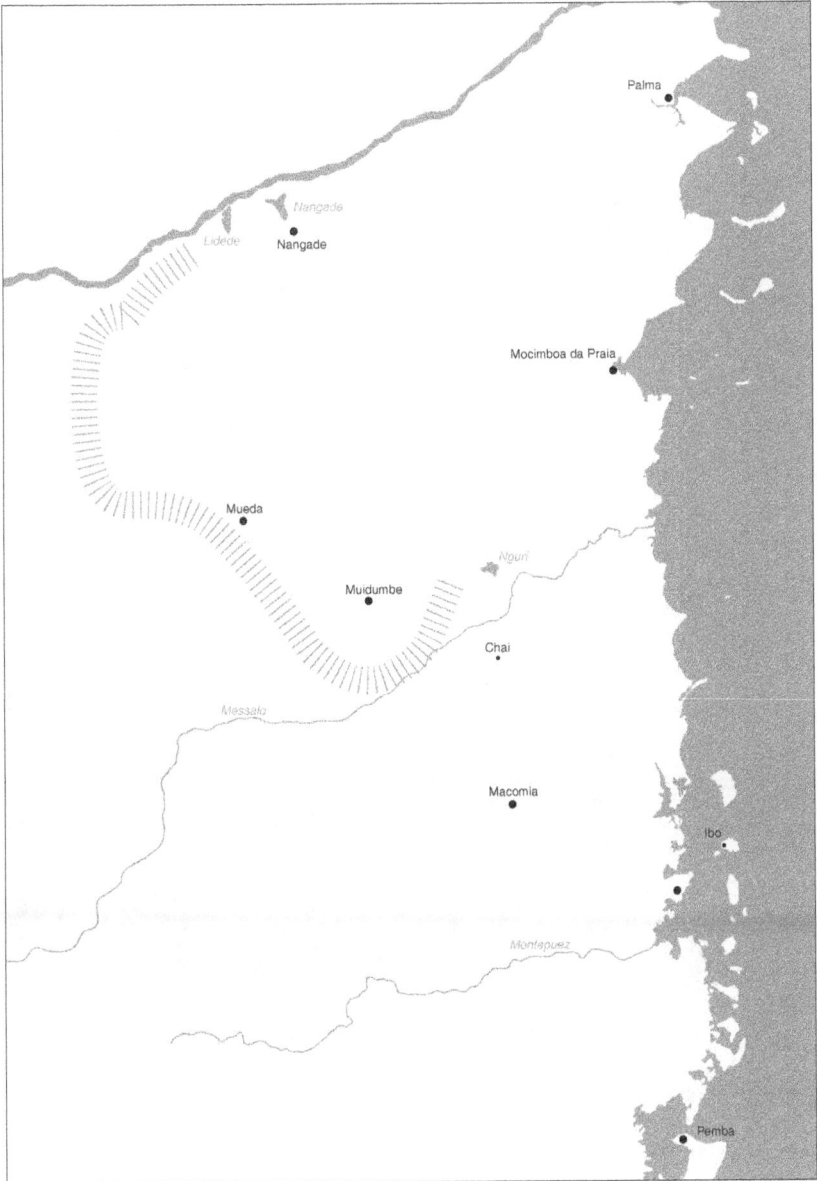

MAP 1. The Makonde Plateau *(map by Sabina Favaro)*

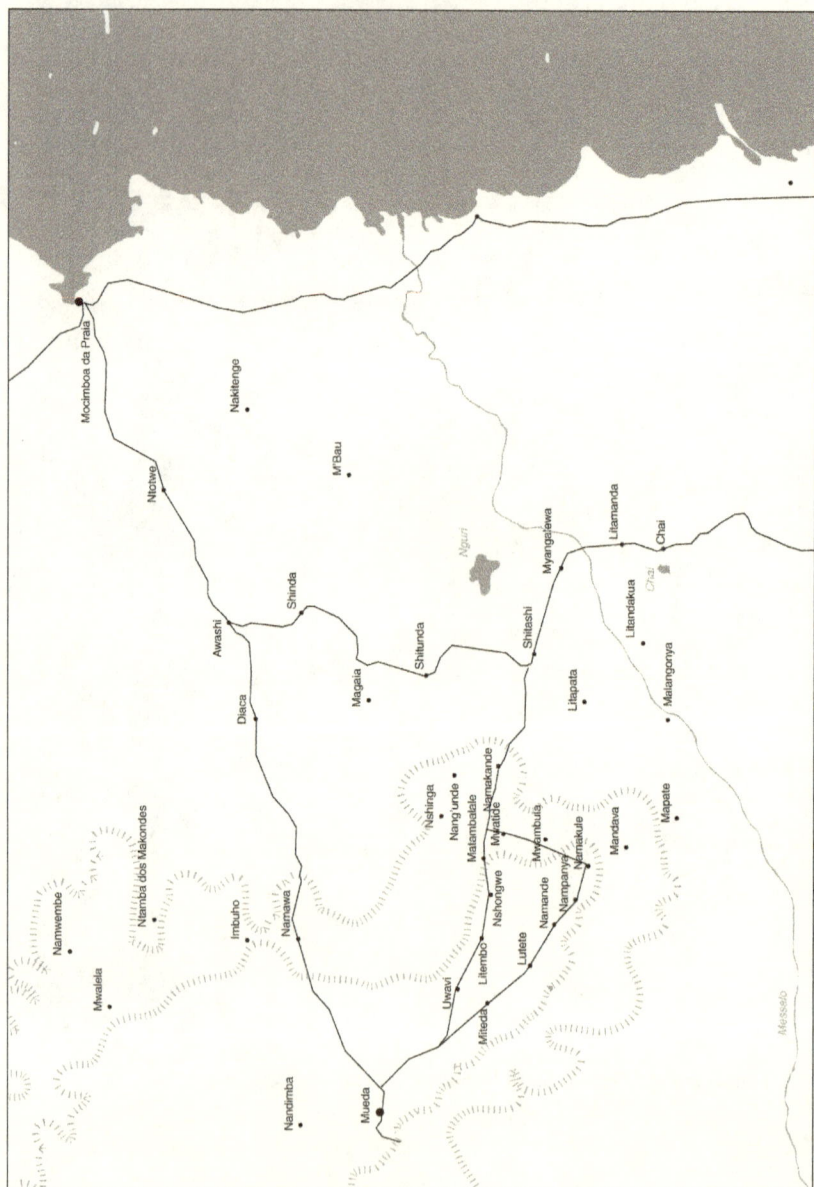

MAP 2. Muidumbe, the Messalo, and the Iyanga Plains *(map by Sabina Favaro)*

INTRODUCTION

# Rhythms of Change

| | |
|---|---|
| Namakule leka aikele Marikano | If in Namakule stayed the Americans |
| Vilambo uti vyapanda | In all countries abroad |
| Ikandyumanga ishipa yashimapiko | Mapiko's fame would expand |
| Tundamanyia mavetu | We tell you, my friends |
| Wetu tundiwika | We have arrived |
| Amunatulole liu lyankondo | Don't look askance at us |
| Wetu tuvamapiko | We are mapiko people |

—NMA/Nshesho/Namakule/2004

1. ON THE threshold of the third millennium, an elderly rice culti-
vator from the northern Mozambican district of Muidumbe focused
his creative energies on matters of masquerading and endeavored to
think something new. He sought inspiration in the past. He recalled
the time in his youth when he had seen a contest between the masters
Nampyopyo and Shumu, which had dragged on for days. He could
still picture the *Germans* taking their hats off to salute, *Smoke's* huge
head puffing white fumes, the *Prostitutes* with their smooth pregnant
bellies, the heavy *Buffalo* pissing and charging; he could still hear the
drums moaning, the horns blowing, and the songs calling the masks'
names. Throughout his lifetime, he had seen the ancestral masks
being ceaselessly reinvented. Shumu, Nampyopyo, and the other
old masters had died, together with their characters; a new generation had cultivated aesthetic abstraction and athletic perfection; the
national liberation struggle had brought realism, unity, and political
watchwords; the demise of socialism had left behind disorderly tattered beasts roaming the villages thirsty for money. Drums had come;
drums had gone. Time and again, youths and elders alike had shaken

off the old and tried out the new. Time and again, called by the blast of antelope horns, dancers had gathered under the leafy roof of the mango trees, warmed up their drums on crackling burning straw, intoned songs of defiance, and challenged their rivals with tricks and styles. What would the new millennium bring about? The elder sat in the large veranda of the house that he had built on the main road of the communal village, looked at an old tire lying in the courtyard crammed with work materials, and smiled.

2. This study is a microhistory of mapiko masquerades of the northern Mozambican Makonde. It reconstructs in great detail the transformations of a single tradition over a relatively short period of time (ca. 1920–2010), exploring its changing aesthetics and practice, the thought and personalities of its protagonists, and its relevance as an idiom of collective consciousness.

*Mapiko* masks are carved in wild kapok (*ntene*)—a tropical wood that is soft to the knife when wet and featherlight when dry—in such a way as to resemble a head.[1] They are worn like a helmet, covering the head to the nape. The dancer watches through the mask's mouth and inclines the head downward to give the illusion that its half-closed eyes gaze and flicker (fig. 1). Painted in natural colors—ochre, gray, brown, yellow, silver, and black—they represent human, animal, or fantastic figures, both men and women, Makonde and not. Their aesthetics is marked by a double inclination to naturalistic perfection and grotesque exaggeration: here embodying the elegant features of a beautiful woman or a hieratic elder; there indulging in protruding eyes, large ears, bumpy foreheads, or menacing teeth. This "grotesque head" allure might account for mapiko's rather modest fortune on the international tribal commodity market, for, as an amateur collector in Mozambique once remarked, "Who wants to put a dead man's head on their dining room table?"[2]

But mapiko were not meant to be appreciated as still objects. The word itself covers a different semantic spectrum than the English *mask*.[3] Etymologically, it is linked to the verb *kupika*, alluding to the transformation of a sorcerer into a magical beast. The plural form *mapiko* refers to the dance of masks, which occurs to the rhythm of drums and songs; the singular *lipiko*, to the dancer-spirit, once his body is completely covered in a costume of which the wooden headpiece is

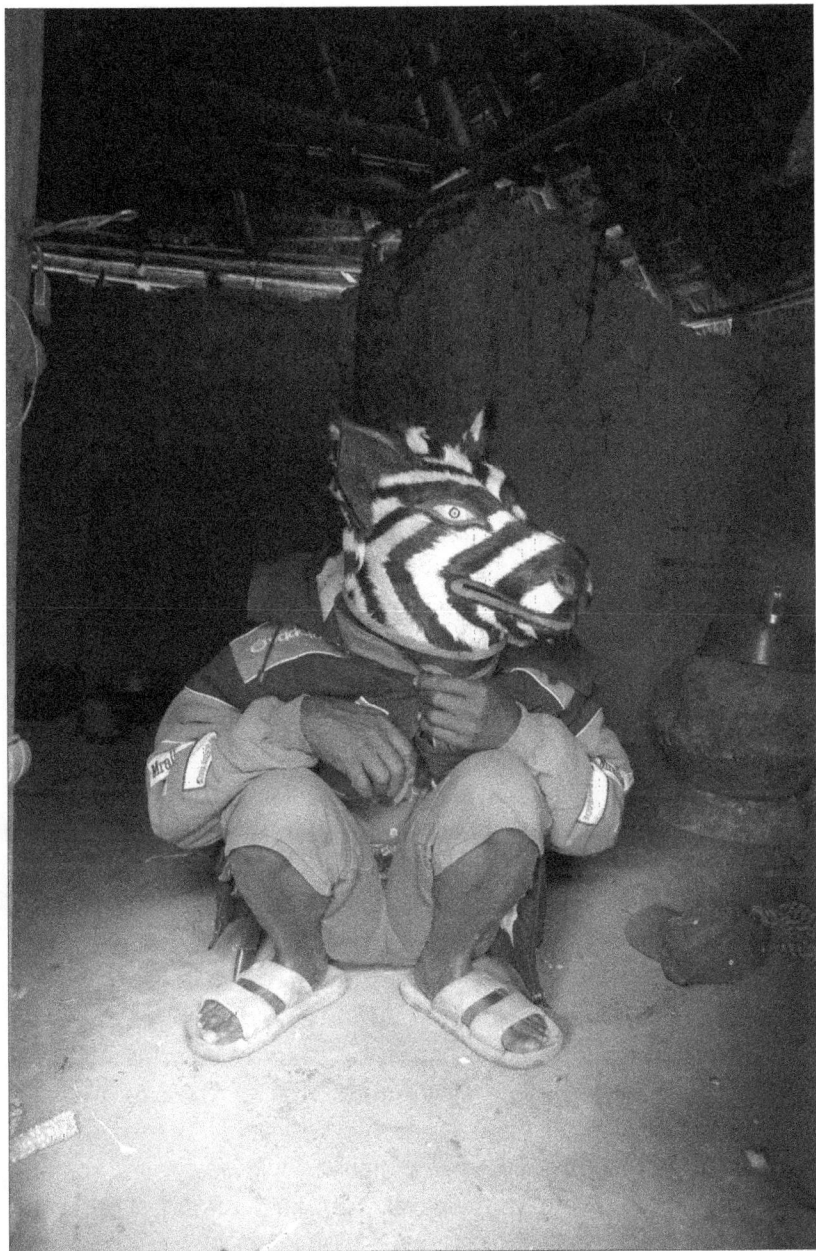

FIGURE 1. Playing with a *ling'anyamu* mask *(Rui Assubuji, Matambalale, 2009)*

but a part. The name *mapiko* applies to various forms of masquerading, some of which do not even involve a headpiece. Masks-as-objects, when still and not dancing, are referred to as "heads" (*myuti*); when their figurative power is to be stressed, as "faces" (*ding'ope*). Both are euphemisms of the initiated, for mapiko are covered by secrecy (*shipii*) and deserve respect (*ishima*): women and children can see them only on the dance-field. *Mapiko* goes together with action verbs, such as *kupanga* (preparing, arranging, organizing—referring to the dressing of the masked dancer and metonymically to the whole performance), *kuvina* (dancing), *kwomba* (drumming), *kwimba* (singing), *kutamba* (partying, animation), and *kupikita* (playing)—a verb that mapiko people (*vamapiko*) use to describe all of the above.[4] There is no mask without drums and songs, and the masks themselves appeal to the senses: above all, their dance must be pleasurable (*ing'oma kunogwa*).

As a corrective to the colonial-era overemphasis on masks as objects—the ultimate collectible signifier of African primitiveness—this study focuses less on carving and more on performance: on the dancing, drumming, singing, and partying that bring the masks to life, as well as on the shifting regimes of ritual practice that regulate their local usages. While following the play of masks, we heed Fredric Jameson's categorical imperative: "Always historicize!"[5]


3. In the past fifty years, the performative approach has brought a host of new insights to the study of African masquerade, dance, and ritual. Extending the metaphor of theater to objects previously understood as magico-religious was the most effective strategy to unmake the legacy of colonial primitivism. Rituals, dances, and masquerades were shown to be sophisticated expressive idioms, arenas for power and identity negotiations, institutions that mold gendered and cultured subjectivities, and sites of knowledge production.[6] Their logic was revealed to be analogous to that of performative activities in industrialized societies, from face-to-face interaction to politics. Concurrently, the vocabulary shaped in the analysis of "primitive" ritual—such as *liminality*, *passage*, and *segmentarity*—was used to gain an understanding of a variety of phenomena across times and spaces. The performative approach also paved the way for the study of historicity. Exploring the nooks and crannies of ritual practice and aesthetics, performance scholars were led to acknowledge change, even when they did not thematize historicity per se.

The breakthrough in the historical study of African dance came with Terence Ranger's *Dance and Society in Eastern Africa,* an unassuming book that endeavored to apply the methodological lessons of European popular culture research in an African context.[7] Ranger reconstructed with unprecedented rigor and unmatched wealth of detail the historical trajectory of the militaristic Beni *ngoma;* furthermore, he argued that popular culture offers important insights into underclass collective experience. The latter lesson was absorbed better than the former. Somewhat paradoxically, Ranger's work inspired a host of anthropological studies on African popular culture, which focused on urban artistic production and its political significance with a presentist approach. In 1978, Johannes Fabian heralded the "loud and colorful bursts of creativity in music, oral lore, and the visual arts [. . .] pioneered by the urban masses" and "carried by the masses in contrast to both modern elitist and traditional 'tribal' culture."[8] These urban art forms were considered expressions of underclass consciousness, which, following a classic Marxist teleology, was seen as emerging with urbanization and detribalization.[9] The anthropological scholarship on popular culture thus gave new currency to old primitivist ideas about the apolitical stasis of rural African societies, reproducing the dichotomies—urban/rural, modern/traditional, detribalized/tribal, worker/peasant—that were at the heart of the colonial world:

> Traditional arts [. . .] belong primarily to the rural-based, predominantly oral peasant cultures inherited, with continuous modifications, from the pre-colonial era. Popular arts by contrast are essentially modern and urban-oriented and represent a new culture. [. . .] The newness felt to be characteristic of popular arts is not merely the result of the gradual internal changes always taking place in indigenous cultures, neither is it an involuntary effect of the blanket impact of foreign rule. The syncretism of the popular arts is actively and selectively sought.[10]

Under the influence of performance and popular culture studies, the field of African art history revised its paradigms, overcoming the legacy of primitivism and producing sophisticated histories of changing forms.[11] The best example of this new scholarship is Zoë Strother's *Inventing Masks,* which provides a meticulous analysis of the dynamics of invention in Pende masquerades.[12] Original and pathbreaking as it is, this work still lingers on the threshold of historicity. While it individualizes the process of invention, restoring the faces and intentionality of mask creators, it largely relies on the ethnic subject ("the Pende mind") that Sidney Kasfir so deftly critiqued.[13] The question of historical consciousness is left to the final pages, leaving the reader wanting to know more about the ways in which Congolese political upheavals played out in the domain of masquerading.[14]

A tendency common to both popular culture and African art studies is to locate the spark of change in the colonial encounter. This is partly dictated by the quasi-total absence of sources on the precolonial period, especially on ephemeral matters of song and dance. But it also stems from an unquestioned assumption, the old idea that cultural change in Africa must be prompted by secularization or reaction to conquest.

4. Against such emphasis on external influence and secularization, this study argues that the riveting changes that have characterized the twentieth-century history of mapiko sprang from a principle internal to this institution itself: ritual rivalry.

Many authors in different African contexts, including Ranger and Strother, have observed a relationship between dance rivalry and innovation. Only Kelly Askew has explicitly thematized it, arguing that in the context of East African dance, the one is tied to the other. "If one is to best one's rival, the strategy proven most effective is to appropriate and incorporate something new, be it of local or foreign origin."[15] Askew's insight is very pertinent to the case of mapiko. From the outset of my fieldwork in the Makonde Plateau I was faced with both novelty and rivalry. Masks and other dances were proliferating at a fast pace, with styles unknown even to my guide and companion, Atanásio Nhussi, self-declaredly the best mapiko dancer in the country. Groups competed with boastful energy in state festivals and initiation rituals. The first mapiko song that I ever learned was a challenge cast in a mixture of Shimakonde and Kiswahili:

| Lo' mavetu amutamba | Look, my friends, you don't party |
| Leo leo | Today, today |
| Matambalale lilongwe | Matambalale is the headquarters |
| Leo leo | Today, today[16] |

This first impression would be confirmed by historical inquiry, which made manifest that both rivalry and innovation had been there since time immemorial and that the one had stimulated the other in decisive ways. As it turned out, all inventions in the domain of mapiko were conceived as competitive challenges — generational, gendered, personal, or between groups bound by kin or locality. If rivalry is undoubtedly the motor that stimulated masquerading creativity, how should it be understood? I followed two complementary paths: one structural and the other historical.

From a structural point of view, one could register a homology between dance competition, on the one hand, and the rivalry between men and women that is the mainstay of Makonde puberty rituals, on the other. The work of Gregory Bateson was crucial in illuminating this connection. For Bateson, ritual competitive performance is generative of social difference — a process that he calls *schismogenesis*.[17] This idea can be fruitfully applied to both puberty rituals and dance competition, which throughout the period under consideration produced various forms of difference — gendered, generational, of kin, and of locality. Thus, rituals of passage and dance competition are shown to obey the same logic. This argument lays to rest the idea that creativity in ritual art emerges only with disenchantment, once it is divested of its sacredness and turned into secular spectacle. Quite on the contrary, the engine of innovation is to be located within ritual itself. Johan Huizinga and Mikhail Bakhtin also provided grounds for undoing the narrative of secularization and for demonstrating the deep affinity of ritual and dance competition. In *Homo Ludens*, Huizinga subsumes competition and ritual under the concept of play and observes that play "loves to surround itself with an air of secrecy." For Huizinga, play takes two forms, the competitive and the representational; when they come together, play "becomes a contest for the best representation of something."[18] Similarly, Bakhtin argues that the distinction between ritual and theater is a product of the bourgeois world and that they are both figures of the primordial carnivalesque.[19]

From a historical point of view, one had just to lift one's eyes beyond the narrow confines of the Makonde Plateau, overcoming the "one tribe, one style" paradigm that has so strongly dominated African art history, and look to the East African landscape.[20] There, rivalry has been woven into the fabric of social life for centuries, in a variety of spaces and practices: provocations between moieties in Swahili towns, joking relationships between ethnic groups, rituals of passage and dance festivals. All these competitive institutions can be understood as instances of schismogenesis—a task beyond the scope of the present study. *Mashindano* dance contests (from the Kiswahili verb *kushindana*, "to compete") have been especially prominent on the Swahili coast and intensified after the ending of slavery.[21] Against this background, mapiko dance rivalry stands out in its rightful importance; moreover, it can be framed within a regional cultural history.[22]

The literature on East African dance competition puts a special emphasis on fashion. At least from the late nineteenth century, both coastal and upcountry dances have been swept by periodic waves of fashion—a phenomenon observed also in the domain of dress.[23] The same occurred in mapiko. Innovation was prompted by visionary and influential individuals, who pursued fame and victory over their rivals. The most successful of these inventions were copied by less imaginative contenders and congealed into established genres, which stayed in fashion for a period of time, until they were abandoned, transformed, or sometimes resurrected (*kutakatuwa*) by younger generations. Such genres thus came to be associated with the specific social groups that had embraced them, especially age groups. This is also a figure of schismogenesis: the collective identification with a specific genre is a form of producing social difference.

This dynamic between individual creation and genre, fueled by ritual rivalry, has been a constant in the history of mapiko. It drove the masquerade's transformations through the "fast cycles" of Mozambique's turbulent twentieth-century trajectory—from the ending of slavery and colonial occupation; to the great adventure of the revolutionary nationalism, whose epicenter was the Makonde Plateau; to the uncertain times of neoliberal postsocialism.[24] Ritual competition made mapiko attuned to these conjunctures, keeping it always, as the title of this book has it, in step with the times. The formula and the argument that sustains it are meant as a thorough refutation of the "denial of coevalness" that is the enduring legacy of colonial anthropology.[25]

5. At the same time, the emphasis on schismogenesis is intended as an intervention in the debate around tradition that has been at the heart of contemporary Mozambican historiography. The terms of this debate were cast in the language of revolutionary nationalism, the political option chosen by the country's liberation movement and post-Independence single-party Frelimo (Front for the Liberation of Mozambique). Inspired by

the ideology of the New Man, Frelimo held the cultures of the Mozambican peasantry as corrupted by "five hundred years of Portuguese colonialism" and embodying a "feudal traditional mentality," which was to be radically transformed through mobilization and (re)education. Tradition should be purified of all residues of obscurantism, tribalism, and sexism and made into a new national culture. Such language exerted a powerful influence on a new generation of engaged historians, who studied the peasantry's political behavior in terms of class consciousness and considered their traditions as a hindrance to social change.

A critique of this discourse came from the discipline of anthropology—more specifically, from the vitriolic pen of Christian Geffray, a student of Claude Meillassoux who had spent some time in the electrifying milieux of the Centro de Estudos Africanos at the Universidade Eduardo Mondlane.[26] Trying to make sense of the civil war that was ravaging the country—and that the intelligentsia understood as "destabilization" and "armed banditry"—Geffray suggested that Frelimo's antitraditionalism had created a deep disaffection in the Mozambican peasantry. The peasants who supported the contras movement Renamo (Resistência Nacional Moçambicana) did so in the name of the cultural institutions that, for better or for worse, had regulated their lives for centuries and that Frelimo had disparaged and tried to eradicate, especially chiefship.[27] Riding on this argument, historian Michel Cahen depicted Renamo as a protraditionalist "coalition of marginalities."[28] Geffray's argument also set the tone for a new anthropological scholarship that emerged after the demise of socialism—a disciplinary return of the repressed, if any. Following in his wake, anthropologists set to demonstrate the resilience of traditional authority and magic mentalities—the two targets of Frelimo's repressive intervention—arguing that all attempts to govern rural Mozambicans would fail if policy makers did not become conversant in the peasants' own enchanted interpretations of historical change.[29]

The polarization of this debate, which followed the Cold War's fault lines, had three lasting consequences on the young field of Mozambican historiography.[30] The first was to foreground class and culture as the two main analytic categories, thus foreclosing the study of political identity along more complex lines.[31] The second was to produce a representation of the peasantry as a political other. For the revolutionaries, peasants had to be educated out of their mentalities; for the revisionists, they had to be understood in their cultural difference; both agreed that they were somewhat estranged from the political processes of which they were supposed to be protagonists. The third consequence was to narrow the focus of cultural inquiry to matters of customary authority and supernatural belief, disregarding dance and other expressive forms. Social historians who carried out sophisticated studies of Mozambican dance as anticolonial resistance either did not explore the trajectory of these dances in the socialist age or touched on the topic in dismissive terms.[32] The ethnomusicological work on Mozambican dance by researchers of the Arquivo do Património Cultural (ARPAC) studiously evaded all political questions.[33] Otherwise, no in-depth study has been carried out on Mozambican song and dance, which is the country's self-proclaimed foremost cultural heritage.[34] This is altogether more surprising given the rich literature on performance and politics in other countries in the region.[35]

The analysis of mapiko in terms of schismogenesis does not merely demonstrate the potential of such a "traditional" institution to generate viable social identities across historical periods; it also highlights the various forms of political subjectivity, affiliation, and affect that emerged throughout the twentieth century in the social space under consideration. Each of the genres, analyzed in relation to a specific historical conjuncture, refers to specific configurations of political subjectivity. Methodologically, this reveals the productivity of looking at dance at a reduced scale. This is the fundamental lesson of microhistory: things are different when seen close-up.[36] Political identities mediated and expressed by mapiko genres are more complex and fragmented than the class or cultural subjects produced by the analysis of chiefship and witchcraft. They run along lines of generation, gender, and kin; they refer to specific social spaces; they are constituted through historically contingent projections and imaginations; sometimes, they are completely idiosyncratic. Dance conveys the complex affective matter of politics; microhistorical analysis brings to the fore its irregular fault lines.

The case of mapiko is especially productive in this respect. Because the Makonde Plateau was the cradle of anticolonial guerrilla and socialist revolution, mapiko aesthetics was permeated by political symbolism as none of the other song-and-dance Mozambican traditions were. Such aesthetics provides an invaluable entry point to explore questions of political subjectivity, from anticolonial rebellion to revolutionary passions, from gender frictions to postsocialism. The analysis of mapiko aesthetics is especially revealing of the ways in which various social groups responded to the political interpellation into a new national-revolutionary subject—*tuvenentete* "we, the People"—during the liberation struggle and in the post-Independence period. The "frelimization" of mapiko reveals a collective investment in a socialist utopian subjectivity, which laid to rest the idea of an apolitical or estranged peasantry. At the same time, mapiko players used the symbols and aesthetics of socialism as weapons of competitive rivalry, to bolster specific local identities; in the process, the symbols were not necessarily subverted, but appropriated in a game with different stakes. The dynamics between these two poles—politics and play, identification and appropriation, conjuncture and *longue durée*—is what makes song-and-dance a productive terrain to apprehend matters of historical consciousness and subjectivity.

6. Excavating a microhistory of masquerading raised several methodological challenges. As often happens, beginnings were determined by chance. As I was about to initiate fieldwork, driven by a rather vague interest in the relationship between dance and nationhood, the Mozambican government launched a grand Second Festival of Popular Dance (2002) to celebrate a decade of peace. I let myself be sucked in, following the event as much as I could. The festival left me with a powerful impression of the kaleidoscopic richness of Mozambican dance, as well as of its imbrication in the state's apparatus of classification and valorization. On the festival stage, dance groups were leveled into a homogeneous entity; instructed by officers of the Ministry of Culture, they acclaimed the Party and intoned platitudinous songs on prescribed themes. Popular dance was there to touch, yet remained elusive, materialized in the mask of a political spectacle that made it at once sensuous and silent. The choice to focus on a single tradition, rather than carrying out multisite fieldwork as I initially envisioned, was also a reaction to this populist appropriation and to the homologated discourse that it produced.[37] Delving into the historicity of one form, I reckoned, would be the best way to dig behind the pervasive politicization of popular dance in Mozambique and to understand the complexities of a whole field. I chose mapiko.

Already during the festival, I settled in the small district of Muidumbe, at the southeastern edge of the Makonde Plateau, the region's epicenter of dance creativity. There, I had a house built for me on the land of the local administrator; I experienced village routine; and I followed ritual and political events with some sense of being a local. Meanwhile, I travelled in the neighboring districts and villages to research local genres and to interview specific individuals, accompanied by two field assistants: Mario "Malyamungu" Matias, the son of a Frelimo guerrilla and a dancer of masks; and Evaristo "Angelina" Januário, a pupil in a local school. We hopped from village to village by foot and slept in borrowed huts, to have a more direct experience of life and landscape.

I would lie if I said that I followed a predefined methodology. I had absorbed enough Feyerabend as a philosophy undergraduate.[38] Mainly, I dived in for as long as I could.[39] In retrospect, I would describe my research method as based on the attempt to establish a virtuous circle between three endeavors: the aesthetic analysis of specific genres, the ethnography of ritual performances, and oral history. The first was posited on recording and transcribing a massive amount of songs, listing dance styles, discussing aesthetics with mapiko players, and, of course, watching and filming performances.[40] The second consisted of the observation of many political events (national and local holidays, festivals, elections) and masculine and feminine initiation rituals, twice as a spectator (early 2002, late 2003) and once as an involved participant (2004–5).[41] The third amounted to interviews of two kinds: collective, with members of specific dance groups, which established a general overview of the history of genres; and individual, with persons identified as protagonists of the history of mapiko.

The virtuous circle between these three endeavors relied on embodied nature of the knowledge that I was pursuing. The more I understood the aesthetics of mapiko and its genres, the more I acquired the codes and language of performance, the more ritual and dance got under my skin, the more people responded to my inquiries with interest, detail, and precision. Interviews would be punctuated by fragments of performance that anchored memories into historical actuality. People played with their mouths rhythmical sequences related to dance styles (*vikuvo*) of long-dead genres or stood up to dance them.[42] Some descriptions were verbal-art performances in their own right. While in the early phases I kept song recording and interviewing separate, I later built interviews around recording sessions. In this way, songs functioned as mnemonic hooks to talk about masks, evoked recollections that in a normal life-story interview would remain buried, and provided cues for discussion of lyrics, music, and genre.

Audiovisual recordings gave me the opportunity of in-depth formal analysis. They also defined the field activities of my small research brigade. "The white who passes to take dances" (*njungu apita atwalanga ding'oma*) "and his crew" (*na vanemba vake*), thus we were called. The word *taking* has obvious overtones of vampirism, but film and sound actually helped to restitute part of what we were extracting.[43] In a later stage of fieldwork, I produced films (first in the form of tapes, then DVDs) for the groups that I worked with; and I provided the regional branch of Rádio Moçambique (RM) with a selection of music, which was put on the air. This was particularly appreciated by performers, as it boosted their renown and prestige; concurrently, it mitigated immaterial suspicions concerning my activities.[44]

The volatility of oral history is well known. One could imagine that the attempt to historicize the evanescent matter of song and dance, especially in a highly competitive context, would result in a kaleidoscope of incoherent versions or that memory would be significantly shaped by social position and power. Quite the contrary, the picture that emerged out of dozens of interviews was remarkably coherent. Aesthetic judgments varied dramatically; less so, facts. The old technique of cross-referencing was particularly useful. Dancers, singers, and carvers tended to boast about their own achievement, but when faced with conflicting versions—say, of histories of invention—they most often conceded and concurred. Second or third interviews with the same persons would produce new in-depth information, sometimes because people had been left to think about the questions that I had asked. Weaving this web of cross-verification, I repeatedly returned to a handful of elders who demonstrated deeper knowledge of and interest in matters of play—such as Mustafa, from whose perspective I have introduced mapiko in the first pages and whose personality and inventions will be revealed in the final ones.

Concentrating my efforts in establishing a virtuous circle among formal analysis, ethnography, and oral history, I resorted much less to written sources. A practical reason was the paucity of such sources, which are mostly silent about dance and song. Secondary literature and contemporary accounts offered a solid historical frame, as well as occasions for critical engagement—especially colonial-era ethnographical writings and Frelimo publications. The sound archives of Rádio Moçambique (Pemba and Maputo) and ARPAC were an invaluable source from which to reconstruct the aesthetics of postcolonial mapiko. Most important, working from the ground up and relying on oral history was crucial to reconstructing a history of mapiko from the point of view of its players—a history of subjectivity more than anything else.

7. The methodological challenges that I addressed indirectly in the field became outright theoretical problems in the phase of writing. How was I to project back in time the knowledge of contemporary performances that I acquired from fieldwork, without falling into anachronism—the historian's capital sin? How would I harmonize in a single narrative the various voices and visions of mapiko players, doing justice to each individual without losing sight of collective dynamics? How should I connect the description of stylistic change to matters of historical consciousness? Could I historicize mapiko genres without falling into the pitfalls of historicism—without turning each of them into an allegory of a specific epoch?[45]

I was aware that all writing impasses conceal epistemological problems but also that epistemological problems find practical solutions only in writing.[46] Each of my difficulties boiled down to the same problem: the articulation of regions of the real that obey partially independent logics (the individual and the collective, form and consciousness, generic conventions and historical epoch). I found a solution in the writing technique pioneered within the microhistorical school that Jacques Revel dubbed "play of scales" (*jeux d'échelles*).[47] Instead of connecting different levels of analysis through an explicit apparatus of mediation, the microhistorians rely on sudden shifts of scale and perspective; in this way, the articulation occurs intuitively and without falling into reductionism. The micro can be juxtaposed to the macro, aesthetics read against the background of social change, without subsuming the one into the other.[48] From a textual point of view, play of scales is sustained by narrative parataxis—by the juxtaposition, rather than subordination, of the various elements of the plot. The articulation of the text in small numbered sections—which is a recurring feature of microhistorical writing and which I have adopted here—is geared to produce this paratactic effect.[49]

Following this principle, the historicity of mapiko genres is explored here in its multiple and contradictory aspects. Formal coherence is contrasted with the haphazard circumstances of invention, ideology with practice, politicization with playfulness, epochal meaning with discordant interpretations, rhetoric with ambivalence, verbal bravado with lyrical obscurity. Each genre is analyzed in relation to the historical moment in which it was invented but also to deeper chronological sequences. Each genre thus emerges as a thick knot of temporal layers and historical experience, which can never be totalized but only traversed narratively. The technique of play of scales enabled me to articulate this complexity and to interrupt the task of historicizing when it is on the verge of turning into allegory.

Narrative parataxis and play of scales are also akin to the aesthetics of masquerading itself. Masked dancing cannot be experienced as a whole. If you stand near the drums, you will not be able to hear the singing. If you mingle with the singers, you will lose sight of the dancer's footwork. If you pay too much attention to the masked dancer, you will be so captivated as to forget all the rest. If you stand in the front line, you will perceive details: the breathing, the metal rattles, the mask itself. But only from above—say, from the perspective of a child sitting on the branch of a mango tree—can you apprehend the shape of the dance-field (fig. 2) and follow all the participants' movements. Polyrhythm and syncopations inscribe disconnection among masquerade performers themselves. If you play in the drum orchestra or sing in the choir, you cannot watch the dancer, or you will fall out of rhythm.

FIGURE 2. The dance-field (*Rui Assubuji, Litamanda, 2009*)

Only the lead drummer dares watch the mask, bridging between the two domains; to do so, he must keep so concentrated as to lose connection with the rest. There is no possible unified way in which the whole can be kept together. A famous Igbo proverb makes of this aesthetic fragmentation an epistemological principle, which is a folk version of the microhistorian's play of scales: "The world is like a mask dancing. If you want to see it well you do not stand in one place."[50]


8. The most elusive challenge was indeed to put into words the sensuous beauty of masquerading, which for thirteen years sustained my passion. Many have tried; few have succeeded, even in part.[51] Lacking the skills for musicological or choreographic notation and finding impressionistic description always to fall short, I chose an indirect approach. I wove into the fabric of my text, sometimes surreptitiously, the voices of mapiko people talking about their art: descriptions, anecdotes, idioms, aesthetic judgments, critiques, boastings, and song lyrics that—stripped of music as they may be—still carry echoes of the dance-field. The reader interested in listening and watching mapiko more directly will find audiovisual material available on a dedicated website.[52]

But music and dance, with their broad range of kinesthetic associations—the smell of burning leaves on antelope hide, the sweaty thick heat, the sweetish fiery taste of cashew moonshine, the pushing and pulling—can also seep into text following less explicit paths. Achille Mbembe commented, on his own work, "A good reader of texts can hear the sounds of Congolese music late in the night behind many a chapter of *On the Postcolony*."[53] Writing each chapter of this book I have listened to the sounds of masks, over and over—so much that I hope you, reader, can hear them.

# PART ONE

⌐⌐

# Directions

WRITING ABOUT Africa always entails a confrontation with the epistemological legacy of colonialism. The colonial text is marked by the taint of complicity and of primitivism; yet it is there that one turns first in the elusive quest for meaning and origins. Such is the privilege — and the burden — of the first inscription. Deconstruction of colonial epistemology is paramount, but if it is not to be a sterile exercise it must lead into the more interesting task of reinterpretation. This part begins with a critique of colonial-era ethnographies of mapiko, then proceeds to discuss fundamental anthropological questions to establish the coordinates for the historical reconstruction that follows.

Chapter 1, "The War of Sexes," takes as its object the work and legacy of anthropologists Jorge and Margot Dias, who interpreted mapiko from a functionalist perspective as a mystical weapon used by the men in a war for gender supremacy. The chapter discusses the Diases' texts, shows how their theories and observations are in conflict, contrasts their analyses with other contemporary accounts, and demonstrates their long-lasting influence on Frelimo's texts. Overall, the chapter argues that such functionalist interpretation posits a fracture between ritual and theatricality, whereby the first is considered as original and the second as derivative.

Chapter 2, "Passage, Secrecy, Rivalry," sets to recompose this fracture by addressing a central problem in the anthropology of masquerading: ritual secrecy. After probing various interpretations and drawing on my own field research as well as on the history of Makonde ethnogenesis, the chapter argues that ritual secrecy is a performative game geared to produce social difference, especially gendered and generational. Ritual secrecy and dance competition are thus shown to obey the same logic. While this anthropological groundwork is of crucial importance to reorient the historicity of mapiko, the chapter concludes by highlighting its limits, arguing that theoretical generalizations cannot substitute for oral history when it comes to the interpretation of mimesis and performance.

# 1 ⮜ The War of Sexes

*The Colonial Library and Its Afterlife*

| | |
|---|---|
| Shimadengo | A form of work |
| Kila shinu shimadengo | Everything is a form of work |
| Ata shimapiko shimadengo | Even mapiko is a form of work |
| 'Tulola wetu | Look at us |
| Twaleke kushu ku-Nampanya | We came from far away, from Nampanya |
| Akune kwashi? | And where are we? |
| Shimapiko shimadengo | Mapiko is a form of work |

—NMA/Nshesho/Nampanya/2004

1. THE ROVUMA River flows from the interior of east-central Africa into the Indian Ocean at the height of a coastal headland named Cabo Delgado by the Portuguese. Digging its way to the coast with unsteady activity, the Rovuma has carved the contours of two high plateaus, wide and jagged, overlooking each other across the shallow bed of the river, north and south respectively and about a hundred kilometers inland. Rivers divide and connect; they make for natural pathways and borders. So it was with the Rovuma. The bed of the river served as a corridor for the caravans connecting the East African interior to the Indian Ocean trade networks, certainly since the fifteenth century and possibly since the eleventh. The polities that developed along the Rovuma were shaped by the tenor of this trade: in spices, cloth, and gold first; then in ivory and slaves.[1] The river saw fortunes amassed, empires rise and fall, populations settle and disappear. In the course of the conflict over the control of the Indian Ocean trading space, Cabo Delgado was chosen as the conventional boundary between the zones of influence of the Portuguese, on the south, and of the Omani, on the

north. Eventually, the Rovuma would become the borderline between German East Africa and Mozambique.[2] The two twin plateaus, whose history was made by the river, were divided by it.

The southerly plateau remained uncharted on European maps until the mid-nineteenth century. Its inhabitants were known as Mavia or Mawia, a derogatory denomination meaning "the irascible" in Chimakonde, the language of their northerly neighbors. The Mavia had a regional renown for being "the most exclusive tribe in East Africa," "fierce and inhospitable," and *washenzi kabisa* (complete savages).[3] The first European "discoverer" set foot on the plateau in 1882, "excited [by] the desire to break down the barriers by which the tribe seemed to be fenced in, and to learn something of their nature and customs." As a result of a few days spent among them, British consul Henry O'Neill found the Mavia "hospitable" and "generous" and attributed their reclusiveness to the impact of the illicit slave trade, which had achieved degrees of terrifying intensity in the region. The Mavia lived in fortified enclosures, barricaded with "a thorny underbush, every crevice in which appeared to be filled up so carefully that it became an utter impossibility for man, or beast of any size, to penetrate it" and hidden in the middle of the plateau's impenetrable bushes, connected by narrow circuitous paths meant to baffle the unacquainted. Any presence of strangers was signaled by alarm sounds. The gates of these enclosures were constantly guarded and "carefully closed at sunset."[4]

O'Neill was disappointed in his hope of discovering "some curious customs special to this tribe, which had earned for itself such a name for exclusiveness and idiosyncrasy." Besides the widespread practice of facial scarification and the use of the lip plug (*pelele, indona*) among women and, more rarely, men, he could "fix upon nothing to distinguish them from neighbouring tribes." He concluded: "[T]hey [the Mavia] appear to me to be a branch of the Makonde."[5] Thus, on the two twin plateaus, ethnographic reason assigned two twin populations, distinguishable by minor differences in custom, practices of the body, and language.[6]


2. In 1957, Portuguese ethnologist Jorge António Dias was charged by the Ministry of Overseas Affairs with the Mission on the Study of the Ethnic Minorities of the Portuguese Overseas (MEMEUP). Based on a first reconnaissance carried out in the summer of 1956, the mission—composed

of Jorge, his wife, Margot, and literary scholar Manuel Viegas Guerreiro—chose as the main topic of inquiry "a little-known ethnic group"
of Mozambique: the Makonde. From 1957 to 1960, the trio spent
several months in the field, producing the four-volume monograph
*Os Macondes de Moçambique*, which has been described as the most
prominent work of Portuguese colonial ethnography.[7]

Dias was indeed an innovative figure in Portuguese ethnology. Trained
in Germany between 1937 and 1949—where he met Margot, who was
also an ethnologist—and then in the United States in the 1950s, he
managed to displace the dominant paradigm of Portuguese physical
anthropology in favor of scholarship more in touch with international
debates. He was especially influenced by functionalism, the culture
and personality school, and *Völkerkunde*. In 1956 Dias was appointed
chair of ethnology at the University of Lisbon, and in 1965 he founded
the Museum of Ethnology, building on materials connected to his
Makonde expeditions. Most Portuguese contemporary anthropologists
recognize him as their "immediate ancestor."[8]

The honor of being the research subjects of such an illustrious
academic fell to the Makonde largely on account of their reputation for primitiveness. The Makonde Plateau had been pacified in
the course of the military operations of World War I (1917), the last
patch of land in Mozambique to be subdued. In 1921, a new road was
opened and the plateau was brought under the rule of the Companhia do Nyassa, a multinational chartered company to which Portugal
had outsourced the exploitation of the northern third of its Mozambican colony.[9] In 1929 the charter was withdrawn, in obeisance to a
more aggressive and unified politics of empire promoted by António
de Oliveira Salazar's dictatorship in Portugal. The plateau was included in the vast Circumscrição dos Macondes. In the 1930s, Christianity and forced labor came hand in hand to strengthen the grip of
colonial occupation.[10] The Makonde perpetuated in the social space
of the colonial state the reputation of aggressive savagery that had
kept at bay intruders during the time of the slave trade. They were
feared and respected by the "neighboring tribes" and held in high
consideration by colonial officials as trustworthy and single-hearted.
As it turned out, some "curious customs" indeed distinguished them
from their neighbors (at least within the borders of the Portuguese
colony): a vibrant carving tradition and the practice of the peculiar
helmet-shaped masks called mapiko.

When the Dias brigade set foot on the plateau, the only literature produced on the Makonde consisted of travelogues and notes written by colonial administrators. Numerous artifacts—masks and carvings—had been collected and shipped to Portugal or sent to Lourenço Marques and Nampula. The team set to inquire into the tribe's way of life following the customary headings of the classic ethnographic monograph.

3. In the "cradle to the grave" section that constitutes the major part of the bulky third volume of *Os Macondes*, on ritual and social life, mapiko plays an exclusive role. The dancing masks are described as the heart of puberty rituals, which are deemed "the central institution of Makonde people, around which everything gravitates": "The ceremonies of puberty, masculine (*likumbi*) and feminine (*ing'oma*), which differ with respect to their rituals and mysteries, have *mapiko* as their common element. The *mapiko* masked dancer features in almost all important festivities of initiation ceremonies, to such an extent that it turned into a sort of symbol of these celebrations. [. . .] He is the key-element of mysteries, and it is around *mapiko* masks and dances that all the secrets of men turn."[11]

As with most forms of ritual masquerading throughout the world, the practice of mapiko was covered by strict rules of secrecy. The masks were said to be fearful spirits of the dead, evoked from a grave by the men. The women, the children, and the noninitiated should respect a series of proscriptions concerning the masks: behaving as if they believed in the masks' supernatural origins, showing fear, and hiding in the houses when the masks are in sight. The Diases provided an explanation of mapiko's practices of secrecy couched in a functionalist framework. The masks' mysteries, they argued, should be read in the context of a "war of the sexes" as a strategy for men to maintain supremacy over women in a matrilineal society: "For all we could observe, living amongst the Makonde, we are brought to affirm that *mapiko* has been the most powerful weapon that men used in this struggle against the women's prestige and supremacy; and that they transmitted it, from generation to generation, through puberty schools."[12]

The idea of masks as "agents of social control" was not new: it had been put forth by a missionary, George W. Harley, in a study on the Liberian Poro masking society (1950) and was then refined by functionalist anthropologists. Harley observed that elders and big men exercised power and claimed obedience through the symbolic set of proscriptions concerning masks and that the ownership of "big masks" reinforced the authority of chiefs.[13] The Diases' reformulation of Harley's hypothesis was premised on two misconceptions: that women are in power in matrilineal societies and that Makonde women actually feared the mapiko and ignored their secrets.[14] The fable of the "war of sexes"—strong because simple—would deeply influence subsequent understandings of mapiko, well beyond the confines of academia.

4. If the Diases theorized *mapiko* as a "magical weapon" in the war for gender supremacy among the matrilineal Makonde, artistry and mimicry erupt through their detailed descriptions of actual performances.[15] The dance of masks comes across as a spectacle with refined music and choreographies:

> The musicians tune their instruments, approaching them to the fire, and strike them until they are satisfied with the pitch of the sound. In general, in *mapiko* the big drums are struck with the hands, and the small ones with thin and long sticks.
>
> In front of the orchestra, a large space is dedicated to the dancers. The young women who want to participate in the dance dispose themselves in two lines, on one and the other side. Behind, the crowd of spectators gathers. [. . .]
>
> At a certain point, the drums with their vibrant rhythm give the signal for the beginning of the dance. A *mapiko* appears and takes position in the middle of the terrain. The *chinganga* player starts to play a rhythm of obstinate triplets. The other drums also start. The main drummer's rhythm commands the different dance steps: *likambale, imbwani, alupu, linda.* [. . .]
>
> The dancer is soon tired and the main drummer calls: *tayali?* (ready?). He answers: *tayali!* (ready!) The first: *ngumalile?* (should I finish?); the second: *malila* (finish!)[16]

The "war of sexes" supposed to be the masquerade's social truth is also sustained by a dramatic performance, in which the women participate actively: "The women, from both sides, in two lines, perform a slow and hieratic dance, with movements of the hips and the arms. They assume a serious expression, and, in certain moments, when the low drums signal the coming of the *mapiko* and his dance in front of the orchestra, their heads and their torsos hang low, as if they couldn't look at the dancer."[17]

This pantomime of fearfulness, in which the men and the women cooperate, coexists—with no apparent contradiction—with a playful atmosphere and farcical interludes: "The comical element was represented by a hunter with arrow and bows. In his gourd, he kept a mirror and a cooking knife, with which he pretended to shave himself, for the public's enjoyment. [. . .] As always amongst the Makonde, he represented his comical role with the uttermost seriousness. We never saw him smile or laugh."[18]

Like many other spirit possession dances, African and not, mapiko appropriate foreign elements into their dramatic texture—especially those belonging to the colonial master—with a distinct carnivalesque touch:

> Nowadays, to these festivals has been added a compact choir of men and boys, with books, papers, or newspaper in the hands, who sing and gesticulate as if they were reading and commenting. In front of them, a man directs the choir as if he was an orchestra director, or a school master. They preferably use what is foreign to their culture: a woman's plush dress, an explorer's cap, a fireman's uniform, a coconut hat, the coat of a British sergeant, a kofiò on the head. This travesty gives them the pleasure and joy that, in other countries, people experience masquerading for *mardi gras*. And here is a *mardi gras* that, in the dry season, repeats itself continuously and fills them with delirium. The market of used clothes coming from the United States can satisfy whatever kind of fantasy.[19]

In fact, if war appears at all in the Diases' description of mapiko, it is not between the sexes, but rather as rivalry between the lineages competing on the dance floor:

> The men scream more or less these words: "Mwenu makoko, mwe mundapanga mapiko kulingana na mwetu. Manguluve mwe, mapiko kumanya tuvana maliya" (you [are] animals, you don't know how to [be] *mapiko* like us. You are pigs, we know *mapiko*, you are not right!). And they impetuously exclaim the village's *likola* [matrilineage].
>
> The group who is on stage with the *mapiko* screams the name of the *likola* [matrilineage] of the village *nanolo* [elder] in which the party is realized. Sometimes, other men join the

group, screaming sentences that appear incoherent. Once they said: "We want our women." Other times: "You don't know anything, we know everything. Today, you learned." Or also: "You are an animal, you'd better leave," etc. etc.[20]

Mimesis, rivalry, and revelry—the Diases saw quite clearly but could not thematize the interconnectedness of these elements. The passages in which they praise the Makonde's ingeniousness and taste for theater are numerous, not only concerning mapiko but also with respect to the dance of the *vanalombo*, which opens the masculine puberty rites. "Undoubtedly, these people have an irresistible taste for dance and for pantomimic figuration, in which their ludic and theatrical force expands."[21]

Contemporary scholarly accounts of mapiko also highlight performative rivalry:

> Today, we believe, it is nothing but a sort of tournament between the inhabitants of different villages, or perhaps better a dance of competition between the '*mapicos*' of different clans.[22]

> Being, as it is today, a competitive dance, all the various *mapico* have one objective to achieve, that is, to keep training—be it the dancers or musicians, as well as the men and women who work as escort or accompaniment—so as to have more possibilities of winning the contest. [. . .] When there is a contest between the performance of the various *mapicos*, there are some who, while singing in choir, bend down and seem to write on the ground; which is not what actually happens, because with this constantly repeated gesture they only want to say, in a disparaging tone, that the value of their rivals is equal to the soil that they grab and toss away in contempt.[23]

For the Diases, however, ritual logic is what counts, and such amateurish descriptions are thus reprimanded: "The inadvertent traveler who watches these festivities notices only the *mapiko*, and doesn't even get to realize that it is just one of their elements[, . . .] an aspect of the rich and varied ceremonial which accompanies the period of the initiations of adolescents."[24]

5. Another one of these "inadvertent travelers" had made his way to the Makonde Plateau, bound to an *Adventure in Search for African*

*Art.* In 1955 British collector and amateur historian Robert Dick-Read traversed the Makonde Plateau and stopped at the mission of Nangololo, with the objective of acquiring masks and sculptures. There, he encountered mapiko:

> [I]t was like no other [dance] that I ever saw elsewhere in Africa. The whole village, men, women and children, were assembled in an open clearing out in the bush, arranged in a horseshoe around the arena. At the open end of the horseshoe were the drummers beating out a fantastically rapid, high-pitched rhythm like the sound of hailstones pattering on sheets or corrugated iron. For some time the drummers played while the women around the arena clapped and sang to their rhythm. Suddenly into this cacophony of sound [. . .] sprang the Lipiko—the dancer with the mask—who rushed in from the bush, beating his feet upon the ground, prancing round the line of women who now cowered away from him in silent fear. For several minutes, while the drums beat on incessantly, the awesome figure of the dancer charged the terrified crowd, stopping short as he appeared to strike them."[25]

The art merchant observed that most of the masks were tied to the representation of alterity: they "portray people other than their village."[26] Montfort Father Vloet from Nangololo, "an old Dutchman, short and bent, with long white hair," took pains to explain that in times gone by, mapiko had been a "war dance."[27] The masks used to represent "powerful enemies" from the neighboring tribes, which the Makonde would summon from the bush and symbolically defeat— a patent example of "sympathetic magic."[28] After the brutal pacification imposed by the Portuguese and the end of internecine wars, this sympathetic magic had been redirected to other usages. For instance, by mimicking in masquerading social virtues (a harvesting woman) or vices (a sorcerer, a "bugger"), the Makonde wished to sympathetically encourage the former and magically chastise the latter. From Malinowski back to Frazer, masking mimesis remains a function of the primitive mind:

> The most extraordinary example of sympathetic magic I witnessed was on an occasion when a lipiko came prancing into an arena wearing a mask of none other than "Kwini Elizabeti Yapili

wa Waingilesa"—Queen Elizabeth the Second of England. The Queen was referred to by name, and though the mask itself was no flattering work of art, there was no doubt whom it was supposed to represent from the crown onto its head. The dance that Her Majesty performed was as fast and furious as any of the others, but they treated this mask with particular respect, and everything about it indicated that the Makonde wished they were her subjects.[29]

6. "Imperialist nostalgia"—that is, the "mourning for what one has destroyed"[30]—and the correlative delusion of "imagining that one's real object is not there, in what is happening around, but in what has already and forever disappeared" are constitutive of ethnology.[31]

The apparent decline and loss of tribal purity struck the Diases in another form of masquerading: night-masks (*mapiko ashilo*, or simply *shilo*, "night"). Toward the end of initiation rituals, after the boys had been submitted to one of the final ordeals in which they must recognize and unveil a fabricated lion, they were introduced to mapiko ashilo. Built with bamboo structures and covered with cloths, they represented wild animals of a spiritual nature (such as the lion, the hyena, the leopard, the rhino, the buffalo, the monkey, and the wild pig) or entities classified as spiritual animals (such as the car [*mbutuka*] or the terrifying Nandenga, a giant demon [*lishetani*] of the wild). These spiritual animals danced during moonless nights, such that their silhouettes make an eerie impression.

The practice of shilo appeared to Dias very similar to that of the *nyau yolemba*, the nocturnal masquerades of the Chewa-Nyanja people living around Nyassa Lake. This allowed the anthropologists to establish a diffusionist connection between the Makonde and the Maravi—a people who had migrated from the Congo Basin in remote times—and hence to account for the presence of masks in northern Mozambique.

Observing playfulness and theatricality in shilo, the Diases drew upon the trope of decline and disenchantment:

> We believe that this custom represents a phase of transformation of *chilo*, which lost its mythic value, and transformed itself into an amusement (*folguedo*) associated with the puberty rites.

Many women continue to feel a certain fear, the young ones are scared, but truly, the profound mystery that once enshrouded the *mapiko* complex, and *shilo* especially, lost its force. The circumstance of many Maconde women going to Tanganyika, where the rationalist attitude is quickly gaining strength over the previous mythic thought, is sufficient to undermine the belief in the truthfulness of the *chilo* animals. This was not the case in times of old. Some Maconde elders recount that when the lion, the rhino or the buffalo entered in the scene with their roars, the atmosphere was one of authentic panic.[32]

7. Anthropological explanation—to paraphrase Paul Valéry—is a prolonged hesitation between function and meaning.[33] These two options and their various theoretical declinations continue to delimitate the horizon of possible anthropological questioning: *How does it work? What does it mean?*

Theories of masquerading are caught in such a hesitation. Explanations in terms of function consider dancing masks as elements of a ritual process. The focus here is on secrecy rather than representation, on concealing rather than revealing: ritual secrecy is thought to contribute to the social reproduction of segmentary groups or to further gender or generational domination. Interpretations in term of meaning dwell on the masks' surface—on carving and performance—connecting masquerades to myths, cosmologies, and systems of thought, generally (and cross-culturally) concerning the dead and the wild-animal kingdom.[34] Recent research on masquerading within the "modernity of ritual" school has forgone questions of function, in favor of an expressive reading that no longer dwells on traditional cosmologies but instead charts the collective interiorization of historical processes.[35]

We can identify the tension between interpretations in terms of sense and function in the colonial-era texts that we have read. Both the Diases and Dick-Read consider representation in mapiko as an epiphenomenon of function. For the Diases, the masquerade serves the social function of regulating the struggle for supremacy between men and women; for Dick-Read, it is a way of symbolically mastering the tribal enemy. But play, theater, and performance are everywhere to be seen. What to do with this fact? How to reconcile the masquerade's farcicality with the assumed seriousness of ritual logics? To explain the preponderance of farce and play, both anthropologists—the professional and the dilettante—recur to a narrative of decay, in which theatricality emerges with disenchantment. Once upon a time, mapiko was a fearful ritual—the women *really* believed in the masks' spiritual nature, the dance was *really* frightening, the tribe *really* thought it could conquer its enemies through sympathetic magic—but now all this is gone or dwindling.[36] Theatricality and playfulness emerge in this space of modern disbelief: once the masks are divested of their sacred power, one can play with them.

The Diases' interpretation of mapiko reflects the backwardness of Portuguese ethnology—enthralled by functionalism when it was already on the wane—more than the primitive mentality of the Makonde. The third volume of *Os Macondes* was published two years after the English translation of Mikhail Bakhtin's *Rabelais and His World*, a book that opened up a space to think laughter and parody within the sacred. Bakhtin vividly described a culture in which religiosity and the comical were intertwined—the European Middle-Age popular farces and carnival—suggesting that the separation of the comic and the sacred was specific to Christian religiosity and bourgeois subjectivity and that originally an all-embracing and ambivalent ritual laughter was at the heart of religious experience.[37] In carnival, the bodily and spiritual elements are conjoined in an aesthetics of "grotesque realism," wherein orifices, digestion, sexual organs, and regeneration are prominent. There is no way of imposing divisions within this primordial wholeness: "[T]he basic carnival nucleus of this culture is by no means a purely artistic form nor a spectacle and does not, generally speaking, belong to the sphere of art. It belongs to the borderline between art and life. In reality, it is life itself, but shaped according to a certain pattern of play."[38]

The original proximity between theater and the sacred was also observed in Francophone studies of African possession cults, especially Vodun religion. "Trances usually take place in series, resulting in a spectacle that resembles the *commedia dell'arte*," observes Luc de Heusch. "All theater is located in-between possession and simulation."[39] The obfuscation of this essential unity, for which de Heusch used the expression *sacred theater*, was due to the influence of the Catholic Church, with its religiosity revolving around asceticism, disembodiment, and gravity. Increasingly henceforth, scholars began to defend the idea that in masquerades, "ritual and entertainment are [. . .] indivisible."[40]

A folklorist by training, Dias did not ignore the phenomena discussed by Bakhtin: "The burlesque element appears in the middle of ritual, like it happened amongst us [. . .] in the Middle Ages, with the miracle plays."[41] Nonetheless, when speaking of the primitive Makonde, Dias assigned the ritual and the burlesque to different phases of historical development.

8. The Diases had chosen the Makonde as subjects of research not only because of the tribe's backwardness but also for murkier reasons. The Ministry of Overseas Affairs was preoccupied with signals of anticolonial sentiment taking hold on the plateau and demanded that the anthropologist put an eye to the situation. In their labor migrations to Tanganyika, where they worked mostly on sisal plantations, the Makonde were being influenced by pernicious ideas concerning independence. Various protonationalist organizations, born out of mutual help clubs based in Dar Es Salaam, Zanzibar, and Tanga, were beginning to acquire followers in Mueda, notably the Mozambique African National Union (MANU).[42] During the first four years of research, Jorge produced confidential reports for the ministry, in which he commented, in a rather unspecific way, on the raise of nationalist consciousness among the Makonde.[43] But the group's excursions would be interrupted by a dramatic event.

On 16 June 1960, a political manifestation held in the colonial town of Mueda, the administrative center of the Makonde Plateau, was repressed in blood by colonial troops. Two years later, MANU was absorbed within the nationalist movement Frelimo, founded in Dar Es Salaam under the auspices of Julius Nyerere. Frelimo's leadership judged that the Makonde Plateau was to be the battlefield of a guerrilla war waged against the Portuguese. The Armed Struggle for National Liberation (Luta Armada de Libertação Nacional) was to last ten years (1964–74), during which Frelimo radicalized its political approach to become a Marxist-Leninist revolutionary movement. During ten years—so the tropes go—the guerrillas fought the colonial regime by hiding in the plateau's bush thickets; marching by day and by night; smuggling goods from the nearby Tanzanian border; mobilizing and training military recruits; attacking the enemy with guns and bazookas; resisting napalm and propaganda falling from the sky; growing food, educating, and organizing; and building a new society on the ashes of the old one. The thick

Makonde bushes were the first parcels of land freed from colonial domination, the mythic *zonas libertadas* (liberated zones) where Frelimo's project of social regeneration was piloted. Together with other dances associated with anticolonial strife—such as the miner's choir *makwaela* or the war dance *xigubo*—Makonde masks turned into national symbols.

Three years after Independence (1975), Anna Fresu and Mendes de Oliveira, two theater professionals, visited the province of Cabo Delgado to carry out research, being one of the many scholarly brigades (*brigadas*) in search of the revolutionary peasant.[44] First they worked with war refugees from the communal village of M'bonje on a theater production on the history of anticolonial resistance. Then they traveled north, to reconstruct the evolution of Makonde masks and rituals. Their book *Pesquisas para um Teatro Popular em Moçambique* (Researches on popular theater in Mozambique)—published in 1982 by the state magazine *Tempo* and prefaced by the country's president, Samora Machel—describes the passage from ritual to theater with explicit reference to the work of the Diases.[45] The interpretation of mapiko's historicity is expounded in a chapter titled "The Appearance of the Comical and the Everyday in Makonde Ritual":

1. Originally, the *Mapiko* was part of Maconde initiation[; . . .] its main function was to scare women, so as to maintain the men's dominance over them.

2. Afterwards, there was a progressive introduction of comic and everyday aspects in rituals.

3. In the confrontation with colonialism, *Mapiko* acquired the functions of critique of colonialism, through satire and making fun of the colonialists. [. . .]

4. During the Armed Struggle of National Liberation, *Mapiko* acquired the function of critiquing colonialism, and introduced the function of mobilizing people for the armed struggle and the organization of life in the liberated zones.

5. After independence, the evolution expected did not take place. The majority of dancers restricted themselves to dancing old stories; they indiscriminately use the same masks. The only visible alteration was the substitution of songs with slogans or *vivas*. [. . .] Not only do they not reflect the growing

consciousness of problems, but they don't serve as a mobilizing and catalyzing element to solve these problems. These
functions should be stimulated within the correct perspective
of the development of popular culture.[46]

According to Fresu and Oliveira, and via the Diases, the masquerade was once a ritual geared to further gender domination. In time,
and as a consequence of the colonial encounter, ritual drifts toward
theater. Its irrational aspects are gradually overridden by a more caustic look on society. The "comical element" appearing "in the midst
of religious ceremonies" accelerates this movement of secularization
and skepticism. Through farce, people start questioning the religious
interpretation of life. "This process leads to the autonomization of the
comical in function of social critique."[47]

This description of this movement "from ritual to theater" is at once
prescriptive. The Party's "correct perspective" demands indeed that all
ritual forms become "popular culture." But the expected transformation has not fully taken place: the new revolutionary consciousness is
not visible enough in the spectacle of masks. In a patronizing conversation with masters of puberty rituals (*vanalombo*), the researchers try to
persuade them to forgo all ritual aspects of their dances, which should
become a comic and educational spectacle inspired by the aesthetic
principles of socialist realism. The stubbornness of the ritual experts
provides the occasion for a melancholic comment on the opportunity
lost: "Combined with many other educational factors and consciousness campaigns, they would become accustomed to seeing them dance
in the field, during the festivities, so they would desist from identifying
the *Vanalombo* as priests, and would see them now as good dancers,
mimes and acrobats."[48]

9. The revolutionary narrative of change was the same as that of the
colonial ethnologist: it only inverted the moral connotation of its elements, introducing a perspective of utopian regeneration. For the ethnologist, Africa's precolonial past was the uncorrupted origin of tribal
authenticity, and colonialism a moment of transition in which traces of
this authenticity could still be seen but were already contaminated by
European modernity and doomed to disappear. The story is one of sorrowful and inevitable decline. For the revolutionary, authenticity had

been lost the very moment the colonialist had set foot in Africa, and cultural practices had been corrupted and turned into forms of collective false consciousness, made to serve tribal and masculine domination. However, the transformations wrought by the liberation struggle have the power to bring back the precolonial golden age: "At night in the liberated areas the people of the villages gather by the fire and sing and dance in complete freedom, as in the time before the arrival of the Portuguese. The old people tell the children about the crimes the Portuguese practised against the people, when they occupied that territory. They tell them about episodes in the liberation struggle, the courage of our guerrillas."[49]

It should come as no surprise that practices such as mapiko were understood within the colonial ethnographic mold. The Diases' explanation of masking secrecy as a war between the sexes seeped into official Frelimo discourse because it fit the portrayal of tribal Africa as a world of superstition and exploitation. What could have been mapiko's function but to take part in the age-old game of obscurantism and domination that only the coming of socialism could annihilate?

The question is more complex when it comes to the interpretation of mimicry, farce, and theatricality. For the Diases these were minor aspects of mapiko, which merely indicated an ethnic propensity of the Makonde for "pantomimic figuration." For the Marxists, mimicry and farce are the forms through which political consciousness is articulated by people who cannot do it otherwise—Eric Hobsbawm's famous "inarticulate rebels."[50] Aesthetics was read allegorically, as the figuration of collective political passions. The transformations occurring during colonialism were interpreted as a formative phase of political consciousness, still inchoate and merely embodied, which prefigured the combat for liberation. The most apparent sign of this inarticulate class consciousness was the farcical representation of white people, especially agents of colonial power. African ritual parody of colonialism had received a great share of international attention with the release of Jean Rouch's ethnographic film *Les Maîtres Fous* (1955) on the West African Hauka possession cults. Perhaps inspired by Rouch's film, Frantz Fanon theorized this incipient political consciousness erupting in culture and arts as a restructuring of perception: "We might in the same way seek and find in dancing, singing and traditional rites and ceremonies the same drive, and make out the same changes and the same impatience. Well before the political or armed phase of the national liberation struggle, an attentive reader can thus feel and see the manifestation of a new vigor, the combat approaching. [. . .] In renewing the purpose and dynamism of crafts, dance, music, literature and oral epos, the colonized restructures his perception."[51]

The bifurcation between function and meaning was thus neatly organized into a moral political teleology. Ritual belongs to the obscurantist past, theatricality to the radiant socialist future. These ideas were shared by revolutionary leaders and influenced the operation of state power. The realm of socialist utopia would be open only to the traditions that had achieved the required transformation: from superstition to rationality; from inarticulate to explicit class consciousness; from ritual to theater. The adjective *popular* was used as the marker to indicate this transformation—to qualify the traditions that underwent it or were in the process of undergoing it.

The allegorical interpretation of masquerades is not a prerogative of Marxist thought: it is a possibility inherent in the structure of masquerading itself. Middle-Age European theological treatises, for instance, condemned popular masquerades as *similitudo*, allegories of the devil.[52] Perhaps, though, masking mimesis remained elusive to the Marxists as it was to the medieval theologians, too complex to be reduced to a "politically conscious viewpoint."[53] Indeed, the dilettante anthropologist interpreted the mimesis of the white master rather differently from the Marxists: for him, the mapiko of Queen Elizabeth II, far from being a parody expressing half-articulate anticolonial consciousness, conveyed the Makonde's wish to be her subjects (expressed through sympathetic magic)!


10.  When I set out to research the history of mapiko in the early 2000s, the Diases' monograph was the only serious fieldwork-based research that had been carried out on the masquerade. In the 1980s and 1990s, a few articles appeared, written by scholars close to Frelimo, which substantially repeated Fresu and Oliveira's reinterpretation of the colonial text.[54] Fieldwork touching on mapiko was carried out in Tanzania: among the Makonde of Newala in the 1970s and among Mozambican Makonde emigrants in the 1990s.[55] The growing number of exhibitions on Makonde blackwood carving did not add substantially new information on masquerading.[56] Harry West's ethnography carried out in Mueda in the late 1990s mentions mapiko only cursorily.[57]

An exhibition on mapiko at the Sevilla Expo '92 was accompanied by an English translation of passages from the Diases' monograph.[58] The Diases' interpretation of mapiko as a ritual of feminine subjugation became normative and was widely appropriated not only by Marxist intellectuals but also by local mapiko practitioners, especially in Maputo. Alexander Bortolot's dissertation, based on fieldwork carried out in the second half of 2004, is posited on the same modernist teleology, arguing that the drive to depict the contemporary emerges in Makonde arts as a consequence of the colonial encounter.[59]

The colonial library inscribed into the historiography of mapiko a founding disconnection between ritual and mimesis, function and sense, whereby the first is seen as original and essential (and geared toward a precise social function, the control of women), the second as derivative and accessory. The Marxist intellectuals reframed this disconnection within a moral narrative of regeneration and enriched it with another layer: the idea that dancing mimesis is an allegory of collective political passions. Before we delve into mapiko's twentieth-century historicity, it will be necessary to undo this teleology and try to "reconnect the disconnected," thinking in more organic terms the relationship between ritual and mimesis.[60] To do so, we must confront head-on the core mystery of the masks: the question of secrecy, of its meanings and functions.

# 2 Ꝡ Passage, Secrecy, Rivalry

*An Excursion into Anthropological Theory*

Nyagwe nyagwe
Shipii shapetu
Shapa-Nampanya
Aunaulange
Ndikwauli' gwegwe

My friend, my friend
The secret of our homestead
Of Nampanya
Don't tell it around
I am speaking to you

—NMA/Nshesho/Nampanya/2004

1. IN THEIR central articulations, Makonde puberty ceremonies, both masculine (*likumbi*) and feminine (*ing'oma*), are similar to other analogous practices described in the ethnographic literature on east-central Africa.[1] During the phase of separation—the "launching" (*kujela*)—initiates (*mwali*, pl. *vali*) are subjected to a series of ordeals (*shipito*, pl. *vipito*, from the verb *kupita*, "to pass") and "treated" with various magico-medicinal substances (*ntela*, pl. *mitela*). Meanwhile, the masters of ceremonies (*nnalombo*, pl. *vanalombo*) dance (fig. 3) and instruct the initiates' families with secret teachings (*midimu*, sing. *ndimu*).[2] At the end of this phase, which extends over two days, on the way to the bush, the boys are circumcised. In the liminal period, the initiates are secluded from their families for a long period of time: the boys hidden in a bush cabin, the girls in a hut at the margins of the hamlet. There, more secret teachings are imparted to them, and they are subjected to more ordeals and undergo an apprenticeship (*kulumya*, "to learn") in the skills that will help them through their adult lives—such as cooking, hunting, and house building. Finally, "the rites come out" (*likumbi/ing'oma kujaluka*). The initiates are brought out of their place of hiding, with the assistance of another ritual specialist

FIGURE 3. Dance of the *vanalombo* (Sandra Lourenço, Mwambula, 2005)

(*nnalombo wankamangu*), and submit to the final ordeals, which once included scarification and tooth chipping. Newly dressed and drenched in perfume, they are reintegrated in the community as reborn adults. Revelry follows, in which excesses in alcohol and noise, dance, and cross-dressing are tolerated if not encouraged.

Puberty rituals are governed by strict rules of secrecy, which exclude the women from the secrets of masculine rites, the men from the secrets of feminine rites, and children and strangers from both. Ritual spaces, whether in the bush or in the village, are carefully insulated from snooping. Masters of ceremonies see that the ritual order and the rules of secrecy are enforced, protecting the initiation hut (*likuta*) from sorcery attacks. Most of this ritual secrecy, as often is the case, conceals nothing. However, the order and unfolding of each of the ordeals; the contents of the instructions imparted to the initiates and their parents; and the sex-related choreographic practices such as male circumcision and the practical demonstration of sexual intercourse—done with a stylish ceramic dildo (*nkungunyale*) to the girls and with a pierced viscous fruit (*lipudi*) and a hammer head (*inyundu*) to the boys (the former symbolizing the attractive vagina of a young girl, the latter the stiff and cold one of an old woman)—all make the object of careful concealment from the one side, ignorance and prurient curiosity from the other.

The secret of masks is one with the secrets of initiations: it is part of them and represents them metonymically. Women and men both make their masks. The women's *vitengamatu*, made in clay, dance only once a year in the final coming-out ceremonies (*nkamangu*) of feminine puberty rites, held in the thick of the bush and almost paranoically guarded from intrusion. They are never danced in public, and men die without ever seeing them. The men's mapiko, on the contrary, are public and dance for both boys' and girls' initiations. But there, on the dance-field, they are bestowed with an aura of secrecy and danger, for a lipiko is said to be a ghost dug from a termite mound (*liyoka lyuki' ndaimba kushushulu*), dangerous and fearsome for the women and children.

The masks' secret is disclosed to male initiates during an epiphanic moment taking place toward the end of the seclusion. The boys are suddenly awoken and exposed to the lipiko. They must run toward it (passing between two lines of whipping and shouting men), grab it, and unmask it. The initiates—especially the leader of the group, "the hare" (*shingula*)—experience the ordeal as a progression from terror to surprise and relief:

> There is a specific time to pass the mapiko. The ordeal (*shipito*) of mapiko. The masters prepare their lipiko. "Oh-oh-oh!" The lipiko stands in front of the house. The masters of ceremonies (*vanalombo*) arrive. "Here, nobody will escape. Shingula, go and grab the lipiko!" And now, you are afraid. Because, that time we used to say that the lipiko comes out of a grave. That it is a ghost (*liyoka*). They would take some *ntamba*, and a white cloth. And that is what we believed. You go, and you fear death. "How will I do?" When you pass, you pass through the: *Sha-Sho! Jé-jé-jé!* [onomatopoeic for whipping and screaming] Bah! Finally! This is how this thing is done. *Aba . . .*[3]

2. "Once upon a time, when a child died during the rituals, the mother was presented with a pestle at the moment of coming out. She would know immediately that her child had died." I was invariably told this story when inquiring about puberty rituals. *Os Macondes de Moçambique* also reports it. I thought of it as little more than an antiquarian curiosity. However, the memory of this custom encapsulates something crucial about the rituals: the inherent possibility of death, the idea that the initiates are akin to the dead.

Puberty ceremonies turn children into adults: *kulumuka*, "growing up," is the meaning generally attributed to likumbi and ing'oma. Ritual coming-of-age is staged as an encounter with death. The rites' tripartite structure—separation, liminality, and reintegration—corresponds to a symbolic death involving the whole community. As an outcome, the children, undifferentiated beings themselves associated with the dead and the spirit world, are turned into adult men and women, into social beings responsible for their capacity for reproduction and future inheritors of the cultural order.[4] *Vanamako* and *vashungu*, the uninitiated, become *vali*, boys and girls ready to marry.

Masks bring about this encounter with death quite dramatically. Masks are transculturally associated with death and animality—the latter representing a threshold between the world of the living and the world of the dead, human life and mere life.[5] The ordeal of unmasking constitutes the climax of puberty rituals. The initiate is faced with an incarnate symbol of death, the mask, and is asked to relinquish fear, to reach and unveil the mask. The reward is full participation in the world of adulthood.

Touching the question of secrecy, though, things become more elusive. Why are rituals secret? Why are masks secret? Discussing the work of ethnologist Martin Gusinde on the Big Hut ritual of the Patagonian Selk'nam and Yamana, Michael Taussig observes, "Unlike later anthropologists—British social anthropologists and U.S. functionalists, for instance—he was intellectually honest enough, at the end of the day, to admit that he *finds himself mystified as to what function the secrecy served*. An obvious contender was male dominance. But then, he could not see any need for the men to deceive the women in order to control them through fear."[6]

Let us begin by putting to rest the "obvious contender," *pace* the Diases and the Marxists. Masks do not further gender domination. The men do not need the masks to control the women, and the women actively and willingly participate in the game of secrecy.[7] For all adult men and women, masks and initiations are covered by a public secret, "that which is generally known, but cannot be articulated."[8] In order to be dominated through the terror of masks, women should have believed that the mapiko were terrifying ghosts evoked by the men. But how could they not know about the human nature of the masks, considering that they danced their own masks in the secret of the bush? Pointing out this paradox during interviews and conversations elicited amusement and verbal gimmicks, even brazen denial. To maintain the fiction, some invented the most adventurous explanations, undone by great bursts of laughter:

—Because you dance your own thing in the bush . . .

—Ahi-ahi, we go to the savannas! Let's go, mothers-of-a-child!

—Now, you didn't imagine that the thing of the men was like yours . . .

—In the nkamangu we tie up a mapiko, with clay . . . It's called *shitengamatu*. But it isn't a mapiko like . . .

—Did you call it a mapiko?

—Yes, because of imitating [the men]!

—And you didn't realize that it's the same thing . . .

—No. Because we saw that the thing the men dance with was very strong. Even if it dances in a group, and it falls, it doesn't break. Now, ours is made of clay: when it falls down, *pwi!* [it breaks] And now we didn't understand: why the one of our friends doesn't break? So now we thought that it must really be a bush beast![9]

Others confessed candidly:

—We knew very well.

—Did you believe that the lipiko was a ghost?

—No one believed it! We didn't believe it. We knew that we are elders, and this is our secret. That was our secret, together with our men.

—Now, this secret, was it a form of respect (*ishima*)?

—Mmh! Respect, together with our men.

—And children like this one, did they know?

—Once upon a time, they didn't. Because us, the elders, we knew: that which dances is a person. But we said "it is a ghost dug from a termite mound" in order to hide it from the little children. We concealed it. Us the elders, we knew.

—Now, this secret, this respect . . . how do you see it, what does it mean?

—[silence]

— [another woman] He asked: this respect that was ordained like this, what did it mean? Answer!

— *Baba*. There is no meaning, only mutual respect (*kwishimana*). Them, to respect us; and we, to respect them. To have a great secret together, them the elderly men and us the elderly women; and our secret to be like this: one and the same. So that the children don't know. Mmh. If you ask for its meaning, it is mutual respect.[10]

The division of labor between the men's public dance of the wooden mapiko and the women's bush performance of clay vitenga-matu was played out for the sake of the children—girls and boys who would be exposed to two equally terrifying secrets in the most momentous passage of the rituals.[11] To what effect?

In a discussion of Hopi Katsina masquerades, psychoanalyst Octave Mannoni interprets the sequence of unmasking as a way to teach the children to transcend naïve belief in spirits: to instill the knowledge of spirituality as a matter of symbols. The spirits are not *behind* the masks, but *in* the masks. Unmasking is a form of Hegelian sublation (*Aufhe-bung*), a practical lesson about the "labor of the negative." The boys learn that "the spirit is not something which is hidden behind the mask, the spirit dwells in the mask itself: the symbolic function, the ritual form, thus has more weight than its bearer [. . . and] the mask is only a signi-fier which expresses an internal, invisible spirit, a mystical preserve."[12] Secrecy has almost a cognitive function: it exemplifies this conceptual leap between the children's naïve belief in spirits and the adults' under-standing of the spiritual power inherent in the symbolic form.

While never referring directly to Mannoni, Taussig's evocative *De-facement* arrives at similar conclusions. The arts of masking and secrecy, with their complex tricks involving sound and visuality, are a way to instill in the initiates a practical knowledge about the labor of the nega-tive, of demonstrating the power of the symbolic form. At the same time, masking provides a sensuous representation of the fundamental divide between man and woman. The arts of deceit, which "in an-other time" were the domain of women—and that essentially belong to them, the sex of mysteries—have been entrusted to men through a tragic reversal. In Selk'nam myth, the women were once the masters of all secrets, until the men stole the secrets by carrying out a matri-cidal massacre. Similarly, a Makonde etiological story wants the men's mapiko to have been taken out of the women's initiation. Partaking in the game of secrecy, men and women reenact this original crisis and represent, for the initiates and for themselves, their relationship as one structured by irreducible conflict.

3. If the secrets of masks were such only for the uninitiated, who really believed in the spiritual nature of the lipiko until the dramatic moment of disclosure and unmasking, the game of secrecy and respect engaged adult men and women in ways that exceeded the educational function. If the game was staged for the children, the adults played it wholeheartedly and intensely as if their lives depended on it; it pervaded their everyday beyond the time of initiations, sustaining a playful but deepseated antagonism.

In his seminal monograph *Naven* (1937), Gregory Bateson proposed the concept of *schismogenesis* to account for the forms of competitive behavior that he observed in the New Guinea Iatmul puberty rituals. Schismogenesis, which literally means "generation of difference," describes a "process of differentiation in the norms of individual behavior resulting from cumulative interaction between individuals."[13] For Bateson, the Naven ritual worked to produce gendered and generational difference within Iatmul society. Through competition, the still-unformed boys and girls are turned into men and women, the cognitive and emotional experience of ritual working to accentuate gender difference. In the terms of contemporary social theory, we would translate Bateson's thesis as one concerning the relationship between competitive performance and subjectivity. Indeed, Bateson himself referred to structures of personhood intermediate between individual psychology and the group mind (the latter he considered "almost meaningless") and employed the concept of performance to account for the formation of these structures: "We have seen that the women are an audience for the spectacular performance of the men, and there can be no reasonable doubt that the presence of an audience is a very important factor in shaping the men's behavior. In fact, it is probable that the men are more exhibitionistic because the women admire their performances."[14]

For Bateson, Iatmul initiation rituals are but a case of a general dynamics: schismogenesis embraces phenomena as varied as intimate relations between individuals, the progressive maladjustment of neurotic individuals, culture contact, and modern politics.[15] Schismo-genesis occurs in two forms: *complementary*, when it generates forms of behavior that gradually differentiate and adapt to each other (as in the case of gender difference); and *symmetrical*, when it generates a similar behavior that can ultimately escalate in open conflict (as in the case of the arms race or boasting).

In Makonde puberty rituals, the game of ritual secrecy generates a dynamics of fierce schismogenetic rivalry between men and women. The atmosphere of initiations is one of mutual envy, provocation, and suspicion, in which men and women are constantly brought to com-pare their respective domains and to act as spectators of the others' performances. The choreography of initiation and the secret songs taught to the boys and the girls, in which they learn to insult (*kutu-kana*) the opposite sex, are all geared toward exacerbating this rivalry. On a Saturday afternoon, the women dramatically leave the village to go and perform their nkamangu deep down in the bush. The drums can be heard from the village, and they say, "You can't watch"! (Ac-cording to a popular etymology, the name of the feminine mask itself, *shitengamatu*, means "open your ears," a provocation addressed to the men, who can only listen to their drums). On Sunday, the men dance their mapiko. "Yesterday, they beat us. Today we are going to beat them!" "Why can't we follow you there?" "Because we have hanging penises and you have a crack between your legs!" "Women have the most powerful secrets because they are all witches!"[16] This is not a war for supremacy but a form of producing gendered difference.[17] Rivalry induces the boys to be boys and the girls to be girls; it shapes them into form; it teaches them their places; it inculcates the characteristics of the gendered self and other. Like circumcision, it removes all symbolic traces of bisexuality or androgyny. Empty as it is, secrecy divides: there are things between husband and wife that will never be spoken.

Interpreting secrecy in terms of schismogenesis allows us to draw a connecting line between puberty rituals and those aspects of masquer-ading that the Diases dismissed as inessential, especially mimicry and competition. To explore this interpretation, let us have a closer look, as it were, into my fieldwork notes.


4. The lowlands of ku-Iyanga lie east of the Makonde Plateau, a long stretch of savanna that traditionally served as a hunting ground for the

plateau people. Close to the coast, the Makonde intermingle there with the Islamic Mwani people, whose language they use for commerce and even domestic conversations.

In August 2002, I was prompted to carry out research in ku-Iyanga by Vicente Muanga, a sculptor and trader born there and living in Maputo who desired to visit his family villages. "There are mapiko there that will leave you wide-mouthed!" Vicente also insisted that we should not travel alone. "We will walk by foot, sometimes at night, for long stretches." In the months following my arrival, I had settled in the district of Muidumbe, located in the southeastern part of the Mueda Plateau, renowned for the richness of its dances, especially masquerades. There, I had become especially close with two persons: Maly-amungu, a boastful dancer of masks in his thirties, and a daydreaming teenager known as Angelina. They were the steadiest elements of a small crowd who frequented my house in the evenings for drinks and conversation. One night, Vicente invited them both on our ku-Iyanga trip and they accepted.

We began by working with a group of elders in the administrative post of Mbau. The elders had two masquerading genres in their repertoire. The first was a real rarity: a reenactment of an ancient genre called *dutu*, whose invention in the 1920s had marked a watershed in the practice of mapiko. These elders were ostensibly the only ones left who knew how to strike the drums, sing the songs, dance in the manner required by the genre, and paint scarifications on the masks with wax derived from a local wasplike insect. During an interview, the elders explained to us that they had been introduced to this genre of mapiko long ago, in the 1930s, by their fathers who had invented it. After a decade or so, they had moved on to new form of masking, introduced by their own generation, which they then danced for almost four decades. Upon becoming old, they reverted to dutu. They wanted to show to the generations of their grandchildren how their elders danced, but they also wished to differentiate themselves from their sons, who all danced the form of masking that they themselves had invented in the 1940s.

The second genre that they showed us was specific to the lowland areas: a long spectacle featuring several mask-characters, each with its own song and ambivalent moral message. The group called it *shike-lya*, but it was a variation on the regional style called *nshindo*, derived from the night-masks that the Diases had seen disappearing. During the shikelya performance, an uninvited guest showed up on the dance ground. A monkey mask, alone, began dancing to the rhythm of the elders' drums. The mask caught the attention of the crowd with feats of agility and dancing prowess. It climbed a tree and danced on a branch. The angered elders tried to chase the monkey away, but the young man who hid beneath it had already won his share of visibility and recognition. The monkey mask was also a novelty, as it did not feature in the elders' large collection.

Vicente's interest in visiting his home villages was also commercial: he wanted to buy masks and sell them in Maputo at higher prices.[18] The local nshindo group with their many headpieces, Vicente thought, would provide an opportunity for cheap, mass purchases. (I had already been a victim of his trading skills the year before, when he had sold a mask for an outrageous price to the inexperienced kid that I then was. "This mapiko has been danced by women in the nkamangu," he added, to increase the head's symbolic appeal.) In Mbau, Vicente stored the mystic goodies in the house where we were staying—an imposing array of disembodied potentialities lying on the floor. One day, a young woman came to bring us food in the house, but was unaware of what we were hiding there. Upon seeing the heads, she was startled and let the pot drop on the floor and break, spilling its contents. She looked away and stepped back, cloaked in modest shame. Was her fright sincere or performed? Was that shock or respect? The morning when we left Mbau, headed for the village of Nakitenge, an elderly woman called me quietly into her house. She wanted to sell a clay shitenga-matu mask. While I had tried hard to distance myself from Vicente's business endeavors, I gave way to the desire of possessing a token of the women's secret. Inspecting the head hidden in my bag, Malyamungu exclaimed, "I must tell you, this is the first time in my life, the first time I ever see a thing like this . . ."

In Nakitenge, we worked with another nshindo group, and again Vicente bought dozens of mapiko. We were staying in the house of his paternal aunt. *Baba nkongwe* (woman-father) was aware of the masks, and utterly unimpressed by them, as she herself was a master of the nkamangu. She walked freely in and out of the room where the heads were stacked. One night, after one too many glasses of *sura* (palm wine), seeing Baba nkongwe enter and leave the secret chamber where we were drinking, Malyamungu burst into a fuming invective: "You, Vicente, you are not a Makonde! You, lowland people, you have been corrupted by these Arabs, here on the coast! You are like

Arabs! You don't know a secret anymore! This fills me with shame. A woman, here, like this . . . Had we been in Muidumbe, blood would have been spilled! Machetes! If I'd told your mothers in Muidumbe, they wouldn't let you sleep in their house! In Muidumbe, they would machete you, I swear! I swear on my mother's crotch!" We all laughed at the spirited performance, but Baba nkongwe was herself ashamed.

At the end of our trip, we stopped in the city of Nampula, headed to Maputo and loaded with information and artifacts. We showed our guests, a Makonde couple from Nangade, some of the footage shot in Mbau. When it came to the dressing of the masked dancer—which I had filmed in detail, though keeping the dancer's face out of the field of vision—the woman became exceedingly curious, and the man annoyed. "So, this is how they do it," she said, craving more. The spiritual nature of the lipiko was not a source of concern for either of them, but the practical secret concerning the dressing of the dancer was one that the man deemed worthy of protecting and the woman of discovering. After we left, the husband promptly concealed the DVD from his wife's inquisitiveness.

Through the game of secrecy, gender, generational, and regional differences are enacted and produced—at once playfully and seriously. For if the women perform their fear and the men their wrath with more than a hint of irony, the feelings thus aroused are real enough to make one drop a plate, the other go into a fit of rage; one be shameful, and the other hide away a film from his wife.


5. Puberty rituals and their attendant secrecy cannot be reduced to schismogenesis. Their historical resilience is connected to their malleability: to the capacity of doing and meaning different things in different times. Besides accentuating gendered difference, they induce the initiates to be courageous and withstand pain; they help in dealing with family neuroses; they teach basic livelihood skills; and—not to be underestimated—they endow the initiates with all the necessary magic protections for their adult lives in the form of *mitela* (plants, medicines).

It is indeed the fear of mitela that grounds the game of ritual secrecy in real emotions. For if the women know that the mask conceals a dancer, they are wary of the magical power of both the mask and its wearer, which might be triggered against snoopers. Masters of ceremonies boast about the efficacy of their "mines" (*dimina*) in killing intruders; those who stumble on a forbidden object fear for their health:

Me, myself, it made my head ache. It happened that I looked inside a mapiko. Now, that lipiko went to dance, and as he approached this side, that lipiko did me like this: the *dinjuga* [iron bells] went *dingili!* I left immediately the dance-field. All my head was aching. I was afraid! I took a fright. And I had to leave and go home and lie in bed, and my head was aching until the morning of the day after.[19]

Interpreting ritual secrecy as a social game does not discount real belief in either ancestors or spirits. As Atanásio Nhussi put it in a performance on puberty rituals, the Makonde Plateau is "the place where there are bridges with no rivers and where everybody believes in life after death."[20] This belief is most solidly rooted in the practice of ancestral supplication (*kulipudya* or *kulumba shonde*) performed on the graves of the deceased, more so than in mapiko masks, which refer to the domain of ancestral spirit only symbolically. The mask can stand for the spirit of the dead only after it has led the initiate through a process of radical disbelief, in which its fictive nature has been exposed. The two—belief and unbelief—are inseparable, and their cognitive conjunction is what makes masks mysterious and enthralling across spaces and times.

If we grant, however, that puberty rituals engender schismogenetic dynamics—that the competitive game of secrecy shapes persons as differentiated social beings—this assumption must still be historically specified. If schismogenesis is a universal process rooted in human biology, as Bateson argues, it still manifests itself differently in different historical moments, embodied in various social institutions and charged with various emotional and existential tonalities. The schismogenetic dynamics exemplified by my early-2000s fieldwork sketches refer to a time in which the stakes of the game were somewhat diminished—in which the shaping of social persons was assigned only in part to ritual and masks. The game was still serious, generating emotions of shame and curiosity, fear and defiance. But the existential tone of ritual schismogenesis was much more dramatic in the turbulent times of the Indian Ocean slave trade, when Makonde ethnicity coalesced.

6. The origin of the Makonde has constituted a small mystery to those interested in the dynamics of ethnogenesis and migration in this portion

of East Africa.[21] Jorge Dias formulated the conjecture of a "long march to the East" of a population native to the southern Lake Nyasa region, sometime in the seventeenth century, as a result of severe droughts and warfare. Before, these proto-Makonde would have been part of the Maravi confederation, a great tributary empire that extended far and wide around the lake.[22] The connection between the Makonde and the Maravi was supported by morphologic similarities between *mapiko* and *nyau*, the masquerades of the Chewa-Nyanja populations most directly linked to the Maravi. The rules of secrecy of the two masquerades, and their relationship with initiation rituals, Dias observed, are very similar; furthermore, both nyau and mapiko are organized around a basic division between daytime masks, representing the dead, and nighttime masks, representing spiritual bush animals meant to scare and chastise the women and the noninitiated.[23] Unlike *nyau, mapiko* appeared not to be danced at funerary ceremonies, but the difference seemed minor enough to support claims of a direct genealogical connection.

The diary of António Bocarro's journey from Tete to Kilwa in 1616 might lead to a different interpretation of the connection of the Makonde with the Maravi empire.[24] Traveling under the services of the king of Portugal on a well-worn trade route, Bocarro recorded in detail the meeting with the chiefs and the gifts offered to them, so that "the adventurer, who makes it, may know about the road and the expenses."[25] The large territory that he traversed, from the gold fair of Tete in the upper Zambezi to Kilwa Island in today's Tanzania, was ruled by a variety of chiefs, all imbricated in tributary relations with the Maravi empire. While drawing a precise line between political allegiances and ethnic formations based on Bocarro's account is difficult, one may reasonably suppose that groups of Maravi had settled along this commercial way.[26] With the crumbling of the Maravi empire, these populations would have been cut off from their political center and had to readapt to the conditions of the Rovuma region, which from the early eighteenth century onward was increasingly defined by the slave trade, either by constituting independent chieftaincies or by reverting to segmentary acephalous political systems. The Makonde, Yao, and Matambwe people of northern Mozambique could be the result of this process of disintegration of the Maravi empire. Linguistic evidence supports this hypothesis: the cluster of Makonde and Yao languages are mutually understandable and closer to the Nyanja-Chewa languages than to the unrelated neighboring Makua cluster.[27] If this hypothesis is correct, Makonde ethnicity emerged as the result of the breakdown of one of those African *regna* that were the common political form before colonialism—"geographically huge but strong state formations," dominated by a warrior elite and composed by people of diverse languages and customs.[28] There is no reason to doubt the genealogy that connects mapiko to nyau and the Maravi, and beyond, to the Congo Basin from where the Maravi originally came; mapiko's peculiar helmet-like shape could thus be related to similar southern Congolese masks.

Diffusionism, however, does not lead any further in understanding the historicity of cultural practice and ethnicity in the region. The traits that might have made one group appear different from the other (practices of bodily modification such as the lip plug, tooth chipping, and scarification; the morphology of initiation rituals and masquerading; systems of kinship and social organization; specific customs) circulated in a fluid social space: they were widely exchanged and appropriated.[29] The mobilization of these practices is integral to the wider process of the reconfiguration of northern Mozambican societies in the context of the Indian Ocean slave trade; it can almost be considered as the slave trade's cultural dimension.

In the centuries that followed the downfall of the Maravi empire, each society took a distinctive path to face the challenges of the slave trade. The Yao reorganized in aggressive chieftaincies and become the main raiders and long-distance traders.[30] In the second half of the nineteenth century, they massively converted to Islam, forgoing many of the cultural practices, customs, and alimentary habits forbidden by the Koran, especially scarification and masquerading. Coastal Makua groups adopted similar strategies, with their cultural consequences: after having extensively practiced facial scarification and tooth chipping, they abandoned these practices in the course of the nineteenth century, together with masquerading, which is attested by extant masks and residual practice.[31]

The Makonde took the inverse path, entrenching themselves in a remote plateau to resist the ravages of slavery. The first mention of the Mozambican Makonde as a separate ethnicity dates to the early nineteenth century—precisely the years in which slavery was on the rise in the Rovuma Valley—and refers to raids carried out by the "small Makonde kingdom" against "slaves in the fields."[32] The etymology of the name *mmakonde* (pl. *vamakonde*) is uncertain, but all interpretations seem to point to a geographical meaning. Jorge Dias connects it to *likonde* (pl. *makonde*), "drylands," and *kukonde*, "being fertile," both being appropriate to the plateau, which is waterless but fertile during the rainy season.[33] The word *likonde* (pl. *makonde*) also indicates a type of grass growing in the southern plateau area, which might define it metonymically.[34] Another possible interpretation is that *makonde* is a vernacularization of the Kiswahili term *makonde*, indicating remote lands allocated to slave communities, on which only staple crops could grow.[35] Be that as it may, the name Makonde (*vamakonde*) certainly indicated those who inhabited a place, the plateau known as ku-Makonde (*ku* being a locative particle).

The plateau was open to all people who would renounce the proximity of water in order to find refuge from the slave trade, hiding in the maze of thickets known as ku-Makonde. Rules of belonging were inclusive: a person from the lowlands would be made Makonde by undergoing scarification and teeth chipping, as well as committing to master the language.[36] There was no need of passing through puberty rituals again: a Makua initiation, say, was considered sufficient, so long as the person accepted having Makondeness inscribed on the flesh. Many Makonde matrilineages thus trace their origins to Makua and Matambwe ancestors who took the way of the plateau. For instance, the lineage that Montfort missionaries encountered in 1929 when they first arrived on the plateau actually descended from a Matambwe elephant hunter from the Rovuma River region named Shiebu, who had settled there in the late nineteenth century. The name of the lineage was originally Vamatambwe, but it was changed to Vanang'alolo because of the appetite of its members for wild partridges (*ng'alolo*, which the missionaries misspelled as *nangololo*). The Vanang'alolo eventually allowed a group of Yao traders to settle on their lands; with them they coexisted in peace, exchanging the customary provocations that link the two groups in a joking relationship (*uvilo*).[37]

Makonde ethnicity was defined by the retreat onto the plateau area as a defensive stance against the slave trade; by correlative segmentary acephalous social organization; and by the rebuttal of Islam and the intensification of cultural practices characteristic of *washenzi* ("barbarian, savage, non-Muslim") such as bodily modification, extensive consuming of all forms of meat, and masquerading. These practices can be considered as strategies of social differentiation, adaptation, and reproduction, rather than merely as ancestral cultural features. Although scarification had a magical, aesthetic, and sexual dimension—"how sweet to caress a *dinembo*-covered belly"[38]—it also served to mark belonging. Makonde persons could recognize each other's bodies far away from home, living or dead, free or slave by merely looking at each other's skin. Slavery (*ushagwa*) was the commonest theme of provocation in joking-relationships: "You're a slave! My father bought you!" "You're the slave of slaves: your father was my mother's slave!" and so on.[39] "Slave-lands" (*kuna-vashagwa*) is what all territories beyond the plateau were called; and "slave masquerades" (*makomba amashagwa*) was the term given to the face-masks danced by the Makua, Yao, and Ngoni. The peculiar helmet shape of mapiko masks, which could be genetically connected to Congo Basin masks, can thus also be considered as the result of schismogenetic differentiation with the face-masks of the neighboring Makua and Yao.

The myth of Makonde fierceness and savagery was possibly propagated by the Makonde themselves to scare away intruders from their refugee stronghold. It would eventually survive the times of the slave trade, fostered by colonial exoticism and local lore: the Makonde, who are avid consumers of all sorts of bizarre meats, who always carry knives and machetes, who are quickly angered and prompt to kill, who are feared by the tame and treacherous Makua, who will not work as maids but make for excellent night guards, who can be stern enemies or loyal friends . . .[40]

We are now in a better position to understand the attachment of the Makonde to practices abandoned by their neighbors—masquerading and bodily modifications—as well as the existential tone of ritual schismogenesis at the time. A refugee group such as the Makonde was faced with the constant threat of annihilation: a very concrete prospect, if one considers the Matambwe's doom.[41] If the symbology of death that pervades puberty rituals has broader cosmological resonance, it might also be an expression of the angst and dread that are characteristic of the historical world of the slave trade, more specifically, of a refugee society threatened by disintegration. These emotional tones would continue to permeate initiation rituals and the social fabric that they help produce. Half a century after the ending of slavery, Jorge Dias observed that "the dominant emotion amongst the Maconde in general is fear more than piety or love."[42]

7. Let us now peep back into Vicente's baskets, full of mapiko masks. What do we see? Masai and Americans, dogs and hares, Makua and

Mwani, drunkards and womanizers, fishermen and hunters, lazy and avid, witches and crippled, young and old, men and women. If ritual secrecy produces social difference through competition, masking mimesis represents it in all aspects: difference of gender, generation, lineage, ethnicity, religion; between human and animal, self and other, vice and virtue. In this respect, mapiko is by no means special. Most spiritual dances across the world focus on the representation of alterity. In fact, the cipher of sacred theatre—of that primordial wholeness where laughter, representation, and ecstasy are not separated—might very well be the mimicry of otherness. How does anthropological theory approach this fact?

In a broad-ranging study of ritual arts south of the Sahara, Fritz Kramer argues that the mimesis of otherness is at the core of an indigenous African aesthetics.[43] Contrary to the assumption that sees "primitive arts" as abstract, for Kramer the aesthetics of African possession cults is grounded in realism. The depiction of otherness expresses a "view from without," which does not interpret the other's cultural world but congeals its essential characteristics, in the process almost turning the other into a monster. African realism is not a committed satire, as the Marxists wanted it. For Kramer, this view from without is apolitical: "[T]he outside observer maintains an essential distance, doing so precisely by making his replicas—and in some cases even himself—similar to that which he observes and not [. . .] by passing critical judgment."[44]

However, clearly the mimicry of otherness in ritual arts has a broader scope than the sub-Saharan African region considered by Kramer. In a book published in the same year as the English translation of Kramer's study, Michael Taussig discusses the mimesis of otherness that occurs in South American ritual statuettes. Inspired by Walter Benjamin's musings, Taussig contends that the relationship between mimicry and alterity is somewhat inscribed in the colonial encounter—a spiraling game of savages mimicking Westerners who hold that savages are the masters of mimicry.[45]

But the link between mimesis and alterity is clearly also older than colonialism: it is an almost universal feature of ritual arts. René Girard found in this fact a proof of his anthropological hypothesis concerning the scapegoat mechanism as the foundation of human culture. For Girard, human desire is triangular: we always desire that which somebody else desires. The triangular nature of desire drove primitive human communities into what Girard calls a "mimetic crisis"—a moment of generalized envy that burst into a fight of all against all, as in Bateson's symmetrical schismogenesis.[46] The mimetic crisis could be solved only by killing one of the members of the community as a scapegoat. All human culture, for Girard, is inspired by the traumatic memory of this original mimetic crisis. The depiction of otherness in masks is interpreted as yet another reenactment of the crisis: they represent "monstrous doubles," selves devoured by the desire of what the other desires.[47]

What does the mimesis of otherness in ritual arts index? A form of sympathetic magic? An incipient form of political critique? An indigenous African realism that does not pass judgment on what it mimics? A game of mirrors between colonial primitivists and newly discovered primitives? The survival of the traumatic memory of an original mimetic crisis? Dick-Read's, the Marxists', Kramer's, Taussig's, and Girard's interpretations are so divergent as to almost nullify—or ridicule—each other. Ritual mimesis eludes the crossfire of anthropological theory. It is tempting to summon the concept of schismogenesis to make sense of the enigma. Could we interpret ritual mimesis as a way of producing social difference through representation? To what avail? Can all of Vicente's masks fit into one theoretical basket?

The major flaw of all the above theories is that they do not take into consideration performance, genre, and historicity, as if the meaning of ritual mimesis could be decided in the abstract. But masks take on life in elaborate spectacles, and one cannot assume that their meanings remain unchanged through time. In fact, the only reason to assume so would be the desire to attribute some kind of essence to the dancing subjects, such as the "realist Africans" or the "mimicking subalterns."

The concept of schismogenesis has been useful to reconnect aspects that in the colonial library had been dismembered: ritual, secrecy, competition, and mimesis. But these connections do not point to an essence, only to a pattern. If there is one law pertaining to human institutions, it is that they change, together with their meanings and functions. The same must be true of mapiko. After this excursion into anthropological theory, we must abandon the quest for origins and move to a historical analysis that stays closer to the thought and practice of mapiko players themselves.

# PART TWO

⤸

# Cosmopolitanism (1917–62)

In African nationalist political discourse, literature, and academic production, the colonial era is painted in somber tones—as a time of chains, despair, humiliation, and folly, redeemed only by the sentiments of rebellion and the practice of resistance that it generated. How do such heavy times appear when seen through the prism of play? The oral history of mapiko that is the object of this part, from colonial occupation (1917) to the formation of Frelimo (1962), is marked by cosmopolitan artistic vibrancy, creativity, and festive effervescence. In this period, the foundations were laid for everything that would follow: mapiko diversified in competing genres; its aesthetics was enriched and refined; participation was extended beyond the boundaries of lineage; and influential individuals emerged as leaders of flamboyant ensembles. The curiosity for the foreign is the hallmark of this era. More than anything, mapiko players looked beyond the confines of the plateau in search of inspiration, appropriating the exotic in their quest for fame, while at the same time making sense of a broader world through the dance of masks. Four chapters explore this colonial-era cosmopolitanism from various angles and with increasing intensity of detail.

Chapter 3, "Meat Is Meat," discusses a rupture in mapiko practice that occurred in the 1920s, marked by an emphasis on aesthetic perfection and abstraction, by the recruitment of group members according to artistic talent, and by the emergence of new genres with generational resonance. The chapter argues that this break was prompted by the intensification of dance rivalry after colonial pacification and by the appropriation of coastal competitive culture.

Chapter 4, "Masters of Play," follows the track of the masquerade master Nampyopyo to have a closer perspective on mapiko in the colonial era. Focusing on this "exceptional normal" case, the chapter discusses vernacular conceptions of aesthetics, transformations in mask ownership, the influence of European patronage of Makonde carving, and the summoning of dance ensembles in the state rituals. Finally, the chapter introduces Nampyopyo's rival Shumu and describes their lavish masking contests.

Chapter 5, "Lowland Nights," moves down to the Messalo Plains southeast of the Makonde Plateau. There, the elder Lipato invented a new genre of night masquerades: a parade of dozens of characters danced on the occasion of funerary ceremonies and focused on the depiction of otherness. This genre would eventually include a public demonstration of the activities of sorcerers. The chapter analyzes the relationship between charactering and otherness, ambivalence and grieving; it also provides a poignant example in which masking creativity, far from being prompted by disenchantment, was underwritten by increased anxieties concerning witchcraft.

Chapter 6, "Migrant Tunes," dwells on the aural matter, discussing the elaborate poems that renowned "song carvers" composed specifically for mapiko performances. Spiced up with words in Kiswahili—the language of labor migrancy—these songs anchored the dance of masks in historical actuality, providing a vivid picture of unrest on the eve of the anticolonial struggle. The chapter explores the multilayered meanings of such songs, the competitive contest in which they were performed, the trajectories of their authors, and their musicality.

# 3 ⤚ Meat Is Meat

*Modernism in the Aftermath of Slavery*

| | |
|---|---|
| Nshenji kabisa | Thoroughly savage |
| Makalia banga ntima | Makalia has a naughty heart |
| Mtoto walaya | A kid from overseas |
| Anshema muje kwimbanao | Calls a friend to sing together |
| Wetu tukannola | When we see him |
| Tunshema nshagwa | We call him a slave from the |
| Ku-Makugwa | Makua-lands |
| Nshagwa ni nshagwa | A slave is a slave |
| Nshagwa shani ku-Namande? | What kind of slave, in Namande? |
| Mpolo wakwetu 'ndaigwinika | Our mask-hiding-place is famous |
| Mpaka Tanga | As far as Tanga |

—"Nshenji kabicha," Makonde Kawe Group[1]

1. THE HISTORY of mapiko that can be written relying on living memory begins with an upheaval at the zenith of Portuguese colonialism, whose sense is captured by a telling Shimakonde expression: *nyama ni nyama*, "meat is meat."[2]

> Everyone who liked could come and enter. Everyone who wanted could join on the dance-field. Then, it is called meat-is-meat. Because it means: the meat of this lineage, the meat of that lineage, they can be mixed. This is why you say meat-is-meat.[3]

> I answer, you answer, he answers. From where you come, I don't know. But you prepare [the masks] with me. *Wa! Nyama ni nyama!*[4]

57

Before meat-is-meat, mapiko masks were organized following the lineage partitions of segmentary Makonde society. Each hamlet (*likaja*), home of a portion of a matrilineage (*likola*), would prepare the masks (*kupanga mapiko*) to dance at specific times of the year, in connection with the coming out of masculine and feminine puberty ceremonies.[5] Groups from other hamlets and lineages would be invited to join on the dance-field and to confront each other's skills in dancing contests, but the members of each lineage group would not intermingle. The triumph of a mapiko ensemble went to the glory of one lineage, and a hamlet headman (*nang'olo mwene likaja*), against the others.

This social configuration changed in the years following the subjection of the Makonde Plateau by the Portuguese. Then, heads of mask ensembles began to enroll new members based on their artistic talent (*ulanda*), irrespective of their lineage. The revolution of meat-is-meat—the loosening of lineage logics in the organization of masked dancing in favor of artistry—made possible the emergence of new sophisticated forms of masquerading. Inventiveness and excellence in dancing, carving, drumming, and singing were sought after and cultivated. The long seclusion in masculine puberty ceremonies, during which boys would be exposed to the secrets of the masks, became an occasion for exploring their talent and to carry out an intensive training of the gifted ones. Talented boys could be enrolled in mask ensembles, as drummers or singers, even before their coming-of-age. The meat-is-meat ensembles could thus offer the most shining performances, unrivaled by lineage-based groups.

In the same years in which the discovery of tribal masks by European modernist artists such as Picasso and Braque prompted the invention of fauvism and cubism, a modernist revolution was taking place in the practice of mapiko.[6] Emerging in a remote periphery of a lesser colonial empire, this modernism in the arts of masking was marked by a shift from "filiation to affiliation" and by an emphasis on aesthetic perfection and novelty, much like its European counterpart.[7] How is one to historicize this major cultural break?

2. The first stumbling block is the lack of written sources that would allow one to reconstruct with some degree of detail the aesthetics and practice of mapiko in the years that preceded the meat-is-meat break. One can blame the colonial ethnographers' primitivism as well as the

economism and antitraditionalism of subsequent Frelimo researchers (dance was not on the agenda of the historical brigades that visited the plateau from the 1980s onward); be that as it may, the situation is such that reconstruction must perforce be conjectural.

The only hard evidence useful for such an endeavor is the head-pieces collected by Europeans from the late nineteenth century onward and preserved in museums. Stylistic analysis reveals a rupture circa the 1930s, marked by geometric abstraction of form.[8] The new carving style, richly documented by extant masks, is characterized by downward-angled slit eyes; a prominent chin, drawn on a line perpendicular to the neck, with the face at a sharp angle; thick rhomboid lips; small ears; and scarifications drawn with wax or in relief.[9] The few extant head-pieces that predate this style are more various: the oldest are round or cylindrical with closed eyelids; others are oval-shaped, with downward-slanting eyes and rhomboid lips; still others are half-helmet shaped. A separate group is constituted by hare-like humanoid masks with elon-gated ears—a theme that bridges styles and is reproduced in oval and round forms.[10] An overall feature that cuts across styles, at least until the 1950s, is semiclosed eyes, which refer to the "living dead" nature of the ancestral spirit that is represented. If the sculptural evidence confirms that a stylistic break occurred between the 1920s and the 1930s, it throws little light on the practice and meanings attached to the older masks. The hard lessons to be learned from the performative approach to the study of masquerading are not only that headpieces are subordinate to performance—that they are created to fit the dancer's vision—but also that performance itself cannot be inferred from the analysis of masks. More than its form, what gives meaning to the mask is the dance that brings it to life and the songs that anchor it to historical actuality.

A more indirect source of evidence is collective memory. None of the elders that I could interview was old enough to have witnessed the times preceding the conquest of the plateau; however, they inherited some knowledge of a style of masking, which would be later resurrected (*kutakatuwa*) by the master sculptor Nampyopyo of Nang'unde and by others, wherein the masks were tied to specific characters, announced by a song, and accompanied by a commentary, whether moral or etio-logical.[11] This character principle applied to both day- and nighttime mapiko: the former represented ancestral spirits summoned from the grave, brought by the men to dance in the settlements; the latter, wild spiritual beasts (*vakoko*) invading the hamlet and tamed by young men.

In times of old, the dance was meant to be dramatically scary, with the lipiko "rushing at people and throwing sticks at random"[12] and even dancing at a distance from the hamlet;[13] nonetheless, the mask was conceived as a spirit with a specific personality, conveyed by a song and a spoken commentary. When Nampyopyo and others resurrected and expanded this character modality in the 1940s, elders knew that they were tapping into an older and more original form: "Thus danced the grandfathers of our fathers."[14]

Comparative evidence strongly supports this idea. The depiction of characters, as well as the division between day- and nighttime masks, is at the heart of all masking complexes of the region. Makua and Yao facemasks from the Rovuma River region are "all representational and each costume depicts a particular person or animal," the dancers being "actors specializing in demonstrating a variety of aspects of community life."[15] Many of the face-masks collected by Karl Weule in southern Tanzania in 1908 represent ethnic others, especially Europeans or Oriental types.[16] Makua wooden face-masks from Nampula are less varied but still embody several mythical characters connected to puberty ritual teachings.[17] Nyau day-masks are satirical representations of village types, and even the more abstract feathery *kasinja* have important mimetic elements conveyed through performance.[18] All night-masks of the region—Makua, Yao, Tanzanian Makonde, and Chewa, as well as our *shilo*—are based on the depiction of morally characterized spiritual animals. Characterization is also at the heart of the more remote, but genetically related, Chokwe Makishi masks;[19] farther away, of southern Congolese masks; and more generally of all masquerade traditions of the central African matrilineal belt.[20] At the risk of making a sweeping generalization, one could in fact argue that most masquerade traditions and spirit possession cults in Africa are based on some form of characterization, however abstract, layered, and composite the representations thus produced may be.[21]

Extant mapiko masks do not give us the means to reconstruct the outlines of ancient danced characters, except for the hare type that still survives today and is connected to the symbology of initiation rituals (*shingula*, "the hare," is the leader of the male initiates [see chap. 2, sec. 1] and the trickster of oral storytelling). The majority of old masks represent women, and according to the Diases, "[O]ld Maconde confirm that in the past [feminine masks] were even more numerous than today."[22] The Makishi example makes clear that such stereotypical feminine masks can be invested with many characterizations. One piece collected in the early twentieth century wears the iconic red fez that Fritz Kramer associates with alterity, representing possibly an Arab or an Islamized Makonde (fig. 4).[23] Other ancient masks still conjoin features of ethnic alterity, such as fluent beards and Muslim hats, with Makonde scarifications—a clear indication that the latter did not necessarily imply the representation of a Makonde person and that the piling-up of different features within a single mask was possible. As we will see, masks of scarified Makonde elders could be used in performance to metaphorically characterize things as diverse as a flood and a centipede (see chap. 4, sec. 8; chap. 5, sec. 3).

Something that we know for sure about this older form of masking is that it was animated by the iconic elongated drum *nneya,* which gave

FIGURE 4. Alterity *(mapiko mask, Mozambican Natural History Museum, ca. 1900–1920)*

name to the performance itself, and that its rhythm was fast and its dance short: *"Tilikili-ti, tilikili-ti, ki-kili, ki-kili, kiliki, tu!* Us, here! And that's it."[24]

3. It is indeed in terms of drumming, not masking, that mapiko practitioners (*vamapiko*) recount and conceptualize the transformations of their tradition:

> I am telling the history of mapiko. The history of mapiko: firstly, the elders of long ago used to play with a nneya. And one *shinganga*. No *ligoma*, no *likuti*. They went on . . . with their elderliness. They eventually abandoned it, as they thought it had become tasteless. That nneya, it had become tasteless.
>
> And they sat and invented the likuti. They introduced the likuti, and they used to play with one nneya, two or three *vinganga*. They went on organizing mapiko with likuti . . . In the end, they left it. They saw it as outmoded now. They invented the ligoma, with the *ntoji*. With vinganga. And one nneya, in the middle. To form one ensemble, with many people [playing]. And they went on . . . until today.[25]

Two rhythms structure the mapiko performance: a reiterative base percussion (*kukudula*), generally played on more than one drum; and a soloist percussion line, which "commands" (*kububuwa*) the movements of the dancer, generally played by one person on one drum. The latter is the most important, and commanding-drum rhythmical sequences are memorized by performers in the form of codified syllabic phrases. *Nneya* (pl. *mileya*), *likuti* (pl. *makuti*), and *ligoma* (pl. *magoma*) are three drums that have been used, at different stages, to command (*kububuwa*) the mask (fig. 5), as follows.

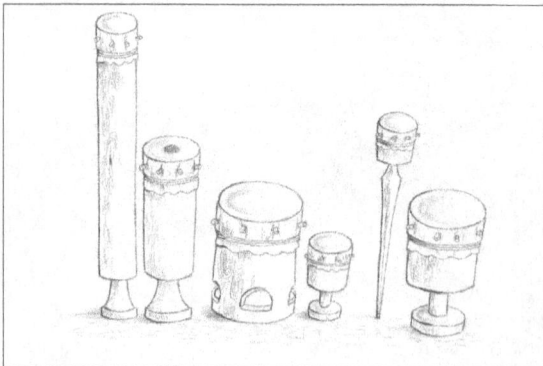

FIGURE 5A. Drums (*drawing by Pascoal Mbundi*)

FIGURE 5B. The drum orchestra *(Rui Assubuji, Litamanda, 2009)*

I. MILEYA. The first drum was used in the genre practiced before the 1920s and based, as I have surmised, on an idiom of spiritual characters. The elongated nneya—a drum difficult to construct, carved out of a log of hardwood buried in the ground and pierced with a harpoon—was accompanied by a few small chalice-shaped vinganga, which produce a characteristic high-pitched sound, especially when covered with python skins. The performance was fast and furious, but there would be more than one mask dancing during the same afternoon.

II. DUTU. The old idiom was wiped out in the early 1920s and swiftly replaced by a new genre commanded by the large drum likuti.[26] This genre was highly abstract. As headpieces, it favored geometric masks of Makonde elders, masculine and feminine, or aestheticized representations of otherness. The dance was devoid of mimetic elements. The mask was called from the bush in a stylized way, with drumming, songs, and the sound of the antelope horn *lipalapanda*. The main performance was divided into two distinct movements: the playful *lishesho* and the more rapid *nshakasha*. Songs, animation, or extra gimmicks filled the pauses between the two movements. The masks danced in turns, but some of the most daring groups put various mapiko to dance in synchrony. The drum orchestra was expanded: more vinganga played the base percussion, with the nneya in their center, while the commanding role was taken by the large chalice-shaped *likuti likumene*, struck with a thick flexible stick. From the onomatopoeia of the piercing sound of this drum, which could be heard as far as ten miles away, the genre was also called *dutu: Du-tu! Du-tu! Du-tu!*

III. NSHESHO. The third genre, which emerged in the 1940s, expanded the formal potentialities of its predecessor.[27] The dance steps of the lipiko were codified in specific mimetic styles (*vikuvo*), each with a more or less precise referent, such as the movements of an animal, a particular gesture, a social situation, an episode of local history, or steps adapted from another dance. The masks were increasingly naturalistic and polished. The songs were intoned by a choir, with harmonies influenced by mission music. The two movements were prolonged and the pace slowed down. The performance of styles and songs worked independently from the mask worn: you could have, say, an Arab's mask, dancing a Makonde feminine dance, to songs referring obliquely to forced cotton production. More vinganga were added to strengthen the base percussion, and a new duo of drums was used to command: the low-pitched ligoma and a small likuti, both struck with the hand.

This genre was called *ashinemba* (youth style), because it was practiced mainly by younger people; *aligoma*, because of the leading drum; or *nshesho* (also *nshesha*), because the first movement was much longer and elaborated.

The new genres that emerged after the meat-is-meat break brought along a new conception of masquerading, whereby abstraction and the autonomy of form—carving, dancing, and singing—superseded the mimetic representation of a character. The performance was complex and elusive, an intersection of different forms that did not necessarily have to converge. Each of these forms could now be developed separately by the more talented people—master carvers, singers, dancers, and drummers—and brought to aesthetic perfection. The meat-is-meat principle itself was initially associated with the dutu genre, as if abstraction in performance was to be accompanied by abstraction in participation. In nshesho, a direct mimetic element appeared in codified dancing styles (vikuvo); however, it was largely detached from the mask and the song.

The two new genres also introduced a differentiation based on generation. The antique mileya cut across ages and regions. Innovation must have occurred within a fixed template—in the form of masks, dance styles, or characters introduced, which would not, however, substantially alter the performance template. Instead, the new genres constituted a radical break: they each had different performance styles and required different skills; they were mutually exclusive; they diffused in abrupt waves of fashion; and they were closely associated with the generations that had introduced them.

4. This swift diversification of mapiko can be understood as a transposition of the slavery-era schismogenetic dynamics into the realm of dance competition. Portuguese peace (*paz portuguesa*) was a somber euphemism for colonial domination, but the expression was not devoid of meaning in the case of the Makonde. Military conquest and effective colonial occupation put an end to raids and lineage wars (*ding'ondo dyanyanyamala*). The violence of the colonial state was more methodical and slightly more sublimated; order was demanded and brawls discouraged. As commandment penetrated the everyday of subjects, the thick walls around hamlets became useless. To connect administrative posts, larger paths were built, on which people, by daytime, could

travel almost confidently, fearing more the voracity of the leopard than that of a human being. Tentatively, a larger public sphere—in which people could exchange news and ideas and could argue and discuss without the immediate impending threat of being captured and sold to a slaving caravan—began to take shape.[28]

Antagonism between lineages and generations was ingrained in the schismogenetic logics of precolonial Makonde society, embedded in social institutions, such as the expectation that cadets carry out provocations (*ushaka*) against rival matrilineages to capture valuables or women.[29] With Portuguese pacification and the end of internecine wars, these rivalries were to be played out in the dancing arena. Announced by groups of women who ran from hamlet to hamlet singing *kwaula ntumi*, "to tell the lion," the coming out of initiations became occasions for different mapiko groups to come together and test their dancing skills on the occasion of initiations or the new state festivities or simply during the weekend.

During the long seclusion of masculine initiation rituals, the boys were exposed to the various facets of mapiko: drumming, singing, dancing, and, no less important, the dressing of the masked dancer. Rolling a fringed cloth (*ingonda*) around the lipiko's pelvis strongly and securely; fixing around its arms and legs a black cloth by using small bits of wood (*vigwali*, from *kugwala*, "to dress") and raffia rope, in such a way as to be tight and elegant—these were difficult tasks, mastered by few (fig. 6). The best drummers would be enrolled to play for mapiko groups even before their coming-of-age. Good dancers were put to the test during the period of initiation. Some youths would be multitalented, learning drumming, singing, and dancing all at once. Artistic talent was considered a hereditary gift, and explorations were carried out to discover one's inclinations:

> Because there is the talent (*ulanda*) that you are born with. That is, it's in the belly of your mother. And you will become a talented artist (*nnanda*). Now, there they tell you "this and that," like in school; if the teacher tells you "this and that," you understand immediately. But the others don't understand.[30]

Lack of any talent was expressed with the disparaging word *udagwa*, which implied more broadly the inability to live a good sociable life—a sign of the importance of performance in Makonde notions of personhood.

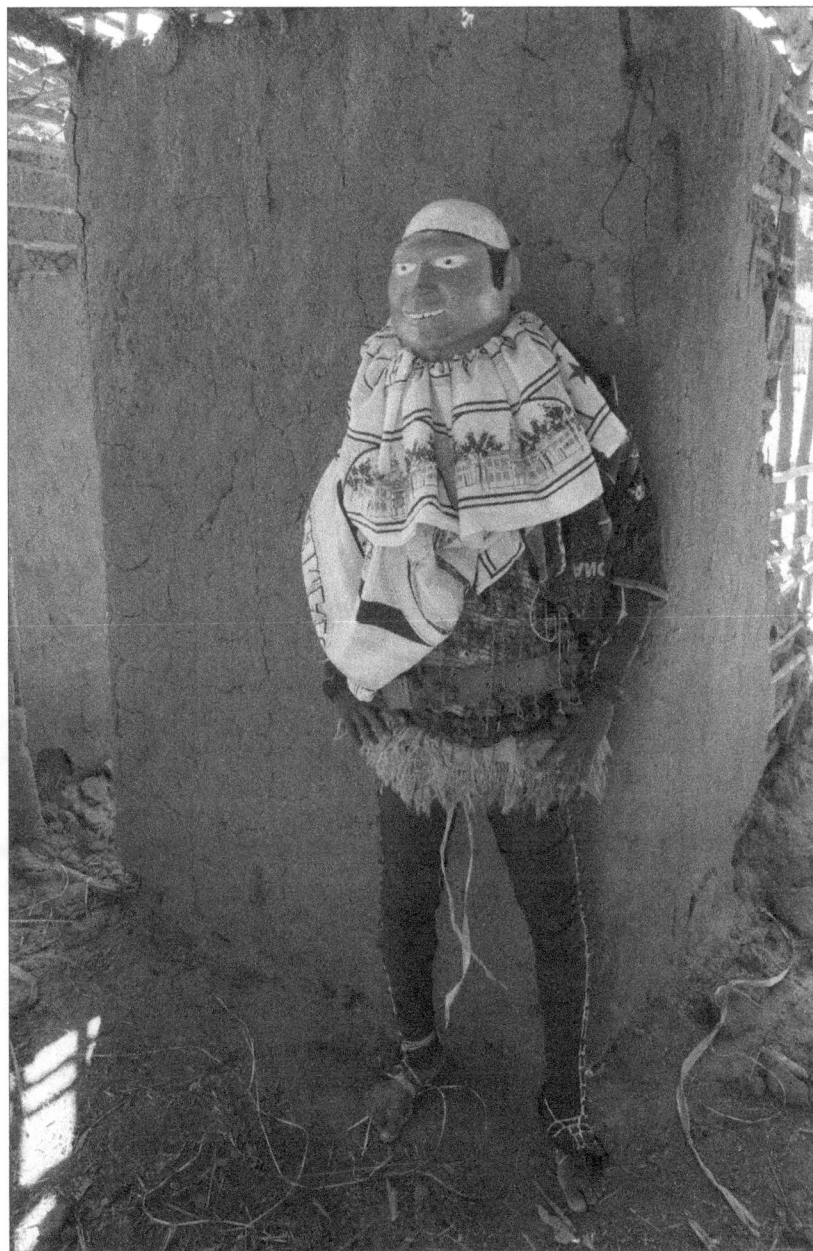

FIGURE 6. Just prepared *(Rui Assubuji, Chai, 2009)*

The invention of new forms and genres of mapiko took place in the exploratory space of initiation rituals, as a way for youths to express their generational defiance: "[T]o deny what is your father's, and you do your own."[31] Generational defiance coalesced, so to speak, in the main two genres introduced after the meat-is-meat break: dutu, with its loud drum and abstract dance style; and nshesho, with its grand choirs and mimetic choreographies. Both these forms emerged as the result of experiments pioneered in the bush by young initiates, performed on the public dance-field, and then widely imitated.

Groups of one genre competed with their equivalents: dutu versus dutu, nshesho versus nshesho. Irrespective of the form, the atmosphere on the dance-field was heated. Provocations were hurled from one side to the other, in the form of elaborate songs of derision:

| | |
|---|---|
| Yashinto kulepa ing'ope | Hyacinth's face is stretched |
| Lundomo lwamwina mene lundipandamoka | The bottom lip falls down |
| Mwaa walijega lyanakuluwo lya-Kungumu | Because of the hernia of your big brother, of Kungumu |
| Yashinto nshagwa | Hyacinth is a slave |
| Nshagwa wapakaja wakushunga dimbudi dya-Yangua, kwetu | A slave of our hamlet, who pastures the goats of Yangua, our homestead[32] |

The arts of melodic insult were perfected as the others and turned into a specific genre, euphemistically called "songs of self-defense" (*dimu dyalishililidya*). Here, on a seemingly dispassionate recitative, the singer describes his adversary's "lack of talent" (*udagwa*) in procreating:

| | |
|---|---|
| Kalapano nnole mwanapo ajó | Kalapano, look at your son, there |
| Pujungu undishanga umwene | He's rubbish, you yourself are horrified |
| Unno' mwanao kummweka dyeko | Look at your son while he laughs |
| Kalapano mwanao kunyata | Kalapano, your son is ugly |
| Aika' panangu kwavailana pamo na ndyagwe | He sits in the veranda with his wife; they are a good match |
| Vakalalana kenga mapiko ashimakonde | They look at each other, like mapiko of the Makonde |
| Kalapano nkongwe kunyata | Kalapano, even your daughter is ugly |

| | |
|---|---|
| Tuninkubali indona yashimakugwa yakalibobe | We trust she wears a Makua lip plug, all flattened |
| Indivaila kutenda lyuniko ye | It would make for a perfect lid |
| Uvaleka dashi? | How do you procreate? |
| Kalapano mwanao andinyata | Kalapano, your son is ugly |
| Kumeo andibavakanga kenga litundu lyadingalau | His face is full of holes, like a termite's nest[33] |

Practices of bodily modifications with schismogenetic value, such as scarification and teeth filing, were dragged into the aesthetic game of rivalry, display, and boasting. An uncut person would not be able to find a spouse, and lineages bragged (*kunema*) about the beauty and perfection of their incisions, evoking forbidden practices of capturing women (*shinantwala*):

| | |
|---|---|
| Tangesa tunshiba | We speak of Tangesha |
| Tangesha mwali wé, Tangesha | Tangesha, you girl, Tangesha |
| Vanemba vanamando dinembo kulinganana | The Vanamando boys, their graceful tattoos |
| Kenga shinu shao shakunamela | Like something to show off with |
| Mwali nakutwala mwali | Girl, I snatch you, girl |
| Mwali nakutwala twende kó kwetu | I snatch you, girl, let's go to my place |
| Kaja kwake Mando | In the hamlet of Mando |
| Ndiyo | Yes[34] |

Besides innovation carried out in the protected space of initiation rituals, youth defiance also took a more unruly and unpredictable form. The innovation, which emerged in the 1940s, was at first called *shiwa-nagweka*, "going around alone." These were masks hastily put together in the time of initiations by young unmarried men (*vanemba*), which went around the hamlet dancing to the sound of other groups' drums. Sometimes these daring youths outshone the real mapiko of the group that they vampirized. Later on, *shiwanagweka* became *mashalagwe-sha*, "those that make you delay" (from *kushalagwesha*, "to be late"). A group of youths accompanied the perambulating mask by singing and striking hoe blades with irons (*vitali*); the mask was commanded with a new drum, the *ntoji* (or *ntojo*). Even louder than likuti, the ntojo was easy to carve and very light. The mashalagwesha groups intercepted the people who were going to see the "real" mapiko, making them delay. Both shiwanagweka and mashalagwesha were acceptable forms of youth provocation, carried out in the reveling climate of puberty rituals, characterized by performances of inversion. The youths accepted the derisory name, but no serious group would ever like to be called a *lishalagwesha*. Even the most innovative elders shunned this form:

> He listens to the drums of his colleagues, and he dances like them. Things started to go awry because of mashalagwesha. The meaning of *lishalagwesha* is the puberty rituals (*ing'oma*); without that, they don't dance. They know, there is a ritual there. And with their ungainliness (*udagwa*), they go and ruin the rituals.[35]

Dance provocation often degenerated into bloody brawls, symmetrical schismogenesis escalating into open warfare (see chap. 2, sec. 3).[36] Together with drums and masks, the machete was a necessary implement in the excursions of mapiko ensembles—a fact that elders today tell with detached humor. Somehow, masks offered protection from extreme mimetic conflict. In the dances known as *likumbi* or *mmaka*, where people would perform mapiko dance steps without masks, violence was extreme:

> People killed each other. If someone danced ungainly (*na udagwa*), people pointed him out. And the machetes, *ka! ka! ka!* Some died right there. Killing each other on the mapiko playground. "You, you're the sons of who?" Killing each other.[37]

5. The volatile nature of schismogenetic competition granted mapiko a substantial autonomy from the attempts of control carried out by the main agent of colonial ideology: the Catholic Church, which established itself on the plateau in 1924 and whose activities were strongly favored by forced labor policies.[38] As is often the case, the missionaries' attitudes toward heathen practices went through two phases: first, outright rejection and iconoclasm, which yielded poor results in terms of conversions; and second, a more astute approach, which aimed to separate the wheat from the chaff and was driven by the double aim of transformation and absorption.[39] Ancestral supplications and initiation rituals were the main targets of this second phase. "Asking favors" (*kulumba shonde*) of the ancestors was reinterpreted as an indirect, inchoate way of addressing prayers to God, with the ancestors functioning as saintlike intermediaries:

| | |
|---|---|
| Vapadili pavaulike valienda | The fathers, when they went |
| Kummupa nkono kulailana | They shook hands, goodbye |
| Nangu mwanda kwetu ku-Lishiboa | I go to my land, to Lisbon |
| Lo panyuma pandikuleka | Back here, where I leave you |
| Kushomya aunaleke | Keep on studying |
| Vanang'olo vashindashomya | The elders used to study |
| Kushomya kwao | And their way of studying |
| Kulomba shonde kwannungu | Was to ask favors of God[40] |

Puberty rituals were organized at the mission in a substantially shortened way and purified of all sexual content. The overall strategy, as the Diases bluntly put it, was to "keep in its formal aspect many of the fundamental elements used in pagan rituals; the content was changed, keeping the wrapping."[41] The first part of the ritual, involving circumcision for the boys, was left to the work of the vanalombo initiation masters; after this initial moment in which the church averted its eyes, the initiates were sheltered at the mission for the entire liminal phase of seclusion. Christian prayers and rosary discipline substituted for the moral-sexual teachings imparted by vanalombo, who were nonetheless allowed in the mission's precinct. A nun or a priest visited the initiates daily, to check on their physical and moral health. The final *nkamangu* ceremony in which boys and girls are symbolically initiated into sex (see chap. 2, sec. 1) was eliminated wholesale.[42]

The missionaries attempted to domesticate mapiko along the same lines, through a double strategy of iconoclasm and absorption. In the mission of Nangololo, a mapiko mask sat on the desk of a priest's office, openly defiling the rules of public secrecy and respect.[43] At the same time, the missionaries organized mapiko groups to dance in the mission's precinct, with songs inspired by the gospel's teachings and purified of all insulting and provocation.[44] The experiment of appropriation was short-lived, as the priests did not count on parallel schismogenesis going awry. In the late 1950s, a mapiko contest held on mission grounds turned into a brawl, sparked by surreptitious taunting and provocation. The priest himself was thrashed, and mapiko would not be danced under the steeple for decades to come.[45]

The priests' inability to interpret the disconnected mimesis produced within the nshesho genre led to another well-remembered incident. In the late 1950s, in the hamlet of the *vanang'alolo* close to the mission, a Catholic mapiko dancer devised a mimetic dancing style (*shikuvo*) on the communion. A lipiko carved in the image of Jesus Christ administered to the crowd small slices of white cassava, symbolizing the holy bread, in a carefully devised choreography. A mission priest who witnessed the performance unmasked the dancer, tied him to his motorbike, and dragged him all the way to the mission, about a kilometer away. With the original shikuvo, the dancer wanted to "beat the other groups," but the priest saw it as a reviling parody. The boundaries of syncretism were clearly marked, and the sense of appropriation unidirectional: the church could absorb selected elements of heathen ritual but not vice versa. Meanwhile, the chastised man, considering that the conjuncture of masquerading and religion had brought on him pain and shame, ceased to practice both and retired to a life of farming.[46]

Overall, the missionaries' misunderstanding of mapiko was what determined the failure of their endeavors.[47] Just like the colonial ethnographers—and, later, Frelimo's modernizers—they believed secrecy to be sustained by naïve belief, mimesis to be nothing but parody, and competition to be an inessential nuisance, thus failing to understand their structural interconnectedness.

6. The explosion of dancing creativity that marked the meat-is-meat years was indeed not posited on the enfeeblement of secrecy: the two went rather hand in hand. As genres multiplied, the game of secrecy thrived, fueling competition with schismogenetic passions and turning the women into the best spectators for masculine boasting. Elders give a nostalgic account of those times, in which the women vividly performed their terror for the masks: "In times of old, the women would fear . . . They wouldn't approach the mapiko closely. They would stand at a distance. Others would run and hide in their houses! They would fear like this!"[48]

This nostalgia is condensed in a short story, which is served as the standard appetizer to the ethnologist in pursuit of mapiko. During the colonial times, so the story goes, the identity of the dancer was carefully protected. A few days before the masks were prepared, the person selected to dance would say goodbye to his wife and to the population of the hamlet more generally: "I must leave on a trip to the hamlet of the sons of so-and-so," "to sell this or buy that" or "to see that maternal uncle (*njomba*) of mine." The dancer would pack his things and hide for a few days, either in the secret place in the bush where the masks are kept and the lipiko is prepared to dance (*mpolo*) or in the house of some lineage familiar in a nearby hamlet. He would then dance as a spirit during ceremonies or just for the weekend, unbeknownst to his wife (and the women more generally), and come back in human form only a few days after the mapiko spectacle. "My wife, the travel dragged on. The family is fine. My uncle sends regards. Look what I brought back for you!"

The dancer's body was carefully and completely insulated, to prevent the women's guesswork. In dutu meat-is-meat ensembles, even the hands and feet of the dancer were covered with *mmala*, gazelle skin. But, of course, women would know. "When you see your husband dancing, how not to recognize him?" Intimacy and masculine boasting did the rest of the work. "You are in bed with your wife, and right there you want to tell her: 'You know what? That was me, today, dancing in the mask. Did you see how I triumphed?' And she: 'Really? You?' And right there you feel empowered (*na dimongo*, "strong"), a man."[49]

The outer layer of mapiko secret—the fact that the lipiko is a man and not a spirit—was such only for the children and the noninitiates. For all others, women included, it was a public secret: a social game by which the women must behave as if they did not know, showing respect for the masks as a space of adult manhood and thus giving value to the performance. The identity of the dancer, though, was a secret actually concealed not only from the women but also from the men who did not belong to the group, who did not have access to the group's mapiko hiding-place.

But the appetizer story also reveals the intensity of dance movement. Traveling between the many lineage hamlets punctuating the Makonde Plateau and lowlands during the era of colonial pacification was intense enough to be plausible as a justification for a person's recurrent absences. Despite the efforts put into concealing the masks' outer secret—despite the mmala skins and the performance of respect—travel, trade, competition, and lust for fame contained the seeds that might crack its inner secrecy: that might expose this or that individual as the talented (*nnanda*) or ungainly (*ndagwa*) dancer.


7. If the intense circulation between hamlets was a direct effect of Portuguese peace, colonial occupation prompted another movement of people, more massive and less leisurely: labor migration toward

neighboring Tanganyika. Escaping the brutality of the Nyassa Company first and the policy of forced cotton cultivation later, migrants sought work in the sisal plantations of the nearby British colony.[50] There, they were exposed to the vibrant culture of dance competition (*mashindano*) that has been prominent on the Swahili coast for centuries. Etymology is an unsure matter, especially when it comes to languages such as Shimakonde that have been barely studied in their diachronic dimension; despite this uncertainty, many words connected to the early colonial practice of mapiko suggest a link with this coastal culture of dance competition.

In the antique mileya genre, the performance had no internal subdivision. The mask came, announced by a song, danced, and left the dance field. By contrast, the new genres invented in connection to the meat-is-meat break were divided into two movements, called *lishesho* and *nshakasha*. Both these names point to a coastal origin. In the first movement, the masked dancer presents some of its dancing skills, almost to warm up the public. Lishesho is about beginning and introducing: "Lishesho is a way of beginning (*shitunduvangilo*), in order to show people: this lipiko is going to dance now."[51] The word comes from the Kiswahili verb *kucheza*, "to dance, to play, to have fun"; on the coast, it is used specifically in the expression *kucheza ngoma*, "to dance a ngoma."[52]

The second movement, called *nshakasha*, contains the most recognizable and codified mapiko choreography. The small-drums (*vinganga*) orchestra attacks with obstinate triplets. The main drummer calls the mask with a specific rhythmic sequence. The lipiko responds with coordinated foot stomping (*kukomela*), which leads him to turn and to move backwards, toward the drummers. This backward movement is propelled by a fast and precise shaking of the pelvis (*kunung'unula*), which transmits down to the feet. This shaking makes the iron bells attached to the raffia corset—themselves called through a loanword from Kiswahili, *njuga*—vibrate prominently and rhythmically.[53] The movement terminates in front of the main drummer. After performing more dance styles, the lipiko turns, performs the backward movement again, and concludes with a swift swirling movement in which he swings his arms and turns his body (*tapwito*) and which must terminate in synchrony with the drum orchestra and with the screams exalting the lipiko's lineage: *Vanantumbati, wetu!* This very stylized movement was performed almost in the same way from the 1950s on, judging from the short ethnographic films shot by Margot Dias.[54] It is considered the most difficult gesture to master.

Our colonial ethnologists interpreted the nshakasha as the attack and flight of the angry lipiko: as the moment in which the spirit summoned from the grave is chased away and vanquished by the men in order to instill fear and a sense of protection in the women (for the Diases) or to sympathetically master the tribal enemy (for Dick-Read after Father Vloet):

> From time to time, the men of the group gather together, doing menacing gestures, and address some words or short sentences to the *mapiko*. Then, they advance some twenty meters in the direction of the latter, vociferous. Suddenly, as if taken by fear, they run towards the drum orchestra, jumping. The *mapiko* follows them, as if he wanted to catch them, with a movement of the leg a bit stiff, but extremely fast. He is on the point of catching them, but he turns back and executes a dance in which the legs jump very quickly, all the body moves, making the rattles sound.[55]

Nshakasha is a choreography to which elders today cannot find any cosmological foundation, except for the fact that pelvis shaking (*kunung'unula*) is characteristic of *shinalombo*, the puberty ceremonies masters' dance, and thus obliquely refers to sexual intercourse. The men's words and "menacing gestures" are nothing but codified—and carefully crafted—rhythmic poetry (*vikuvo*, "styles"), addressed with the hands held high in the direction of the lipiko, which by all means is the cathectic center of the performance. I saw no jumps but only the running to and fro of the men, who prepare the terrain and the atmosphere for the momentous nshakasha. But, of course, I might have arrived too late on the scene; a direct representation of a spirit attack, brutal and scary (remindful of René Girard's ideas about masks as the reenactment of a "mimetic crisis"), could have already been sublimated into an abstract, aesthetic choreography, function converted into expression.[56]

The nshakasha movement, however, was introduced after the 1920s break, together with the dutu genre, as the movement did not feature in the old mileya masks. In an aesthetic trust characteristic of dutu, two or three mapiko could even be put to perform the nshakasha at once, with the challenge of drawing straight lines in their backward movement and to terminate in perfect synchrony.[57] Etymologically, *nshakasha* could be related to the verb *kushakashea*, "winnowing," in Shimakonde, based on the analogy of movement. In Kiswahili, the verb *kuchakacha* means "pounding." But *chakacha* is also the name of a famous ngoma in vogue on the Swahili coast, first as a feminine initiation dance, then as a form of popular music, that Makonde might have encountered in their travels.[58] Rather than the result of a decay of ritual, the nshakasha dance step might very well be the vernacularization of a regional hit.

Finally, even the word *ishima*—which, as we have seen, is the key vernacular concept referring to the ritual respect that women must pay to the masks (chap. 2, sec. 2)—is a loan from the Kiswahili *heshima* ("honor, dignity, awe, reverence", a word with Arabic origins); this is yet another proof of the importance of cross-border cultural contact in the meat-is-meat phase of the history of mapiko.


8. In Kiswahili, the expression *nyama ni nyama* is a playful way of saying "don't ask what it is, just eat it," or "all meat is good." As a metaphor applied to masquerading, *nyama ni nyama* evokes aesthetic universalism (talent is talent, regardless of lineage); the nefarious appetites of sorcerers (for who else speaks of persons in terms of meat?); and the reduction of humans to mere bodies, all practically exchangeable. Four decades of scholarship on "moral economies" have taught us to connect dense metaphors such as *nyama ni nyama* to their possible material referents. The slave trade immediately comes to mind.

In East Africa, slave raiding and trading ceased de facto only at the beginning of the twentieth century. On the Swahili coast, this period was marked by the multiplication of *ngoma* (dances, drums) and especially by the appropriation of hinterland dances into the coastal repertoire as acceptable and desirable forms of cultural expression.[59] As ritual dances practiced by former slaves were drawn into the coastal public sphere, a vivid culture of competition coalesced. Ngoma groups mingled and flaunted their dancing skills in colorful mashindano festivals, animated by entrenched rivalry and provocation. In the urban spaces, new extravagant forms emerged, such as the *beni* military dances. Yet even these fashionable urban forms had clear connection with upcountry practices: indeed, the European battleships paraded in Beni were called *vinyago*, that is, "masks, masquerades."[60]

The few historical studies that describe the transformative dynamics of hinterland ngoma traditions point to a symmetrical process of appropriation, of coastal dances by hinterland people, taking place in the early twentieth century. The most well-documented case is the one of the Tanganyikan Kerebe, whose traditions underwent dramatic cultural transformations in the 1920s, propelled by the appropriation of coastal competitive culture.[61] The emergence of new interethnic dances such as *muganda* and *kalela* is part of the same dynamic.[62]

These two symmetrical movements of appropriation allude to a fusion of horizons between the coast and the hinterland, Swahili and *washenzi* (savages), freemen and slaves, former raiders and former game. The postslavery world was no longer divided into two asymmetrical halves—free people and slaves, coastal Islamized people and hinterland washenzi; it was a space in which humanness could be affirmed as a common ground.[63] It is only natural that this commonality would be tested out on the terrain of dance: competitive performance of a schismogenetic nature was *the* cultural practice common to coastal and hinterland people—in the former, as rivalry between city moieties; in the latter, as ritual competition between genders, generations, and lineages, as well as in the widespread practice of joking relationship (*utani*).

The meat-is-meat break can also be interpreted under this light. While coastal people were appropriating slave dances, the Makonde reshaped the practice of mapiko, which in many ways signified their image of "savages," by appropriating the language of coastal ngoma. All the new mapiko genres that emerged after the 1920s were also referred to as *ding'oma*, "dances," and choreographic movements drew on Swahili styles and names. Meat-is-meat can thus be considered as equivalent to the processes of "detribalization" that took place in coastal ngoma such as Beni.[64] Clearly, it was not an effect of the transformation wrought by urban life on traditional society; rather, it was the voluntary choice of a hinterland group restyling itself as cosmopolitan.


9. Genre would be the most significant and long-lasting stylistic legacy of the meat-is-meat break. Henceforth, invention in mapiko would appear in the guise of new genres spreading in waves of fashion—each with its own identifying stylistic features, practices of secrecy, generational range, and overall mood; each part of a field charged with feeling and value, which exceeds masquerading and embraces other forms of expression. These genres were called "families" (*likola*), "dances" (*ding'oma*), "styles" (*mitindo*, Kiswahili), and later on "types" (*itipo*, a

vernacularized Portuguese word) or simply identified through the genitive form (*mapiko lashinjilo*, "a masquerade of such-and-such").

Shimakonde provides a variety of verbs and metaphors to describe the historical transience and salience of masking genres. Genres can be tried (*kulingangila*), launched (*kujela*), learned (*kulipundisha*), imitated (*kujedya*), bettered (*kwanjedya*), and transformed (*kubadilisha*); they can rise to fame (*kuumanga*), circulate (*kudingula*), and spread (*kulyandadya*); they become insipid (*kudidimanga*), age (*kunyakala*), go to ruin (*kubyaika*), and eventually are abandoned (*kuleka*) and forgotten (*kulivaliva*)—for the youngsters, even shitted away (*kunkagali*); or else they are passed on to new generations (*kwimyanga*) and resuscitated (*kutakatuwa*) to be danced again. Mapiko genres seized the spirit of the times and conveyed the generational incommensurability of experience that is a major marker of modernity, wherein "the temper of each new generation is a continuous surprise."[65]

Thinking meat-is-meat in reference to the end of slavery—as a form of displacement of schismogenetic dynamics into the aesthetic domain and as part of a regional construction of a new cultural *koiné*—allows us to historicize this break without reducing it to a mere story of secularization and disenchantment. Within this interpretation, meat-is-meat is part of a specific strand of modernism, the one that upholds cosmopolitanism, universalism, and freedom. But this level of generality is still unsatisfying. We must now move closer to the individuals and groups who imagined and promoted these momentous changes. Who were they? How did the forms that they invented become of broader significance? Which ideas informed their practice?

# 4 ᔟ Masters of Play
## Late-Colonial Aesthetics and Practice

| | |
|---|---|
| Ulanda i wakuvadela | Talent, you can't carve it |
| Ni kuvalekwa nao | You are born with it |
| Shinguma omba ligoma | Shinguma, strike the drum |
| Tuvapundishe vanu vakamanya | Let's teach those who don't know |
| Patuja wetu panyuma petu | When we go home, there behind us |
| Valipundishe vakamanya | Those who don't know, they'd better practice |

— NMA/Nshesho/Nangade/2004

1. AMONG THE mapiko masters of the colonial era, the one whose name has consistently resisted oblivion is Nampyopyo (chap. 3, sec. 2). Everybody who has grown up in his times knows of him, and most remember his most famous masks, the *Germans-in-the-Hamlet*. In Pemba, a statue of Nampyopyo greets the visitor right at the entrance of the Mbanguia Cultural Centre, an old institution of the provincial capital that hosts the dance group Mapico Moderno. Nampyopyo is remembered for his unique and bewildering masks, and the statue establishes a link between that inaugural creativity and the new urban "modernization" of mapiko.

Nampyopyo was one of the promoters of the meat-is-meat break. Today, most people have forgotten the meaning of the expression *meat-is-meat* in relation to mapiko and think of it as a mere play of words. But those who have heard the idiom, even without knowing its meaning, associate it unfailingly with the name of the old master. Nampyopyo? *Nyama ni nyama!* The Diases, who otherwise kept mapiko artists in anonymity, mention Nampyopyo, testifying to the fame that he enjoyed in his times. In their monograph, he features not as a person but as a misspelled name of place: "We must not forget that the village of *Naupyopyo* is famous amongst them for its enormous capacity of creation and improvisation of drums for playing (*chikokulu*)."[1] The anthropologists, however, did not leave a visual record of Nampyopyo's masquerades.

Who was Nampyopyo, and what did his mapiko look like? We will begin to explore the thought, practices, and personalities of late-colonial mapiko masters by following the tracks of this rather atypical character.

2. Nampyopyo son of Nkondya was born in the hamlet of the Vannuma, close to today's communal village of Nang'unde.[2] By a twist of fate, the group of trees that signals the abandoned hamlet lies a few hundred meters away from the place where Frelimo's central operative base was located in the final phase of the anticolonial war. The elder's grave is framed by a *maule*, a circle of trees planted on the occasion of a major masculine puberty ritual (*likumbi lyamaule*, fig. 7).[3] On the tombstone, only the date of death is inscribed: 19 July 1967.

Nampyopyo died old (*nang'olo*), but not an elderly man (*liputa*): at sixty or seventy. Hence, his date of birth can be estimated at the close of the nineteenth century. We can imagine him growing up as a child in a fenced enclosure, fearful of the night, when man-eating spirits and raiders loom; undergoing puberty rituals during the First World War; carrying out raids among lowland "slaves" as an adolescent cadet; and marrying shortly after the plateau was subdued by the Portuguese.[4] Nampyopyo belonged to the last generation that saw the elders' *mileya* masks being performed; he was also among the youths who pioneered the new abstract *dutu* genre. Of these early moments of Nampyopyo's life, we know nothing: his talents and inventions have been swallowed up in the great river of anonymous tradition and collective memory.

Eventually, the playful boy became an "elder master of the lands" (*nang'olo mwene shilambo*), a figure who exerted his authority over various neighboring hamlets of the same lineage, especially on questions of land tenure, but was not directly co-opted in the Portuguese system of indirect rule.[5] "He wasn't a man of many wanderings" and lived most of his life in this native hamlet. There, Nampyopyo put his innate carving talent to good practical use, learning the craft of making

FIGURE 7. *Maule (Rui Assubuji, Nampanya, 2009)*

firearms. He specialized in the muzzleloaders ironically called *espera-pouco* ("wait-a-little-bit," as you would say to the enemy in the awkward time when you reload the weapon). Even in the times of Portuguese peace, this kind of commodity was highly valued, to such an extent that the bride price was often referred to as "paying the arquebus."[6] Nampyopyo was also able to craft hoes, knives, and faucets (*muundu*). He worked mostly independently, sometimes solicited by the colonial government, and was wealthier than most of his peers. He married thrice and had numerous offspring.

Inside the influential man, the playful boy lived on. At the height of his powers, in the 1940s, Nampyopyo founded the meat-is-meat group par excellence. He summoned the best dancers, singers, and drummers within a twenty-kilometer range (we must bear in mind that at the time distances were covered by foot and the bush was thick and filled with dangerous animals) to play with him:

> As dancers: Namiva of the Milangi, Kunyuma Ungo and Nang-wigwa Ntondo of the Mwitambedi, Likwimbi Makanga and Mpalamba Mpunya of the Munnanga, Mushimbalyulo of the Muluvango, Shileu of the Vashimaladi and Utoi of the Valula. As singers: Mpululu of the Vamilangi, Mpilimba and Misila of the Vamwilambe, Umwago of the Vatambedi, Masheka Nshegwa of the Vannuma. As drummers: Shivambwe of Mwa-tide and Kulematete of the Vamyumba. As carver and dancer, Nampyopyo himself.[7]

The group in which these talented men were enrolled was not a dutu ensemble: it was a resurrection (*kutakatuwa*) of the oldest style of mapiko, the one commanded by the drum mileya and based on the principle of the mask-character. In times of old, each hamlet would own and perform a small number of masks; but now, Nampyopyo carved a large number of masks, which performed in sequence, so as to produce an orchestrated spectacle of characters. In essence, he trans-formed the old template of mapiko into a unique genre, of which he was the established master.

The spectacle lasted a whole day, sometimes even two, and each mask was performed only once. The instrumentation was minimalis-tic: one or two small chalice-shaped *shinganga* played the base rhythm, and a few mileya alternated in commanding the movement of the masked dancer. Today, people say that Nampyopyo's arsenal consisted in dozens of masks, but only a few characters stuck in the memory of those who watched or performed with him. These memories are attached to the aural matter of song, rather than to the visuality of the headpiece, mainly because the former was more stable than the latter.

Amongst the first masks to dance in the morning was the *Coastal Woman* (*nkongwe mmanga*) who does not greet her guests under the mango tree, for fear that they might steal the fruits—which grow in abundance on the Makonde Plateau but are a prized commodity on the coast:

| | |
|---|---|
| Kutangangadika nkongwe mmanga | The coastal woman laments |
| Aushikale aushikale | You shouldn't sit, you shouldn't sit |
| Pamingela | Under the mango tree[8] |

Then came the mask of the fake friends, *Those-Who-Laugh-with-You* but betray you behind your back. The mask was characterized by an allegoric squinting eye:

| | |
|---|---|
| Mwenyekanao | Those that laugh with you |
| Valalanga navadya' venu | Are sleeping with your wives |
| Vanyunalila avó | Those that you suspect |
| Nanga shinu | That's nothing |

Then, a series of characters whose features have been washed out by time: *Nnembe*, a bearded elder from Miteda who was a personal friend of Nampyopyo's; *Ugomwa*, the recently converted Makua who does not wear a fez (*akanagwala kopio*); *Mandova*, the native policeman; the *Prostitutes* (*malaja*), Makonde women with a lip plug and belly covers signifying their pregnancy; *Bavola*, with a hanging lower lip (*lindomo lindikangamoka*); and the *Partridges* (*vanambili*), Makua women with a nose ring and large headdresses.

The most famous masks came toward the end of the performance. The *Germans-in-the-Hamlet* (*majelemani nkaja*) were a couple of white people dressed in fine clothes, their masks devised in such a way as to have a removable wooden hat that they could take off and put back, to salute the audience:

| | |
|---|---|
| Ndota nangu ndiwena | Me, I travelled |
| Nangu ndiwena somo | I travelled, my friend |
| Ku kaja kwa-Likwalele | To the hamlet of Likwalele |
| Ku kaja Matambalale | To the hamlet of Matambalale |

| Kweli kweli somo | It's true my friend |
| Nankodya njungu ndikidiki | I found a little White man |
| Majelemani kwetu | Germans in our homestead[9] |

3. The emergence of Nampyopyo's group was enabled by the meat-is-meat break—by the possibility of recruiting talented players beyond the confines of hamlet and lineage. At the same time, the group dramatically worked to redefine concepts of mask ownership and agency.

Shimakonde expresses the concept of ownership with the polysemic word *mwene* (pl. *vene*). Firstly, *mwene* signifies "owner" in a material sense, as in *mwene shipula*, "the owner of the knife." More broadly, it can indicate the "master" of a territory, as in *nang'olo mwene likaja*, "elder master of the hamlet," the lineage authority overseeing a specific hamlet. More generally still, *mwene* is connected to a sense of moral responsibility, as in *mwene malove*, "the one who personally uttered these words."[10]

Before "meat is meat," the ownership of masks—to be *mwene mapiko*—was entirely entrusted to the owner of the hamlet (*mwene likaja*). Even if he was not himself a talented artist, he would act as the "owner of the mask's hiding-place" (*mwene mpolo*), overseeing the carving of headpieces and the acquisition of dancing implements, launching and organizing puberty rituals, managing the rivalries with other groups, and working to keep good harmony between all the members of the *mpolo* (those who play in a group). In homage to the elder-owner, his name would be shouted defiantly at the end of each mapiko performance: "Us, here, from the lands of so-and-so!"

In a meat-is-meat group such as Nampyopyo's, ownership was defined not by lineage but by more elusive qualities. First, there was the capacity to provide patronage. Mapiko necessitates many implements. While masks and drums could be fashioned from natural materials—wood and animal skins—the cloths that cover the lipiko's body and the metal *dinjuga* iron bells had to be purchased. Nampyopyo's relative affluence was crucial in establishing his ownership of a group that required obtaining and managing masks and materials in great quantity. Second, there was tolerance and respect. Members of Nampyopyo's mpolo were allowed to carry on dancing in their own nshesho ensembles, some of which still functioned along lineage principles. Being the owner of a multilineage group required mediation and modesty. Wary of offending sensibilities of this or that lineage, Nampyopyo made the performance of his masks end with a wordless shout. Third—and perhaps more important—Nampyopyo's artistry won the admiration and respect of his fellows, his established reputation as a multitalented *mmapiko* what made participation in his group prestigious.

4. Those who witnessed Nampyopyo's talent describe it in terms of representational accuracy. His foremost skill was carving: "He would watch a face . . . Like you are now, he would watch you well . . . Then go there, and take it [the mask] out: like yourself. Him? He would make you precisely like you are: with a beard and all." The master often impersonated the masks that he had carved: "And there to dance, the same! He would . . . complete the work himself." "He himself was a master (*nnanda*) of dancing: he was accomplished in all talents."[11] Nampyopyo's self-proclaimed successor, the elder Mustafa Mwana Bonde (see chap. 11, sec. 2), employed a photographic metaphor to describe his master's feats: "Nampyopyo won with the faces (*ding'ope*). The one who knew how to make a perfect picture (*ipisha*): that was Nampyopyo."[12]

Nampyopyo's masks were not created to serve a particular function: they were done for the sake of perfect representation. They had the power of astonishing with their precision, but they were not tied to any form of social or magical efficacy. True, some of the characters put across a moral point, like the classic *Those-Who-Laugh-with-You* and sleep with your wife. But in other cases, the moral point was obscure, almost imperceptible. Was the depiction of the Mwani woman, afraid that her guests might steal her mangoes, a critique of avarice? Or was it the snapshot of a foreign custom? Certainly there is no moral lesson in the most famous of Nampyopyo's masks, the Germans, who elegantly arrive, take off their hats, show off in their clothes, and leave to the sound of a playful song. This is representation stemming from observation, tied to a knot of historical experience: the arrival of German settlers in northern Mozambique in the aftermath of the First World War, when Germany lost its East African colony.[13] But the depiction of the elegant Germans is void of moralizing or social critique: it is the product of curiosity and the will to capture for the sake of capturing.

The Diases referred to Nampyopyo's masks as "drums for playing" (*chikokulu*, which actually means "festivity"), perhaps anxious to set apart his creative effervescence from "serious" ritual mapiko.

Nampyopyo's masks, though, were no less dangerous than their parent genres. They were even more so, from a ritual point of view, as young initiated men were barred from the masks' hiding-place (*mpolo*), which was open only to the middle-aged. "You had to have a beard to enter there."[14] This extreme secrecy not only increased the mpolo's prestige but was also intended to exclude volatile youths from the secrets of mask preparation. Nampyopyo's masks were appreciated for their perfection and beauty (*kwalala*), but their capacity to baffle, dazzle, and stupefy is what made them famous and inimitable. They would beg the question: "How are they made?" The verbs most consistently used to describe them—*kukamadyanga*, "to be complicated," and *kujowa*, "to be danger-ous"—are also euphemisms for the invisible powers of sorcerers.

Beautiful (*kwalala*) and dangerous (*kujowa*), Nampyopyo's masks were nonetheless—as the Diases rightly remarked—playful and enter-taining. They elicited smiles (*kumamweta*) as well as stupor and ritual respect (*ishima*). If Nampyopyo was a great man (*munu nkumene*), powerful and rich; a talented one (*nnanda*), born with the gift of mi-mesis; and a complicated one (*munu wakukamadyanga*), endowed with invisible sight and magical powers; he was also, and foremost, a "playful one" (*munu wakupikita*). This Makonde instantiation of *homo ludens* is certainly the most stable signifier associated with the practice of mapiko throughout the twentieth century. "To play" (*kupikita*) is the verb most consistently used to describe all the activities that surround masquerading. Following Huizinga, the concept of play encompasses all other specifications we have identified—beauty, danger, and com-plicatedness. This "playful man" emerges as the subject of mapiko: of invention, of competition, and of talent, as well as of the game of ritual secrecy. Rather than constituting an odd exception, Nampyopyo might have led us to flesh out the key vernacular categories of mapiko prac-tice and to connect them to a concept—play—which bridges domains of aesthetics and ritual.

5. From a historical point of view, however, the emphasis on repre-sentative perfection in Nampyopyo's mask could be, at least in part, an effect of the encounter with European conceptions of figurative art. In the years in which the meat-is-meat break was revolutionizing the practice of mapiko, a new form of art was created on the plateau: blackwood sculpture. The invention was prompted by the colonial

encounter but built on a preexisting tradition.[15] After conquest, the Nyassa Company enforced the hut tax that made it infamous in the whole region. As a consequence, Makonde women began wearing around their necks small gourds (*dinyumba, mitete*) containing the tax receipt, for fear of being found wanting and then imprisoned or brutalized by company agents. These gourds were closed by finely carved stoppers, most often representing the scarified head of a Makonde elder. Makonde ritual and utilitarian carvings had raised interest among collectors since the late nineteenth century, but these small head-shaped artworks became more noticeable because they were exhibited on women's bodies. Missionaries and colonial officials appreciated them, inquired about their makers, and commissioned enlarged copies of these figures, which they wished to be carved in the more precious and resistant African blackwood (*mpingo*).[16] The sculptures reproduced quite faithfully the scarified heads that closed the tax gourds, gradually reshaped to resemble the classic European form of the bust.[17] Elated by the results, the missionaries commissioned sculptures with new subjects, by and large naturalistic depictions of characters peopling the Makonde everyday: the smoking man, the peasant carrying a hoe, the drummer, the woman at the well. In time, the sculptors appropriated and twisted the naturalism elicited by the missionaries, adding new themes to the gallery of village still-life, such as the famous carving of the *assimilado*, with scarifications and suit, smoking a cigar. While the missionaries' attempts to domesticate mapiko met with failure (see chap. 3, sec. 5), the promotion of this new sculptural genre was an unabashed success. Makonde blackwood sculpture enjoyed a growing fame, first in the Mozambican colony and then in the world at large. Exhibitions were organized, in Lourenço Marques and overseas, beginning in the late 1930s.

If Nampyopyo's wealth mostly derived from his work as a firearm artisan, he was also involved in the production and promotion of Makonde carvings, in a phase in which blackwood had not yet taken over as the privileged medium.[18] Statuettes of women figures carved in soft *ntene* wood, supposedly of a devotional nature, are widely attested in collections since the late nineteenth century. Under the same influences that prompted the emergence of blackwood carving, this tradition was expanded to cover a similar range of everyday subjects.[19] Nampyopyo was among the protagonists of this transitional genre. Carved in ntene and painted in glossy colors, his pieces especially favored the depiction of modern subjects: they "always sported suits and ties."[20] The statuettes were commissioned by the colonial administrator and collected by two Portuguese men who went under the Makonde names of Nabadula and Magomba.[21] Nampyopyo coordinated a small number of carvers who produced similar statuettes that he then sold: two lived near today's village of Namakande, and one was his own son Nshemo Nampyopyo Nkondya. All of them worked without remuneration, as a token of admiration for Nampyopyo and to bask in the shadows of the master's fame. Moreover, and perhaps most important, the status of carver implied an exemption from forced labor.[22] The genre of painted softwood figures enjoyed a great popularity until the 1950s, when it was superseded by blackwood carvings. Nshemo himself, who more than anybody else inherited his father's carving gift, abandoned this genre in the 1950s and moved on to the more remunerative and technically challenging blackwood.[23]

The fortune of Makonde sculpture attracted new attention to mapiko masks as collectable and displayable objects. By showcasing Makonde sculpture together with the masks, the new impure form could be legitimized and rooted in the authentic ritual one. Collectors and buyers were increasingly drawn to the plateau to acquire both masks and sculptures. The hamlet of Nampyopyo was also well-known by missionaries and the colonial government for its masks. Indeed, in its vicinity, the collector Dick-Read was directed by Father Vloet in his quest for African art in general and mapiko specifically (see chap. 1, sec. 5).[24] Following a common pattern, the commodification of masks valorized their mystery and shock effect rather than their beauty, horror rather than smoothness:

> Though there were no windows, sufficient light filtered through the doorway for me to see that the hut appeared to be quite empty. [. . .] But then Gogo, reaching up under the darkened eaves brought down a bundle wrapped in several layers of black cloth, and unraveling this with great care, he revealed a mask. It was an extraordinary, helmet-shaped object, rather terrifying, and ugly beyond belief.[25]

The dichotomy between beauty and danger, naturalism and shock, which seemed to point to a Makonde vernacular aesthetics, appears now in a different light: inscribed in, and maybe produced by, the colonial gaze; assigned to different objects, the polished wood carving and the terrifying mask.[26] It is also suspiciously remindful of the dichotomy that structured romantic aesthetics, which opposes the sublime and the beautiful, the awe of nature and the quiet beauty of civilized art.[27]

In the subsequent history of Makonde blackwood sculpture, fearfulness reappeared on its polished surface. In the 1960s, a new sculptural genre was invented by Mozambican Makonde expatriates in Dar Es Salaam: "demons" (*shetani*) with twisted forms and fragmented, almost cubist, bodily structures. The invention was prompted by a challenge that sculptor Samaki Likankoa launched against his patron, Mohammed Peera: the sculptor carved his first shetani as a provocation for having been fired for scarce productivity and drunkenness; the unexpected commercial success of this first piece made the rest.[28] The new genre borrowed from imaginaries of devils and djinni (*majini*) rooted in coastal Swahili culture and responded to curio buyers' exoticist expectations of African magic. But the genre's central aesthetic category was, again, complicatedness (*kukamadyanga*). Just like Nampyopyo's masks, a good shetani must baffle the beholder, must prompt the question "What is this?" or "How was it done?"[29] The decomposition of body shapes serves to generate this feeling of bemusement, wonder, and doubt. While the production of shetani was mainly aiming a foreign market, their consumption on the plateau was accompanied precisely by such an aesthetic response.[30]

Does the dichotomy between beauty and fearfulness, naturalism and complicatedness point to a vernacular Makonde aesthetics? Or is it the result of a set of complex flows and exchanges—European patronage of Makonde blackwood carving, exoticist imaginaries related to the commodification of masks, and visual influences rooted in Indian Ocean culture? Or both? As often is the case, the question of aesthetic universals and particulars is bound to remain open.

6. An important figure in the history of Makonde modern carving, Nampyopyo was closely involved in another process of colonial valorization of "native arts": the summoning of dance groups in the spectacle of state power. In the late 1950s, as a recognition of his fame, Nampyopyo's group was brought as far as to Mocimboa da Praia—taken and driven back by truck—to dance for a state ceremonial, on the occasion of the visit of a "white elder." The troupe that Nampyopyo put together

for the event included a few selected women singers and dancers—yet another proof, if needed, of the public nature of masking secrecy in those days.[31]

Nampyopyo's ensemble was not the only one to be summoned to the important festivity. Other mapiko groups took part, and they were recruited following the meat-is-meat principle:

> One year they called us to a festivity in Mocimboa. "There is an elder coming." I went. No group went as it was. Two or three people from here; from Muidumbe two people; and so on, in each place. We got together in the car. And go! This kind of mapiko was called meat-is-meat. I went to that festivity. A festivity such as that was not organized again.[32]

People recruited in such a way, upon indication of the customary authorities, rehearsed together in the city before the spectacle. Co-option in the cultural spectacles organized by the colonial state was compulsory, but the participation was not deprived of enjoyment:

> We were dominated by the Portuguese government. But for us, playful people (*tuvakupikita*), if they called us, we went. The native authorities (*makulungwa*) said, "Mapiko, mapiko, let's go, a white elder is coming to visit." And no one refused, because we liked playing.[33]

> If you weren't sick, you would rejoice.[34]

We must register a radical disconnection between the meanings that the two parties—the colonizer and the colonized—attributed to the event and to the participation of dancers therein. The colonial master summoned the troupes to provide a visual justification of its might: to frame savage dance within the rational order of state spectacle; to reabsorb native exuberance within the parade of power; and to provide a sensuous representation of the specific ideology of Portuguese colonial rule, luso-tropicalism, the idea that Portugal and the tropics are made for each other. This aesthetics rested on an economy of desire and exoticism that remained largely obscure to the dancers, who appropriated the event in the great game of competition and schismogenesis and did not even understand the name or position of the leader that they celebrated.[35] As despised as the colonial government might be, being selected as the most representative troupe in the master's ceremonial of power was a sign of recognition, something to claim and boast about as a victory.

7. Following the traces of Nampyopyo, we have ended up encountering a unique genre that was in fact a reinvention (or "resurrection") of the old mask-character template. But I have said little about the two abstract genres that were introduced together with the meat-is-meat break: the *likuti*-driven dutu and the *ligoma*-driven nshesho. Overall, these two genres were the most widely practiced in Nampyopyo's time: the first by people from his generation, or slightly younger; the second by their sons. Yet we have little other than fluctuating names to describe their aesthetics: names of groups, dancing styles, carvers, dancers, drummers . . . This lack of detail says something of the economy of dance competition and its effects on memory. Competition produces innovation; novelty is baffling and brings crowds of spectators to those who muster it. But it also produces the contrary: imitation. As soon as a winning novelty has been introduced—one that briefly provides fame (*shimbili*) to its inventor—it is immediately appropriated by competitors. As styles are shuffled around by the engine of competition, their origins are forgotten and they become of public domain.

Within mapiko practice, there is a fundamental difference between initiating (*kutunduvanga*) or inventing (*kulyaidyanga*) something new; resurrecting (*kutakatuwa*) something ancient that had been abandoned; and imitating (*kujedya*) what is already out there. Invention and resurrection are highly praised: they are the sign of talent and vision. Imitation is what is left to those who, bereft of creativity, still desire to impress their audiences on the dance ground. Accusing a rival of unoriginality is a common provocation:

| | |
|---|---|
| Kwomba nshesho wetu kwalala | Our way of drumming the nshesho is beautiful |
| Kila munu pavele kumwamweta | Everybody who's there smiles |
| Wetu tuvalanda | We are talented |
| Lude' Mwatidi vanditwala | The village of Nampanya, they stole |
| Likodi lyetu | Our recordings |
| Lude' Mwambula vanditwala | The village of Mwambula, they stole |
| Likodi lyetu | Our recordings |
| Wetu tuvalanda | We are talented[36] |

The abstract genres introduced after the meat-is-meat rupture were more open to innovation than the old mask-character template, but they were also more prone to imitation. The breaking up of the unifying frame of the character encouraged experimentation with dance styles, masks, and songs. At the same time, it made stealing (*kutwala*) a style easier, without having to copy the whole character. The descendants of the elder Nandindi from the hamlet of the Vanang'alolo claim that he introduced the way of concluding the *nshakasha* with a caper, hitting the ground with the mask (*tapwito walipondo*). Or was this invented by the Vanshandani group? Who first carved the stunning three-faced mask that was later danced in the village of Miteda?

The process of invention of the two new main genres that emerged in the times of Nampyopyo, the abstract dutu and nshesho, is unclear. Determining even the approximate geographic location in which the two genres were introduced is impossible, so quick was the process of diffusion and appropriation. Those inventions that were unsuccessful or short-lived had even less possibility of being remembered. Later in my fieldwork, I was perchance informed of the existence of an intermediate genre between dutu and nshesho, in which both the likuti and the ligoma drums were used. The innovation, pioneered in the Messalo lowlands, did not manage to conquer the heart of a generation, as the two other genres did, and was quickly abandoned and forgotten.[37]

The mimetic choreographies (*vikuvo*) that were the landmark stylistic feature of the nshesho genre clustered around a variety of themes: from the appropriation of other dances' dance steps to the imitation of animals to the representation of elements of daily life. Apart from those that were continued in later practice, few stuck in popular memory as did the one of the holy communion, which had raised a missionary's iconoclastic fury (see chap. 3, sec. 5). When they did, they can be recalled as rhythmic sequences played with the mouth:

> —There was "Planting the manioc in the field" (*mpande imbwani muligweu*). Here there was a manioc, and there a hoe. *Dikidi-ki! Dikidi-ki! Dikidi-dikidi-dikidi-di! Likili-likili-likili-likili . . . Dikudi! Dikudi!* And there he plants . . . *Di-ki! Di-ki! Ko!* Ooooh . . . and that's it.
>
> —Another style?
>
> —Another style was "The airplane above" (*ndege muwa*). *Krrr, krrr, krrr.* Oh! *Dikili-dikili-dikili-di.* He's commanding the mask,

that is coming . . . The airplane above. *Dikili-dikili-dikili-di. Ko!* Oooh . . . And it's the airplane!

—The airplane above. Another one?

—[*Laughs*] Another? *Baba*, I forget the other ones. And I am someone who did things myself. And who used to know: this comes from there, and that comes from there.[38]

Styles could be named but were also interchangeable. The mask of Elizabeth the Second described by Dick-Read (see chap. 1, sec. 5) was danced in a nshesho group of one of Nampyopyo's players; he could recall the mask, but no specific dancing style was attached to it. Showing to elders a photographic album containing numerous masks kept in Mozambican and Portuguese museums yielded little results. This mask? It might have been used in dutu, but then maybe also in nshesho . . . Wasn't this the work of *njilo* from *kuna-nyamani? Mene, wako!* This was from that other guy![39]

Nampyopyo's resurrection of the old mask-character template, at a time in which it had been largely abandoned in favor of the new abstract genres, was also a strategy against imitation, in order to acquire a unique and lasting renown. While all other groups were copying each other's styles, masks, and dances, the old master towered with his peculiar re-creation, which he protected through the rules of secrecy and respect. And a successful strategy it was, as the characters and the name of their maker resisted oblivion and inscribed themselves in collective memory.

8. As it turns out, however, Nampyopyo was not the only one to have resurrected the old mileya masks. He had some imitators in the hamlet of Untonje of the Vanambala, close to today's Mandava, and in the hamlet of kuna-Ntengo, close to today's Namakande.[40] The latter group was led by the elder Ashalela, who was one of the two carvers of painted ntene figures operating under Nampyopyo's patronage. Ashalela's group functioned on a lineage base: only people from the clan of the Vamyoni could participate, although some came from neighboring hamlets of the same lineage. New group members were recruited at the end of the puberty rituals, and initiates could introduce new mask-characters with their songs and personalities. Ashalela had an arsenal of a dozen mapiko, which danced to the sound of four *vinganga* and

one *nneya*. The most famous character was an ironic depiction of a Makonde elder who puts too much faith in ancestral supplication:

| Nalinga imbula | I will try the rain |
| Kulumba shonde | Hunt for favors |
| Mavangu kwitika | My friends, answer! |

The group ceased its activities in the 1950s, undermined by the spread of the new fashions of dutu and nshesho. Nampyopyo's sons dismiss Ashalela's masks as derivative: "There were some who just imitated (*kujedya*), in Ashalela's place . . . But they cannot be put on the same level with Nampyopyo."[41] Some of the players of Ashalela's ensemble, while agreeing on the unoriginal nature of their own work, told me that there was someone else who competed on par with Nampyopyo: the elder Shumu from the hamlet of kuna-Nkungulu, in the Messalo lowlands.[42] As much as Nampyopyo's name is steeped in fame, the one of Shumu is all but forgotten, even in his home region. "Shumu who? No, not here . . ." It took a few weeks' work and some walking to identify one of Shumu's last living players, an elder named Anogwa, who in turn directed me to two other people who were involved in the ensemble. Once it was uttered, the name of Shumu triggered powerful memories in those who had seen his masks.[43]

Shumu's group was in many respects similar to Nampyopyo: it was a grand meat-is-meat ensemble whose players were recruited in a large region around today's village of Myangalewa; it was based on the mask-character principle; it used nneya as a commanding drum and vinganga for the base rhythm; and it was extremely secretive. Unlike Nampyopyo, Shumu was neither a carver nor a wealthy man. He was a simple peasant, and his role as mask owner was organizational. He invented the characters, together with their songs; commissioned the carving of the headpieces; selected the drummers and the dancers; and choreographed the whole spectacle. It was solely on account of his vision that many talented men heeded his call.

Unlike Nampyopyo, Shumu's masks did not have a smooth naturalistic quality or pretense of resemblance. His work leaned toward the frightful side: shock, stupor, and complicatedness. His most famous character was *Lo' lyoi*, a huge headpiece cemented on the inside, holding burning maize cobs that produced large puffs of smoke:

| Lo' lyoi | Look at the smoke |
| Kwa-Magama akó | There in Magama |

The effect sought was at once to puzzle and to scare: "You would flee! Those mapiko? You would see those mapiko and run away!"[44] "Those were mapiko of provocation, of the elders."[45] Two other masks that conjoined ingeniousness and fearfulness were the *Shimmyae*, in which a live cat was wrapped in a cloth to simulate the screaming of a newborn baby, and the *Buffalo* (*Nyati*). This latter was a reinvention of the nocturnal mask with the same name, in a form that could dance by daytime, entirely covered in animal skins, and with carved head and legs. Like its nocturnal equivalent, it would roam around, urinating, defecating, and then charging the audience.[46]

The evocative "gashing" (*Shikishiya*) was an abstract representation of fearfulness:

| Igwa ku-Memba akuno | Listen, here in Memba |
| Kushikishiya | Gashing |
| Kushikishiya Mwalu Mwalu Mwalu | Gashing in the Messalo |

The *Centipede* (*Shangolo*) was surrealistically incarnated in human form, as a Makonde elder with a large hole in the face—a connection that demonstrates the impossibility of interpreting headpieces outside of a detailed history of performance and genre:

| Lipinde Shangolo | The centipede rolls in |
| Ushwele ne' ushwele | Sunrise today sunrise |
| Pindiku' shangolo | The centipede stretches |
| Munnole mwanalilo | Look at his manner of sleeping |

Unlike Nampyopyo, Shumu's work did not fall under the eye of the colonial authorities. His hamlet was far from the main roads, from the missions where blackwood carving was being invented and initiation rituals reshaped, and from the centers of colonial power. Only a narrow *machila* (man-carrier) path could bring the white man there. Out in the sticks, Shumu's ensemble did nonetheless travel around with his masks, even reaching the plateau and challenging Nampyopyo.

Upon a second interview, the sons of Nampyopyo admitted the existence of Shumu and conceded that the two met in dance contests. The rivals competed at least twice: once in the lowlands and once on the plateau. "Shumu, in the Messalo, Nampyopyo, on the plateau.

When they met, it was a fight. Like they do with football today."[47] Some claim that Shumu won in both occasions, largely on account of the number of masks that he could muster. "Nampyopyo could take out masks to play one day or two, and that's it. Over. But Shumu . . . he would dance the first day, until sundown, *pi!*; the second day, until sundown, *pi!*; the third, fourth, fifth . . . until the sixth day. All different masks. The other, he couldn't."[48] "Forty big baskets full of masks": with such an unwieldy baggage Shumu was said to travel, moving at night, so as not to be seen.[49]

Shumu's group was organized following a strict division of labor. The preparation of masks worked like a chain of assembly: a first group, which included Shumu, dressed the dancer; a second group attached the mask; and a third one brought the lipiko by hand to the dance-field. Anogwa's role was to paint scarifications on the masks with wasp wax. Hidden in the bush, far from the dance ground, he drew from morning to sunset. "They brought me food there." But the result was worth the hard work:

—Nampyopyo didn't have many masks. We beat him at kuna-Nkalau [*laughs*].

—Had he come there?

—He got tired (*andidoba*). There, there, *pushove*, there . . . We beat him, and he shook Shumu's hand. [. . .] Shumu had powerful magic. He had many masks.

—Like, how many?

—More than a hundred! And each mask with its song and with its style.[50]

What desire drove, what energies sustained these extravagant contests of masks, held in times of hardships and uncertainty? What kind of man was Shumu? "He was a black person, like this (*munu wakudimba, doni*)." "And what were his thoughts like?" "Just artistry (*ulanda, tu*)."[51] Shumu passed away a few years before Nampyopyo ("He was still alive, and organizing masks, when the war of Shibiliti was fought," that is, in 1960).[52] With the two masters died a unique genre, perhaps the most lavish episode of the whole history of mapiko. It is impossible to know which one of the two rivals—the famous or the unknown, the naturalist or the surrealist—came up with the idea of resurrecting the character template into a multiday parade of masks. The spirit of their invention, however, lived on in another peculiar genre that emerged in the lands of Shumu—the lowlands of the Messalo River, where the template of mapiko based on the mask-character was to be reinvented, cultivated, and conserved for many years to come.

# 5 ↶ Lowland Nights

*Ambivalence in the Face of Death*

| | |
|---|---|
| Uwavi | Witchcraft |
| Vina matakodao | Dances naked |
| Inyama yamunu kunogwa | Human meat is tasty |
| Kunogwa nshimamanela | Tasty when you chew it |
| Tuke tukavine uwavi | Let's dance witchcraft |
| Muti wamunu vashema mpila | A person's head, they call it a ball |
| Lidodo lyamunu vashema ipimbo yakuwanela | A person's leg, they call it a walking stick |

—NMA/Nshindo/Myangalewa/2004

1. THE GENESIS of Makonde ethnicity was tied to a geographic entity: a plateau that served as a refuge, or stronghold, during the dangerous times of the slave trade. People who took shelter in the plateau's maze of thickets had to renounce the proximity of water. A Makonde myth of origin tells the story of a couple living in the Rovuma River, the woman of which manages to give birth to a healthy child only by abandoning the swampy lowlands and climbing the dry plateau.[1] The myth frames the geographic difference between plateau and lowlands into an axiological opposition of "purity" versus "danger." This opposition is two-sided: it refers to the salubrious plateau, largely free from malaria and sleeping sickness, versus the unhealthy lowlands; but also to the plateau as the land of the freemen versus the lowlands as the realm of slavery.

Makonde women fetched water from the large cracks that interrupt the plateau, whose contours are indented, especially on the eastern side. Each Makonde hamlet was located within walking distance from these fissures—between five and fifteen kilometers. A steep path would lead down to the lowlands, where springs restitute the rainwater that seeps through the plateau's permeable soil. Makonde livelihood depended on these ravines and lowlands (*dibondi*) situated in the plateau's proximity. Used without further qualifications, the verbs "descending" (*kwalela*) and "raising" (*kwamboka*) refer to the daily excursions between the plateau and nearby lowlands, where one could find not only water but also building materials such as bamboo, ironwood, and rock.

Farther beyond the plateau lay the dangerous lowlands where sickness and slavery lurked. To the north, *kundonde*—the Rovuma River lowlands traversed by trading caravans and raiders. To the east, *kuiyanga*—wild savanna fields where elephants and lions roamed. To the south, *kumwalu*—the lowlands adjacent to the Messalo River, being a pathway to the lands of the Makua, who lived farther south of the river. To the west, the plateau gradually sloped down into the deserted badlands that lead to today's Nairoto, in Montepuez District. The lowlands of kundonde, kuiyanga, and kumwalu were raiding terrains for the Makonde, who would venture eastward to hunt game, northward and westward to capture women from the Makua and Matambwe.

When colonial conquest put an end to slavery, raids, and warfare, Makonde lineages began to resettle in the lowlands of kundonde, kumwalu, and kuiyanga, where they intermingled with those living there: the remnants of the Matambwe, to the north; the coastal Mwani, to the east; and the Makua, to the south. This process of lowland resettlement intensified throughout the twentieth century. As a consequence, dialects of Shimakonde originated in these areas, demarcating them as somewhat distinct social spaces: Shindonde in the north, and Shimwalu in the southeast—the former characterized by lexical borrowing from Shimatambwe, the second by phonetic and lexical peculiarities.[2] While all the speakers of these dialects continued to identify themselves as Vamakonde, they also developed a sense of regional belonging, sometimes calling themselves Vamwalu or Vandonde, as opposed to Vantadala, the plateau people (*kuntadala* being an alternative name for *kummakonde*, "the plateau"). Those who decided to stay on the plateau—sticking to the original Makonde vocation, as it were, even when its historical rationale was over—largely saw lowland people as impure, half-breeds, or second-class. The axiological distinction between "pure plateau" and "dangerous lowlands" extended well into the postslavery period. Later on, both Frelimo and Renamo soldiers used the Messalo lowlands as a hideout, fueling its reputation as a space of danger.

2. Scholars of the Makonde have largely overlooked the lowlands, unwelcoming because of endemic malaria and bereft of the "tribal purity" allure associated with the plateau. Had the Diases carried out research in the Messalo and Iyanga lowlands, they would have obtained a rather different picture of the historicity of *shilo* night-masks, which they described as corrupt and waning under the blows of rationalism and modernization (see chap. 1, sec. 6).

Before the meat-is-meat break, shilo night-masks were integral to masculine puberty ritual teachings. The boys were initiated into the technique of constructing animal silhouettes with flexible bamboos and cloth. These beasts (*vakoko*) were danced in nightly sallies, during which the women had to hide away in the houses. As in parent masquerades in the region, the category of "beast" encompassed real animals, fantastic spirits (*mashetani*), and technical marvels such as the car, the bus, the airplane, and the helicopter.

Night-masks were also danced during *matanga* funerary ceremonies. A widespread institution in east-central Africa, matanga consists of a night of vigil that culminates in a morning communal meal. Matanga are held during the dry season, when food is abundant; they begin on a Friday night and terminate on a Saturday morning. The ceremony marks the definitive departure of the deceased to the spirit world and the end of grief, signaled by ritual shaving. The matanga is the last moment in which the family is allowed to be bereaved. The long night encompasses sadness and joy, grief and elation. These mixed emotions are channeled by alcohol and dance. Even in precolonial times, matanga was one of the few ritual occasions in which communal binge drinking was socially allowed.[3]

In the late 1920s, night-masks were abruptly abandoned on the Makonde Plateau. The technique of constructing animals with bamboo and cloth was sometimes taught to initiates, but less and less with the passing of time. No one danced night-masks any more at funerary ceremonies, and the memory of masks dancing at matanga faded on the Makonde Plateau.[4] This was far from being an effect of disenchantment. As is the case with daytime mapiko, no one had ever "really" believed in the spiritual nature of the night-masks: neither the men who fabricated them with bamboo and cloth nor the women, who performed their fear as they did with daytime masks. In fact, the word *believe* itself makes little sense in this context: what does it mean to believe in the mask of a beast-helicopter?

The practice and ideology of mapiko was, however, closely connected to the domain of sorcery and magic (*uwavi*).[5] Etymologically, the word *mapiko* is linked to the verb *kupika*, alluding to the mysterious processes by which a sorcerer turns into a spiritual animal (*nkoko wakumpika*). *Kupika* could be translated as "shape changing," "transforming," "transfiguring," "wonder," or "witchcraft." "Let's go and transform a mask" (*tuke tukampike mapiko*) was one of the ways in which the men described publicly that which in private they called "organizing the masks" (*kupanga mapiko*). Mastery in the realm of mapiko—the ability to summon complicated and fearful visions—was an index of powers in the invisible realm. "You don't shake your pelvis just like this" (*aunanung'unula vila*), you don't dance the masks without magical knowledge, support, and protection. A lipiko could have omens or foresights while dancing. Dancing or drumming prowess was supported by plants or medicines (*mitela*). The fame of one or the other group was boosted through the use of *nshamoko*, a mixture of a particular root with honey, which increases one's appeal. Nshamoko could be given to a dancer or a singer, or put within a drum to ensnare the bystanders and call more crowds to watch. The contests between dance ensembles were punctuated by accusations of witchcraft—especially of launching magic missiles (*shijela*) to injure or confuse the adversary's dancer.

Night-masks were discontinued on the plateau as they became the object of sorcery-related anxieties. The magical energies involved in the production and performance of daytime mapiko could be somewhat mastered, subjected to some sort of public scrutiny—in the moment of preparation of the masks, if not in the unpredictable space of the dance-field. Elders such as Shumu and Nampyopyo established their authority also as benevolent but powerful countersorcerers, proficient in the arts of plants and magic defense. The dancing of masks in the night, though, was beyond everyone's control. For who can see better in the night than the witch himself? And is not night dancing the activity proper to sorcerers? Are not those proficient in fabricating and impersonating night beasts the very same ones who transform into magical lions (*vantumi vakuvapika*) to devour children and women on their way to the well? Heavy suspicions fell on night-mask practitioners, and the masks themselves were swiftly abandoned.

Why witchcraft-related anxieties might have increased in the late 1920s is a matter of speculation. This phenomenon could be interpreted as a sublimation of the horrors of the slave-trade world into an immaterial domain.[6] Or one could consider that the end of slavery marked also the opening up of the Makonde refugee society to a wider world—a process that was as enabling as it was charged with fear and suspicion. One might also connect the emergence of sorcery anxieties to the transformative processes engendered by colonialism. Witchcraft crises often accompany change, especially when brutal and disruptive, and sorcery accusations and countersorcery cults are a marking feature of African colonial modernity.[7] The abandonment of shilo on the Makonde Plateau, sparked by fear and suspicion, can be considered as the dark side of the modernist revolution inaugurated by the meat-is-meat break, as the obscure counterpart to the playful cosmopolitanism that predicated a new cultural *koiné* coming after slavery.

The abandonment of shilo was also reinforced by missionary activity. In explicit opposition to paganism, the Christian religion considers the funeral as a space of serious sadness. Its official ideology has always been inimical to the intermingling of grief and laughter. Dance was explicitly forbidden at the matanga of Christians (or "Christian matanga," *matanga anklistu*), sobered-up ceremonies in which the festive element was expelled and grief was to be accompanied only by prayer and moderate singing.

While night-masks were dying out on the Makonde Plateau—abandoned because of witchcraft accusations and banned by Christianity—they surprisingly flourished anew in the Messalo lowlands. There, shilo was turned into a new thriving genre, called *nshindo*. Instead of fearing sorcery accusations, nshindo practitioners trod the thin line that separates sorcery from countersorcery, providing a daring public demonstration of the activities of sorcerers and protecting their dancing space with powerful antisorcery mines. As much as nshindo is associated with the lowlands space, it is also known as "the dance of witchcraft" (*ing'oma ya-uwavi*), thus conjoining geographic with mystical dangerousness.

3. Nshindo was initiated in the mid-1940s by the elder Lipato from the hamlet of the same name, situated midway between the present-day villages of Myangalewa and Mbau, alongside the seasonal river Mwela, which marks the borderline between the fertile Messalo lowlands and

the Iyanga savanna. The hamlet was very close to the one of Yangua, an important *régulo* (native authority) of the area. Lipato and Yangua founded together the inaugural nshindo group, which functioned with the meat-is-meat principle; the first provided the creative thrust, the second the patronage.[8] Lipato's hamlet was also relatively near to Shumu's (see chap. 4, sec. 8)—about twenty kilometers away on a narrow winding forest path—and Shumu's influence must have been strong in the invention of the new genre. Nshindo can be described as a mélange of the daytime characters that made Shumu and Nampyopyo famous and of night-masks, properly speaking. While Shumu's and Nampyopyo's masks were variable—new ones were constantly invented, and the order of presentation could be shuffled around—nshindo characters danced following a well-established sequence, which obeyed the ritual unfolding of the funerary ceremony.

The dancing space was framed by a wooden enclosure (*lingongo*), which served to protect the dancing space not only from the excesses of participation—especially revelry and drunkenness—but also, most important, from the attacks of witches. The night before the performance, a healer (*nkulaula*) sealed the terrain against malevolent magic, demarcating the enclosure space with his naked buttocks, planting anti-sorcery "land mines" (*dimina*) at the four corners and at the center, and painting the wooden fence with remedies. On the night of the performance, the healer would sit in the enclosure with his gourds hanging close by, as a silent warning.

The masks entered the enclosure one by one. Each one danced, then returned to the hiding-place. In-between masks, the drumming—mostly, of large *makuti*—would not stop; the group members sometimes performed circular dances without masks. The spectacle unfolded as follows.

I. MANGA NA MUNYU. The first character to enter the dance space, just before sunset, was "the Manga with the salt." The word *mmanga* is difficult to translate: literally, it means "person from the coast"; more specifically, it can refer to a Kimwani-speaking person from the littoral adjacent to the Iyanga Plains, but it can also be used to identify a Muslim. All these meanings are overlapping and conflated. In sum, *mmanga* is the quasi-derogatory counterpart of the word *mchenzi* ("savage") used by coastal people.[9] The Manga's headpiece was characterized by a fez, a yellowish complexion, and a quiet smile. The mask came carrying a torch, danced, and then lighted the fires at the four corners of the enclosure that would burn throughout the night. The group's owner (that is, Lipato himself) introduced the mask along these lines:

> —This one, do you know him?
>
> —*Ahii!* No! [*the crowd answers*]
>
> —His name is Manga na Munyu. He comes from the coast. From Mocimboa. He heard that his friend is holding a matanga. There is a matanga at the place of so-and-so. And he said: "*Booo* . . . why didn't you come and tell me? I don't live that far!" And he took out some four hundred [MT], and bought salt, and put it in a plastic bag. Then, he bought a chicken. As a present. "These things are enough." And here it comes.
>
> Then, the mask itself might speak:
>
> —I am the *Manga-with-the-Salt.* The owner of the matanga is a friend of mine. I came here at his place. I didn't eat porridge, and I didn't sleep in a nice place. My friend, today, he robbed me. He was doing a matanga without me! He would have begun and finished without me; and now I come in the middle of things. I apologize to you all. My friend, here's a chicken. Kill it, so that people can eat it. And salt. Put it in the sauce that people will eat. [. . .] But now, I don't want to invite myself. I gave you the salt, the chicken, and the fire, and now I go, and I won't come back again. That's it.[10]

II. Low-lying masks. After the first mask and until midnight came the night-beasts proper, made of bamboo and cloth, also called low-lying masks (*mapiko apai*): the buffalo, the elephant, the snake, the car, the truck, *nnandenga,* and so forth. Each mask was introduced by a song, most of the time simply inviting people to watch: "Come and see the pangolin" or "Come and see the helicopter; it throws fire" or "Women, don't run away, come near and see the crocodile."[11] Sometimes the song constructed a minimalistic story around the beast:

| | |
|---|---|
| Nyati nyati | The buffalo, the buffalo |
| Wakubyaa nannume | Killed by the man |
| Wakumbula nkongwe | Finished off by the woman |

The song could also play with the physical qualities of an animal in surrealistic ways. For instance, *kabwele,* a bush antelope with a swaying pace, was made into a dancer of fancy Congolese rhythms:

| Kabwele jó alivalenge kumanya | Kabwele, this one, it turns out to know |
| Lumba lumba | The rumba, the rumba |

III. LESSER MASKS. The wee hours after midnight (*shilo shi-kumene*) were filled by playful "small masks" (*mapiko madikidiki*) danced by youngsters. Here, the space was left open for improvisation and experimentation. The same rudimentary mask could be used to impersonate this or that character, to support this or that song. Anyway, no one could distinguish clearly, as the night would be dark and the souls elated by the spirits.

IV. GREATER MASKS. One hour before daybreak, the disorderly parade of lesser masks was interrupted by the first of the daytime "big masks" (*mapiko makumene*): the Ngoni's morning star. The mask referenced the fishermen of Ngoni descent who settled around Nguri Lake in the aftermath of the southern African upheavals of 1815–40, with their habit of waking up before daylight to go fishing in canoes. The mask's song was a poetic description of the increasing brilliance of the star in the hours before dawn, conveyed through onomatopoeic intensification:

| Manemba | My friends |
| Ngugwene vya ngango | I saw something that did *ngango*! |
| Lyalosha, lya-Vamangoni | The morning star of the Ngoni |
| Ngugwene vya . . . | I saw something that did . . . |
| muli | something that comes out of a hole |
| piuwo | a faint light |
| ka | small explosion |
| mba | something that stands out of a background |
| ngali | an explosion |
| ng'aa | rays of light falling down like a firework |

After the *Morning Star* and until the end of the ceremony, other greater masks appeared in the enclosure. In the beginning, these were only three: *Kushenga Lidi* ("voice of brilliance"), a beautiful Makonde woman; *Vyungula*, the *Hares*; and *Liwambe*, the *Flood*:

| Liwambwe nelo liwambe | My friends |
| Kushanya akó | There, above |
| Kubondi akó | In the lowlands, below |
| Kushanga wetu | Woe on us |
| Tunyeme manemba tunyeme | Let's leave, boys |

The mighty *Flood* was represented metaphorically by a gigantic mask of a Makonde tattooed elder—yet another proof that headpieces cannot be interpreted outside of their performative history.

V. MALONJE. The final character, the *Baobab Fruit* (*Malonje*), came after the communal meal and marked the end of the ceremony in quite a physical way. To the sound of a surrealistic call-and-response choir—*Malonje?* Answer! *Malonje?* Answer!—the mask rushed into the dance-field armed with a cudgel and hit madly around, physically swiping the matanga of all lingering guests—drunks and gluttons, sleepy and lazy—leaving the family alone for the last intimate moments, the last thoughts and the last tears.

4. The historian of African dance has the advantage—and the risk—of proximity. For as arduous as it is to imagine the atmosphere and feeling of colonial-era masquerading, one can integrate oral history with the observation of recent genres and forms. In the early 2000s, Nampyopyo's and Shumu's masks were alive only in the memory of few, and only two dutu groups survived—one of which performed very sporadically, the other being almost indistinguishable from a nshesho.[12] But nshindo was thriving, the legacy of Lipato distributed across communal villages in the districts of Muidumbe and Mocimboa da Praia, ku-Mwalu and ku-Iyanga. Since Lipato's times, the sequence had been enriched by dozens of new characters. The time frame of the dance was also expanded: no longer terminated by *Malonje*'s cudgeling, it now carried on for twenty-four hours, from sunset to sunset.

It took me a while to overcome the "plateau complex" and descend to the lowlands. I was first exposed to nshindo in Nakitenge, Vicente Muanga's village (see chap. 2, sec. 4). Vicente was a nshindo fan, and he insisted that we see it. He immediately made a fan of me, too. I was captivated by nshindo not only because of the intensity of round-the-clock masquerading but also because it gave me the opportunity of observing in action the mask-character template, which had been abandoned in all other mapiko genres. I could watch the dance again in June 2003, when a group from Myangalewa ascended to Muidumbe to perform on the occasion of the Second Festival of Popular Dance. In 2004, I carried out systematic research in the lowlands, working with six out of eight existing nshindo groups, photographing masks, noting the names and songs of characters, and filming eleven performances as well as the construction of night-masks.[13] On two occasions I was invited by nshindo groups to participate in their excursions to dance at matanga in different villages.[14] My experience of nshindo and matanga has influenced my historical reconstruction not only of this genre but also of Nampyopyo's and Shumu's masks. Let me now bring this experience more to the fore: in the form of some morphological observations, rather than in the genre of the fieldwork sketch; synchronically, rather than diachronically; and mixing freely among the various performances in which I took part.[15]

A nshindo character emerges at the intersection of four media: the CALL-SONG, the MASK, the DANCE, and the narrative PRESENTATION (*kuvalanga*, "to tell"). Except for songs, which are transmitted and reproduced quite faithfully, the other media allow for latitude of improvisation.[16] Two or three features identify a mask as representing a certain character—Manga's fez, Liwambwe's huge head, and so forth—while the rest is left to the carver. Instead of being codified in styles (*vikuvo*, "rhythmic sequences"), the dance is described and transmitted in terms of actions (*vitendo*). The narrative presentation follows a vague script but is largely left to the verbal skills of one lead speaker, who dialogues with the choir and the matanga guests. The drums go still and the presenter explains, "We are going to see masks . . . each style with its name (*shikuvo na lina*)." What is produced at the intersection of these media? Besides the low-lying masks of animals that form the bulk of the early night entertainment, the major masks can be broadly divided into three categories.

I. A first group of masks are *moralistic*: they impersonate vices, which are overtly stigmatized. The scrooge is thus called into the enclosure:

| Epu-epu | *Epu-epu* [Onomatopoeia for mouth-cleaning] |
| Ntondo ndakwima shangu | The day after tomorrow I will deny you mine |
| Tunsheme washoju jó | Let's call him a scrooge, this one |
| Pakanywa pó | In the mouth there |

The mask is marked by one defining feature: a crooked open mouth. It dances while waving a maize cob in front of its mouth, and the choir goes, "*Epu! Epu!* He swipes! He swipes!" The presenter explains:

—You are watching here actions (*vitendo*) . . . This one, he had a friend. But his friend, he didn't come. He said, "Go there by yourself." They organized a trip to Chai. As they were going to Chai, his friend bought some bananas. [*To the choir:*] Is it not like this, boys (*manemba, i momo?*)

—[*The choir:*] Precisely like this (*momo*)! Go on! You never lie!

—And like a true friend, he offers: "Take some!" Now, the other, in Litamanda, he buys some dried maize for four hundred *metical.* Isn't it, boys?

—Precisely!

—And he eats it alone. He refused to give to his friend, *kobó!* He's called: "The day after tomorrow I will deny you mine."

Theft is described indirectly. There is the mask of a beautiful Makonde woman, who came to the matanga and now does not find the plate that she brought. She is searching and searching; and there, her friend has a plate that looks just like hers . . .

| | |
|---|---|
| Shani ashi, shani ashi | This plate, this plate |
| Kulingana | It looks like |
| Kulingana, kenga shangu | It looks like mine |

Along the same lines, there is the critique of the too-promiscuous woman (the "minibus," *chapa cem*); of the old man who marries a young girl (*ntwa' mwali*); of the woman who cannot cook ("I don't want to marry, *sha!*"); of the drunkard Mwanjojo, whose belly does *be! be!*

II. A second group of masks embodies professional *habitus*, which is taken at the point of becoming obsession and eventually backfires on its owner. This was the fate of Kumbwanano the trapper, greedy for meat:

| | |
|---|---|
| Kumbwanano | Kumbwanano |
| Nang'olo aju | This elder |
| Lindikanda liliva | Hit himself with a trap |
| Mmuti mó | On the head |

The mask enters with a stick and runs around to set snares everywhere. A large red crack runs across his lip, face, eye, and forehead, signaling that the obsession with meat and hunting went awry. The narrator admonishes the crowd directly, while the mask nods, dully satisfied in its devouring passion:

—Me, there is something I want to tell. I haven't told it yet.
    This one . . . Let's leave this thing of traps! Those bush rats,

those traps, those monkeys . . . you go and set your traps. But you must know how it all ends. Look at this one! This one, he's a real trapper. He set his own trap. At *kunamamba*. Isn't it, boys?

—Precisely!

—At *kushivimbi, kunamamba*. He sets it, *ka!* And as he leaves, truly, it catches a monkey. On the second day, he goes to check it. He's taken something. He goes there to take out the animal, and the trap backfires! *Gwe!* Isn't it, boys?

—Precisely! You never lie, you!

—He's a real trapper! In his house, he refuses to eat vegetables. Every day, bush rats, *ntotwe, ntavala, viluma*. That's him.

The elder *Ndemba*, "who eats honey in the bush," is a bee hunter with a prominent bump on the forehead—again, an obsession that led to self-injury.[17] A beehive is put in the enclosure; the mask tries to take out the honey and is repelled by the bees, until he succeeds and eats the sweet prize, rubbing his sting. *Mingoko* is an avid fishermen "who jumped into the pot" (*andilijela nshilongo*) to eat the fish that he brought back to his wife: a conjunction of habitus obsession and gluttony. But something went wrong: a large fishbone got jammed in his throat, and "his tongue stuck out."

III. Finally, there is the broad category of the *other*, ethnic and fantastic: Europeans, Arabs, Makua, Mwani, spirits, and animals. The *Masai* are depicted as sellers of fraudulent traditional medicines. The smoothly carved masks engage in a long theatrical sketch: they lay out their medicines from their gourds; they get their first patient, massage her belly, cut her body with razor blades, and then make her rise, healed! The *Masai* dance elegantly and quietly, waving their walking stick, while the song exalts their physical alterity:

| | |
|---|---|
| Masai lo' | Look at the Masai |
| Kwavalakadile | Whence they came |
| Vakongwe na valume | The men and the women |
| Uti vagwa' dyaleni | They all wear earrings |

*Shinengo*, the lesser bushbaby—a nocturnal primate with prominent eyes—is made into an overly voracious reader, a swot. This is why his "eyes came out" (*meo tungulungo*)! In another, more fantastic version, the bushbaby was sent to Lisbon to have his eyes replaced with a cat's, after too avidly watching a football game.

5. Nshindo characters are located at the intersection of alterity and morality. The exceptional and the bizarre—the host of odd animals, strangers, and madmen that make up most of the nshindo masks—are framed within a moral narrative that stigmatizes vices such as gluttony, avarice, laziness, jealousy, arrogance, and vanity. Such moral discourse is a constant of peasant societies, in which scarce resources require strong values of solidarity, of low-population groups in which the struggle for life and death is intense and pervasive.[18] Morality also familiarizes the foreign and makes the stupefying intelligible.

But nshindo's moral tales are never wholly moralistic: they are unmade by the atmosphere of laughter that surrounds them (fig. 8). The carving style is always grotesque: there is no smooth naturalism in nshindo masks, only roughly cut surfaces, spirit-dark complexion, and ugliness. The songs are elliptic, playing with onomatopoeia and images. The presentation is admonishing but thoroughly complicit. Is the moral tale that is being told true, or is it a joke? "Isn't it like this, boys?" the nshindo presenter asks his choir. "Precisely! How could you lie?" the choir responds. Is the public asked to condemn vice, to identify with it, or both?

Echoes of Bakhtin's "people laughter" resonate loudly here. This is a laughter that is festive, collective, and above all ambivalent. "Folk humor denies, but it revives and renews at the same time. Bare negation is completely alien to folk culture." This laughter "is gay, triumphant, and at the same time mocking, deriding. It asserts and denies, buries and revives." Its essence is "to present a contradictory and double-faced fullness of life."[19] At the root of carnivalesque laughter is the joyful acceptance of death and change, embodied in the figure of the pregnant death. This laughter embraces "the very act of becoming and growth, the eternal incomplete unfinished nature of being." For it, "death is not a negation of life seen as the great body of all the people but part of life as a whole—its indispensable component, the condition of its constant renewal and rejuvenation."[20]

Nshindo characters perform moral ambivalence at the very moment in which grief is abandoned, in which the cycle of death and rebirth is joyfully accepted. Ambivalence saturates the atmosphere of matanga,

FIGURE 8. Laughter *(Rui Assubuji, Litamanda, 2009)*

when it is animated by the nshindo masks. The night is dense and long. The grieving of the women inside the house, the ritual lamentation, the tears—which become so prominent in the Christian version of the ceremony—are all but silenced by the drums, striking without interruption. The drinking is massive. The Messalo lowlands are a factory of moonshine sugarcane liquor (*nipa*): dozens of liters are consumed by the guests and the drummers, as well as by intruders who help themselves to the flowing alcohol. Eating of newly harvested food is copious, and people hide in dark corners for elated encounters. "It is a gay funeral."[21]

Themes of Bakhtin's grotesque realism are abundant in nshindo. The thrashings, in the iconic mask of *Malonje* the cudgel-man and in its later reincarnation, *Nandulumbuka*, the crazy one who comes armed with bow and machete. The drinking, eating, and copulating body: take, for instance, the mask of the native authority *Majembe*, who got drunk by eating too many green peas, and the depictions of the sexual appetites of men and women, young and old. Or consider the mask of the hernia (*Liyega*), who enters with a huge protuberance dropping from the groin. "He didn't want to go to the hospital to get cured, and now he needs to be operated here." Is meaning conveyed by the moral message, or does it lie in the sympathetic laughter that punctuates the grotesque operation, in the joyful jumping of the liberated mask?

In nshindo, we touch a deep root of peasant society, with its cycles of death and rebirth, its morality unmade by laughter, its cosmic relativism, its grotesque body. We touch a mode of representation that brings about at once assertion and denial, celebration and critique, sadness and laughter. This mode of representation cannot be confounded either with naturalism or with irony, because it manages to achieve both: a precise description, inspired by an all-embracing passion for the existent, and a caustic critique, driven by communal values and ideas of social change. This is neither first nor second degree but both at the same time, or perhaps a gesturing toward a utopian third degree of meaning. As we will see, nshindo would conserve this representative mode and revitalize the whole tradition of mapiko with it, when political reformers tried to bend the masquerade to their principles of univocal seriousness.


6. At the same time, the genre of nshindo is very much the product of a specific location—the lowlands of *kumwalu* and *kuiyanga*—and of its

history as a liminal space. Details of costuming and instrumentation are revealing in this respect. In daytime mapiko, the cloth that covers the body of the dancer is tightened through the use of little bits of wood called "wearers" (*vigwali*), around which a string is tied. This results in small bumps that elegantly punctuate the legs and arms of the lipiko. Heavy metal bells (*dinjuga*) hang from the *lutove* corset. In nshindo, the costume is tightened by raffia ropes that cut horizontally across the dancer's arms and legs. The dancer wears around the ankles light rattles made from dried fruits called *meeve*. Sometimes, the loincloth *ingonda* is substituted with a long raffia skirt.

These three costuming features—horizontal raffia ropes, meeve foot rattles, and raffia skirt—originate in the face-masks that were danced in the region mostly by Ngoni people around Nguri Lake but also by the Makua south of the Messalo. The Ngoni had appropriated these masks from the Makua people upon their arrival in the region. Before colonial conquest, the Makonde referred collectively to these dances as "slave masks" (*makomba amashagwa*—the word *makomba* indicates specifically a mask that covers the face). In the 1940s, the Makonde who had settled in the Messalo lowlands (*vamwalu*) began to appropriate facial "slave masks" within their repertoire of genres.[22] Makua masks were reinvented into a new genre called *nantyaka*; the Ngoni's into a similar genre called *majoji*. Both involved the use of a large feathered crown around the mask (*linjonda*). Sometimes these genres retained the original song lyrics in Emakhuwa or Chingoni, but many new songs in Shimakonde or Kiswahili were also composed. Facial masks were associated with a light, playful quality; with lesser secrecy and danger; with comicality, capers, and jokes. Their main dance feat was foot stomping, rhythmically underlined by the meeve rattles and whistling. Also, because of the material structure of the face masks—in which the mask's eyes correspond to the dancer's eyes and the mouth to the mouth—the slave's makomba could speak, something that was strictly forbidden to the helmet-shaped mapiko.

Meanwhile, Makonde masters began to sell the secrets of mapiko to the Makua living in the southern side of the Messalo. The Makua desired to enrich their initiation rituals with the most fearful masks of the Makonde, and the latter were willing to cash in on their reputation of being "thoroughly savage." The genre taught to the Makua would be the most recent *nshesho*. A few Makua ensembles of this kind emerged in the early 1950s, dancing mostly at initiation rituals. "They would dance, *gwe!* Some would know well."[23] However, these dynamics of exchange would be short-lived: they were truncated in the 1950s, when the Makua and the Ngoni abandoned the practice of masks as a consequence of Islamization.[24] The masks that originally belonged to the Makua and the Ngoni lived on as playful genres in the Makonde repertoire, exerting an important influence on the aesthetics of nshindo. This is also why secrecy rules in nshindo were less stringent than in other genres. "Elders didn't get angry. Because those were like slaves' masks."[25]

7. It was in Litamanda, one of the farthest Makonde settlements south of the Messalo, that nshindo was taken to new heights. Lipato visited the area and impressed two youngsters, one named Ligulunyule and the other Shalele Mawasha, who decided to follow in his footsteps. "Lipato came here, for a matanga. We watched, and we wished to learn. And we carved masks, until we started dancing. And we established our mask hiding-place here."[26]

The group of Litamanda expanded Lipato's idea in both scope and time frame. Instead of being interrupted by *Malonje*'s blows, the spectacle continued until sunset. A host of new characters were introduced and some of the old ones reinvented. The greater masks now occupied the whole day, from daybreak to dusk—dozens of characters, with their own song, actions, and ambivalent morals. When the sun was about to set and the light dimming, the new nshindo ended with a no less astonishing climax than the old *Malonje*, a fearful representation of the deeds of sorcerers:

| | |
|---|---|
| Uwavi-e-ke | Sorcery |
| Tuke tukavine uwavi | Let's dance sorcery |
| Vina matakodao | Dances bare-buttocked |

The mask of the sorcerer is red and silver: red the closed eyes and red the cross on the forehead, silver the complexion. The head is misshapen, with a prominent backward-crested nape, topped by a thin strip of hair. It is called *Shipindi*. On his head, *Shipindi* carries a pitcher containing a remedy, which he sprays on the crowd with a whisker tail, while the *makuti* strikes a slow, hypnotic rhythm. People back off, in fear. Is the remedy sorcery, or is it antisorcery? Behind the mask come *Shipindi*'s helpers: a group of eight or ten naked boys, their bodies painted in white spots, like masters of ritual ceremonies. They enter cautiously onto the dance field, on their toes. When inside, they begin shaking their bodies, their hands moving quickly up and down, scratching the skin from the chest to the thighs. It is precisely like this, in this itchy nervous way, that sorcerers dance. *Shipindi* slowly circles the enclosure, spraying the remedy. The presenter repeats again and again, lest what is to be seen is misunderstood: "Leave sorcery! Sorcery is ugly!"

There follows a theatrical representation of the activities of sorcerers.[27] Many sketches can be performed, but they all turn around the same plot: a devouring hunger for human meat; a nightly attack during which a victim is abducted and his meat collectively devoured in a cannibalistic feast; the sorcerers that "injure themselves" (*kulibyaa uwavi*) by stepping on an antisorcery mine planted by a healer; and *Shipindi* raising them from the ground with a more powerful medicine and making them dance again the itchy dance of witchcraft, until they run away from the enclosure never to return. Sprinting away one by one in the thick dust, the naked sorcerers spread their buttocks and show the body part most closely associated with dark magic and destruction. "Whoever hasn't seen an asshole, here it is!"

Again, my knowledge of the sorcery mask and theater is shaped by the performances that I watched. I saw the best *Shipindi* in the village of Nakitenge, incarnated in a geometric headpiece, perfect in its ugliness, splashing the remedy with hieratic movements, crouching and balancing with assured elegance, resurrecting his mates by rubbing his buttocks all along their spines. In Myangalewa, the depiction of the *Shipindi*'s helpers was most theatrically vivid: eyes and tongues rolling in lust of flesh; the sorcerers breaking out in random fights, throwing dust at each other and even hinting at sodomy (*shilumelume*, "between men," an activity possibly more secretive than sorcery itself); all culminating in the communal distribution of flesh, swallowed greedily and with shivers of pleasure. In Litamanda, I could see the original "sorcery" as it was thought by Mawasha himself, who coached a group of young people and would nod in approbation or shake his head in reprobation when the modifications to the script that he had once devised were too drastic. The assistants come into the circle first, crawling between the legs of a lead sorcerer and preparing the entrance of *Shipindi* with its jar. They sit, forming a star, holding with their inward-pointed feet a closed pot. Crosses hang from their necks (fig. 9). They argue, discuss, and scream at each other, calling each other names such as *likabuli*, "tombstone." They want to devour the flesh in the plate. In Mawasha's

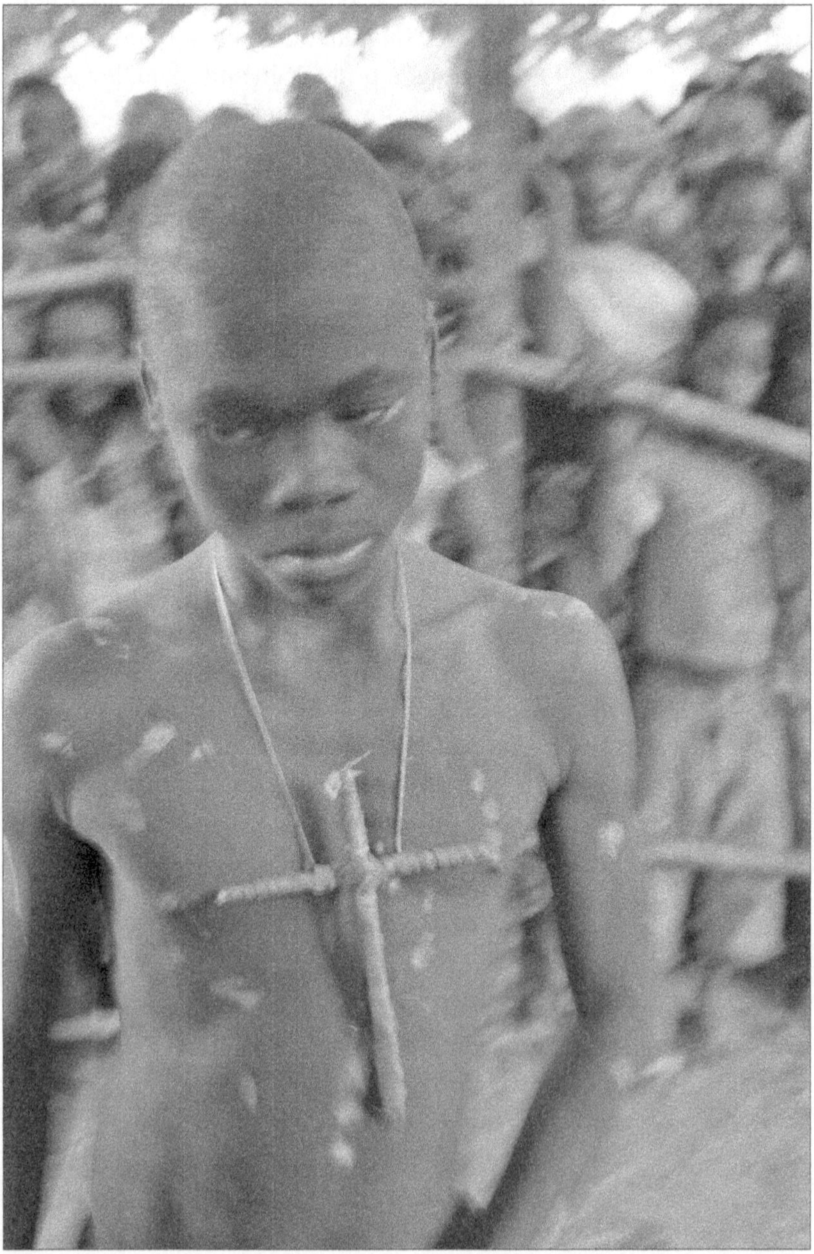

FIGURE 9. The sorcerer's young acolyte *(Rui Assubuji, Litamanda, 2009)*

times, songs would be sung before the flesh is swallowed with deep shivers, from mouth to mouth around the circle:

| | |
|---|---|
| Vavetu Myangalewa vanditauka | Our friends from Myangalewa, they defied us |
| Tukavine uwavi | Let's dance sorcery |
| Uwavi pa-Litamanda apó | Sorcery at Litamanda, there |

In Mawasha's mind, the representation of sorcery was meant to be an open condemnation: a demystification that, by exposing publicly the misdeeds of sorcerers, would keep people away from the temptations of dark magic. In this respect, nshindo deserves a place among the antisorcery movements that punctuated colonial modernity in Africa, testifying at once to the spread of sorcery anxieties and to a broad reconfiguration of the idiom of sorcery itself, seen now more consistently as an antisocial force. However, the daring presentation, of course, opened the question: "If they know so well what sorcerers do, are they not themselves sorcerers?"[28]

The preparation of the nshindo dance ground as a countersorcery space is meant to testify to the good faith of the dancers. The space of nshindo is thoroughly "mined" against sorcery, with a complex preparation that involves an egg and powder, in such a way that "if a sorcerer tries to attack us, if he tries to attack the boys that dance, he will die him/herself." But who shields the terrain in such a way? "We call a healer; but this healer is himself a sorcerer."[29] In many ways, nshindo exposes the ambivalence inherent to sorcery, whereby good and evil, healing and injuring, sorcery and countersorcery, construction and destruction are always at risk of turning into their opposite.

Drawn into the peculiar idiom of nshindo—in the atmosphere of laughter that at once embraces and critiques—the denunciation of witchcraft appeared as all too sympathetic, if not complicit. Seen from the plateau, the mask of the sorcerer came to represent metonymically the whole genre of nshindo, a nocturnal dance of witchcraft, and the dangerous and impure lowlands in which the genre was cultivated. For nshindo practitioners, it became the unwieldy banner of their art, treading the fine line between the acceptable and the subversive, the festive and the deadly.

8. After my first visit in the lowlands, I returned to carry out research in ku-Iyanga in July 2003, again in the company of Vicente Muanga. The

day after my arrival in the village of Mbau, I was summoned by the post chief. I had presented the documents that qualified me as a researcher to the relevant structures, the village secretary and the village head of culture, so I was somewhat surprised by the urgent convocation from a higher authority. After reading my papers and hearing about the motive of my visit, the post chief sighed in relief. "I was very worried by what I heard, and I wanted to check personally. But if things are like this I wish you all the best with your endeavors." According to a rumor, he explained in a somewhat embarrassed tone, this white man (me) would pay five hundred *contos* to young men willing to take off their pants and run naked in front of a camera. It was not difficult to reconstruct how the rumor originated: five hundred contos was the price that I had paid to the Nakitenge group in order to film the performance, and it was also the price that a nshindo group generally charged at the time to dance for a ceremony; the part about the pants and the boys probably derived from the stupefied question that I posed when I heard about the sorcery dance: "Do they *really* dance naked?"[30] In the space of a few months, the rumor had taken on a life of its own. While visiting Nakitenge again, I was approached by a young man, who, emboldened by shame, exclaimed abruptly, "I am ready to take off my pants; prepare your camera!"[31]

In the second half of the twentieth century, the Messalo lowlands have witnessed waves of witchcraft rumors, which sometimes resulted in scapegoating violence: rumors of lion and elephant men; of organ and child trafficking; of blood-suckers and plague-spreaders; of nightly helicopters powered by human flesh; of oil fields hidden under the sandy dunes.[32] The plateau has not been immune from such rumors, but in the less controlled space of the lowlands they ran rampant; moreover, they were projected onto that space by plateau people themselves: "These things happen there, in the Messalo." The lowlands are also the space in which the most powerful sorcerers and healers have operated: those able to combine the legendary Makonde lore for plants (*mitela*) with evocations based on the manipulation and recitation of the Koran, which they learned there from Makua colleagues. Plateau people travel to Litamanda, Litandakua, and Mbau to consult these hybrid and powerful healers, to be treated and protected in ways that are impervious to the monochord knowledge of plant-based plateau healers and witches. But these are also places where the unequipped and the feeble fear to tread.

Faced with these spiritual dangers, most nshindo practitioners continued to expose the misdeeds of sorcerers through their ambivalent and festive theater, arguing that they were fighting against, not contributing to, the spread of witchcraft and that the Messalo needed the exposure and the demystification more than any other place. Others withdrew. This was the case with the group formed in the village of Mbau in the late colonial period by elders who had played with Lipato. First, they changed the name of the dance to *shikelya*; then, under the influence of the healer and witch-finder Alivémwako, they eliminated the representation of sorcery from the performance altogether.[33] Other groups continued to dance the mask of sorcery, but only at funerary ceremonies and only in the lowlands, omitting the naked dance when performing on the plateau or for the state. *Shipindi the Sorcerer* thus retired in the intimate, and consonant, space of the matanga ceremony of laughter and departure.

9. *Shipindi* is a proper name, referring to a man who existed when nshindo was invented. "Shipindi was a powerful sorcerer, an elder who used to live in the Messalo area."[34] He was wicked, ugly, and blind in one eye—or so the tradition has him. The mask was carved in his likeness. Most nshindo practitioners cannot recollect the actual person, but the proper name stands there as a reminder that the moral story is historically grounded.

Like *Shipindi*, many typified nshindo characters originated in the memory of a real person, taken at once in its singularity and its generality. Sometimes the features of the person inspired the mask template (like Nampyopyo, some nshindo carvers were talented portrayers) but the individuality of the subject was sublimated into an ambivalent moral representation. Such is the case of *Esho*, an elder who was fond of riddles, who is typified as an old man whose feet are eaten by *matakenya* worms—a vivid representation of traditionalism and backwardness. But the name and the mask evoke the features of a real person:

| | |
|---|---|
| Watana dinano nyani jó? | Who is the one that poses riddles? |
| Esho | Esho |

Most nshindo characters are constructed through such a sublimation of a person into a moral template. Memory is made into myth, the individual turned into the general, idiosyncrasy into collective value.

The proper name is the point of resilience of memory itself: that which anchors the moral message in historical actuality, into a "this really happened." The genre of nshindo can be thus considered not only as a repository of a specific representative mode based on ambivalent laughter but also as an archive of memory taken at the point at which it is about to turn into myth. Seen from this angle, the composite gallery of nshindo characters captures the peculiar historical experience of a group of people, the lowland Makonde, settling in a liminal social space. This experience was marked by the encounter with alterity; by feelings of curiosity, anxiety, and puzzlement; and by the desire to represent and capture it all in dance: the Ngoni fishermen, the Mwani who carries salt from the coast, the medicine-selling Masai, the hungry Makua (*ndalo*)—a mask that specifically refers to a famine that took place in the 1950s in the area south of the Messalo. This could also be the reason why the character template, discarded in the plateau in favor of more abstract genres, thrived in the lowlands: because it lent itself to the representation and typification of alterity in a composite social landscape.

But sometimes history looks too hard—or too far—for causes and reasons: in the realm of finality rather than in the one of accidents. Such was the wisdom of the elder who remarked, "Here in the Messalo, there are too many mosquitoes. By night, we don't manage to sleep; since we don't sleep, we dance. And that's why there are so many nocturnal dances here. Plateau people sleep by night; we can't!" This historical interpretation—an environmental determinism of sorts—is captured by nshindo itself. One of the night-masks originally danced in Lipato's group, which became a mainstay of later performances, represents the most dangerous beast to roam the Messalo lowlands:

| | |
|---|---|
| Njanjema! Njanjema! | Mosquito! Mosquito! |
| Dukukuka | It oscillates |
| Dukukuka, ndó! | It oscillates, it's full of them |

# 6 ∽ Migrant Tunes

*On the Threshold of Nationalism*

| | |
|---|---|
| Nikaikala ngushiba kwetu | If I sit and tell of our home |
| Kwetu ku-Mwidumbi | Our home Muidumbe |
| Shilanga shavangan'olo | The elders' song-poems |
| Kuvalanga vinu | They told things |
| Kulapa vinu | They lamented things |
| Kulambalela vinu | They inquired into things |
| Leka tuleke | Let's leave it there |

—NMA/Shilanga/Mwambula/2005

1. THE MASK-CHARACTER template, exemplified in the reinventions of Nampyopyo, Shumu, Lipato, and Mawasha, referred to history somewhat obliquely. The genres of both mileya and nshindo produced representations anchored in historical experience: of personality and behavior, of social alterity, of puzzling phenomena recast as ancestors or spiritual beasts. But the historicity thus evoked was overridden by the aesthetic thrust of each genre: by the will to stupefy with perfect or shocking representations, in mileya; by ambivalent morality, in nshindo. History is readable there as remainder or trace, as the proper name that survives the moral typification, as the memory of the encounter or incident that sparked first the observation and then the representation. Behind each mask there is experience, but the mask transforms it into something else: beauty, danger, or moral lesson. Even Nampyopyo's *Germans*—which stemmed directly from, and referred precisely to, the historical conjuncture of the First World War and its aftermath—could be seen as just another representation of white people as colonialists.

One might expect even less historicity to exude from the abstract genres that emerged after the meat-is-meat break, the likuti-driven dutu and the ligoma-driven nshesho. Once the mimetic unity of character was broken, the mask and its dance operated as free-floating signifiers, open to an array of discordant interpretations or perhaps resistant to interpretation altogether. Dancing a variety of styles, what did the mask of Queen Elizabeth the Second convey (see chap. 1, sec. 5 and chap. 4, sec. 4): admiration, desire, critique of a possible new colonial master?

Freed from mimetic reference to the mask, though, mapiko songs became a new vehicle through which historicity was embedded in the play of masks—in a much more articulated, direct, and precise way than in the old character-based template. Take for instance, in this dutu song, the depiction of a fight sparked by an incongruent motive, poignantly exposing the persistence of schismogenetic dynamics in postslavery Makonde society:

| | |
|---|---|
| Kuvabyana elo | They killed each other, yes |
| Vana-Nshaka | The sons of Nshaka |
| Shilambo shaku-Bamela | In the country of Bamela |
| Kutunduvanga naku-Bamela | It started at Bamela's |
| Mashamba nanung'une kugodolana | Mashamba and his little brother fought |
| Kumalilila pana-Mpalembe | It only ended at Mpalembe's |
| Mukava na uwavi lipungule | If you are bewitched, keep it down |
| Aunavone kukamanana mwanda wamandyoka | Didn't they fight on their way to collect manioc |
| Mela vanu vaposhe | Mela had to rescue the people.[1] |

Examples abound of these historically minded songs, which colonial-era performers remembered lucidly at the time of my fieldwork, as sometime-important repertoires. How did these songs emerge? How did they come to play such a prominent role in ritual masking? To what kinds of historical experience do they refer?

2. Listening synchronically to a large corpus of songs in Shimakonde, consisting of more than a thousand items recorded in the field or collected from various sources, one can make a broad distinction between four categories. There are secret ritual songs directly connected to the various phases of puberty rituals; popular public songs, which are the

domain of everyone and whose origins are lost beyond any possible recollection; and songs that are connected to a specific genre of dancing,
and possibly to a specific group.[2]

The latter make up the large majority of the corpus. Stylistic mark-
ers, both lyrical and musical, set apart the songs belonging to each
genre and connected to one or the other dance. A song for *ligwalema*,
an ancient funeral dance, cannot be confused with a song for *nshaila*,
a circular dance of elderly women; a *linjolo* song cannot be sung for a
*nkala* dance. In this category, the process of composition is partly individual and partly collective. In each group there are masters of lyrical
and melodic invention who also generally lead the singing (*kushamalela*) in the moment of performance. These masters craft a song, alone
or in well-established duos, and propose it to the group in a rehearsal
session (*kulingangila*, "trying out"). There, other group members can
propose modifications, whether minor or major, or can reject the song
altogether if the lyrics seem unconvincing, the melody weak, or the
tone not fitting the conventions of the genre. Once the song is performed on the dance-field, it is subject to imitation and appropriation
by other groups. A particularly successful song—crafted by an individual, launched by a specific group, and imitated by others—can become
part of a genre repertoire associated with a specific dance. Often groups
complain about imitation—"Those guys have stolen our songs!"—but
being imitated is also a sign of success and fame. The repertoire of one
specific dance group consists of about ten to thirty songs, about half of
which will be unoriginal (or partly original) and the rest composed by
the group but still marked by lyrical or melodic similarities with songs
of the same genre. Imitation also implies distortion: if a good listener
can catch (and copy) a melody of a rival group, in the noisy space of the
dance-field one or the other verses can escape him; the gaps are then
filled through creativity.[3]

A fourth category of songs is composed by people who play a specific soloist instrument, such as the bow-violin *kanyembe*, the wooden
xylophone *dimbila*, or the zither *ibangu*. Songs performed by singers
accompanied by solo instruments tend to be more idiosyncratic, longer,
and less imitable, although these individuals can perform adaptations
of popular songs, and their compositions can be taken up within dance
genres in a shortened form.

The fields of music and text crisscross irregularly. To begin with,
there are many more lyrics than there are melodies. Some groups have

one landmark melody to which many lyrics are adapted; some melodies are borrowed, sometimes quoted, by one or more other groups; other melodies almost define an entire genre. Imitation of music is more common, and more tolerated, than imitation of words: a catchy tune is a catchy tune, and one is allowed to grab it. The only boundaries to imitation are set by genre: you do not sing a dutu song in nshesho, or vice-versa. The role of music in the composition and reception of songs must thus be understood within an analysis of genre: it resides not in the specific blend of this or that melody in conjunction with this or that lyric—for the combination is often haphazard—but in the set of conventions that determine which lyric can fit to which music (the latter are often composed first) and which kinds of songs are fitting to which kinds of dance.

This is how singing has worked in the broad field of Makonde dances, at least from the 1920s onward, when the field witnessed a multiplication of forms and genres. The meat-is-meat break, specific to the practice of masquerading, must be framed within the explosion of dance creativity that swept the hinterland of the Swahili coast in the first decades of the twentieth century (see chap. 3, sec. 8). Mapiko masks thus became embedded within a larger, and constantly shifting, field of song and dance, of which they were the centerpiece but by no means the sole element. New dances sprang into existence together with the new masks; new songs circulated within and in-between genres, sustained by a spirit of festive and fierce competition. When mapiko ceased to represent spiritual characters—in the now-mainstream genres of dutu and nshesho—and it became one among many ngoma, a new array of songs was composed for each of the two new genres. For the drum needs the dance; the dance needs the song; and the song is the unit through which the dance itself is thought and measured.


3. Cutting across barriers of genre and individuality, Shimakonde singing is characterized by a cardinal aesthetic principle: what makes a song beautiful is the combination of economy, euphony, and ambiguity. A beautiful lyric is created when a few words, possibly rich in ideophones, produce multiple layers of meaning, a text that is phonetically dense and difficult to decipher.[4] This intersection between elegance and obscurity is a constant of African orature.[5] It is probably rooted in the structure of initiatic songs—apparently simple lines, with a deeper

meaning referring to the secrets of sex and puberty. It is also typical of Kiswahili poetry, which is based on the notion of *mafumbo*: ambiguity, metaphor, double meaning.[6]

Consider this dutu song:

| Likambe wenda kundila | Likambe went to the field |
| Nankodya nkoko aekele | He found a sitting beast |
| Wako njomba mene omba | Uncle, why don't you shoot? |
| Wako baba mene omba | Father, why don't you shoot? |
| Kwela-wé | Climb |
| Kwela, kwela muwa | Climb, up high[7] |

Apparently, the story is quite straightforward. Likambe, one of the group's drummers, went to the field, where he saw a mysterious beast sitting. Likambe wondered: how can a beast sit? This is magic, an omen (*mwiko*)! Or perhaps he saw something weird in the beast, something unnatural. Likambe took a fright, and instead of firing his gun he climbed the nearest tree—what a laughable coward—and what an admirable example of self-irony! But one must consider the polysemy of the verb *kwomba*, which literally refers to drum playing and metaphorically to gun shooting, and of the verb *kwela*, which means "climbing" but also "ascending," going up. Seen in this light, the last four lines of the song can be read as a covert provocation launched by the young generation toward their elders, through the newly invented genre of dutu. Father, uncle, you don't play (you don't know anything, you old thing), it is us now who go to the top, achieve mastery, become famous:

| Wako njomba mene omba | Uncle, you don't play |
| Wako baba mene omba | Father, you don't play |
| Kwela-wé | Rise |
| Kwela, kwela muwa | Rise, rise up high |

This widespread dutu song provided a tougher hermeneutical challenge:

| Mwali Kashiano wayangele leka | Cassiano girl, leave this diviner stuff |
| Ndavina kumakalogwe | I dance at Makalogwe |
| Nangu nindukuluwo | I am your nephew |
| Nikakulola nikwona dyoni | If I look at you, I feel ashamed |
| Leka tulambele-e | Let's search . . . |

| Jambo ke-ke-ke | Hello, *ke-ke-ke* |
| Ndalilola nangu nshilolo | I see myself in the mirror[8] |

What would the lyrics mean? Most of the people who have sung the famous song could not answer the question; this includes some associates of the composer, the famous Rashidi from Lusheni. Vicente Muanga came up with a subtle interpretation.[9] The Cassiano girl is bewitched. She wants to consult a diviner to identify the evildoer. But an elder kinsman (or kinswoman, for the gender is not specified by the term *ndukuluwo*, which can be used to address an uncle, aunt, or grandparent) tries to discourage her: "Cassiano girl, leave this diviner stuff." I trust you, "I am your own niece." But the grandparent feels awkward while looking at the girl Cassiano: "When I look at you, I feel ashamed." Notwithstanding the advice, the girl Cassiano goes to the diviner, accompanied by the overzealous grandparent. The voice now is the diviner's, who begins his investigations to find out the source of the bewitchment: "Let's search . . ." The diviner takes a mirror, on the surface of which the sorcerer's face will appear. And who is s/he? None other than the grandparent who discouraged the girl Cassiano from going to the diviner, and who looks at the mirror: "I see myself in the mirror"! The sense of the refrain becomes clear: the person who dances at Makalogwe is the grandparent him- or herself, dancing the dance of sorcery to injure the nephew.

I was myself captivated by this interpretation, which is wholly justified by the text. But I was left to wonder whether the lyrics could convey a different meaning when I encountered another song in Rashidi's repertoire that features Kashiano and a mirror:

| Lashidi wone | Look at Rashidi |
| Kashiano kwenu andiwika | Kashiano arrived in your homestead |
| Lashidi andilundukanga | Rashidi dropped his lip |
|   ainjila ing'ande watwa' shilolo |   he entered the house and took a mirror |
| | |
| Kashiano shaida akuno | Kashiano, you must come here |
|   ungupundishe shilolo ngumanye |   teach me the mirror, so I know |
| Nakushonga mwimbo tayali | I am going to carve you a song immediately |
| | |
| Watwa' lishanjo | Take a rattle |
| Vatoto Vashipondo kwa-Lusheni | The Vashipondo kids from Lusheni |
|   vanditawala shauli yamwimbo |   rule because of songs |

What was Kashiano, "Rashid's healer," teaching about the mirror?[10] How to use it for divination? Or simply how to use it—a self-ironical joke not uncommon in the times of provocation and boasting?

Listening to mapiko songs is nothing like reading their lyrics. In the dance-field, amid the rumble of drums and the cheering of crowds, songs are perceived in waves, as verses or at best as phrases. The attention paid is fragmentary, as spectators move from one spot to another, following now the lipiko and then the drummer; first a gimmick and then a song; now this group and then the other. As much as a song-master might craft a subtle narrative, its immediate impact comes from the power of each verse, or groups of verses, and the specific synergy of words and music therein. The fortune of a song rests on the evocativeness of its lines, rather than on the hidden narrative, which ultimately might not survive the song itself. While the "original" meaning is known only to a few (in some cases, only to the composer), the song generates alternative interpretations that should not be considered as false or meaningless. The song's power lies in its potential polysemy. Some read *Mwali Kashiano* as a song about the vanity of a young girl, dancing and admiring her beauty in a mirror; some as a critique of the faith put in diviners (which, among all categories of dealers in magic, is the most mistrusted); most remember the name of a place, Makalogwe, carried across by a haunting two-note descending melody.

4. *Mwali Kashiano* and *Likambe* exemplify the songs crafted to fit the new modernist abstract dutu genre: incisive and multilayered pieces, with catchy eerie melodies and simple rhythmic patterns. They were often embellished with descending scales, sometimes sung over filler syllables—*ke-ke-ke* or *nge-nge-nge* or *ge-ge-ge*—which also gave the name to the genre at large.

Another type of songs came to dutu via a tortuous route, as a result of the disappearance of one of those total social institutions characteristic of segmentary acephalous societies. In preconquest Makonde society, salutations were very formalized, especially among elders. Greeting was a verbal art in itself. The arrival of a visit was met with an invitation to sit down on an *igoli* bed, in the shade of a tree, in the space reserved to the men at the center of the village (*shitala*). *Karibu. Ikala, nang'olo* ("Welcome. Sit down, elder . . .") Then proper greeting (*kuudyanga*, "the asking") would begin with a long codified exchange of compliments, opened by the formula *Nandele?* ("News?"), to which one would answer, *Nakwaneka. Ungwauli' wako* ("I am good. Tell me yourself.") or *Jii nguleka nguvalange* ("Good, let me recount."). After this formulaic opening, the actual telling of stories would start: "I have come from the hamlet of so-and-so; someone from my family is sick; I have heard from so-and-so that this lineage made war on that other," and so on and so forth. Especially between elders, these stories and bits of information might be sung, rather than spoken. The words were improvised on a descending recitative melody, opened and closed with the formula *Shilanga-o*, which signaled the end of the story and handed over to the interlocutor to sing. The word *shilanga*, translated as "conversation" or "poem," gave also the name to these recitative songs of salutation and exchange of information.

Shilanga also might be sung in the judicial meetings that settled disputes internal to a lineage. The arguments pro or against the accused were sung, rather than spoken, in the same improvised but elaborate way. As in ancient Greece, truth and rhetorics, knowledge and beauty were not considered opposites but instead were viewed as intimately bound.[11] Shilanga can be interpreted as a way of avoiding extreme schismogenetic conflict in a fragile segmentary society. Encounters between elders of different lineages and resolutions of internal disputes were delicate moments, which could lead, respectively, to lineage warfare or fission if some words of salutation were understood as carrying across a provocation (*ushaka*). Ritual formalization brought calm and control to these potentially explosive moments of friction.

With colonial occupation a wholly different judicial system was put in place, based on sheer force first, then on indirect rule. Shilanga rapidly disappeared, both as a form of salutation and as an aesthetics of the law. Makonde salutations remained long, elaborate, and formulaic, but they were no longer sung. *Vilanga,* however, migrated into the heart of the modernist dutu genre, as long recitative songs performed before the beginning of the dance and in the pause between the masquerade's two movements. The essential characteristics of the songs always reported some news, ephemeral or dramatic, in narrative form. Their verses were not repeated—repetition (*kuujiya*) is another crucial feature of Makonde (and African) music—but were sung only once and at a rather fast pace. Song-masters could also inscribe their authorship in the work of art itself, commenting about the process of compositions (in meta-songs, as it were) so as to project their fame:

| | |
|---|---|
| Ndashikia namwimbo wakwetu wé | I am going to sharpen a song of our homestead |
| Mwimbo wamalidadi | A stylish song |
| Kashiano mwimbo wako wenda mbele | Kashiano, your songs go forward |
| Lashidi kuna-Lusheni | Rashidi from Lusheni |
| Manemba ida saa sita tushonge uwó mwimbo | Boys, come at twelve, to compose a song |
| Vandilunga ing'opedi pamwembe | They mixed the initiation medicine under a mango tree |
| Kweli wé | Goodbye |
| Vandipata mwimbo wambone | They got a good song[12] |

The masters of dancing and rhythmic innovation in the dutu genre have left little trace: the former to protect their identities; the latter because their styles were too quickly imitated to preserve the memory of their inventors. Thanks to these self-praising refrains, dutu song-masters have somewhat defied oblivion, as their names were inscribed in an imagined geography of talent: "There was Rashidi at kuna-Lusheni, Nampunda in Litamanda, Juakali in Shitunda, Mpavelo in Myangalewa, Rosário in Nshinga, Nshebwa in Mwambula, Namwalu in Mbau . . ." (fig. 10).[13]

FIGURE 10. Rosário Kanteke listens to himself *(Paolo Israel, Nshinga, 2004)*

5. Playful showing off (*kunema*) is a cardinal aesthetic practice of mapiko, and of Makonde dancing in general, solidly anchored in the principle of competition. A winning *mmapiko* is never modest: he boasts about his qualities before the show and embeds boasting in the performance itself. A classic boasting gesture, for instance, is for the lipiko to touch his *lutove* corset, make the *dinjuga* iron bells tinkle, and raise his arms to the sky, as if to say, "See how much weight I carry on me; nonetheless, with the strength of my chest and lungs, I dance with lightness."

In such a spirit of boasting, mapiko master singers began to embellish their songs with words and expressions in Kiswahili, the language of labor migrancy. Colonial conquest had set in motion massive waves of labor migration to Tanganyika (see chap. 3, sec. 7). Upon returning home, migrants brought back a rich baggage: the experience of life in large villages; the encounter with new forms of alterity, especially the Maasai, who figure prominently in Makonde carving and masking; the exposure to ideas concerning independence, which were much stronger in the British colony; the practice of associative life, especially in the cities of Dar Es Salaam and Tanga; the fascination with cosmopolitan cultural forms and fashions, from Congolese rumba to modern clothing; and fluency in the great vehicular East African language, Kiswahili. The latter knowledge metonymically captured all the former experience: speaking Swahili was a sign of worldliness and prestige, of having travelled and lived beyond the river, ku-Ng'ombela, in Tanganyika. Adorning songs with Kiswahili words was "like a sauce: if you want it to taste good, you put in oil and coconut and other things. If you sung Kiswahili you would win a lot. Because people didn't understand anything. And they would admire: '*Baa*, see how he knows . . .' They saw you as a person of mastery."[14]

*Ke-ke-ke* songs were embellished not only with the usual Makonde kinship terms (*mama, njomba, dada*) or words of ritual supplication (*shonde*) but also with Kiswahili syllables such as *ndiyo*, "yes." Words in Kiswahili would be conjugated à la Makonde, using the vehicular root and the vernacular grammar structure and producing a mixture that was understandable only to the migrants themselves or to Kiswahili-speaking Makonde.[15] Master singers did not care much that their message get across, that the lyrics would be understood by the public. What was important was to boast about one's worldliness and—within the aesthetics of "complicatedness" (*kukamadyanga* [see chap. 4, sec.

4])—to baffle the public with extravagant language mixing, as in this song, spiced up with both Kiswahili and Kimwani:

| | |
|---|---|
| Saide andimwasha simba amu mwina | Saide left a wounded lion lying low |
| Wakipola | So that it cools down |
| Pakutangola tsipa kwetu | When we talk, we bring fame on us |
| Saide andasema apiga isonjo | Saide said: We must ring the signal |
| Waje watoto wa kimando | For the kids of the commando |
| Wafike peshi wa muwe simba | Come quickly, there is a lion here |
| Huyu simba wene nyama gani bwana? | This lion (*simba*), what kind of meat is it, mister? |
| Kwa-Shimakonde vamwamba ntumi | In Shimakonde it's called a lion (*ntumi*)![16] |

The songs themselves could comment on the travels of the master and on the forms of practical knowledge that these travels resulted in:

| | |
|---|---|
| Mangela dodo | A big *dodo* mango |
| Kuntamba moja kulujado | In Mocimboa [it goes for] one *cruzado* |
| Andilingana kwetu | It is not like that in our lands |
| Ndiyo | Yes |

In the meta-songs of boasting, the process of composition itself was called, in the Swahili fashion, "carving songs" (*kushonga mwimbo*):

| | |
|---|---|
| Tundashonga mwimbo | We will carve songs |
| Wo-Razaro waku-Nshinga | Wo, Rosário from Nshinga |
| Siku jumapili kwedya ibandela | Sunday we raise the flag |
| Nshinga vanu kuvatema | Nshinga beats everybody |
| Mukalota mwimbo lipundishe | If you want a song, learn it |
| A-shonga | Carve it[17] |


6. Such was the skill in, and the enthusiasm for, embedding verbal arts into masquerading that sometimes songs got the upper hand over masks. "They would drop the drums on the floor, in the midst of a mapiko, and have a song-fight, right there!"[18] Singers had their favorite adversaries: "With Rashidi, in the Messalo. Each ritual we would meet and made each other suffer . . ." "And who would win?" "Myself! Me, I got a lie in the mouth. But Rashidi, alone, if he met somebody else . . . He knew songs."[19]

Let us imagine one of these contests, which certainly never took place in this precise form.[20] It is a Sunday, on the occasion of a great puberty ritual, in the hamlet of kuna-Lusheni on the Messalo Plains, punctuated by clumps of tall *lyumu* fan palms and thick banana shrubs. The song-master Rashidi has invited his friend and rival Juakali from Shitunda to cross styles on the dance-field. Juakali arrived on a Friday afternoon, after having walked cautiously along the thin paths that border Nguri Lake. He was met on the outskirts of the hamlet by a man who led him to the masks' hiding-place, so that he could store there his gear—drums, headpieces, rattles, and cloths. He was then invited to eat in the men's meetinghouse. After salutations and food, he exchanged some jokes with his rival: "Brother, we are going to steal all your women. They are going to cry and lose their cloths and forget to cook porridge." "Brother, you are going to walk out of here hiding your face and looking down."

On the day of the coming out, women's songs tear the night just before daybreak; *mapalapanda* horns fill the morning air. Somewhere in the bush, men are turned into spirits; magic defenses and decoys are set up in the drums, dresses, and bodies. At midday, the likuti launches its guttural call: *Du-tu! Du-tu, tu-tu-tu!* The dance-field is full of people: full-full-full, bursting full! The lipiko emerges from the forest, tinkling in style, enticed by the drum into the heart of the hamlet. The women bow in respect; the children run around in fear and excitement. The groups take turns in dancing: first enter the guests, then the hosts. All are captured by the feats of the talented. From the bush are brought the initiates, anointed in oil; the mapiko drum on, louder and stronger.

After four rounds of dancing, the bodies are tired and no winner has yet emerged. Shitunda is complicated! Lusheni is dangerous! Before the guests' lipiko is called into the circle again, Rashidi steps in, the drums still, and people keep quiet and listen to the master's voice:

| | |
|---|---|
| Luishi njinga shana | Luis is an idiot |
| Nnungu andijowa mwiu | God is really dangerous |
| Shaka shanamwaka pita liwambwe | This year's suffering, a flood came |
| Majele andyalibika | It destroyed the maize cobs |
| Lashidi pundi kuma kutwa' kulila | Rashidi the master came out and cried |
| Nangu shakupona nina' kumanya | I don't know how to heal this |
| Ngwenda kumwe Lijali nitapanda | I am going to Lijali's, to plant |

| mwogo ngulyakalele | manioc, so I can eat |
| Luishi kuka indala ininkolela indimpundanianga | Luis went with a hunger that grew and worked him |
| Maduvano mmanga | Nowadays he's a Muslim |
| Luishi andishilimuka | He converted to Islam |
| Ashwali idini na vamanga | He prays the religion of the Muslims |
| He gwoe | *He*, what a poor guy |

Islam is a growing power in the Messalo lowlands: many are converting, and they try to convince the Makonde not to eat *haramu* meat, especially the bush rats that they so much cherish. Juakali steps into the circle to pick up the provocation launched by his rival, carrying on the theme set by him, but in a lighter tone:

| Nnemba Ndondolo akaenda kushiwanja | The youth Ndondolo, he went to the field |
| Akauja apita watukuta nelo | He came back running, today |
| Nguwene shinu kushiwanja | I saw something on the field |
| Ndamwaulila mwanangu Juakali | I am going to tell my father Juakali |
| Tanganeshe mwimbo | So that he'll make a song |
| Lishee andashangania | The sheik went mad |
| Igwa akula kuna-Mugia | Hear: there at kuna-Mugia |
| Lishee wena na mangundu ndani walikoti | The sheik goes around with a house-rat in his coat |
| Mangundu akulanga | A rat that he is breeding |
| Nshonge mwimbo uwalale | Carve a beautiful song about him |
| Vavave nelo nimmwanalela | His friends today saw him |
| Akula kushiwanja, shiwanja shandege | There in the field, in the airplane field |
| Lingundu andyuma mulikoti aigwili' pai | The rat came out of the coat, fell down |
| Pita atukuta | And ran away |
| Lishee kwinamila pai | The sheik looked down |
| Ananga dyoni | Full of shame |
| Manemba nkanyolange | Hey, boy, let's smash it! |
| Apita watangadika | [The sheik] goes around moaning |
| Lingundu lyangu kwaleta | My rat fled |
| Andyuma ndani walikoti | It fell from my coat |
| Apita alambela shakulya | It went looking for food |
| Vanu vandikanyola | And people hit it |

| | |
|---|---|
| Unji nimpate dashi? | Where am I going to find another one? |
| Vikanniya mwimbo | So I tailored him a song |
| Kuna-Mugia | In kuna-Mugia |
| Juakali kushonga mwimbo | Juakali carved a song |
| Nililapa | I swear |
| Vikannila mwimbo | He tailored the song |
| Lishee andashangania | The sheik went mad |

The two masters are now standing head-to-head in the afternoon heat. They are delighted to listen to each other's compositions, to study the turns of phrases, the narrative twists, the melodic ornamentations. As the drums continue to lie still, Rashidi sings again, keeping to the theme of religion and hunger but hitting now a different target:

| | |
|---|---|
| Jumapili nelo ishiku kubwa | Today is Sunday, a great time |
| Vajungu vakulaya vashomya Kili | The white Europeans read the Kyrie |
| Vanditangola wetu Vamakonde madanganyipu | They say that we, the Makonde, we destroy everything |
| Mukenda kwenu mukapulai mujugwe medi | When you go home, you'd better ask for water |
| Mwaa nnungu nkubwa | Because God is great |
| Inema yapadyoko nanshaidiya | A small blessing will help you |
| Padili kwanjedya kwake kwakushang'apa | And the Father went on with other lies |
| Liduva lyakuvalekwa mwanagwe Yesu | The day when the son of Jesus was born |
| Watonya medi ntuli kuumbala | It will rain *tuli!* it will fill up everything |
| Ndapata inema yamalidadi | I will get a stylish blessing |
| Ishiko yamwisho vanu kuyayala | In the end, people march |
| Vatwa' dinjele vaenda kumashamba vandapandanga | They take the maize, go to the field and sow |
| Yesu nelo kwaaloka | Jesus arrives today! |
| Imbula yaambi padili ndapata inema yamalidadi | With this rain the Father will get a stylish blessing |
| Ishiko shaba kuva liduva | On the seventh day, there is still sun |
| Ushwanga wapadili ndikubali | The Father's lies, I believed them . . . |
| Laishi mwalimu nkubwa | Raishi is a great teacher |
| Watwa' shitabu washonga mwimbo wa-Shimakonde | Who takes a book, carves songs à la Makonde |

| vanu kupulai | people rejoice |
| Laishi apata kushomya apata dyangele dyamalidadi | Raishi was bestowed with reading, was bestowed with stylish [powers of] divination |
| Laishi puundi | Raishi is a master |
| Laishi puundi wana-Nkalau | Raishi master of Nkalau |
| Mwimbo pakushonga anditanganesha | When he carves songs, he summons crowds |

Poking fun at the institutions of colonial power is no challenge for Juakali, who strikes back, maintaining his characteristically playful tone:

| Sentimoja andikashali kubalashia kwetu | Sentimoja pressed charges in the palace |
| Akashalya mwavi | He pressed charges for witchcraft |
| Takataka mwavi | Takataka is a sorcerer |
| Vajungu vandimmunga mwene | But the white man arrested him instead |
| Kunkoma shosholo | They beat him up like a sack |
| Takataka mwavi | Takataka is a sorcerer |
| Mingo lumba shonde | Mingo prays to the ancestors |
| Mwanangu jó mumi | Please make my son be fine |

Rashidi whispers to his rival in the afternoon dust, "Should I carry on with the white man?" The topic is momentous, and there is a sense that the settler's reign is dwindling:

| Njungu Kalavai | The white man Kalavai |
| Amekwenda gwé | He left, poor guy |
| Mambo leo | Today's news |
| Iboma yaku-Mwidumbi | In the district of Muidumbe |
| Vajungu vandishanga | The whites are worried |
| Limeni ipamba, shitaki ata shakula | Grow cotton! I refuse, that's not food |
| Kumwidumbi makulungwa mwikimbia | In Muidumbe, the regulos flee |
| Kalavai nnenda ku-laya kwenu kawike | Kalavai go to Europe, to your lands, get there |
| Ndio nakwenda | Yes, I will go |
| Vajungu vajinga shana | White people are so dumb |

On the last notes of the song, Rashidi makes a sign to the likuti, which comes back in full power with its guttural moan. From the corner of a house, the dinjuga tinkle again; the spirit is ready for another round. Juakali steps back, mentally rehearsing another composition that will leave the crowds, and his rival, breathless.

7. On the twelfth of June 1960, Juakali left his home in Shitunda, at the outskirts between the Messalo lowlands and the savannas of ku-Iyanga, headed to Mueda. Juakali the master, the carver of words, the great and terrific teacher of songs was not going to a masking contest to cross (s)words with one of his friend-rivals. He was headed to a political meeting in which the destinies of the country were to be decided. Faustino Vanomba and Kibiriti Diwane, leaders of a protonationalist organization based in Tanganyika, had entered Mozambique to discuss the conditions of life and labor under colonial rule.[21] They were going to be received by the district administrator in person. A large crowd participated to the meeting, which would turn into the infamous massacre (see chap. 1, sec. 6). Back in Shitunda, Juakali composed a song about the event:

| | |
|---|---|
| Ibalugwa kwaloka ku-Mweda | A letter coming from Mueda |
| Shibiliti walota kuwika | Shibiliti is coming |
| Amekuja mwenyewe Shibiliti pamoja Faustino Vannomba | Shibiliti is coming in person together with Faustino Vanomba |
| Nkutano aramishi ku-Mweda | There is a meeting on Thursday in Mueda |
| | |
| Manemba shamananga tuke tukaigwilile | Boys, they call us: go and listen |
| Mpurtukeshi mbaya-mbaya | The Portuguese are bad, bad |
| Nae akashindwa shaliya | They don't know any law |
| Portugesi uwananga dyoni | They are shameful |
| Shibiliti mmunge | Imprison Shibiliti |
| Faustino mmunge | Imprison Faustino |
| Vandilinga kummunga Shibiliti kunshindwa | They tried to imprison Shibiliti, they failed |
| Vandilinga kummunga Faustino kunshindwa | They tried to imprison Faustino, they failed |
| Upingo kulumuka | The handcuffs broke |

| | |
|---|---|
| Vamakonde anditangola nakupwatekanga | The Makonde spoke full of pain |
| Shibiliti apakiligwa aenda kushinu | Shibiliti won't be taken, he won't go anywhere |
| Mwindi Nshina mbaya | China, the Indian, is bad |
| Lijanga andijela | He threw a stone |
| Vamakonde vandyatika | The Makonde responded |
| Governadoli andinjila mulukoma | The governor took shelter on the veranda |
| Bashitola kutwala | He drew a gun |
| Alamulila ing'ondo, omba | He ordered a war: shoot |
| Piga wé Vamakonde vabyae | Shoot and kill the Makonde |
| Omba wé Vamakonde kutwangaisha | Shoot, the Makonde are annoying us |
| Yuti kupiga | Guns were fired |
| Likola lindyalibika | Families were ruined |

Drawing on the usual mélange of Shimakonde and Kiswahili, the song's first part describes the massacre as many experienced it.[22] People were called to attend the meeting. The administrator received Vanomba and Diwane. The two walked out of the premises as prisoners, to be carried away in a car. But, so the story goes, the handcuffs broke thrice, as if they did not want to have anything to do with the imprisonment. The crowds blocked the administrator's vehicle, until an Indian merchant called China threw a stone that elicited a violent reaction.[23] The Makonde threw back mud, and the administrator ordered the native police (*cipaios*) to shoot. The demonstrators fled in panic, abandoning their bicycles. A jeep with a handful of soldiers and a machine gun arrived on the scene some fifteen minutes later.

I met Juakali in July 2008. In Myangalewa, Luis Amissi mentioned his name as the last living song-master of old. In the early 2000s, Juakali had left the village of Shitunda to settle in Rwarwa, a remote farming encampment near the northern shores of Nguri Lake. We walked there, crossing the wet Nguri plains, arrived at sunset, and presented ourselves to the encampment leader, explaining the motivation for our visit. Two hours later, a worried, stuttering old man appeared. "What do you want from me?" I asked him about recording his songs, putting some on air via the provincial radio, and researching the history of mapiko. Juakali smiled, relieved: "Once, a white man sent me to prison because of a song. And now I thought: again?"

Juakali sang the song about the "war of Mueda" on the mapiko playground. The time must have been 1962, just after Frelimo was founded in Dar Es Salaam. Imaginatively, and anachronistically, the second part of the song puts Eduardo Mondlane—the newly appointed leader of the nationalist movement—on the scene:

| | |
|---|---|
| Tumpige shimu aende Maputo mpaka Pemba | Let's make a phone call, to Maputo and through to Pemba |
| Majibu analoka shinu | There is no answer |
| Majibu aloka Tanzania | The answer comes from Tanzania |
| Monjane akaigwa ing'ondo andikubali | Mondlane, he heard about the war and he agreed |
| Bwana Monjani kuma kutangola | Mister Mondlane stood up and said: |
| Mungulinde kwanja | Wait for me first |
| Ngwende ku-laya Portuguesi | I will go overseas to the Portuguese |
| Nikavaudye ing'ondo vakalota mwiu vangwaulile | Ask them: if they really want a war they must tell me |
| Bwana Mondlane kutango' shana | Mister Mondlane spoke well |
| Ngulinda nangu kwanja | Wait for me first |
| Monjane kupita andikodyana namu Shibiliti koko akó | Mondlane met Shibiliti there |
| Faustino Tiago | Faustino, Tiago |
| Vajungu Portuguesi vankwangaika | The white Portuguese are all worried |
| Portuguesi kutila ulaja kuleka gweka | The Portuguese flee overseas, they leave us alone |
| Vanyopa Mondlane | They fear Mondlane |
| Mana Mondlane alota ing'ondo pamo | Because Mondlane wants a war[24] |

Frelimo was indeed preparing for the struggle. With war in the air, Portuguese counterinsurgency intensified. The state was not as deaf as before, even when it came to native dances. A *cipaio* who overheard the song denounced Juakali; the mapiko master got imprisoned and transferred to Porto Amélia for an interrogation—a history that is told in other compositions. The third part of Juakali's shilanga foretells a future that reveals the sentiments of the singer, a melancholic failed prophecy:

| | |
|---|---|
| Nangu ing'ondo yó angumanya | I don't know anything about this war |
| Ngwenda kwetu akó ngwikala | Let me go back home and sit down |

| Portuguesi kutukuta Moshambiki | The Portuguese flee and leave |
| kuleka shana | Mozambique in peace |
| Vajopa ing'ondo | They fear a war |
| Mondlane alota ing'ondo | Mondlane wants a war |
| Nangu ing'ondo yó angumanya | Me, I don't know anything about |
| | this war |
| Ngwenda kwetu akó ngwikala | Let me go home and sit down |

8. The ornate singing derived from shilanga poems was characteristically connected to dutu, almost to compensate with words (and voice) the greatest choreographic abstraction that characterized the genre. Dutu was devoid of mimetic styles (*vikuvo*), the pace was vertiginously quick, the dance overall abstract, and the role of the likuti drum preponderant in shaping sound and mood.

In the genre of nshesho, mimesis reemerged, through dance styles imitating the movements of animals and episodes of everyday life, or telling stories in visual form (*vikuvo*), and overall through a slowing of pace, which allowed more space for theatricality and representation. Nshesho songs were intoned by large choirs, were shorter and less obscure than their dutu counterparts, and were influenced by the fashions coming from the north—especially Congolese rumba love songs. A new form of verbal art was embedded in the performance of masks: spoken styles (*vikuvo*) in which a defiant rhythmic poem is declaimed first by a lead person, then by the whole choir.

Paradoxically, it was much more difficult to retrieve colonial-era nshesho songs than their dutu counterparts, mainly because nshesho repertoires had been completely overwritten with new songs—and a wholly new vocabulary—that coalesced during the liberation struggle. While soliciting old tunes from nshesho practitioners who remembered many dutu songs, I was told, "The old ones, we forgot them, we don't know them . . . All of our songs are from the year of armistice until today."[25]

The only extant recordings that can give back some of the sound, mood, and lyrics of late-colonial nshesho singing were captured by Gerhard Kubik in October 1962. The 120 minutes of recordings comprise a wealth of precious materials—mostly feminine ritual songs and instrumental music—including two integral recordings of mapiko performances, one from Namawa and the other from Miteda. The Miteda songs draw on fashionable coastal idioms, howling in Kiswahili about lovers, marriage, betrayal, and heartbreak. The group from Namawa begins with similar accents:

| | |
|---|---|
| Nganu wé | Ngano, you |
| Mpenji nalia | My lover, I cry |
| Oh mama | Oh, mama |

But the song immediately following, also in Kiswahili, is an outright incitation to subversion. Inspired by the recent independence of Tanganyika, it prompts Makonde migrant workers to return to Mozambique armed with foresight and Fanonian determination:

| | |
|---|---|
| Mwingereza mwenda kwao | The English went home |
| Murudi namapema | Come back hurriedly |
| Kwangalia mbele | [We must] look forward |
| Na twende namagongo | And let's go with cudgels[26] |

The melody is festive but militaristic, the tone assertive. The recording is concluded by an enigmatic verbal shikuvo:

| | |
|---|---|
| Kwomba akili | Play [with] wit |
| Alo malove | These are words |
| Kwali mashala | Or perhaps a good-day |
| Mchezo uvele apa | The dance is here |
| Akó kulyambila | And that is regret |

Kubik's musical intelligence preserved this fragment of vocal rebellion by locating the microphone close to the singers. In Margot Dias's two-minute recording of mapiko, the voices are a faint inaudible trace overwhelmed by the drums.[27] In any case, the anthropologists charged with the task of counterinsurgency (see chap. 1, sec. 8), the subjects supposed to align power and knowledge, were deafened by their own primitivism. This is what they had to say about the expression of the people that they should surveil: "The lyrics of the song that they sing do not always seem to be in relation with the topic. [. . .] Experience brought us to conclude that those populations still in intimate contact with Nature and not influenced by the values of industrial society encounter in song a form of full vital expression, which dispenses entirely verbal relations from their logical signification."[28]

9. Reading song lyrics as windows into historical consciousness yields a familiar picture of growing discontent and insubordination on the eve of nationalist struggle, of sharpening critical consciousness and verbal bravado, of restlessness and rage. Only a detail of language—the usage of Kiswahili words as boastful weapons of competition—colors such sentiments of protest with a lighter and cosmopolitan emotional tone.

The historicity of music speaks of the same cosmopolitan attitude. From the 1930s onward, Makonde music is marked by a double process of appropriation: of church choirs harmonies on the one hand and of Black Atlantic rhythms reimported on the continent—such as jazz, rumba, and blues—on the other. This double appropriation resulted in an overall influence of tonal harmony and temperate scales. Over the long term, this process of tempering stands out. The break is conceptualized in vernacular terms. Xylophone (*dimbila*) players speak of an "old style," rich in polyrhythms and fantastically intricate, and of a "new style," which imitates the movement in parallel thirds of church choirs.[29] The same break occurs in the passage between dutu and nshesho songs: while the first are largely penta- or hexatonic, the second mimic church choirs, with tonal melodies moving in parallel thirds.[30] But old habits are difficult to abandon, and Makonde thirds sound—as is often remarked—flat to the well-tempered ear.[31]

This overall influence of church choir and pop melodies makes nshesho melodies more assertive, festive, and triumphant—characteristics that they would conserve in their post-Independence trajectory. But one should be wary of overstating the meanings of music, that "grammar without semantics."[32] For the history of Makonde song provides examples of the most fantastic migrations. This lullaby is part of the shared repertoire of Makonde popular songs, falling within the genre of *ke-ke-ke* songs:

| | |
|---|---|
| De-de de-de de-de | *De-de de-de de-de* |
| Nakulela-e | I will take care of you |
| Anyoko andi' kumuto | Your mother went to the well |
| Nateka lyambwambwe | To fetch dirty water |
| Lyambwambwe lyashitala | Dirty water for the men's meetinghouse |
| Auja natangadika | She comes back complaining |
| Kannunnu mala' kulila | Baby, hush, stop crying |
| Malala nikubebe-e | Hush, I will rock you |

Into this very same melody, supposed to have a soothing effect on a baby, new words would be plugged to make the most renowned Makonde war song, which connected old deeds of anticolonial resistance to the ones to come:

| Vashitenda ing'ondo, ing'ondo, ing'ondo | They were making a war, a war, a war |
| Yakulyambola | Of self-liberation |
| Ya-kala | Long ago |
| Ing'ondo | The war |
| Ya-Ngungunyane | Of Ngungunyana |
| Namuje Malapende | And his friend Malapende |
| Vashitenda ing'ondo | They were making a war |
| Yakulyambola Moshambiki | To liberate Mozambique[33] |

# PART THREE

༣

# Revolution (1962–92)

In the historiography of Mozambique, the Struggle for National Liberation posits itself as a radical rupture with the past, signaled by the endeavor to invent a new society and a new man from the ashes of the old ones. This part follows the great transformations prompted by the massive engagement of the Makonde in the revolutionary adventure. On the one hand, it charts the formation of a new socialist aesthetics and practice, embodied in new politicized mapiko genres; on the other, it highlights the resistance of schismogenetic rivalry to the attempts to flatten popular dance into a celebration of power. The coexistence of the new aesthetics and the old engine of creativity creates paradoxical situations, in which the language of politics is used as a weapon of dance competition.

Chapter 7, "Ten Years of War," charts the vicissitudes of mapiko and other dance genres during the liberation struggle (1962–74). The war had a direct effect on dance, which needed to be silenced as a measure of military precaution. But as new dances emerged in times of wartime uncertainty, a new aesthetics and song vocabulary were piloted in Frelimo's training camps and military bases. The endeavor to shape a new subject—we, the People—entailed the destruction of everything old: rivalry, seen as a figure of tribalism; and secrecy, seen as a figure of gender oppression.

Chapter 8, "Youth Power," focuses on the dominant mapiko genre in the post-Independence years (1975–92), performed by the generation that spearheaded the war and permeated the socialist aesthetics. The chapter describes the practice of mapiko in the new revolutionary social institutions—the communal village and the national festival. At the same time, it demonstrates the resilience of competitive provocation, if only disguised in the acceptable language of political commentary.

Chapter 9, "Faceless Spirits," follows the invention and fortunes of a new defiant feminist masquerade introduced upon Independence as an explicit challenge to masculine supremacy. The new genre embodies the trajectory of gender revolution in socialist Mozambique: first triumphantly asserted, then thwarted and twisted into repressed feelings of rage and ambivalence. The new feminist mask was also rooted in a burgeoning late-colonial form of spiritual dance—a paradoxical mimesis of a decayed white lady.

# 7 ↜ Ten Years of War

*Shaping the People*

| | |
|---|---|
| Atulivaliva | We don't forget |
| Myaka kumi vy'ing'ondo | Ten years of war |
| Tunditenda | We did it |
| Ku-Moshambiki indyambola | Mozambique was liberated |
| Tundishumba | We overcame |
| Vyakunannopa namene | Many hardships |
| Myaka kumi | Ten years |
| Ku-Moshambiki indyambola | Mozambique was liberated |

— NMA/Nshesho/Nampanya/2004

1. ANTICOLONIAL STRUGGLES in Lusophone Africa were inspired by the Maoist concept of the "people's war" (*guerra popular*). The central tenets of people's war are the intensive political mobilization of the peasantry; a three-tiered strategy of military offensive, beginning with hit-and-run attacks, escalating to guerrilla conflict, and culminating with total warfare; and the establishment of liberated zones, which are areas taken away from enemy control to serve as sanctuaries for the guerrillas, where a process of radical social regeneration is put in place.[1] The latter is overall the most important, not only strategically but also because it fulfills the crucial political task of all revolutionary endeavors: the construction of regenerated men and women, "delivered from the corruption of previous history."[2] If, as many have observed, the history of the liberation struggle is shrouded in the mists of ideology, it is precisely because of this mythic task that it had to perform—shaping a new people and a new society.[3]

Frelimo chose the Makonde Plateau as the first seedbed of its people's war partly on account of the Makonde political conscientization, made dramatically visible by the 1960 Mueda massacre and then by their transiting en masse from the quasi-ethnic MANU to the new movement.[4] Strategic considerations also played a part: the plateau was in the finest strategic position to support guerrilla warfare backed from Tanzania, close as it was to the border, and covered in dense bush thicket. Already in 1963, groups of Makonde lineages began to abandon their settlements and to retreat into isolated lowland areas, preparing for the storm to come.[5] The first shot of the liberation struggle—fired, as the story goes, on the twenty-fifth of September 1964 against the administrative post of Chai in the lowlands adjacent to the plateau— found most of the Makonde already dispersed in the bush, as the pro- verbial water in which the guerrilla-fish would swim.

2. People's war fell on the Makonde Plateau with the sound of silence. Drums are heard far and wide, and detectability through noise was one luxury that the populations living in the war zones could not afford. In the "branches" and "localities" under Frelimo's control—encampments of precarious huts built under trees in the lowlands adjacent to the pla- teau, constantly threatened by incursions and by the creeping suspicion of treachery—all drums had to shut up and be vigilant, waiting for better times to raise their voices. Mapiko, the loudest of them all, would not be danced for years. The lavish culture of competition and circulation that had developed since colonial pacification was thus interrupted. "It was the time of war, and we were running, *mbule mbule mbule*. The dance of the time was *nkala*. We meet, *e-e-e*; we run away and go."[6]

But constraint encouraged creativity. Already in the first year of war, a new dance was introduced to fill the void: *ngoda*.[7] Invented by the soldier Lingondo, it was a circular dance similar to the ancient nkala, performed to lighten the long nights of soldiery vigil. The name meant "dried maize" and referred to the foot-soldiers' most common food, which was put into old rusty cans to turn them into hand-shaken rattles (*mashanjo* [fig. 11]). The rhythm was invigorating but quiet enough. The menace of enemy attacks demanded constant alertness:

| | |
|---|---|
| Ngwimbanga muda | I sing the times |
| Moda yamaduvano | The mode of nowadays |
| Ye ye ye | *Ye ye ye* |
| Ngoda aunavini' vila | Don't dance the ngoda just like this |

FIGURE 11. Reenacting the "dried maize" dance *(Rui Assubuji, Myangalewa, 2009)*

| | |
|---|---|
| Bila shaleko | Without a sentinel |
| Nsheme nkutano | We call a meeting |
| Mumpigi' Lingambwanda | We test Lingambwanda |
| Lingambwanda wena, kapalaleshe | Lingambwanda, go and spy |
| Ukaigwa vajunganga | To check if they make noise |
| Nawika dao | Don't come like this |
| Ing'ondo | [This is] war[8] |

Concurrently, a more ominous "drum" spread on the plateau: *likulutu*, military training. Youth began to "dance the training" (*kuvina likulutu*) inside the country with wooden weapons, obeying the cacophony of commands of instructors of various nationalities, each of whom taught basic military instructions in their respective languages (Kiswahili, English, Chinese, Arabic, and so forth). Recruits were then sent to Frelimo camps in Tanzania, Kongwa, and, later, Nachingwea; the best would be selected for training abroad, especially in Algeria and the Soviet Union.

The war was sustained by movement: underground commerce, the smuggling of weapons across the Rovuma, and trips back and forth to Tanzania for training. Many stories of affiliation with Frelimo begin with adventurous journeys of hundreds of kilometers through thick bushes, across marshes, hills, and rivers, fleeing from a hamlet to join the guerrillas. In the mid-1960s a new fashion was brought from Tanzania: a modification of the *ibangu* board-zither, an old traditional East African instrument of uncertain origins.[9] Added to the ibangu was a big resonance chamber carved in *ntene* softwood and one or two more strings; thus, the instrument could be made to resemble the guitar. A new fingering technique was devised in order to play the fancy rhythms from the northern coast, especially the rumba, twist, and cha-cha-cha. Renamed *magita* or *magalantoni*, the new instrument became a soldier's favorite.[10]

Intense circulation rekindled the practice of dance competition, if in a more specialized way. Soldiers carried along their *magalantoni* in the marches across the four military sectors into which the province of Cabo Delgado was divided.[11] To their sound, twist dancers pushed athletic boundaries: "They would bend their heads backward to touch the floor; some broke their backs and died right there!"[12] Ungainliness—even when coming from the most famous of dancers—was pointed out and immortalized in song:

| | |
|---|---|
| Lingondo ku-Mwambe | Lingondo at Macomia |
| Vandimpukuza | They kicked him out |
| Vankupushidya, nkala wako aumanyikenge | Your nkala is worth nothing |
| Lingondo ku-Mwambe | Lingondo at Macomia |
| Ankuja na dyoni | Came back full of shame[13] |

After a moment of consideration—both political and of practical opportunity—puberty rituals were celebrated in the precarious war conditions, but in an abbreviated form. No noisy masked dancing could celebrate the entrance and coming out of rituals: ngoda and magalantoni guitars stood in. These transformed ritual occasions brought along intense intermingling. People had resettled in the new branches and localities following lineage lines, but they lived in much stronger proximity. Soldiers from nearby bases also joined in the celebrations:

> We lived in the same locality. Now, if someone worked at the Ngungunyane base, their dances, you get in and you dance. "Our people have arrived!" And he gets in and dances. The people used to dance, and the soldiers as well, all of them together.[14]

The reintroduction of puberty rituals also brought back schismogenetic gendered provocations, which were now viewed unfavorably by the Frelimo leadership, as a manifestation of tribalism and sexism. But one could compose politically correct lines to complain against the unequal application of political directives and use the song as a covert gender provocation; this strategy, inaugurated in the early years of war, would become widespread in later times:

| Kuvangadika | We complain |
|---|---|
| Tuvalume paing'ondo yamapindushi | We, the men, in the revolutionary war |
| Vakongwe munkamangu tunkutukana | The women in the *nkamangu* insult us |
| Tuvalume kulikumbi tukatukana | We, the men, if we insult during *likumbi* |
| Vabulanje kututwala nako' madengo | The branch officials take us and make us work[15] |

Ngoda and magalantoni lyrics poignantly captured everyday life in the liberated zones—the former more abstractly, the second through vivid snapshots. Both evoked the dangers and anxieties of guerrilla warfare; new forms of socialization such as marching, training, the watch, antiaerial combat, and collective cleaning; new emotional investments in the leaders and the nation. Moreover, they consistently demonstrate the multiplication of occasions for amorous adventuring.[16] Like their colonial-era predecessors, ngoda songs were embellished with short hollow words addressing kin figures—*baba, mama, njomba*—or sometimes merely euphonic. In these early years of war, a new word began to punctuate such melodies: *tuvenentete*, "we, the People," the new subject to emerge from the "revolutionary war."

3. In the history of European nationalism, *the people* are at once the culturally homogeneous national subject and the lower rungs of society, the subaltern classes. Giorgio Agamben notes that this duality is inscribed in the linguistic history of the concept itself. In European languages (especially Latin ones), the word "people" (*popolo*) stands for both "the constitutive political subject" and "the poor, the underprivileged and the excluded" broadly defined: "on the one hand, the People as a whole and as an integral body politic, and, on the other hand, the people as a subset and as a fragmentary multiplicity of needy and excluded bodies."[17] These two dimensions of the concept of "the people" generate, respectively, "vertical" and "horizontal" contrapositions.[18] In the first (the people as a political subject), the cut is vertical and the whole body politic is juxtaposed to what is foreign—one nation to another. In the second (the people as subaltern), the cut is horizontal, and the society is divided into a higher and a lower stratum, which can be described in terms of class and/or culture. In Marxist thought, "the People" refers not to the idea of a homogeneous nation grounded in the culture of the humble (as in the Herderian right-wing nationalism) but to the utopian conception of a New Man emerging in a struggle that, in the name of the oppressed, must abolish all oppression. For a revolutionary, "the People" is a concept always twisted towards the future.

The signifier *o Povo* ("the People") was the cornerstone of Frelimo's political discourse from the outset.[19] Its contours and functions are difficult to pin down, but one can identify four broad semantic connotations: the People as a specific social class, the peasantry; the People as the utopian regenerated new subject to emerge from the revolution, liberated from the mental and social shackles imposed by colonialism; the People as the masses, as opposed to their leaders; the People as the nonmilitary population engaged in the struggle in a productive or supportive role. Taken together, this semantic entanglement speaks of the Maoist influences that led Frelimo to identify the peasantry as the class with the higher revolutionary potential (which translated into a mistrust for the city and its inhabitants); of the kinds of charismatic relationships that the movement leaders wished to establish with their subjects; and of the militarization of politics that would remain a lasting feature of Mozambican social life.[20]

*O povo*: how to translate such a dense concept in a language, Shimakonde, that knows no word for "poor" (a Kiswahili loanword is used, *maskini*) or one to define ethnos or citizenship? In which the idea of "people" is captured through the class prefix *va-?* In a society in which belonging was decided not only by blood but also by choice (ascending the plateau and renouncing water to escape slavery) and in which lineage was the main form of political organization? The wits of an unknown poet solved the puzzle by infusing new meaning into an old expression, *mwene-ntete.* The first word is the widespread and untranslatable noun, meaning at once "owner," "master," or "person responsible for" (see chap. 4, sec. 3). The word *ntete* (pl. *mitete*) describes somebody else's hamlet, as opposed to *likaja*, one's own. The plural *venentete* then indicated people living in foreign settlements, as opposed to *vene makaja.* The utopian political subject of national liberation—the People to be—was thus baptized *venentete,* "a stranger to her/himself."

Almost as a physical reflection of this linguistic invention, the practices through which Makondeness had been inscribed on the flesh—scarification and tooth chipping—were forbidden in a political council held in the lowland hamlet of Litapata in 1967. The measure was intended to undermine tribalism in its most evident manifestations but also to safeguard young Makonde coming out from initiation rituals from being targeted by the Portuguese counterinsurgency as potential terrorists.[21] The abandonment of scarifications and tooth chipping marked a break that perceptually divided the old generations, born during colonialism, from the ones that were to grow up in the liberated country. It also signaled a renewed attention of the Frelimo intelligentsia to matters concerning culture.

4. In the first years of war, culture was not especially on the minds of Frelimo leaders. More urgent matters were to be attended to: military organization, setting up a rudimentary educational and health network in the liberated zones, and dealing with internal dissent. As the war progressed, the latter exploded, threatening to tear the movement apart at the seams. In May 1968, the students of the Frelimo school at Dar Es Salaam, perhaps inspired by the global student revolts, protested against mismanagement and military drafting to the combat zones. The Cabo Delgado commissioner, Lázaro Nkavandame, also challenged Frelimo's leadership. In February 1969, Eduardo Mondlane was assassinated in circumstances that are still contentious. An internal

power struggle followed. Frelimo's vice-president, Uria Simango, wrote an open letter in which he accused Mondlane's clique of disposing of political adversaries by stirring up crowds in the liberated zones who would eagerly stone to death anyone who was pointed to as a traitor or a counterrevolutionary.[22] The group that coalesced around Samora Machel dismissed the letter as the voice of counterrevolution itself, expelled Simango and Nkavandame from the movement, and crushed the dissension. The winners described the crisis as a split between a conservative and a revolutionary line; for the vanquished, and for those who would later take inspiration from them, it was one between pluralism and totalitarianism.

The new leadership brought political radicalization, militarization, and a renewed interest in matters of culture.[23] Frelimo's military training camp at Nachingwea became the new vibrating center of the movement's political life. Two main cultural dynamics were put in motion in this phase. The first was the composition of military and revolutionary anthems. Musicians educated in choral singing in missions, especially Protestant, put their skills to the service of the cause. Unlike other struggle-song traditions, such as the Zimbabwean Chimurenga, local imagery and musical traditions made their way only marginally into the architecture of Frelimo anthems: in a turn of phrase, in a peculiar rhythmic syncope, in certain melodic passages, in the structure of call and response.[24] The composition of anthem lyrics was part and parcel of the movement of literary effervescence that took place between Dar Es Salaam and the liberated zones, resulting in the publication of various gazettes and newspapers, such as *25 de Setembro* and *Os Heroicos*. The heteroglossia that was characteristic of migrant songs was forbidden in political anthems. The use of African languages was accepted and encouraged, but not the confusing intermingling of idioms and forms: a song could be either in Makonde or in Yao, in Portuguese or in Kaswahili. Being "correct" applied to grammar, as well as to the political line. Lyrics were subjected to ideological control and, like guerrilla poems, influenced by a "vocabulary of ready-made ideas" shaped by the Frelimo intelligentsia.[25]

> The songs were organized to motivate the anti-colonial combatant. The struggle is tiresome. In order for the people not to become tired, we needed to be motivated politically. All the songs that we composed should speak of the evils of colonialism, Kaulza de Arriaga and what-what-what of Frelimo. Everything was oriented from above.[26]

The second cultural innovation pioneered in Frelimo's military camp was the fusion of local dances into mixed ensembles. Guerrillas from different regions of the country would share their favorite dances, which would be then performed in the concerts that were held at Nachingwea every Saturday afternoon.[27] "This came with a nationalist ideology, anti-tribalist and anti-regionalist. Culture was a meeting point between south, centre and north."[28] Besides the opening up of participation, the concerts required a fundamental aesthetic transformation: to be presented to a public, the dances should be performed in a line and no longer in a circle. Because of the preponderance of Makonde in the rank and file of Frelimo, mapiko was a mainstay of these spectacles. Only the genre of nshesho was performed, however, as it was the only one that the young guerrillas knew.

These experiments were prudently replicated in the liberated zones. In some of the most remote areas, especially at the central base—which was always moving to escape the enemy's vigilance—national holidays were celebrated with dances, especially mapiko. Even there, the only genre performed was the youths' nshesho. The soldiers mingled with the people: "We would prepare [the masks] with the People. Now, on the day when there was a festivity at the base, we would go to the base. We would dance at the district; they would call us 'come and play,' at the time of the festivities."[29]

5. These burgeoning dynamics were brutally interrupted in the liberated zones by the counterinsurgency operation code-named Gordian Knot, which intended to wipe out the military bases of the movement by "combing the bushes" and through massive propaganda.[30] Kaulza de Arriaga, who had learned his lessons in Vietnam, was in command. Launched in May 1970, Gordian Knot brought disruption and suffering: chains of command were broken and bases abandoned; guerrilla groups struck independently, with the sole objective of surviving and bringing losses to the enemy. After five months, however, Gordian Knot turned out to be a fiasco. The expenditure on the operation was huge; Frelimo managed to resist; and Arriaga retreated declaring victory but actually in defeat. After the successful resistance to Gordian Knot, Frelimo tightened its control of the liberated zones. The Portuguese seemed weaker, the guerrillas stronger, and the planes and helicopters farther away. The veil of silence over drums was lifted, and dances

returned with their intrinsic loudness. The two instruments that had animated the long years of silence, ngoda rattle-dances and magita zithers, were replaced with powered versions. Ngoda was transformed into *limbondo*, a drummed circular dance in which people dress in tatters, wear animal-fur backpacks, and violently shake axes or scythes. Zithers such as magita and magalantoni were abandoned in favor of homemade electric guitars that imitated the "correct" political style of soldiers. Their lyrics were written "respecting the watchwords of the party, presenting the correct revolutionary line."[31]

In the aftermath of Gordian Knot, Frelimo also reflected in a more systematic way on questions of culture. A dedicated First Cultural Seminar was organized in Tunduru between December 1971 and January 1972, followed by other seminars of the Department of Education and Culture (DEC).[32] Four broad directives were promoted. First, culture should be mobilized in the fight against tribalism: dances should no longer be practiced along ethnic lines, and all references to lineage and tribe in lyrics should be banned. Second, songs and dances should be used as weapons of mobilization in the struggle against superstition and obscurantism, especially through educational lyrics. Third, culture should be used to further militarization: "In song and dance we solved various problems. When we sing or dance, gestures and words are uniform. It is the question of discipline."[33] Finally, there was the more abstract project of eliminating the "metaphorical residue" in art and literature, which theoretically implied the realistic description of anticolonial struggle but practically translated into a massive imitation of party watchwords and formulas. Within this struggle against metaphor and bourgeois lyrical subjectivity fell the prohibition of "love poems without an explicit revolutionary content."[34] The combined result of this intervention would be "a new culture, national in form and revolutionary in content."[35]

6. Besides these explicit directives, three other ideological influences marked the development of "culture"—the word was used almost synonymously with "song and dance"—as a consequence of the harrowing 1968–70 crisis.

The first was the emergence of the Enemy of the People as a cathectic figure of collective hatred. This was generated by the rift between revolutionaries and counterrevolutionaries in the crisis and was practically sustained by the public execution of traitors and "scoundrels" (*malambi*) in the liberated zones. One who is familiar with the historical geography of the Makonde Plateau knows the names and locations of the abandoned villages (*madembe*) where such stonings were carried out: they stand near to Frelimo bases, branches, or settlements as a silent reminder. Post-Independence mapiko choirs would celebrate these executions in unabashedly proud terms:

| | |
|---|---|
| Shiashya shani? | What kind of politics? |
| Shiashya shani shamutendile Mapelelimo | What kind of politics did you do, you of Frelimo |
| Akumwing'a sheu jó Lasharo Nkavandame | Giving the power to that Lázaro Nkavandame |
| Wetu tuvenintete | We, the People |
| Tuvenintete Vamoshambiki | We the People of Mozambique |
| Tulinkunjugwa Lazaro Nkavandame | We ask him for us, Lázaro Nkavandame |
| Bai, wetu tukampata | And if we get him |
| Tukampata Lazaro jó tundantannola | If we get Lázaro we will execute him |
| Kenga Mandushi tundintannola | Like Mandushi, we executed him |
| Lidembe kuna-Buluna | At the abandoned hamlet of the Buluna |
| | |
| Elo, twita malambi aló | Yes, we refuse the scoundrels |
| Wetu malambi atutamwa | We don't want scoundrels |
| Manang'olo Mapelelimo | You, Frelimo elders |
| Tulambalelele Lazaro Nkavandame | Let's look for Lázaro Nkavandame[36] |

The crisis also reinforced the mythology of the heroes (*vanshambelo*) and leaders, inscribed in collective consciousness by the deaths of major guerrillas—Paulo Samuel Kankhomba, Filipe Samuel Magaia, and of course Eduardo Mondlane, remembered here in a mapiko song:

| | |
|---|---|
| Mondlane | Mondlane |
| Wakubyaite wako | Those who killed you |
| Vanu vamalambi | These people are scoundrels |
| Twala | Take |
| Makalatashi lao | Your posters |
| Andika | Write |
| Lina lya-Mondlane | The name of Mondlane |

| Andika | Write |
|--------|-------|
| Lina lyamaimyo | The name of History[37] |

The third ideological concept that emerged out of the crisis was History itself. An idea of history as a meaningful and progressive order was absent from Makonde language and cosmology before the 1960s. The resistance against the mayhem unleashed by Arriaga was the major sign of the fulfillment of a historical teleology and the symbolic matrix of all successes to come. This and other wartime events became the objects of new historically oriented compositions called "songs of reminding" (*dimu dyakwimyangidya*), such as this widespread mapiko song:

| Likukumbwe / Kunambayaya | In Likukumbwe / Nambayaya |
|--------------------------|---------------------------|
| Tushindaikala p'ing'ondo | We stayed during the war |
| Maimyo | History |
| Tushindanama mandumbwe | We lived on sweet potatoes |
| Shedi Luli | In Lurio base |
| Ashindikala Shepi Mpembe | Stayed chief Mpembe |
| Maimyo | History |
| Tushindanama mandumbwe | We lived on sweet potatoes |

The verb *kwimya* means "to tell a story that should be remembered." Its durative-causative form *kwimyangidya* thus means "to purposefully tell a story that should be remembered."[38] *Maimyo*, the substantive derived from *kwimya*, is usually simply translated as "History," but it conveys the same notion of "history to be reminded." History-maimyo, that is, remembering the deeds of the struggle, was to constitute the new thematic core of a new genre of political singing that would spread well beyond the confines of Frelimo's military camps and literate music composers.

7. The transmission of ideological directives, party watchwords, and formulas in the domain of popular dance was facilitated by the expansion of Frelimo's network of schools in the aftermath of Gordian Knot.[39] In the first years of war, informal Frelimo schools were modeled on missionary education; their programs were mostly left to the initiative of individual teachers. Subsequently, Frelimo created special "pilot centers" (*centros pilotos*) that would provide advanced politico-military training.[40] These centers were placed in the proximity of military bases to defend the children from possible incursions; pupils grew

up with soldiers and were subjected to military rules, routines, and ceremonials. The first directives to integrate culture into the centers' activities came in late 1970. Schoolteachers were instructed in cultural matters in the formation center of Bagamoyo. Activities in the schools included choral singing, theater, poetry, and dance. Among the dances taught to the students was mapiko. The rules of gender were not challenged even in the revolutionary setting:

> There was secrecy. The women couldn't know—even here in the centers. We danced the mapiko but the women only saw the dance. They didn't know who danced. On the day of the concert, the professor disappeared from the center. When we had to prepare the lipiko, we would leave for an area seven kilometers away; we prepared the lipiko there and no one knew. He comes back without the girls knowing, without anything.[41]

Beginning in 1973, the dance makwaela became the elective cultural activity for pupils in Frelimo schools. This was a southern Mozambican variant of a regionwide modality of choral singing, *makwaya* (from the English *choir*), in which European four-part harmony is fused with local musical practices such as "responsorial organization, dense overlapping, and variation of individual parts [. . . in addition to] more relaxed vocal timbres, [and] a more spontaneous approach to vocal exclamations and other sounds."[42] Its origins in migrant labor—especially from southern Mozambique to South Africa—gave it the right credentials for a revolutionary dance. Simple and rhythmical, it appeared ideal for transmitting ideology; its teaching was promoted in the professor school of Bagamoyo. A host of new texts was composed for the pupils of the pilot centers, structured around ideological formulas, dates, and names of heroes and leaders. In the years after Independence, makwaela would become the national school-dance and one of the major forms of reverberation of Party ideology.[43]

Concurrently, makwaela made its way to the core of Makondeness. Possibly in the final year of war, or in the year of transition that followed the armistice with Portugal (1974), the southerly dance replaced mapiko as the main content of masculine puberty ritual teachings. Through a paradoxical chiasmus, while the masks made their way into the heart of national spectacle, the southerly national dance replaced the masks in the heart of Makonde ritual life. A similar dance, called *kurtura* ("culture") was introduced in feminine initiation rituals. From

1975 onward, in the new independent state, Makonde boys presented at the coming out of initiations a Changaan migrant labor dance; arranged in orderly lines, they sang in Makonde or Portuguese of presidents and political directives, war heroes and memorable dates. The slogans and formulas of the Party would henceforth be considered the central values to be instilled in the initiates.

8. Domination (*kutawala*), servitude (*utumwa*), colonial taxes (*ukoti*), forced labor (*shibalo*), the lamentations (*tundipata tabu*) and tears (*tulila kwatulila*), the ten years (*myaka kumi*) of war (*ing'ondo*), the carrying of military materials (*materiale, vyombo*), the leaders (*machepi*), the organization (*kupangana*), understanding (*igwana*), unity (*upamo*), the long walking (*kuwena shilo na mui*), the blood spilled (*myadi*), the geographical metonym of national unity (*kuma Rovuma mpaka Maputo*), the quasi-messianic expectation (*patime panatime*), the roads (*ibalabala*), courage (*ntima*), the invocations to the leaders (*mwenu manang'olo*), perseverance (*kukanyilidya*), the Party (*ishama*), the rejoicing (*kupuwa*), the expelling of the colonialists (*kuusha*), the recitation of dates (*italee*), and of course "we, the People" (*tuvenentete*), revolution (*mapindushi*), Independence (*Uhuru*), and liberation (*kwambola*): these tropes and watchwords would dominate Makonde political singing for many years to come.[44] In this process of tropification, ambiguity and multilayeredness were suppressed. Song production in Shimakonde registers a sharp, almost quantitative decrease of rhetorical strategies such as metaphor, ellipsis, and ideophones in the songs composed in the aftermath of the liberation struggle. The practitioners of these new "revolutionary songs" (*dimu dyamapindushi*) looked with condescension toward more mundane genres, which did not approach their subject matter using the correct words and following the correct line.

Makonde revolutionary singing was constituted around a concept of History (*maimyo*), in which the deeds of the struggle are sung as they were supposed to have unfolded:

| | |
|---|---|
| Shumbo shitandi shindyuma | The first lead was discharged |
| Iboma yaku-Chai | At the district of Chai |
| Kulangalela kaka Chipande | The leader was our big brother Chipande |

| | |
|---|---|
| Pamo na vavagwe | With his companions |
| Tundamanya mavetu | We inform you, my friends |
| Mwenu mukapagwite | You who were not there |
| Mwatulyadile ndugu pa-Chai | How we organized our plan in Chai |
| We' tunamanya | We inform you |
| Tundintuma njetu Chipeda | We sent our friend, Chipeda |
| Wena palalesha | Go, and spy! |
| Palidimbile liduva | When the evening got dark |
| Wetu tundinjila | We entered |

This mapiko song describes the mythic beginning of the liberation struggle: the "first lead" shot by Joaquim Alberto Chipande, the Makonde guerrilla who would later become minister of defense. Sung in a triumphal first-person plural, the song addresses listeners "who were not there"; however, it does not map any direct experience. In the first account of the shot, authored by Chipande himself, the person famously sent to spy on the post of Chai was erroneously identified as Bento Chipeda instead of Bento Pachihi Nalyambipano. The mistake was later rectified in the official record but not in the popular text, which tells the story by the (old) book.[45]

9. Precisely gauging the transformations wrought on mapiko by the liberation struggle is impossible. Like the history of the first shot, the living memories of its protagonists have been overwritten by the official version and made into myth. The archive of song allowed us to reconstruct the massive penetration of Frelimo watchwords and formulas into Makonde orature; the memory of cultural policies provided a sense of the "nationalization" of mapiko in the great adventure of the Ten Years' War.

Most important, however, was the attempt to destroy the motor that had ensured the reproduction and transformation of the masquerade throughout the colonial period: ritual schismogenetic rivalry. This onslaught was carried out from a multiplicity of angles. The first was the outright repression of ritual rivalry: of provocations, as contrary to the socialist principle of unity; of gender frictions, as sexist; of local identities, as tribalist. Instead of the segmentary identities produced by ritual schismogenesis, a new collective subject was imagined, "we, the People," defined by national belonging, utopian regeneration, and cathectic hatred for enemies, scoundrels, and counterrevolutionaries. The second was the erasure of the complex field of mapiko genres in favor of a single genre, *nshesho*, practiced by the youth who were the protagonists of the struggle. The third was the politicization of initiation rituals and the substitution of the southerly dance makwaela for mapiko. Finally, there was the spatial transformation of dance itself, from a circle in which the competitive gazes converge on the lipiko, to a line on a podium, in which the dancers all turn to face the gaze of the Leader. The effect of these changes, however, was less predictable than could have been foreseen.

# 8 ⮌ Youth Power

*Villages, Festivals, and Rivals*

| | |
|---|---|
| Kwalala kwalala | Beautiful, beautiful |
| Antigo waku-Mweda kwalala | The Mueda war veterans are beautiful |
| Uti na vakongwe mwao ni mpomo | All of them, and their women even more so |
| Niyere andiwika | Niyere arrived |
| Na ibandeira yake mmakono | With his flag in the hands |
| Na ikomando yake panyuma | With his commando following |

— NMA/Nshesho/Mueda/2004[1]

1. THE RECOLLECTIONS of mapiko players evoke a fairly flat picture of the years following Independence: one of steady consolidation of the achievements of the Ten Years' War, almost of stasis.[2] The construction of communal villages stands as the great rupture that inaugurated this new age, the "time of the villages" (*paludeya*).[3] As people cautiously abandoned the precarious lowlands encampments where they had spent the war years and began resettling into their old hamlets or forming new ones where the old ones stood, the order came to build "cities in the bush": large communal villages on the model of the Tanzanian *vijiji vya ujamaa*. The houses had to be arranged in straight lines, with spacious plots, around a central square destined for communal activities. The initiative was met with resistance—especially around the location of the new villages—but also, by and large, with enthusiasm.[4] In the space of one year (1976–77), dozens of *aldeias comunais* mushroomed all around the plateau and lowlands.

The social experiments pioneered in the camps and the liberated zones were to be transferred into the conductive space of the village.

This applied also to culture. All lineage dance ensembles were to be abandoned in favor of collective village groups, also called "unity groups," open to the participation of everyone, irrespective of kin or gender. The erosion of lineage as a determining factor for participating in mapiko was on its way already in the colonial period, with the meat-is-meat break; however, the history of that earlier modernism did not register in the recollections of the new villagized groups' leaders:

> Because, we came together, we, the war-makers. Our thoughts are the old ones, the ones of the beginning of the Ten Years' War. That's why we saw that: if we organize mapiko in one lineage, it won't go forward; and if we organize mapiko in one neighborhood, it won't go forward. Now, we thought: It's better to come together and work as a single hiding-place (*mpolo*). We organize the masks, men and women. Each person who thinks "I am talented (*nnanda*), I like mapiko, put me in the mask," that's it, s/he enters in the group and plays.[5]

Songs of provocation, containing insults that could lead to disharmony, were banned. New structures of leadership were put in place. Each group was to elect a chief (*chefe* or *secretário*, "secretary"), a deputy (*adjunto*), and a treasurer (*tesoureiro*), and groups were to be identified and authorized by the competent village structure (*estrutura*), who would in turn provide a register of village dances to the district officer. Puberty rituals were moved to the wet months between October and January and significantly diminished in duration to accommodate the school calendar; overall, they became a much less important occasion for dancing.

Already introduced during the Ten Years' War—in the liberated zones and on the Saturday concerts at the base of Nachingwea—national ceremonials became the mainstay of popular dance in the age of villages. In 1975, Samora Machel traversed the country in a north-south journey, from the Rovuma where the war had begun to the Maputo River close to the capital, holding a symbolic flambeau that represented national unity.[6] At each station, the visit was met with vast crowds, establishing the classic metonymical relationship between the leader and the People. Three years later (1978), a grand First Festival of Popular Dance was organized. The festival staged the country's administrative pyramidal structure: "An entire People will partake, from the circle (*cerculo*), to the Nation."[7] Groups competed first at the level of the village (*aldeia*), then of locality (*localidade*), of post (*posto*), of district (*distrito*), and of province (*provincia*), involving "half a million dancers and about four million spectators." This event, "the largest mass manifestation that ever took place in our Country," was intended as a "demonstration of the capacity, pride and determination of our People in creating and transforming the cultural values inherited from the feudal-traditional society." A selection of the best groups, representing each province, paraded in the capital, Maputo. "From the localities, the free People brought to the great cities—last stronghold of the colonial mentality—the true vigor of popular culture."[8]

Nshesho emerged as the uncontested king of the age of villages and festivals, almost wiping out all other forms of mapiko. A multitude of nshesho village groups were founded, and those villages that happened to incorporate the most talented and famous hamlets were better off: Nampanya, Mwambula, and Namakule in Muidumbe; Mueda sede, Litembo, and Uwavi in Mueda; and then catching up, Lutete, Miteda, Nandimba, Omba, Litamanda, Litandakua, Mwalela, and on and on. Not only was nshesho the genre of the generation that had spearheaded the war—the "war-makers" (*vanantenda ing'ondo*)—it was also deeply consonant with Frelimo's new aesthetics.


2. Despite the introduction of cinema in Mozambican social life in the late 1970s, visual records of mapiko performances are hard to find, buried in the great uncatalogued Kuxa Kanema itinerant newsreel archive.[9] The sound archive is slightly more generous: recordings of 1970s and 1980s Makonde performances are kept in the Pemba and Maputo branches of the Radio Mozambique archives.[10] Listening to them, one is struck by the continuity of nshesho over forty years. A gulf separates the 1962 Kubik recordings from the 1980s ones, in lyrical content, rhythmical patterns, and mood; but the latter did not seem so dissimilar from what I could see at the times of my fieldwork. The Ten Years' War marked a rupture that matched its own rhetoric; the continuity established in the period after Independence bespeaks a successful interpellation into a new aesthetic idiom.

Frelimo's post-Independence resolutions on culture were inspired by a vague commitment to socialist realism, promoted especially in the First National Meeting on Culture, which took place in July 1977.[11] The usual themes are present: the rejection of abstract art as degenerate and bourgeois, the promotion of realistic portrayal and political didacticism. The depiction of the misdeeds of colonialism was also encouraged, the foremost example being a great theatrical representation of the Mueda massacre, the object of the first Mozambican feature film and performed every year, for two decades, on the anniversary of the massacre.[12] More generally, Frelimo aesthetics shared the key features of twentieth-century totalitarian regimes: the veneration for the vanguardist leader; the predominance of monologism and party watchwords; and the nurturing of fear and suspicion, catalyzed in the spectral figure of the Enemy of the People. The latter was inaugurated by Samora Machel's theatrical display of Nkavandame and other traitors during the Rovuma to Maputo journey;[13] it then became a hammering theme of propaganda, embodied in the popular cartoon of Xiconhoca, the Enemy of the People.[14] We can find all of these themes intertwined in an ideologically dense poem by Samora himself that opens the booklet produced on the occasion of the First Festival of Popular Dance:

| | |
|---|---|
| A cultura é criada pelo povo | Culture is created by the people |
| não a cria os artista. | the artists don't create it. |
| A burguesia não produz arte: | The bourgeoisie doesn't produce art: |
| falta-lhe a terra | it lacks the land |
| falta-lhe a inspiração. | it lacks inspiration. |
| O povo inspira-se todos os dias. | The people take inspiration every day. |
| Vejam os camponeses . . . | Look at the peasants . . . |
| A sua música fala da sua vida, | Their music talks of their life, |
| da lavoura, das colheitas, da rega. | of tilling, harvesting, watering. |
| Conta como foi colhido o arroz, | It tells of how rice, pumpkin and |
| a cabaça, | maize |
| a massaroca . . . | were harvested . . . |
| Quando está a trabalhar, a suar | Laboring, sweating under the Sun, |
| sob o Sol, | |
| regando a terra com o seu suor, | watering the land with his sweat, |
| o camponês canta. | the peasant sings. |
| Volta a casa | She comes back home |
| com um cântaro de agua na cabeça, | with a bucket of water on the head, |
| pensa que tem de fazer fogo para | thinking that she has to light a fire |
| cozinhar, | to cook, |
| vive a vida e canta a vida. | she lives life and sings life. |

| | |
|---|---|
| Nas noites, nas horas de descanso, | During the nights, in the hours of rest, |
| quando a Lua-cheia o ilumina, | when the Full-moon lights him, |
| canta ao seu trabalho, conta as suas penas, | he sings at his work, tells his labors, |
| seus sofrimentos, suas esperanças . . . | his sufferings, his hopes . . . |
| canta a felicidade. | he sings happiness. |
| Canta a dança, | Sings the dance, |
| pode ser triste ou alegre, | it can be sad or joyful, |
| uma referencia à história | a reference to history |
| ou um episodio quotidiano. | or an episode of the everyday. |
| Mas, seja como for, tem um significado real. | But, be that as it may, it has a real meaning. |
| Define um inimigo | It defines an enemy |
| e como lutar contra esse inimigo. | and how to fight against this enemy.[15] |

The first lines define a subject of culture: *o povo*, the peasants-People, in opposition to the uprooted bourgeoisie. The bulk of the poem consists of a description of the hardships and enchantments of peasant life in a mode of socialist realism. The long description is terminated by a sudden twist—"be that as it may, it has a real meaning"—that needs the interpretive intervention of the vanguardist leader to be clearly articulated: identifying the political Enemy.

The genre of nshesho echoed Frelimo's aesthetics in striking ways. New polished masks depicted leaders, peasants, and guerrillas (fig. 12). Mimetic dance styles offered vivid representations of rural labor and struggle history, performed with wooden weapons that evoked the times of "dancing the training" in the Ten Years' War (see chap. 7, sec. 2). Choirs praised the Party, addressed the leaders, and invoked the execution of traitors and scoundrels, to be "tied to a pole and killed without pity."[16] The opening up of participation resulted in large ensembles that, all dressed in party insignia, offered a compact spectacle of popular unity. In Pemba or in Maputo, such demonstrations of revolutionary enthusiasm served not only to please the leaders but also to show to the rest of the nation that the communal village was a fertile breeding ground for the socialist New Man:

> Amongst all the dances of Mozambique, today *mapiko* is perhaps the one that underwent the most dramatic alterations. This

FIGURE 12. Samora Machel *(Paolo Israel, Lutete, 2003)*

is because it found its precise role in the revolutionary culture that we want to build. The longstanding experiment of the creation of the New Man in the liberated zones of Cabo Delgado put an end to obscurantism, in which many traditional dances were, and still are, enshrouded. So it is that, while years ago people could kill to defend myths fostered by superstition, today, when we go to those areas where the people are organized in communal villages, we found that the *mapiko* dance is a fundamental element in the intense cultural activity of those villages. Today, the spectatorship is composed of women and children who can all enjoy the cultural richness of this dance, from the masks and the adornments to the dancer's performance.[17]

3. Frelimo's rationale for the construction of communal villages was developmental and socialist. No functional and equitable economy could be built—such was the argument—if people lived in remote and scattered settlements. People needed to be concentrated in places where they could benefit from the state's welfare and education; exert the rights and obligations of direct democracy; practice new forms of socialization; and produce communally and more efficiently, as well as close to the roads so that they could easily trade.

The critique of villagization carried out by radical intellectuals from the 1980s onward, when the project was beginning to show its cracks in terms of economic productivity, bears the imprint of Michel Foucault's thought. James Scott considered the communal village as a panopticon: a tool of governmentality that aimed to surveil, rather than develop, its subjects. The rectangular grids and the spacious courtyards were interpreted as instrumental to creating a field of visibility in which no action could go unnoticed.[18] Christian Geffray saw the communal village as a biopolitical mechanism through which the Party exercised power in a capillary form, from the capital into the individual household, passing through the whole echelon of intermediate structures.[19] While supporters of the communal village picked the school and the hospital as metonyms for the institution, the detractors selected the Party house and its microphysics of power; if the ones highlighted the role of avenues of communication, the others saw grid urbanism as a form of police control; where the ones upheld instrumental reason, the others unveiled discipline. From this latter Foucauldian angle, the Party house casts a deep shadow on the neighboring dance-field, which, imprisoned in the grids of streets, appears more as a space of surveillance than as a free agora of play, commerce, speech, and dance. The accomplished "frelimization" of mapiko can be considered as the product of the villages' disciplinary mechanisms. Through Party structures, cultural watchwords and directives could be capillarized, enforced onto groups by zealous officers who tinged them with their own personal interpretations.

The state festival, miniaturized in the village, was the most pervasive mechanism of transformation and control. The visit of a leader (*dirigente*) or a national holiday would be celebrated through an established ceremonial: the welcoming of the leader at the district boundary; the collective cleaning of the village square; the calling of the popular assembly with the onomatopoeic iron bell *shingwangwa*; the flower offerings at the Heroes' monument; the reading of augural messages from the mass organizations; the gift giving to the leader; culminating with the political speeches. This ceremonial produced the spectacle of a People, whose voice is mediated by the Party in its various emanations and existing in a direct charismatic relationship with a Leader who is legitimized by the heroic deeds of the liberation struggle.

Cultural groups were summoned to partake in such events. A festival was an occasion to get the village's organizational machinery into shape: the district cultural officer would select groups from neighboring villages on account of their fame and political respectabilities; messages would be sent to invite them, to which a reply was expected; food contributions (*nshango*) were organized; rations were distributed and accommodation arranged through neighborhood leaders. Groups entered the village on the eve of the festival, singing their way through the streets. The morning's synchronized sweeping publicly represented a long collective work of preparation.

"Cultural activities" would punctuate all the phases of the ceremonial: poems and songs, to heighten the pathos of the most solemn moments; and dance, to convey happiness and popular participation. Toward the end of the official ceremonial, each group was invited to dance, in a dedicated space below the podium of honor, under the leader's watchful eyes. The most deserving groups were publicly recognized through awards. In the absence of formally established aesthetic directives, groups could only guess what pleased the leaders, sometimes producing hyperemphatic expressions of political enthusiasm that embarrassed critical observers.

Once the official ceremonial was over—generally, in the early afternoon—dance groups were invited to continue their activity freely in the village square. And free dance in the village square, of course, was far from being free. For this open space was, more than any other, exposed to the watchful eye of the Party. Potentially, each individual could be an agent of delation: "This group is singing reactionary songs!" "They are behaving like scoundrels!" "They should not be invited again; they should not be allowed to dance."

4. Looking closely at the moment of free dance, however, one can discern, beneath the frelimization enforced through village disciplinary structures, a different dynamic taking place: the undercover continuation of schismogenetic competition, mapiko's old engine of creativity. A state ceremonial is an occasion to confront rival groups from neighboring villages. At least two or three mapiko groups must be summoned to a festival. Being invited is an honor; being neglected is a slight. The host group receives the guests and shares with them a house in which the mask is prepared. The official ideology banned gendered secrecy as an obscurantist practice: the masks must be unmasked, and they are allowed to perform only as art. However, as symbols of revolutionary struggle, mapiko deserve respect (ishima)—incidentally, the same word was used before to keep the women away from their secrets. The groups of war veterans are venerable and should not be approached lightly; no one should dare to touch a party flag or the mask itself, which stands for the flag.

Under the mango trees, the mapiko dance in a dedicated space. The spot is chosen beforehand, on account of the qualities of the soil: the nshakasha movement requires it to be hard, even, and clean. Other groups may pick their trees but must keep a certain distance. As happened in the colonial era, mapiko groups take turns: each one dances one lishesho and one nshakasha before leaving. The pace is slow. While drummers heat their vinganga on the fire—carefully, because the python skin catches fire easily and is difficult to replace—a well-dressed man cleans up the oval, pushes back the children, and prepares the ground for the lipiko. All inflamed, sharpening a traditional scythe, he exclaims, Makwambalwa paiii! "You drunkards, dooown!" Sanaaa! "Aaart!" (fig. 13).

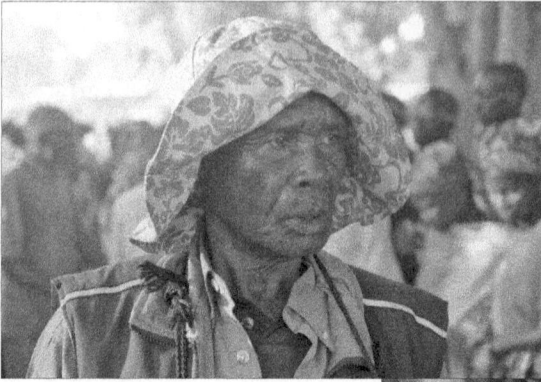

FIGURES 13A/B. Rivals in play: Jerrycan and Peanut-Peanut (*Rui Assubuji, Mwambula, 2009*)

The lead drummer takes position, and the lishesho begins. The singers face the drum orchestra and move slowly backward (or vice versa), gradually opening up a large space in the crowd. Nshesho songs draw from the broader idiom of Makonde political singing. Each group has its own style and repertoire: two or three tunes that are the group's trademark and about twenty lyrics, some of which are sung over many years. By listening to nshesho in action, one can unravel the addressivity of the majestic subject "we, the People" that took the place of lineage—or individuals—in Makonde singing following the Ten Years' War.[20]

Praises of leaders are not necessarily addressed to the leaders themselves: they are a way of reintroducing the competitive element under the guise of socialist officialdom. The qualities of a leader increase the prestige of a group:

| | |
|---|---|
| Mpaka ku-Maputo | Until Maputo |
| Wako nshadolo wetu waku-Nangade | You, our administrator from Nangade |
| Monika undigwinika mpaka ku-Maputo | Monica, you are famous until Maputo |
| Iboma yaku-Nangade | The district of Nangade |
| Tunkulupile Monika atulangalele | Let's trust Monica to lead us |
| Wetu tuvenentete | We, the People[21] |

Revolutionary pedigree is used as a weapon in the game of competition: one district against the other, one village against the other, one group against the other. Behind the majestic "we, the People" hides a more concrete schismogenetic identity, broad enough to encompass a communal village—or the fraction that coalesces around a specific group—but not of the size of a nation. Being invited to an important political meeting, and attracting a leader's attention, is an honor to be boasted about in a subsequent event:

| | |
|---|---|
| Lude' Nampanya lundigwinika kuma Rovuma mpaka Maputo | The village of Nampanya is famous from the Rovuma to the Maputo |
| Tuvamwalimu | We are teachers |
| Anditushema nanangaledi nang'o' Chipande tukaimang'ane | We were called by our leader, the elder Chipande, to meet |
| Lude' Lilondo | In the village of Lilondo |
| Tutende vyetu vyakumanyika | To do our famous things |
| Lude' Lilondo | The village of Lilondo |
| Mama Shopia kutakatuka pakwigwa lidi lya-Vanampanya | Mama Sofia stood up when she heard the voice of the Nampanyas |
| "Ngwenda koko ndavalola Ava Vanampanya" | "Let me go there and watch them These are the Nampanyas"[22] |

Adherence to the precepts of socialism is brandished against other villages. The singers boast as in the times of old; the rivals should bow down their heads in shame (*dyoni*):

| | |
|---|---|
| Kwigwana kwavenentete | Harmony among the People |
| Wetu paludeya yapa-Mwambula | We, in the village of Mwambula |
| Tundilima ibalabala bila shilikali kulamulila | We dug a road without the government ordering it |
| Tundintandola Mwakonda | We elected Mwakonda |
| Alangalele shipinga sha-Upamo | To lead the group of Unity |
| Muve' nadyoni mavetu muve' nadyoni | Shame on you, friends, shame on you |
| Mukanalota upamo nkati mwaludeya | You who don't want Unity in the villages[23] |

In a paradoxical twist, the principle of unity is used as a weapon to foster rivalry. All the Party watchwords and dictates can be deployed in such a way: socialist emulation, revolutionary pedigree, and the sought-after condition of being a war veteran (*antigo*)—we have them, you don't; we do it, you don't. The most powerful—and most paradoxical—weapon is the invocation of Party monologism to silence a rival:

| | |
|---|---|
| Ikanyenje | If it speaks enviously |
| Pakanywa penu je' nkong'o | Put a lock on your mouth |
| Ikanyenje | If it speaks enviously |
| Munno' Nampanya shipambele | Look at Nampanya, a rhino |
| Tundiwika | We are here |
| Munno' Nampanya mushinshiba | Look, Nampanya that you heard of |
| Ikanyenje | If it speaks enviously |
| Mukavikia njeje mpamba yolo | If you introduce provocations, you collect chaff[24] |

The words *njeje* and *iyanje* describe disrespectful and envious speech. Frelimo's imperatives of unity and monologism implied relinquishing such forms of verbal provocations, which might lead to disharmony and strife. The only form of provocation left, then—almost a meta-provocation—is accusing the rivals themselves of njeje and iyanje. Obedience is invoked against bad speech; to silence a rival, the leader is asked to pronounce the ritual formula:

| | |
|---|---|
| Mashala mashala mashala | Salutations salutations salutations |
| Chepi waludeya lwaMweda | Village chief of Mueda |
| Mashala | Salutations |
| Ninkukujugwa namene | We ask you strongly |
| Utaye mashala pashiwanja | Cast a salutation on the dance-field |
| Utumanyie vipita | To inform us of the happenings |
| Nkaja mu-Mweda | In the hamlet of Mueda |
| Akapagwa wanjeje | If there are envious-speech people |
| Tummungalile munnandi | Let's tie them to a pole |
| Tupange mapiko | Let's prepare the masks |
| Bila malove | Without words[25] |

Even more mundane songs are twisted to become provocations. The trope of the woman who is late because she spent too much time grooming so as to be noticed by the dancers is a mainstay of nshesho composition. As in the times of *shinantwala* ("abduction" [see chap. 3, sec. 5]), the game is played for feminine attention. A social critique concerning spousal violence can be twisted to become an aggressive joke:

| Ashindalila numbwangu | My little sister was crying |
|---|---|
| Undipajangila kulombwa dada | You married hurriedly, sister |
| "Nikandilombwa ku Mwambula" | "Had I married in Mwambula . . ." |
| Pole | Patience |
| Aunatangadike namene dada | Don't complain too much, sister |
| Andakukoma nnume ntwao | The man, your husband, will beat you up[26] |

Dance styles unfold against this musical background. When the singers have advanced toward the end of the oval, they turn back toward the drummer. The lipiko comes tinkling and "hurls styles" (*kujela vikuvo*); framed by vocal provocations and self-praises—all in the name of the correct political line—they are also weapons of rivalry. After three or four styles, the dancer is tired. He leans against a group member to breathe. As he rests, a reciter of verbal styles (*vikuvo vyaku-tangola*) comes in, engaging the choir in a rhythmic dialogue. This is boastful poetry:

| Aunatango' iyanje nawetu | Don't speak enviously about us |
|---|---|
| Kulimanya kundikamala namene | To know oneself is very difficult |
| Leka mulimanya | If you knew yourselves |
| Amunatango' iyanje nawetu | Don't speak enviously about us |
| Ata mujunge | Even if you make much noise |
| Mumanenge po' petu sede yaku-Omba | You won't come out from our seat of Omba |
| Kala pankaloni | Once, in the colonial time |
| Nkulungwa wetu Mashongwe bai | Our chief was Mashongwe, that's it[27] |

As the lishesho drags on, other groups become impatient. Do they think that they are going to win, this way, taking so much time? People get bored! You don't know how to share! The last song is an occasion to respond:

| Kaka Gelemani vika shani shamwisho | Brother Germani play the last LP |
|---|---|
| Wetu tulota kunyema | We want to exit |
| Leka tuvapishe vavetu | Let's make room for our friends |
| Tunkwigwa malove tangaleka shipaipai | We hear words being spoken, very low |
| Vatwamba wetu | They refer to us |

| Vamwambula lishesho kutima | The Mwambulas, their lishesho takes time |
| Leka tuvapishe vavetu | Let's leave room for our friends |
| Tunkwigwa malove tangaleka shipaipai | We hear words being spoken, very low[28] |

The lipiko leaves on the sound of this last song, and the choir slowly dances back toward the drum orchestra. When the lead drum strikes the closure, the ground is prepared for nshakasha. Children are pushed away, the oval is redesigned. The tension rises. The first movement put out a challenge; the second will resolve it. No words will be spoken here; all will be entrusted to the mastery of the lipiko and its drummer. For the songs and the drumming are but appetizers: what decides the competition is the lipiko itself. The choir squats in a corner and hums, in a descending melody: *e-e-e, e-e-e, e-e-e.* The lipiko takes position; it is called to *kukomela*; stomps the feet and dances the jerking backward movement. Did it do it in a straight line? Did it end it precisely? The most difficult and intense mimetic styles are played and danced, while the humming continues. Someone from the choir adjusts the lipiko's dress. *Kará-ká, kará-ká, kará-ká!* The vinganga's roar rises; the lipiko gestures to the choir and heads back to finish (fig. 14). As the lipiko spins its *tapwito* on the last touch of the drums, the group springs up and screams the name of the village. Breaths are drawn and the chatter builds up while the next group tunes its drums on the fire.

5. Considering mapiko aesthetics closely, it is equally possible to perceive, below the glaring frelimization, the persistence of older representational modes based on ambivalence and playfulness. Despite their visibility and political deployability, new mask templates such as the guerrilla soldier and the president coexisted with the old ones. While presidents' faces were carved in a naturalistic style, the guerrillas were sometimes treated to the grotesque distortions reserved to ethnic others and social types. As with Shumu's old masks (see chap. 4, sec. 9), ugliness was to inspire awe; moreover, there were many analogies between terrifying bush-spirits and Frelimo bush-warriors.[29] The Enemy was never represented in mask form: playful ambivalence would not dare to tread in that territory.

Many new codified dance styles (*vikuvo*) explicitly referred to the history of the liberation struggle: the AK-47 shooting, the anti-aerial

FIGURE 14. Ready to turn (*Rui Assubuji, Mwambula, 2009*)

combat, the land mine, the flag hoisting, the carrying of the war equipment, the early anticolonial resistance fought with spears and bows (*namashakole*), and the flambeau of unity (*mwenge*). These styles quickly spread across the villages, as part of the basic repertoire of each respectable nshesho group. Sometimes, more specific episodes could be inscribed in dance, such as the style Rui Pinho, representing the violent deeds of a colonial officer working in the Chai post attacked by Chipande in 1964.[30] When they did not evoke war deeds, dance styles referred to various aspects of peasant life: the all-present winnowing (*shelo*) and cultivating (*kulima*); bush-related activities such as hunting, trapping, and collecting snails; the representation of animals such as the hare, the chameleon, the woodpecker, the bat, and the termite; the depiction of social vices such as gluttony, lust, and drunkenness; everyday activities such as smoking and card playing; and the humorous description of the inconveniences of rural life, such as the removal of the *matakenya* foot-fleas or the itch caused by the spores of the wild bean *uwangu*.[31]

This multifaceted representation of peasant life and struggle history responded well to the Party's discourse of socialist realism. However, it stemmed from a much older internal dynamics of the nshesho genre. *Vikuvo*, "dance styles," are driven by a mimetic principle. This is expressed with the verbal form *kummina*, "to dance something" (as in "to portray something"). Such imitation extends to all objects: animals, activities, and moral qualities. The thing to be imitated is captured in its most essential gesture, which is congealed and then represented, sometimes in a very abstract way.[32] Mimetic dance styles were attached to specific characters in the *mileya* genre; they did not exist in the *dutu* genre; and they were resurrected in a more flexible way in the *nshesho* genre. Here, vikuvo were detached from moral typification and turned into abstract representations. This allowed the incorporation of old dances no longer practiced, such as *ligwalema, ndomwa, libwenyu, libadobado, shindimba,* and *shimbambanda.* The essential steps of each dance were condensed into one style and performed by the masked dancer. The repertoire of nshesho dance styles thus constituted a broad archive of memory—of everyday actions, historical deeds, animals, types, and dances—driven by mimetic appropriation.

On the festival stage, dance styles offered an image of a peasantry fully converted to the principles of socialist realism. What the watchers-from-above might interpret as political commitment was driven by a mimetic appetite inherent in the genre itself. Playful ambivalence survived the onslaught of socialist realism, being perpetuated—sometimes even unconsciously—in the performative conventions of a genre. Scratching the surface, the spectacle of revolutionary enthusiasm remained ambiguous and ambivalent; the mask was never completely unmasked.

6. Dance rivalry, which managed to survive the socialist onslaught, was also projected in the ethereal space of the radio. State ceremonials played a crucial role in shaping the social fabric of communal villages, but their impact in terms of a broader public was limited. Sound was more important than visuality in the production of a national imagination. In a country in which the large majority was illiterate and in which visual technology reached only a limited sector of the urban population, the radio was the most effective means of mass communication. Rádio Moçambique—also known as RM, "from the Rovuma to the Maputo"—was created in 1975 in the context of the nationalization of the broadcasting organs. It seeped deep into the everyday: those who possessed a radio set would fall asleep and wake up to the sound of the national anthem; follow the news and listen to the music; invite family and friends to sit by in the idle afternoon hours.

Between 1976 and 1977, RM launched a campaign to collect popular dance, as part of a broader cultural offensive. The majority of recordings consisted of revolutionary anthems and school choirs singing formulaic *makwaela* songs (see chap. 7, sec. 10); other dances could be collected, provided that their song lyrics were revolutionary enough. As the regional branches of RM radios gained autonomy, the collection and broadcasting of popular dance became more systematic. After a short national broadcast, the morning session was held in local languages; in-between the announcements, each announcer played his favorite music. The initial stock of recordings was enriched through the initiative of individual anchormen. Traveling to the field with political brigades, radio announcers such as Akungondo and Nandenga took advantage of the spectacle offered to the leaders to amass private collections of recordings, which they would play back in their radio broadcasts; as a consequence, their names became popular icons.

For mapiko players, the radio became another terrain for competition. Being recorded and broadcast was a sign of distinction. The radio enhanced the value of songs: if on the dance-field they were just one element of the performance, sometimes smothered by the drums, on the radio they became the most prominent. A radio announcer would record the groups whose songs were political to a certain extent but also original and meaningful.[33] Microphones would always be positioned close to the singers. By selecting and broadcasting songs from specific groups, an announcer could convey his own political viewpoint under the guise of popular dance—slipping in a more critical song here and there, for instance. Meanwhile, dancers learned that good songs earned them the prestige and recognition of being broadcast, and they worked to refine their lyrics and tunes.

Through the radio, messages addressed to the leaders could be effectively put across. Dancers are aware that politicians' attention during official ceremonials is at best selective. However, songs are played repeatedly on the radio, and the leaders could thus be reminded of their obligations, recalled to duty by the reference to common deeds:

| | |
|---|---|
| Tunkujugwila manang'olo makomishau | We ask you, elders of the committees |
| Pamukadyana mudikiti mupakanila | When you meet in the chairs to deliberate |
| Antigo vapambedye | Take care of the war veterans |

| | |
|---|---|
| Tukumbukile ku-Nashingwea kwatushinama | Let's remember Nachingwea, where we lived |
| Tukumbukile kuna-Jaria kwatushinama | Let's remember Algeria, where we lived |
| Antigo vapambedye | Take care of the war veterans |
| Mang'amung'amu amwe Mondlane tundyambola | We achieved liberation with Mondlane's wits |
| Ding'ano uti dyavenentete Vamoshambiki | With the wits of all the Mozambican People |
| Antigo vapambedye | Take care of the war veterans |
| Vankuvaleka vana vetu vajaikanga | They leave our sons to get lost |
| Tunkulota kwambola shilambo shetu | We want to liberate our country |
| Wetu tulye shana njula | So that we can eat well our happiness[34] |

If the radio could be used as a megaphone by dance groups, it also worked the other way round, as a surreptitious and pervasive ear. For no one ever knew for sure who was recording what and when, especially during national celebrations. Does that microphone there amplify or capture? Does that guy strolling below the mangoes have a recorder in his pocket? In the end, that man who came here to visit took away (*kutwala*) our songs! Are we going to hear them on the radio? When? On a deeper level, the radio can be considered as a sublimation of the leader's gaze, transferred from the visual to the aural domain: as the great ear of the nation, always present, always attentive, always listening.

7. Showcased in political festivals and broadcast through the radio, nshesho became a national symbol; in the Mozambican public sphere, it imposed itself as the only true mapiko. The nationalization of nshesho was furthered by the physical dispersion of the Makonde. After Independence, Makonde soldiers were allotted to duty stations across the country, as a measure of prudence, so as to avoid a massive concentration of troops that might constitute the core of a rebel army, but also to spread the new consciousness forged in the struggle. Wherever they went, the Makonde built community with a sense of entitlement. "We liberated, we did it ourselves" (*tundyambola tuvene*).[35] "Where were you when we fought the colonists?" In the outskirts of Pemba and Maputo, they settled together in neighborhoods, took possession of the land, and redistributed it to the locals.

Groups of mapiko were organized in these new urban spaces—especially Pemba, Nampula, and Maputo, where the community was strong enough to support the organizational costs. The masks danced for the puberty rituals held for those who could not afford to travel back to the plateau to "put in" their children. Eventually, these groups gained visibility by participating in local festivals and political ceremonials. Gifted Makonde performers took a leading role in the formation of regional groups of dance and song sponsored by the local "house of culture" (*casa da cultura*) or founded under the impetus of individuals. The first and foremost was the group Mapico Moderno, founded by Luis Mbanguia, a war veteran from Quissanga who had came to know mapiko during the struggle for liberation; the group presented a highly theatricized and politicized spectacle of mapiko masks and other dances.[36]

A protagonist of the Nampula's House of Culture group was Cosme Nhussi, called Nantova ("the immortal"), a Makonde veteran with the sulfurous reputation of being a master of *takatuka*—the ability to transfer any wound to the next nearby living being. Nantova was also a mapiko carver and dancer and was husband to several wives.[37] After the armistice he was relocated to Nampula, where he brought his favorite sons Casimiro and Atanasio, begotten with two different Makonde refugee women in Tanzania. The two adolescents had shown an inclination for dance but also for soccer. Nantova told them, "You must choose between the two. But think of this: there is little money in soccer, and your legs will get injured quickly." Both opted for dance. In 1981, Nantova sent them to Maputo, and through his political connections he managed to have them included in the burgeoning Companhia Nacional de Canto e Dança. This state institution had been founded in 1979, building on a previous folkloric group formed during the struggle, which performed a selection of Mozambican dances and had traveled abroad.[38] The CNCD's mission was to provide a representation of the country's cultural diversity: the two brothers, together with the war veteran Augusto Ng'upe, stood in for the north of the country and introduced mapiko, *nnonje*, and other Makonde dances in the company's ballets. In the late 1980s, Casimiro became the lead choreographer of the company. Meanwhile, the two brothers contributed to the establishment of the mapiko group based in Maputo's military neighborhood.[39] At first shunned by the elders—who burned their drums and forbade them to dance—they eventually imposed themselves with their artistry and creative vision. Baptized "16th of June"—an homage to the

Mueda massacre—the group performed on national holidays and festivities, offering a show of revolutionary Makondeness in a metallic and liquored-up environment. Two groups would form later, in the suburbia of Boane and Manhiça, providing an adequate competitive challenge.

Just as mapiko groups in the villages engaged their rivals with revolutionary lexicon, so too did Makonde dancers mobilize their politico-ethnic aura in the new national institutions and urban settings. But the real winner was the genre of nshesho, the only one that the guerrillas knew, valued, practiced, and brought with themselves in their journeys, with its politically correct songs and realistic dance styles.

8. The dominance of nshesho in the communal villages was strong but not exclusive. In the late 1970s and early '80s, new mapiko began to be introduced and some of the old ones resurrected. Among those was dutu, the genre of the meat-is-meat break. Dutu was not played during the Ten Years' War: striking the likuti was too dangerous, as its piercing guttural sound could be detected miles away and would reveal the position of the guerrillas. After Independence, most dutu players entered into the new collective nshesho groups. Some of the old masters, however, resurrected the genre—in the villages of Mwatidi, Nampanya, Namande, and Mwalela on the plateau and in Mbau and Shitunda in the lowlands. The reinvention was motivated by the desire of "having the children who grew up now remember (*kuvaimyangidya*). For everyone who stops by and sees us knows: thus played the elders of old."[40]

The old genre lent itself poorly to the imperatives of socialist realism. The dance could not be changed, and it continued to be short, fast, and abstract. But dutu song masters composed politicized lyrics to be sung to old tunes:

| | |
|---|---|
| Vavetu vatango' iyanje | Our friends who speak enviously |
| Vatango' iyanje na vatanane | Who speak enviously and quarrel |
| We' tundipakanila | Us, we agreed |
| Kupanga mapiko aishama | We prepare Party masks[41] |

But into this new repertoire slipped old obscure songs:

| | |
|---|---|
| Maundi tonya medi | The clouds pour rain |
| Nnungu tonya medi | God pours rain |
| Bwana Nganga alota mwanda jó | Mister healer, he wants to go |
| Vadyoko vakulola | The children are watching[42] |

The master Juakali alone (see chap. 6, secs. 6–7) managed to adapt the long song-poems to the new village dutu. His post-Independence compositions describe, among other things, the introduction of newsreel footage in Shitunda, when people could see Samora and the ceremony of Independence in Zimbabwe; the creation of an administrative post in the context of a general reorganization of local structures; and the group's travel to the city of Nampula, to "show the culture of Shitunda" and "hear the mass in the cathedral." Less inclined to praising, the *shilanga* genre maintained its critical vocation, managing to address the leaders with complaints and requests:

| | |
|---|---|
| Nelo andida baba | Today came the father |
| Andida baba wetu | Came our father |
| Marcelino Dos Santos | Marcelino Dos Santos |
| Wetu po' tunammudya | Herewith, we ask you |
| Vyatutikinganga vyoe ndatumanyia | The many things we don't know, tell us |
| Mashitadolo waku-Kabu | The administrator of Cabo Delgado |
| Apa mwene awena pai | Himself, he goes around walking |
| Avana' mbutuka | He doesn't have a car |
| Vatumila mbutuka wakukatila | They gave him a borrowed car |
| Vene vakavaima mbutuka | The owners refused him a car |
| Nangu ninkwona dyoni | I am ashamed |
| Hi shambone | This is not good |
| Tenda shimbili shakunyata | It makes for an ugly renown |
| Mashitadolo shani aju awena pai? | What kind of administrator goes around walking? |
| Akavé mbutuka | Without a car |
| Madengo andashalagwesha | He will be late to work |
| Tuvenentete tulinkulila | We, the People, we cry for ourselves |
| Shilambo shaku-Kabu wetu tabu, nnemba | The country of Cabo, we suffer, boy |
| Ata chai atukumbila | We don't even drink tea |
| Samani baba | Excuse me father |
| Wetu tunkulila | We are crying |
| Nikakowa ungulivaliva | If I am erring, forgive me |
| Aunangwigwe kunyata | Don't hear my words as bad |
| Wetu tulinkulila | We are crying for ourselves |
| Pameo pako Marcelino utwangangole | In the face of Marcelino, so that he rescues us[43] |

Other dutu songs describe the competition between villages, fought with new languages and media ("the Litapatas lied; they sent a message saying that there are only *mashalagwesha* in Shitunda"). The field of visibility created by the peculiar urbanism of communal villages became a terrain for competition, which is described through military metaphors. Groups march from one village to the other cautiously; prepare their masks in the secretive space of the bush, in an abandoned hamlet; make plans (*milugu*) and send spies to check out the dancing space before they "sneak in" (*kwinjilila*) to ambush their rivals. Or else they flee the battlefield, disheartened:

| | |
|---|---|
| Vashitunda mwanda Mwambula | The Shitundas go to Mwambula |
| Tujugwa lotoli yaku-Mwambula tuvalangila wetu tumanye | We ask the doctor of Mwambula to explain to us, so that we know |
| Vashitunda vandyuka kumapiko nkaja Mwambula | The Shitundas went to the mapiko in the hamlet of Mwambula |
| Vanamande vandipata abali | The Namandes received the news |
| "Twende koko tukavatimbe" | "Let's go there and ruin them" |
| Manemba tukawike pakati ndila | Boys, as we got in the middle of the road |
| | |
| Lidembe lya-Vanshandani | To the abandoned hamlet of the Nshandani |
| | |
| Ipisha yake Yesu | The picture of Jesus |
| Andipanga lipiko lyashimakugwa | He dressed a mapiko, Makua style |
| "Kwanja nintuma shaleko" | "First, let's send a sentinel" |
| "Wena kapalaleshe" | "Go and spy" |
| Shaleko kwida | The sentinel arrives |
| Andimila mwina mwembe | And sits below a mango tree |
| Akunu manyani? | Who is here? |
| Akunu mashove | Here are the youths |
| Akunu Shitunda | Here is Shitunda |
| Shaleko pakati | And the sentinel in the middle |
| Shitunda kuvina | Shitunda dances |
| Shaleko kummwamwatela | The sentinel trembles |
| Vashitunda kumanya | "The Shitundas are knowledgeable" |
| Shaleko kuja | The sentinel goes back |
| Kuja shanganyuma | Goes back stealthily |
| Andyuka ndavauli' vavagwe | Goes to tell his friends |
| "Mapiko kunguulange | "Undo the mask |

| Nangu anguve' mwesho | I don't have the courage |
| Apa vamapiko" | Those are mapiko people" |
| Pa-Shitunda kuvé shinu | Shitunda, that's something |
| Mapiko kumanya | Knowledge of masks[44] |

Most of the village dutu groups disintegrated in the late 1980s, when the civil war cast a dark shadow on the Makonde Plateau. Ultimately only two, from M'Bau and Mwatidi, survived the war and continued to dance into the new millennium, until they likewise gave in to the dominance of nshesho.

9. Guilherme Banga boasts with familiar gestures: he slashes a scythe before his mouth, hits his chest and makes the *dinjuga* iron bells tinkle. He has a dark smooth complexion, elegant downward-angled eyes and mouth, and small ears. The latter, though, do little work. Banga is a war veteran (*antigo*) from the village of Miteda. He is deaf but will not admit it and cannot let go of mapiko. As he warms up to dance the lishesho, the choir sings, over and over: "Boys, let's rejoice, rejoice!" (*Manemba tupuwange, tupuwe*). For what? There is little to rejoice here. The dancing and the drumming do not combine. Banga's steps and the lead drum's beats are out of sync. A young man cleans Banga's ears but to no avail: the mismatch continues. The youth screams: "Elder, not yet!" "Not now, *njomba!*" "Not like this!" The lishesho ends, and Banga continues to dance. "We're done, *njomba!*" The second movement does not go any better. Banga signals to the vinganga drummers: raise your voice! But he performs the nshakasha before the drum calls him. The mimetic styles do not amount to anything. The drummers are down. "We want to finish, *njomba!* Get ready!" Banga goes into a corner and pees: the *ingonda* must be too tight for him. He gets ready for the finale, but his twisted backward movement is performed as the drums are already silent. The choir screams nonetheless: "Miteda! Us!"

The veteran leaves the enclosure amid laughter. It is the end of the afternoon, and the funerary feast warms up toward its momentous finale. The choir, in Manchester United t-shirts, squat down and sing the character's song again:

| Akanaigwa, Guilherme Banga | The deaf one, Guilherme Banga |
| Banga nang'olo wetu nnanda | Our elder Banga is talented |
| E-e-e | *E-e-e*[45] |

After a long silence, the genre of *nshindo* reappeared in the Messalo lowlands in the late 1970s. The old masters of the Lipato hamlet had relocated to the communal villages of Mbau or to Myangalewa. The former founded a group called Shikelya, which briefly rose to political fame upon performing a version of the *Germans-in-the-Hamlet* (see chap. 4, sec. 2) for a visit of Raimundo Pachinuapa in 1977. The latter instructed young acolytes, who took up the lead of the ensembles and introduced new characters alongside the old ones. Among these was the deaf one *Guilherme Banga,* a character based on a real person, "a war veteran from the village of Miteda," but most importantly a parody of the triumphal genre of nshesho.[46] Through grotesque realism—the exaggeration of a physical defect—the performance highlights vanity at the expense of unity, the emptiness of political songs ("let us rejoice"), and the pompous gravity of revolutionary aesthetics. And what can better parody mapiko than mapiko itself?

# 9 ∽ Faceless Spirits
## The Rise and Fall of Feminist Masquerades

| | |
|---|---|
| Siyasha shavamama | The mamas' politics |
| Vamama vandipanga lipiko lyao | The mamas have arranged their mask |
| Vashema lina lingundumbwe | They gave it the name *lingundumbwe* |
| Ingonda andigwadya sana | It wears a gown all right |
| Vigwadyo andigwadya sana | It wears wearers all right |
| Kanji kulivaliva shinu shimu ing'ope | But they forgot one thing, the face |
| Lipiko shani likavé ing'ope? | What kind of mask doesn't have a face? |
| Kudyanga makomba lamashove | It's worse than the youth face-masks |

—NMA/Nshaila/Namwembe/2004

1. SO FAR, this story has been one of men. The women have appeared mostly as walk-ons: as willful partners in the game of secrecy; as the spectators who, by performing fear and respect, make the men's play desirable and important; as the silent presence that gives meaning to the game but remains silent nonetheless. What was the part of women in mapiko, besides applauding, desiring, watching, and mothering talented men?

The women's *shitengamatu* clay masks dance only in the secret of the bush, once a year, and for an audience of women only. I have not seen them and I know little about them; and that little, I will not tell. Why would I break the secret? Shitengamatu never had a stylistic history comparable to the men's mapiko. Its performance remained confined to a single moment of the ritual cycle; for this reason, it had little margin of diversifying its aesthetics into genres. The main transformation was to appropriate the men's wooden masks in the secret *nkamangu* ceremony, partly out of desire for the object and partly because clay masks tend to break easily (see chap. 2, sec. 3). A few women carvers emerged in the late colonial period, when it was difficult for the women to acquire a lipiko.[1] After Independence, if women desired to play with the masculine wooden toy, they could buy it from young carvers or complacent husbands. Or else they continued to use the old-fashioned fragile ceramic mask. In the history of mapiko, women seem condemned to the role of sparring partners. And though the value of the men's performance rests entirely on the presence of women—on the women's complicity, gaze, and desire—it is still the men who carry on the show.

2. Sickened by this state of things and prompted by the new feminist and antiobscurantist Frelimo rhetoric, a group of women guerrillas launched a surprise attack on masculine supremacy in its symbolic core. It was the uncertain year of 1974–75, just after the end of the war and before the declaration of Independence: the year of authority (madalaka), as it is called in Shimakonde.[2] The women were stationed in Beira Base, in the northerly district of Nangade, close to the Rovuma and to today's village of Litingina. As soldiers in a time of transition, they were busy with everyday chores, full of expectations and slightly bored. With a view to the celebration of Heroes' Day, the third of February, they started rehearsing something unheard-of. They prepared a feminine lipiko almost identical to the men's: dressed with cloths held by small bits of wood (vigwali, wearers), with an ingonda gown, two cloths crossed across the chest, and dinjuga iron bells around the waist. Instead of using a wooden mask, they rolled a cloth around the dancer's face (fig. 15). The group was led by one Filomena Ntonya, who danced the unorthodox faceless mask. The invention was called lingundumbwe, a name whose meaning remains obscure.[3]

We do not know how the men stationed at Beira Base reacted to the provocation. In fact, some claim that it never happened in this form and that lingundumbwe was invented in Mueda a few months later by a soldier named Josina Rafael on the occasion of Samora Machel's visit during the Rovuma-to-Maputo journey. Even in this version, the gist of the story remains the same: a group of women secretly prepares a lipiko dressed like the men's but with a cloth on the face and presents it as a bold surprise on the occasion of a grand state ceremonial.[4]

FIGURE 15. Defiant *(Rui Assubuji, Mueda, 2009)*

The invention spread quickly. In the years after Independence, lingundumbwe became the genre of the New Woman empowered by the revolution, a defiant counterpart to the masculine nshesho:

> We started dancing in the year of authority. During colonialism, only the men danced mapiko. [. . .] When we had authority, we tied up lingundumbwe. Because we were to have Independence. When we brought it out to the mango trees, people saw: "The women are rejoicing their Independence."[5]

Lingundumbwe ensembles were composed exclusively of women, who also took up drumming, a role generally reserved to men even in feminine dances. The dance consisted of one long lishesho movement performed on the drilling sound of three or four *makuti*, boosted by *mashanjo* can rattles—an instrument associated with wartime dances, especially *ngoda* (see chap. 7, sec. 2). Toward the end, the pace accelerated dramatically and the lipiko performed an inverted *nshakasha*, moving forward and in a circle, rather than backward and in a straight line.

The aesthetics of lingundumbwe was consonant with the principles of socialist realism and political praise. In the slower part, mimetic styles (*vikuvo*) were performed: including realistic actions or conditions, such as cultivating, soccer playing, festivity, and drunkenness; referring to other dances such as *shindimba*, *dutu*, and *shinalombo*; and even hinting at the secrets of masculine initiation, such as "because of the fish" [*Mwaa wa yomba*].[6] Lingundumbwe songs drew on the idiom of Makonde revolutionary singing, presenting the usual mix of date recitation, invocations to the leaders, and remembrances of struggle deeds. Unsurprisingly, the main figure evoked there was Josina Machel, the war heroine who championed the women's involvement in the struggle:

| | |
|---|---|
| Langale' tuke | Take the lead, let's go |
| Josina tuke | Josina take the lead, let's go |
| Samora nae, akuwatike | Samora, he follows you |
| Mondlane baba kuba' kunyuma | Mondlane baba stays at the back |
| kenga mwalimu waishama yetu | like the professor of our Party |
| Ashilangalela ku-Moshambiki | He used to lead Mozambique[7] |

3. The invention of lingundumbwe was indeed rooted in the political experiences of the Ten Years' War. Women were involved in the

struggle from its outset but, again, mostly in a supportive role: in the years before 1962 cooperating to conceal their husbands' political activities; then in the liberated zones supporting the war with production and smuggling material through the borders. Puberty rituals were used as a space for enrollment of young girls. Older women carried out the political indoctrination of *vali* during the rituals' seclusion phase, so that they would come out as wholehearted militants. Some of these girls were sent to work in the military bases, to help with domestic chores; many fell into the arms of commanders and political commissars, engaging in semisecret relations of concubinage. An unwanted pregnancy would result in the girl being sent back to live with her family in the liberated zones.[8]

In 1966, Frelimo's central committee created a women's corps, the mythic Destacamento Feminino (DF, Women's Detachment). The endeavor gestured toward the empowering of women, without engaging in an outright feminist position; it was nonetheless brave, insofar it challenged a deep-seated chauvinism in the heart of the liberation struggle. One of the first guerrillas who were sent to military training in Nachingwea recalls being held up for days at the border of Tanzania because—she was told—Nyerere was opposed to the idea of women soldiers and Mondlane had a hard time convincing him that this would not bring disorder and lewdness among the (male) troops.[9]

The subsequent history of the women's engagement in the struggle is blurred within the ideological mists of the 1968 crisis. The revolutionary line that emerged victorious accused the reactionaries—Nkavandame and Simango—of withholding gender transformations and fostering a patriarchal ethos, confining the women to the old roles of "producer, re-producer and source of sexual satisfaction."[10] The new leader, Samora Machel, declared the liberation of women as an utmost priority, "a battle inseparable from the development of the Revolution."[11] The enigmatic figure of Josina Muthemba emerged in a leadership role in this tormented transition. Josina had worked at the Instituto Moçambicano in association with Janet Mondlane and had been among the first twenty-five women to be officially trained as DF in Nachingwea. In 1968, Josina participated in Frelimo's Second Congress as a supporter of the revolutionary line. After Machel's takeover, she became his wife and the DF leader. She made an important contribution on women's empowerment in the magazine *Mozambique Revolution* and relentlessly worked at the front in the hard task of mobilizing the masses to unleash a radical transformation of gender relationships.[12]

According to those who listened to her passionate speeches at the war front, her interventions recurrently addressed three questions. First, Josina prompted women to challenge men's dominance and seek gender equality. Second, she mobilized women to contribute to education and taking care of orphans, which materialized specifically in the precious work that she performed in the Frelimo orphanages. Third, in line with Frelimo's antiobscurantist rhetoric, she championed the radical transformation of some of the most backward ritual institutions such as puberty rituals and their attendant gendered secrecy—institutions that, despite some positive aspects, she regarded as contributing to keeping women in a state of ignorant subjugation. While the first two points were embraced with enthusiasm by the crowds that Josina addressed—women's life in rural societies is filled with hardships and the sense of gender inequality acute—the third was met with embarrassed silences and resistance.[13]

Josina's health deteriorated quickly. In 1971 she addressed a large crowd in Itanda, close to Nangade, touching again on the question of rituals and secrecy. During the speech, her voice faltered and she bade farewell saying that she was not feeling well. She then crossed the border and went on to die in a hospital bed in Dar Es Salaam. Her name became shrouded in legend, and her memory was kept alive in the liberated zones. The seventh of April, the day of her death, became the national Women's Day as celebrated in this DF military anthem (fig. 16):

| Nelo ni liduva | Today is the day |
|---|---|
| Lyatulila | In which we cry |
| Lyatunkumbukila Josina Machel | In which we remember Josina Machel |
| | |
| Nae ashindava nanangaledi | She was the leader |
| Wavakongwe Vamoshambikano | Of the Mozambican women |
| Nkongwe waku-Kabu | Women from Cabo (Delgado) |
| Josina Machel | Josina Machel |
| Nkongwe Manyambane | Inhambane women |
| Nkongwe waing'ondo | Women of war |
| Josina Machel . . . | Josina Machel |

If Josina's attempts to undermine puberty rituals did not achieve their intended effect, the war contributed to the erosion of gendered secrecy through its own work of destabilization. DF guerrillas had an

FIGURE 16. Josina's day *(Rui Assubuji, Mwambula, 2009)*

uncertain status, somewhere in-between man and woman; although they underwent puberty rituals, they were sometimes called *namaako*, "uninitiated." The hardships and perils of war pushed the men and the women to moments of intimacy and disclosure: "What do you guys do at the *likumbi?*" "This and that . . . and what about your *ing'oma?*" These moments were rare: soldiers had other things on their mind, and the military's control on speech was otherwise strong. "People spoke with great secrecy. We spoke little. There were intimate relationships, but they were secret."[14]

These relationships existed nonetheless; lingundumbwe could possibly have been born through such confidences. Filomena Ntonya was apparently in an intimate relationship with Jerónimo Vintani, a soldier from Mocimboa who was a master of mapiko costuming and explained to her the technical secret through which a mask is tied up in such a way as to withstand the tensions of dancing. Whether these two characters—Filomena and Jerónimo—are real or mythical is not particularly relevant: the story of two lovers who, in the midst of the fires of war, share the secrets of initiation and forgo tradition iconically condenses an experience shared by many.

4. Stemming from the experiences of the Ten Years' War, lingundumbwe's roots also go back to the colonial period. The Diases describe in some detail a dance called *shinyala*, a vernacularization of the Portuguese word for *lady*:

> These girls represented the so-called *vinyala* (*shinyala* = *senhora*), that used to dance on the Monday following the first day of a *ngoma*. [. . .] Here, [the dancers] were young girls, who however learned to dance with the elder women. [. . .] They advanced slowly with their gaze cast downwards. They gave little steps and stopped. Finally, they arrived close to the drums. A group of women formed around them, which danced with gentle movements of the shoulder blades and undulations of the loins, tapping the feet with the hands open towards the outside, like in some oriental dances. [. . .] Generally, they danced in pairs while a third one sat in a chair.[15]

The movements described here—shoulder blades and loin undulations (*myongo dukuduka*)—are typical of *vitengamatu* masks.[16] The Diases did not make that connection but remarked that "the dance had a prominent ritual character." Very much like mapiko and shinalombo, the women's vinyala was punctuated by carnivalesque interludes:

> Two women began a dialogue that was very funny, not only because of what they were saying, but also for the expressions and mimicry. One of them, while talking, smacked her lips so that the compressed air pushed her *ndona*, which came out a bit from the lip and went back in when she opened the mouth; this was truly grotesque. Then, they spoke as if they had a diction defect, pretending to be very angry. The public was delirious.[17]

The dance, which at the beginning of the ceremony had young girls as the protagonists, eventually captured older women with a magnetism reminiscent of trance possession:

> Little by little, the rhythm of the drums took hold of the women; the older ones experimented [with] some dance steps and finally could not resist any longer. They undid the upper cloth that covered their breasts, tied it in a special way around their waist and began to dance. [. . .] Even a pregnant woman, towards the end of the dance, could not resist. One could see how there was a fight inside her between the desire to dance and the feeling that the state in which she was could not have helped. But in the end the enthusiasm for the dance had the upper hand.[18]

Themselves captives of their ritualist bias, the Diases did not observe or report that vinyala enjoyed a great popularity outside of the context of initiation.[19] In the late colonial period, the two main feminine dances were *nkala* and *nshaila*—both of which were stylish circular dances drummed by men and with a strong singing component. At the same time, shinyala was taken out of its strictly ritual context and brought to the public field of play and competition. Shinyala groups formed, almost as timid equivalents to the men's mapiko. They were called to dance for initiation rituals but performed also for weekends and holidays. "Shinyala comes from afar. In the beginning—because we used to put [the girls in] the ritual—we danced shinyala as they came out of the house. We rubbed white paint all over the face. Then we took it to dance on the field."[20]

Although the vinyala were not the object of ritual prohibitions of secrecy, the process of preparation of the dancers was referred to with the same verb used for the men's masks, *kupanga* ("to dress, to prepare"). The process of transformation was deemed more important than the actual headpiece; though faceless (*bila ing'ope*), vinyala can thus be considered as masks embodying an ancestral spirit.[21] The body of the vinyala was adorned with one cloth tied around the hips and two crossing over the chest. She wore on the head a long sisal wig, straightened and braided, and her face was painted in white. This faceless mask was a grotesque depiction of a white lady who has just shampooed her hair. For this reason, some called it *shampunga*, a wordplay with *shampoo*. The song associated with the character describes it as a decayed lady:

| | |
|---|---|
| Shampunga e-e | Shampoo, *e-e* |
| Avé shinyala kala | Once she was a lady |
| Maduvano nshenji | Nowadays she's a savage |

The dance of shinyala can be located within the regional history of feminine possession dances in which women are seized by the spirits of foreign people.[22] The early twentieth century saw an intensification of such dances, possibly as a consequence of the erosion of the matrilineal systems, which undermined the symbolic prestige of women.[23] Meanwhile, *majini* healing practices of coastal origin came to the interior together with Islam, mingling with older forms of spirit possession.[24] While possession by spirits per se does not exist among the Makonde—possibly because the practice of masks fulfills some of the same psychological functions—the appearance of the infectious drum of the white lady is related to this broad historical dynamic.

Located within mapiko's history of genre, however, shinyala appears as a feminine equivalent of the masculine dutu. Both drew their driving metaphors from the world of slavery: the masculine dutu by affirming the equivalence of all bodies (meat-is-meat); the feminine shinyala by staging a playful inversion in which the "savage" takes the part of the master, herself decayed to the status of "savage." Unlike dutu, shinyala represented a specific character. By becoming public, however, the dance moved toward the formal disconnection and abstraction that characterized dutu. As can be seen from the Diases' description, the dancers performed choreographic styles (*vikuvo*) previously rehearsed with the drummers. A variety of new songs were composed alongside the main one, elliptic and abstract as in dutu:

| | |
|---|---|
| Likangolo wena kashele | The bamboo, go and cut it |
| Lyangu lyó | This one is mine[25] |

Shinyala was the incipient creation of a feminine public mapiko, beginning with the representation of a specific character anchored in ritual practice but slowly becoming a genre with a broader expressive range. This dynamic, however, was interrupted by the armed struggle. With the curtain of silence imposed by the war, the main feminine dances of the late colonial era—nkala and nshaila—were all but abandoned. Shinyala reverted to its ritual function, as a dance of celebration of feminine rituals, less and less performed as the war intensified. Ultimately, women were left to handclap to the men's *magita* and *ngoda*, at best to sing, to the rhythm of wooden logs, a music called *ding'uni* ("wood"). As the war ended and lingundumbwe appeared, it could present itself as something new and revolutionary. But many elderly women drew the connection with the old shinyala. They pointed out a pattern following which the dance movements of "inside the house" (*nng'ande*) and "out in the bush" (*kumwito*)—the secret spaces of feminine initiation—were brought into the open. Filomena Ntonya herself had been a shinyala dancer. These commonalities appeared more important than the changes and the new names:

> These names. . . . we call it vinyala, vinyala, vinyala. One year everything turns upside down and we leave it. And we call it another name. Don't be mistaken: lingundumbwe is one and the same with vinyala. During colonialism, it was another place; under Frelimo, it's something else. [. . .] As we saw that we are going to be free, we abandoned that name, and we picked lingundumbe, and now we got to *utamaduni*.[26]

5. Despite these continuities, lingundumbwe introduced a fundamental element of rupture: the usage of wooden "wearers" (*vigwali*) to tie up the cloths around the body and of the ingonda around the pelvis, in a way that closely resembled the men's mapiko. Both vigwali and ingonda are considered the deepest technical secrets in the dressing of a lipiko, difficult to master in such a way as to make the cloths adhere to the body and the knots endure the dance's abrupt movements. Otherwise, lingundumbwe respected a few fundamental thresholds: it did not wear a corset charged with dinjuga iron bells, which were instead tied around the waist, emphasizing the hips and evoking femininity; it performed the nshakasha but not as a separate movement and in an inverted form; and it substituted a cloth for the mask.

These courtesies were not sufficient, however, and the dance soon awoke the men's wrath. The men considered the invention offensive and encroaching and fought it with all means: in the domestic space, by using marital authority, and sometimes even violence, to forbid the women to dance; and in public, by demanding that the government ban the dance and threatening to drop mapiko if the ban was not enforced. The men considered lingundumbwe as a disorderly dangerous provocation, and the women gave them reasons to argue so:

| | |
|---|---|
| Mapiko letu lo' Josina | Look at our mapiko Josina |
| Iyanje | It's bad speech |
| Kudong'a kwetu kwamashanjo viva | We clap hands with rattles, *viva!* |

The responses to this masculine backlash were varied. Mostly in the area of Nangade, women settled on a watered-down version of lingundumbwe dressed without vigwali. The cloths around the body were instead secured with vegetable ropes disposed horizontally across, like lowland "slave masks" (see chap. 5, sec. 6). Nangade is a district located at the margins of the plateau and exposed to many influences, where the rules of secrecy and respect are not as stringent. By eliminating the most offensive element, the women could strike a truce with the men and lingundumbwe coexisted peacefully with nshesho:

| | |
|---|---|
| Mapiko letu lamangundumbwe | Our mapiko *mangundumbwe* style, |
|   tupange shana Josina |   let's dress it well, Josina |
| Amunavajedye valume | Don't imitate the men |
| Baba Kumposha andyunga nkono | Baba Kumposha shook hands |
| Amunavagwadye vigwali | Don't wear wearers |
| Amunavajedye valume | Don't imitate the men[27] |

Others withstood the aggression and struck back. In the village of Shidwadwa, also in Nangade, the women responded by crossing another threshold, dancing lingundumbwe in two movements with a distinctive nshakasha performed backwards, precisely like the men's mapiko. Because the government did not intervene, the men abandoned their own mapiko and the women won the battle. In Mueda, the ancient group of lingundumbwe sought the government's protection against spousal violence and other forms of pressure. The government intervened half-heartedly, on the one hand protecting lingundumbwe and its dancers, on the other asking the women to be accommodating and to leave space for the men, who refused to perform alongside them on the occasion of festivals.

In the district of Muidumbe, where the government is weaker and the rules of ritual secrecy stronger, the women gave up. In the early and mid-1980s, as the civil war raged in the country, lingundumbwe was replaced with a new dance called *utamaduni*. Musically and choreographically, the two were similar: songs and dancing styles were carried over wholesale from one to the other. Only the offensive elements of costuming were dropped. Three or four girls—dressed stylishly with bandanas, sunglasses, and cloths around the loins—took the lead dancing role, cheered, encouraged, and hand-clapped by the elder women; significantly, they were still called *mapiko*. *Utamaduni* was a translation in Kiswahili of the name of a new educational dance introduced in the feminine initiation rituals after the revolution, called *kurtura* (culture, from the Portuguese *cultura*), the equivalent of the masculine makwaela (see chap. 7, sec. 7); like its ancestor shinyala, it was an initiation dance taken out to the public. Utamaduni groups began to form in all the villages of the Muidumbe region, sometimes more than one in each. The groups clustered around feminine masters of initiation (*vanalombo*) and functioned as support structures for the carrying out of puberty rituals. The women embraced the new dance enthusiastically, without apparent nostalgia for the quasi-mask that they were leaving behind.[28]

Discussing the reasons for the change, many women critiqued lingundumbwe not because it was too provocative but because it lacked originality and was a mere imitation of men. In other terms, lingundumbwe broke a fundamental unwritten rule of the schismogenetic game of secrecy: competition between men and women must always be complementary, leading to progressive gender differentiation and not escalating into gender warfare (see chap. 2, sec. 3). Only in dance competition within sexes—men against men, women against women—can the schismogenesis be symmetrical, with all the risks involved. But lingundumbwe groups did not compete with each other: they openly competed with the men, disrupting their performance and seeking to draw crowds from the nshesho groups. Partly because of the shock of the novelty, partly because of the talent and artistry, they often succeeded in their mission:

> —When we come out to the open and we meet them as they dance, all people leave them and fill up our side. And that annoys them.

—They see you dominating (*kutawala*)?

—*Eeeh*. And we truly dominate. We dominate, truly. In that moment? We dominate. If you are ill, your illness will heal, right there![29]

Utamaduni reestablished the schismogenetic balance. It maintained the fiction that the dancers were not masks, although the dance was of a ritual nature and sometimes referred to as "the ladies' mapiko." The groups competed among themselves, creating broad networks of exchange between villages, reinforced on the occasion of festival and puberty rituals. Within the villages, utamaduni groups twinned with nshesho groups, traveling together to festivals, the men drumming in the women's ensembles and the women singing in the men's. The two genres indeed had much in common: they both abided by the rules of respect and secrecy; and they were both steeped in socialist aesthetics, with their revolutionary songs and realist choreographies. Utamaduni also borrowed from nshesho the lexicon of political provocation—accusing rivals of bad speech and boasting of one's political pedigree. As it gained ground in the villages, utamaduni cut itself a prominent space in the provincial radio's broadcasts beside its masculine twin—an honor never bestowed on the contested lingundumbwe.

Despite the enthusiasm and the re-equilibration, the shift from the defiant lingundumbwe to the more accommodative utamaduni can be seen as a poignant metaphor for the trajectory of the Mozambican gender revolution, which ground to a halt after the first years of Independence. The rise and decline of lingundumbwe echoes the sense of betrayal and shattered hopes expressed by many members of the DF: the melancholic feeling that the empowering years of the liberation struggle were the high point of a downward parabola.[30]

6. This melancholia lurks in both utamaduni and lingundumbwe songs, which are not cast in the bold mold of nshesho choirs but unfold in long and tormented descending scales. The death and legacy of Josina Machel crystallize feelings of forlornness, expressed through the metaphor of orphanhood:

| Malala kwanja nintangashidye | Lie still, so I can tell you |
| Malaililo amwe Josina | The farewell of Josina |
| Mwaka apadile | In the year when she died |

| Malaililo amwe Josina | Josina's farewell |
|---|---|
| "Utamaduni amunaleke | "Don't leave culture |
| Mwenu iyanje leka uwavi leka | You, leave envious speech, leave sorcery |
| Lishunge mene mananshiva" | Take care of yourselves, you orphans" |
| Ata mwiu tuvananshinva | And truly we are orphans |
| Nanangaledi napagwa shinu | We don't have a leader any longer |
| Ata kwatalau napagwa shinu | We don't even have quarters |
| Lishunge mene mananshiva | Take care of yourselves, you orphans |

These feelings resurface on the occasion of the death of feminine leaders such as Maria Chipande:

| Malala kwanja nintangashidye | Lie still, so I can tell you |
|---|---|
| Adi dimu dyatwimba wetu dyakulilanga | These songs that we sing are tearful |
| Tuninnangila Malia mama andituleka | We cry for mama Maria, she left us |
| Shipande baba andipakanyanga | Baba Chipande said |
| "Ushwang'a madada Maria ndyangu napela shinu | "This is a lie, sisters, my wife Maria didn't die |
| Ninkunnindila kung'ande kwangu | I am waiting for her at my house |
| Anangukodya" | She will find me there"[31] |

The dictates of socialist realism demanded that dance groups tell "things that exist and that we see with our eyes."[32] In the majority of Makonde song genres, this translated into the celebration of struggle deeds and much more rarely in topicality. The implicit injunction of praising the leaders was stronger than the explicit injunction of socialist realism, and who dared to describe difficulties and crises realistically? Utamaduni choirs managed to break this double bind. Turning melancholia into anger, they dared to address the leaders with outright expressions of dissatisfaction and bleak depictions of poverty:

| Pamwalela petu pakumene | Mwalela, our home is a big place |
|---|---|
| Katikati Mweda na Nangadi | Halfway between Mueda and Nangade |
| Shivalela vana vananshiva | It is full of orphans |
| Dishikola 'napagwa shinu | There are no schools |
| Ata medi 'napagwa shinu | There is not even water[33] |

Outright rage (*shitundwe*, "nerves") was vented against masculine figures of authority, who were accused of abandoning the rural areas despite the political support received from the peasantry:

| | |
|---|---|
| Shitundwe wetu shipali | Rage, we have it |
| Akunu kwetu ku-Moshambiki | Here in our Mozambique |
| Vakulima vankuvenao shitundwe shoe | The peasants are filled with rage |
| Chissano baba wetu tundakudya | Chissano, father, we ask you |
| Ing'ondo kwetu indimalilika | The war now is over |
| Dibei mene kupungula | The prices won't go down |
| Pacheco baba wetu tundakudya | Father Pacheco we ask you |
| Ushagushi undipita shana | The elections went well |
| Dibei mene kupungula | The prices won't go down |
| Aunatwone kujanda wetu | Can't you see us becoming skinny? |
| Tujanda shitundwe | We become skinny because of rage |
| Kwetu ku-Moshambiki | In our Mozambique |
| Tujanda shitundwe | We become skinny because of rage |
| Wetu kujanda kwoe | Us, we slim down lots[34] |

Songs and dancing styles in utamaduni were widely exchanged. Feminine solidarity was often stronger than the spirit of rivalry, and imitation was not so overtly stigmatized. Relayed by many utamaduni groups, momentous songs swept the villages in waves. A widespread song, for instance, expressed a skeptical view of the invitation addressed by the government to the veterans to register their names in order to receive pensions:

| | |
|---|---|
| Baba Chissano jo kushema | Papa Chissano calls us |
| Vanantenda ing'ondo vaide | The war-makers should come |
| Vakataké pamo | So that they lose together |
| Vakupata vapate | Those who will receive, will receive |
| Vakukatoka vakatoke | Those who will lose, will lose |
| Vakataké pamo | So that they lose together |

These expressions of social critique, which largely remained confined to the genre of utamaduni, took as their favorite object the men. This was a way of prolonging gender struggle after having surrendered the faceless mask. Utamaduni songs targeted especially the self-inflated ego of pension-receiving war veterans:

| Kwalala sana antigo kwaulyona lina lyumile | What beauty do you see when your name comes out |
|---|---|
| Kwalala sani baba? | What kind of beauty? |
| Paushiswalalanga panangu pangu nikwona | When you dragged yourself on my porch, I saw you |
| Kwalala sani baba? | What kind of beauty? |
| Paushinyambikanga navana vako | When you were tattered in front of your children |
| Kwalala sani baba? | What kind of beauty? |
| Paushitaa ugwala navamaringwe nangu ndikwona | When you poured drinks with the maringue people, I saw you |
| Kwalala sani baba? | What kind of beauty? |
| Antigo ida ida | Veteran, come come |
| Ungupe yela yangu tukana' kulala pamo | Pay me my money before we sleep together |
| Ungupe yela yangu tukana' kuje' lishesho | Pay me my money before we shoot the dancing styles |
| Ungupe yela yangu tukana' kuje' nshakasha | Pay me my money before we dance the nshakasha[35] |

The critique of men sometimes exceeded topicality to take a broad existential tone:

| Muduniani ukalola | In the world, if you consider it |
|---|---|
| Vatubyaidya wetu valume | Who kills us, it's the men |
| Nkati mudunia | In the world |
| Vanyaku' mapinde valume | Who carries the bows, it's the men |
| Vanyaku' mashoka valume | Who carries the axes, it's the men[36] |

7. In her inaugural text on the liberation of women, Josina Machel remarked that women should perform an important role in the Department of Security, being "constantly on the look-out for enemy infiltration."[37]

As Mozambique rapidly moved from Independence to civil war—initially fostered by the neighboring white supremacist governments, then taking a life of its own—the phantasmic Enemy of the People received a very concrete face: the one of the *contra* movement Renamo (Resistência Nacional Moçambicana). Initially, the Makonde Plateau was scarcely affected by the war, which unfolded farther south. In 1984

Renamo extended its operation to Cabo Delgado province.[38] In 1990, Renamo bands occupied the Messalo lowlands, from which they subjected the villages built on the edge of the plateau ravines to bazooka fire. In 1991, the rebels hit at the heart of Frelimo, climbing the plateau areas of Muidumbe and occupying the historical Mission of Nangololo for three days, until they were fended off by organized groups of popular militias. Shortly thereafter, peace came (1992), followed by the ballot box (1994).

The end of socialism brought, among other things, a new discourse of reconciliation that left no place for figures such as enemies, traitors, spies, scoundrels, bandits, and *xiconhocas*. The denunciation of the political Enemy was at the heart of Frelimo's aesthetics, and Makonde dances struggled to give it up. Reconciliation was experienced by many as betrayal or surrender. But dance groups had to adapt to the new rules, also considering that the radio would not air explicit anti-Renamo songs. Nshesho groups continued to vaunt the execution of counterrevolutionaries at the time of the struggle (see chap. 7, sec. 6). Women refused to give up the denunciation of enemies in general and of Renamo in particular. Using Samora Machel's name of "hyenas" (*matunu*) or other euphemisms drawn from the animal domain, scathing attacks on Renamo continued to be at the center of utamaduni songs well into the democratic period.[39] Defying the precepts of reconciliation, painful memories were brought out, which sometimes did not correspond to lived experience but relayed propagandistic films projected by local officers on the occasion of elections:

| | |
|---|---|
| Atuntamwa Jakama atuntamwa | We refuse him, Dhlakama, we refuse him |
| Vitendyo vyake vyashitutenda | The actions that he did to us |
| Jakama ashindauma mwanda | Dhlakama used to go out |
| Akawika mudyaludeya | If he arrived at villages |
| Kunkodya mwana kutwa' luvani kunjanikila | Find a child, take a bayonet and skewer him |
| Mwene mwanda | And then leave |
| Atuntamwa Jakama atuntamwa | We refuse him, Dhlakama, we refuse him |
| Jakama akauma mwanda | Dhlakama if he went around |
| Akawika mudyaludeya | And arrived at villages |
| Kukodya ing'ande kutwala moto kushashakedya mwene mwanda | Find a house, put it to fire and let it burn, and then leave[40] |

Women remained attached to socialist aesthetics even more than men did. They were the keenest and steadiest participants in state festivals. Following the old ritual practice of "telling the lion" (*kwaula ntumi*, [see chap. 3, sec. 5]), they went out announcing the visit of leaders and national days, circulating at the break of dawn around the villages, singing and dancing. They volunteered for collective cleaning and defended the symbols of the Party against the possible disrespect brought by masculine drunkenness. Representatives of the Mozambican Women's Organization (OMM, Organização da Mulher Moçambicana) were the most vocally supportive and the most visually homogeneous, all wearing the inevitable cloths with the face of Josina Machel or the OMM emblem. They heeded the call of the Party, justifying the social critique and the refusal to let go of the anger against the Enemy as deep-seated fidelity.

Feminine cultural groups called *likulutu* ("military training" [see chap. 7, sec. 2]) enacted the feats of women guerrillas during the liberation struggle. Dressed in military uniforms, they demonstrated marching, carrying of materials (*materiali*), assaults (*ashatu*), and anti-aerial combat (*anterea*), as well as more elaborate theatrical sketches. The old deeds of vigilance and punishment were directly plugged into the democratic present. Marching in national ceremonials, all dressed in uniforms and with wooden weapons, likulutu groups intoned their stern signature tune:

| | |
|---|---|
| Ngupita nguwenawena ndyaludeya | I roam the villages |
| Kuvalambela vanambili | Looking for partridges |
| Kwavapulike navona avó | I can't see where they crowd |
| Lude' Lutete nindiwika | I arrived in the village of Lutete |
| Kuvalambela vanambili | Looking for partridges |
| Kwavapulike navona avó | I can't find where they crowd |
| Tunkande tunkande tunkande Jakama | Let's stomp stomp stomp Dhlakama |
| Tunkande-e-e | Let's stomp him[41] |

On the occasion of elections, women organized symbolic puberty rituals to propitiate the victory of Frelimo candidates.[42] The women's attachment to the old socialist order—and the punishment of counter-revolutionaries that was at its core—extended beyond the domain of aesthetics and ritual. During the elections in 1994, 1999, and 2005, women's groups taunted Renamo supporters; forced them to lie on their beds for hours holding Frelimo pamphlets; and went around in triumphal processions in the villages after an electoral victory "looking for partridges," sometimes even lynching them or burning their homes.[43] Far from being the prerogative of men, political violence in the democratic period was symbolically channeled and physically carried out largely through the agency of women.

8. On the occasion of the festivities for the fortieth anniversary of the first shot of the liberation struggle, in the district of Chai, a likulutu group from the nearby village of Kabu enacted a series of historical sketches about the Ten Years' War. In the final one, a woman was discovered by a popular committee as she was stealing a blanket to keep her sick child warm. "Traitor!" the committee cried out. The woman begged for forgiveness, to no avail. Popular stoning was the appropriate punishment. This was a version of Antigone, staging the insoluble conflict between two moral imperatives: the law of the city versus the ties of blood. Here, though, the sketch was bereft of any compassion for the culprit: it celebrated the punishment as a righteous feat and without any apparent sense of tragedy. The woman was rightly executed; the story just evokes the hardships of war.[44] People applauded as the traitor fell down. Under another mango tree, a dozen meters away, a nshindo group from Kabu was performing its parade of ambivalent morality.

We have so far followed Bakhtin's views of ambivalence, which interpret it as a philosophical attitude of "jolly relativism," the embracing of contraries and a dialogical approach to truth. Psychoanalysis provides a darker genealogy. Ambivalence there is the result of contradictory feelings toward a figure of authority—love and hate, identification and rejection—wherein the second term is always repressed and surfaces in violent ways, often vented against substitutive targets.[45] This second form of ambivalence is at the heart of all totalitarian aesthetics, based on the celebration of leaders, the scapegoating of enemies, and the repression of political critique. It emerges very clearly in the case of women, in which the process of identification was thwarted by the death of Josina and the continuing prominence of men in political life.

It is not difficult to interpret the women's nostalgia for the socialist order as stemming from a disillusion with the gender revolution that faded out in the years after Independence, and the rage against the Enemy as the venting of repressed ambivalence, the transfer of a dissatisfaction that could not be channeled toward its real target—the men who continued to hold power, foster chauvinism, and withhold gender transformations. This interpretation is easy, perhaps even facile, considering that women have been mobilized as symbolic supporters of the nation in different settings in postcolonial Africa, from Malawi to Tanzania and beyond.[46] But I am a man, and what do I know?

# PART FOUR

〜

# After Socialism (1992–2009)

The demise of socialism, more than a phenomenon that can be inscribed in a linear chronology, is a figure of mourning. It announces the death of a collective mode of life, which lingers on as anachronism; it interrupts the future and tinges the past with nostalgia. In Mozambique, the end of socialism coincided with the coming of peace after the civil war (1992) and the ballot box (1994). In the heartland of the revolution, the enthusiasm for peace and democracy was soured by the perception of a surrender to the enemies of the People, as embodied in the legalized party Renamo, and more generally to a political culture of disorder. This final part explores the invention of new mapiko genres in the aftermath of socialism until the first Guebuza presidency—a period marked by exhilaration, anxiety, and nostalgia and by the rediscovery of carnivalesque ambivalence as an aesthetic alternative to socialist seriousness.

Chapter 10, "Don't Go Astray," begins with the flamboyant genre of animal masquerades invented in the year of peace, which quickly spread among the generation of youths born in the first years of Independence. To understand the genre's historicity, the chapter moves back to explore its ancestor, a large-eared jester character introduced after Independence. Both genres are rooted in collective generational experiences, yet came about through haphazard histories of invention.

Chapter 11, "Puppets and Machetes," describes two masquerades invented in the new millennium: a machete-carrying youth genre, and the unique creation of an eccentric old man. The two forms provide complementary viewpoints on life in postsocialist communal villages, marked by the increasing influence of global media and by the perception of a lapse into an (old) new world of predation and violence.

# 10 ⌘ Don't Go Astray
## Democracy and Disorder

| | |
|---|---|
| A-e video | A-e video |
| Matambalale video | In Matambalale, videos |
| Tunkulodya video | We are showing videos |
| Wako dada 'nalombwe | You sister don't get married |
| Tupwashalane mpwerule | Let's help each other for free |
| Tunkupeja namoto | We hasten, with fire |
| Ana' kummwona nkoko | Who has not yet seen a beast |
| Nelo nnole | Today, watch it |

—NMA/Mang'anyamu/Matambalale/2004

1. DURING THE civil war, the Makonde Plateau was isolated for many years. Since Renamo had entered the Cabo Delgado province in 1984, communications were difficult and traveling was restricted to military convoys. As Renamo set foot in the Messalo lowlands in 1990 — burning, sacking, and occupying the communal villages of Mapate and Mandela—the plateau was cut off from the provincial capital and left like an anguishing island on a sea of flames. With the end of the war, routes and channels opened up again. In 1997, the renowned photographer Sérgio Santimano made his way to Mueda, like others in those years, on a quest to reconnect with the debris of the revolution. Following an acquaintance, he hitched a ride to the village of Matambalale in the district of Muidumbe. There, he saw mapiko that left him wide-mouthed: a bunch of wild animals—lion, rhino, monkey, leopard, buffalo, and crocodile—dressed in tattered sweaters and wearing old sneakers, dancing energetically to the sound of hoe blades. He photographed the masquerade, which, he was told, was a novelty in the

village. Santimano was left to wonder about the new animal mapiko. He thought, "These people must have been so tremendously isolated, so cut off from everything because of the war, so given to nature (*entregues à natureza*) that they had almost turned wild. The only thing that they must have seen in years is wild beasts, and that's what they dance."[1]

A few years later, in January 2002, the animal masks surprised Atanásio Cosme Nhussi (see chap. 8, sec. 8) and myself when we first went to the plateau to carry out fieldwork. Atanásio had not visited Cabo Delgado for years. Apart from stories of wondrous mapiko heard from his father and a brief youthful experience of *mashindano* in southern Tanzania, he knew no other genre but the triumphal nshesho of puberty rituals and revolution, of which he was himself a master.[2] He had been to Mueda again in 1994 to dance *Ode a Paz* ("Ode to Peace"), an educational ballet choreographed by his brother Casimiro, meant to explain the functioning of democracy. In the ballet, a lipiko played the part of a treacherous candidate using his power to influence the electoral result.[3] Local mapiko players attended the rehearsal and warned him to dress the mask properly and respectably, which he did with their assistance. He left the plateau with an impression of the place as a stronghold of traditionalism.

The animal masks popped up in a corner of the communal village of Vintequatro de Março, on a festive wet Sunday in which puberty rites were coming out, announced by the sharp piercing sound of hoe blades, rounded off by a deeper drum. The tattered animals performed acrobatic feats and gimmicks, rolled on the ground, and scared the bystanders; a large crowd followed them, and wherever they stopped to dance they were tipped. Now and then, the dancers slipped off into corners and porches to have a drink of strong acidic palm wine, or hid in the bushes and quickly raised their masks to have a puff of a cigarette. The song lyrics were boastful and polyphonic, spiced up with Kiswahili and Portuguese words as in the old times of migrant song-carvers. The dance, we were told, was called *mang'anyamu* —a word that Atanásio could not make sense of. As we approached the itinerant troupe to film their prowess, the elated drummer Malyamungu confronted us, asking for money to "take" (*kutwala*) the dance. We paid, filmed, and made friends. Based in Mwambula, the district's main village, the group was one among many dancing mang'anyamu. After Santimano had visited the plateau, the animal masks had spread around like wildfire. Atanásio arranged with the group to teach him the dance, so that he might introduce it into the repertoire of the Companhia Nacional de Canto e Dança (CNCD). Disappointed with the CNCD's recent turn to contemporary dance, Atanásio took the animal masks as examples of what real African contemporary dance should be about: globalized, momentous, and hip but still stemming from the roots (*de raíz*). "They call it traditional," he mused, "but *this* is our contemporary."

As Atanásio left for Maputo, Malyamungu became my research assistant (see chap. 2, sec. 4). A year later, in June 2003, I went with him to the First Festival of Mapiko organized by the Provincial Directorate of Culture in Mueda, on the anniversary of the massacre. Only "real" mapiko groups—meaning, ritually and politically correct nshesho— were allowed to perform at the festival; contemporary accretions such as mang'anyamu were deemed inauthentic and excluded. After the festival, we interviewed Joana Makai, the elder who had presided over the jury. To tease Malyamungu, I inquired about the exclusion of the animal masks. The elder answered contemptuously: "These came out now-now. They have not even ten years . . . These dances, they are not dances that are worth something (*kawaida*). Now, when a *ling'anyamu* comes out, it impresses people, because of being many. Now, these, now . . . *nada*." Malyamungu laughed. A stranger sitting in Makai's yard overheard the conversation and commented loudly, "That's democracy!" (fig. 17). Makai took up the cue and elaborated further: "True.

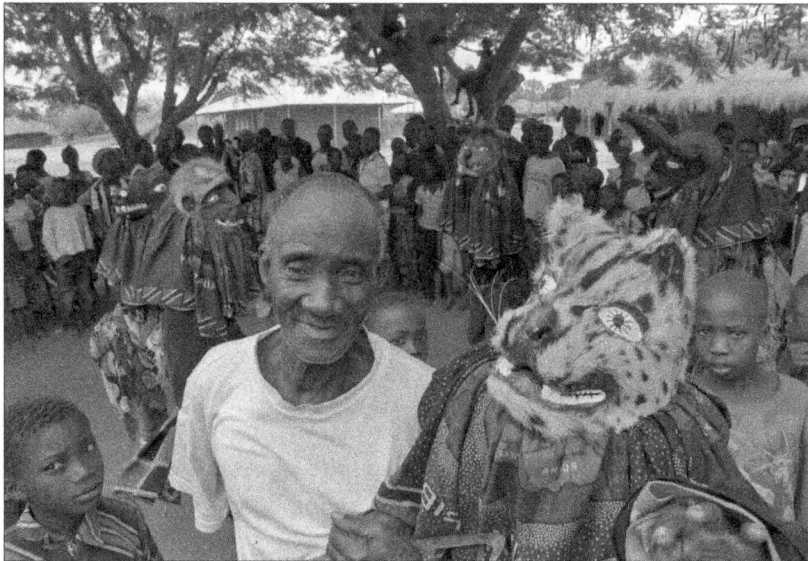

FIGURE 17. A tolerant elder: Luis Amissi (*Rui Assubuji, Myangalewa, 2009*)

Because you see, democracy is like this: everybody can act as they see fit. Now, if you look at matters of culture in such a way . . ."[4]

Whence did mang'anyamu emerge? Was it the result of isolation, almost a regression to a feral state, as Santimano imagined? Was it a hip product of cultural globalization, as Nhussi wanted it? Or was it a degeneration induced by democratic pluralism, as Makai implied? What did mang'anyamu mean for those who practiced it? Why had it spread so momentously throughout the villages in the postwar period?

2. To answer these questions, we must take a step back and consider a much older and enigmatic character. Large-eared mapiko headpieces appear in great numbers in extant collections. They are characterized by a dark-gray complexion, protuberant white eyes, a pointed chin and prominent cheekbones, worry wrinkles (*shinyadinyadi*) on the forehead, and broad enigmatic smiles. Some of these pieces are geometric and essential; others, realistically grotesque, with huge dentures and distorted features—but they clearly belong to the same type. The large-eared masks are known in the literature as *nijale* or *neijale*. Experts have been at odds in interpreting them. Some have observed a resemblance with the humanized hare masks described by Karl Weule in southern Tanzania (see chap. 3, sec. 2); others have ascribed them to the category of the *shetani*, the devilish spirit of Makonde modern carving; and still others have interpreted them as elder figures.

This large-eared mask comes from afar. Its ancestor was a character called *Mbangi* ("the dumb"), which was deployed as a decoy during the "old wars" (*ding'ondo dyanyanyamala*), which led to the Portuguese conquest of the Makonde Plateau (1917–21). *Mbangi* would be prepared and sent out from the thick of the bush to dance grotesquely as a column of Portuguese soldiers passed. The soldiers watched, perplexed by the bizarre apparition, without realizing that it was the prelude to a deadly ambush. "They used to take out this mask, and it goes around *shiti-shiti, linyo-nyo*. The white people go, 'Bah, what's this?' And as they said 'what's this?' that's it. They are killing them."[5] The Makonde attacked with arrows and arquebuses, and the large-eared decoy gave them time to aim and flee, but in the end it could do little to prevent the occupation.

As the mask's military usage faded into tradition, *Mbangi* was reinvented as a comical character that danced at *matanga* funerary ceremonies. "It was a mapiko of laughter: [*screaming*] 'Here comes

Mbangi, this one!'" [*Mbangi, aida Mbangi jó!*].⁶ As nshindo flourished in the lowlands, *Mbangi* was incorporated into the great ambivalent parade of animals, vices, and social others. It was especially in vogue in the area of ku-Iyanga, at kuna-Mbudi, where it was mastered by one Bulashi Nkonde, and in the group of Lipato himself. The large-eared mask also had a life of its own in the genres of dutu and nshesho, in which it was appropriated and danced outside of its original characterization. During the Ten Years' War, *Mbangi* was silenced together with all the other drums.

In 1976, two veterans from the communal village of Mapate, called Nang'oma and Faustino Kabu, travelled to M'Bau and saw the large-eared mask dancing at a funerary ceremony. They liked it and sought to reinvent it in their own village. At the beginning, the character was merely farcical: it climbed a tree and danced on top of it, and performed other gimmicks. "It was something for laughing, not something for dancing with artistry (*ulanda*)."⁷ Some of its styles were inspired by a local colonial-era mask called *Kalilambe*, which had a mobile mouth and could eat food and drink; others, by another local mask, *Namwombwe* the beekeeper.⁸ Eventually, the invention was enriched and refined. Two new masks were carved: one of a beautiful woman—who wore a pregnant belly under her clothes, which she would eventually show—and the other of a child. The three characters, which constituted a family, were named *João Anabadula Neijale, Fátima Aju Lekashipya,* and *Gong'o Gong'o João Anabadula. Neijale* was "an elder with a skin-bag, who sets traps, forges metal and crushes ticks; and who smokes tobacco in a pipe as he does all that, because he is an elder. An old man."⁹ The woman pranced around showing her pregnant belly, and the child performed comical sketches.

*Neijale* was in every way a nshindo character. It was dressed like one, with black cloths kept together by horizontal vegetable strings; it danced a long lishesho to the sound of *mashanjo* can-rattles and *makuti* drums commanded by the loud *ntojo*; and it offered a grotesque representation of peasant activities, with the large-eared protagonist struggling to light a fire or smother metal. After the mimetic dancing styles, the rhythm underwent a sudden dramatic acceleration, in which the mask performed a quick shaking movement with the pelvis and the arms, which also made its large-eared head turn around. The name *Anabadula*, meaning "he cannot break" or "he doesn't share," contained a moralizing critique against laziness and avarice; so did the wife's name, "she cannot keep secrets," alluding to feminine loquacity. As in nshindo, the three characters were introduced by a verbal explanation from the group's secretary, Mangongo. Removed from the nshindo parade, the mask became a dance on its own. Like its ancestors, it was meant to cheer up the vigil night of matanga, but a more important role was in store for it.

3. In Milan Kundera's definition, kitsch is "the inability to admit that shit exists."[10] For Kundera, kitsch is the rejection of contradiction and meaninglessness: it is the opposite of Bakhtin's grotesque realism of orifices and bodily debasement. A strict correlative of socialist aesthetics was to expurgate contradiction from the sensorial field, or rather to sublimate it and condense it in the figure of the Enemy of the People. Ambivalent laughter and multisidedness had no place within socialist seriousness. Neijale managed to put them back on the scene.

In 1976, Nang'oma and Kabu danced around the Messalo area with the large-eared mask. A talented young man from the neighboring village of Litamanda, Januário Nandodo, saw it at a ceremony, liked it, and founded a new neijale group that revolutionized the dance's original conception. Nandodo began with the name. The word *neijale* means "don't go astray"; in the intentions of its inventors, it signified an invitation not to leave the dance-field ("Stay, don't leave") but also a boastful assertion of the magnetic qualities of the dance ("You won't be able to leave"). Building on the expression's polysemic potential, Nandodo reinterpreted it with a political twist:

> Neijale, its meaning: during the War of Ten Years, we were in the bush. And there were political meetings. At the end of these meetings, they used to say, "None must go astray!" (*Anapagwe munu wakujala*). So we thought that "none must go astray, in the meeting"; let's start a dance; let's use the name of "don't-go-astray" (*neijale*). None must go astray.[11]

The character itself was thus reimagined as a disobedient soldier who would "go astray," deserting the meeting to attend to more mundane matters — not necessarily a traitor but a disengaged and selfish person. To signify its soldiery status, the new *Neijale* always went around with a long carbine (which also referenced its previous use in the war of conquest fought with arquebuses [fig. 18]). The masks' big ears were also reinterpreted along these lines:

FIGURE 18. Don't go astray *(Rui Assubuji, Litamanda)*

> The big ears . . . It's a man that skips the meeting. "None must go astray," now he goes to the fields. It's called a man with enlarged ears *(munu wakutumbula matu)*. This is why we did so: a man that doesn't hear that there is a meeting.[12]

Nandodo was a talented drummer, singer, and xylophone player. His reinvention propelled the fame of neijale, prompting the neighboring villages of Chai and Nkoe to initiate their own groups. A master carver from Nkoe produced smooth polished versions of the large-eared masks, which he sold to these bourgeoning ensembles. Soon neijale went on to climb the plateau *(kwamboka)*. Nandodo taught it in the villages of Nshinga and Mandava; the group from Mapate, in Nshongwe. The dance quickly spread to Mwambula, Miteda, and Nimu; to Awashi and Nantadola in the district of Mocimboa; northward to Nangade and as far as Dar Es Salaam. In this diffusion from the Messalo to the plateau, Nandodo's version was the one that took hold. The links with nshindo all but disappeared: the wife and child were dropped from the majority of the ensembles, and the masks were no longer introduced by an explanation. As the character's first names became lost, the name of *Neijale* came to stand for the whole genre. Thus, the character of the backward elder was transformed in a parodic representation of soldiery laziness and disobedience—a playfully ambivalent version of nshesho's gloomy scoundrels, counter-revolutionaries, and traitors.[13]

New styles were added to the original realistic depictions of peasant activities such as hunting, trapping, smoking, and catching snails. Most of them were marked by bodily comicality, such as "the adultery" (*ugoni*), "hide-and-seek" (*namunu*), "defecating" (*kunya mavi*) and "accuse me" (*ntambudyange*). The landmark dancing style of the Litamanda group was "Mandushi's father" (*tatake Mandushi*). The choreography's name referred to the iconic scoundrel Mandushi, a colonial-era native policeman whose execution by stoning during the liberation struggle was remembered widely in popular song (see chap. 7, sec. 6).[14] Neijale's traitor, however, in no way resembled the empty-eyed wretches that Samora Machel carried along in his journey, holding them to public scorn and asking, "Do you want to see how a hyena looks?" Two large-eared masks engaged in a comical sketch, one representing a superior, and the other a clumsy and lazy soldier unable to obey orders or escaping them altogether. The sketch, which could last for half an hour, was the highlight of the performance and ridiculed military life more than it condemned the misdeeds of the infamous traitor. The ensemble from Nshinga had an even more provocative *shikuvo*, which was devised specifically for a headpiece with a lock on the mouth. The lipiko went around pointing at people and then touched the lock on the mouth, as if to ask, "Can you really speak?"

Neijale's sound drew heavily from ngoda, the dance that was in vogue in the first years of the Ten Years' War, before the officialization and tropification of Makonde orature. The *mashanjo* can-rattles, iconic of the years of silence, were shaken alongside *makuti* drums. Political praise was rare; many songs cast an ironical shade on the glorious history of the liberation struggle:

| | |
|---|---|
| Wako Donato wé | You, Donato, you |
| Shaleko shavakongwe aunakulupile | Don't trust the women's watch |
| Kukana' 'vamanya | They are not constant |
| Maduva mavili namatatu lyamba ugoni | Two, three days; on the morning it's adultery[15] |

Moral messages were not spelled out in the dualistic mode characteristic of nshesho; they were ironic and ambivalent, calling for paternalistic rebukes rather than pitiless punishments:

| Kwiva kundinyata | Stealing is ugly |
| Twa' shipula kummwing'a mwene | Take the knife and give it to the owner |
| Liduva lyavakwona vene | The day when the owners see you |
| Kwiva kundapwateka | Stealing will hurt |
| Kwiva amunavalele | Don't get used to stealing |
| Kutangadika anyoke Anabadula | Anabadula's mother complains[16] |

Neijale managed to challenge seriousness in another realm: it reintroduced masked dancing at funerary ceremonies on the plateau after this had been undermined by missionary activity (see chap. 5, sec. 2). The years after Independence were conducive to such an endeavor: following the infamous 24/20 ordinance, priests from Nangololo and Nambudi, suspected of having collaborated with the Portuguese intelligence during the war, were forced to abandon the missions within twenty-four hours and not carrying more than twenty kilograms of luggage. Antireligious sentiment was fueled; condemned heathen practices struck back with a vengeance; and death became once again the occasion for playfully ambivalent dance.

The return of nighttime masquerading on the plateau raised suspicions among nshesho practitioners. Was it a form of smuggling-in dangerous forms of lowland sorcery and political insubordination, the two often going hand in hand? Neijale was mostly danced by youths born during the struggle, who called themselves "the sons of Mondlane" or "the youth" (*mashove*, from Portuguese *jovem*), referring to Frelimo's Youth Organization (OJM, Organização da Juventude Moçambicana):

| Viva viva | Viva viva |
| Mashove twode | Let's follow the youths |
| Palitamanda | In Litamanda[17] |

Were these youths trying to undermine the prestige and authority of the war-makers? Was the dance of the large-eared buffoon a threat to order and monologism?

These doubts and suspicions were harbored by many. Neijale ensembles were, however, tolerated on account of their availability to be mobilized in political meetings in a more flexible way than the cumbersome nshesho groups. When a meeting was called hurriedly, and some group had to dance in another district to welcome (*kumpokela*) this or that leader, the neijale youths were there, with their handful of drums and rattles, ready to jump on the back of a truck and go. This pleased senior nshesho masters:

Those ones, we thank them. Because, some other times, when a meeting comes suddenly, now, you find the mapiko groups, their *vinganga* are not in a good state [because the skins are ripped]. Them, they pass, they dance and they go, and thus honor a political meeting. We don't forbid them.[18]

Of all the neijale groups, Nandodo's one was the best equipped for political mobilization, and it was regularly summoned for the festivities of the First Shot (*primeiro tiro*) in nearby Chai. In 1979, Nandodo transformed it into a polyvalent group called "25th of September" (the date of the shot)—on the model of urban ensembles, adding to its repertoire *dimbila* (xylophone), *utamaduni*, *nnonje*, and another dance called *kapera bai* ("if you die, it's over"). Other groups had worse experiences with instant mobilization:

| | |
|---|---|
| Neijale waku-Mapate | Neijale from Mapate |
| Andyuma mwanda ku-Nang'unde | He left and went to Nang'unde |
| Vandinnadya muarmazem | They put him to sleep in a warehouse |
| Kalibu kaka-o | Welcome big brother |
| Inyumba yangu yo-yai | This one is my room |
| Shitanda shangu shosha ashi | This one is my bed[19] |

In a similar vein, Malyamungu disclosed two years after I met him that he had once been a neijale dancer and that he had quit because of the poor conditions of political mobilization:

Once we had to receive President Samora, who had come to visit. We started dancing at dawn, on an empty belly. We danced the whole day, without pause and without eating. When it was over, Samora shook our hand personally. As he left, they told us to stop dancing, they didn't give us food, and they put us to sleep in a latrine. Right there I took my mask, I kicked it, and I broke it in pieces. I never ever danced neijale again.[20]

4. After the fortunate invention of neijale in the years of post-Independence euphoria, the 1980s were barren years. The shadow of war loomed large. It is fitting that the most substantial innovation of this period was a funerary dance, *bwarabwà*, consisting of lyric-heavy melodies sung to the rhythm of hoe blades struck with irons (*vitali*), or glass bottles. *Bwarabwà* songs could be topical, moralizing, or broadly philosophical.

Samuel Mandia, a master of *magalantoni* during the Ten Years' War (see chap. 7, sec. 2), emerged as the uncontested king of the genre, adapting the wartime instrument to the new style and composing a set of songs that enjoyed a broad popularity through radio broadcasting. The mood was sorrowful; even the ironic twists were cast in a dark coat.

The years of the civil war also saw an explosion in the production and consumption of the liquor known as *nipa* or *lipa* ("pay"), obtained through the fermentation and distillation of various fruits. These brews were already fabricated during colonialism, but their use was regulated by social norms that restricted it to specific festive moments such as puberty rituals and funerary ceremonies. In the first years of Independence, the socialist campaign against alcoholism made drinking a shameful practice, but moralism relaxed somewhat during the 1980s, possibly because of political directives valorizing traditional food and homemade brews.[21] The phenomenon quickly exploded. Nangade became an area of production of the more noble cashew variety (*kashoko*); the lowlands of Muidumbe, a factory of the cheapest and strongest one, made with sugarcane (*mmugwa*). Socialist imperatives demanded that alcohol consumption not disturb the orderly appearance of communal villages. "Down with alcoholism!" was the classic revolutionary slogan, and the traitor Xiconhoca was always depicted with a bottle of liquor protruding from his pants. Dedicated enclosures were thus built in the villages; there, people could become scoundrels for one day, drinking and talking obscenity away from the sight of others. Significantly, these enclosures were named *Maringue*, after the location of Renamo's operational base in the province of Sofala.

The culture of drinking encouraged the multiplication of *mashalagwesha*, juvenile improvised masks that dance for the coming-out rituals. While in the colonial era these masks were challenges posed to the elders by talented youths, who would demonstrate their skills by vampirizing other groups' drums (see chap. 3, sec. 7), the new mashalagwesha were driven by thirst. They circulated in the villages, partying around the houses that had received a new initiate, hoping to be served a drink or offered some coins. Their aesthetics was poor and their means minimal: irons (*vitali*) to mark the base rhythm and a *ntoji* to command the mask. In breach of all conventions of secrecy, they covered the body with a sweater or some used pants and a long-sleeved shirt. Similar to nshindo's nightly lesser masks (see chap. 5, sec. 3), they consisted of crude representations of characters performing a single dancing style and introduced by a song: *Naugwalwa*, "with-a-drink," who falls asleep on the floor after too much drinking; *Simba Bwabwa*, "the little-lion," who shoots arrows blindly . . . They lasted the space of a few initiation seasons and left little trace beyond the performers' euphoria.

The "slave" facial masks previously danced by neighboring Yao, Makua, and Ngoni people and appropriated by lowland Makonde in the 1940s (see chap. 5, sec. 6) also reached the plateau in the 1980s, especially the *nantyaka* and *machapila* variety. Both were characterized by a large feather crown worn around the mask; by raffia gowns; by the use of a whistle; and by songs in Kindonde, the Makonde dialect from the Rovuma River, and Kiswahili. The former wore foot rattles; the second danced on stilts—a landmark feature of Tanzanian Makonde masking since the nineteenth century. In the district of Nangade took hold the half-mask *lingoti*, which specialized in capers. Like mashalagwesha, most face-mask groups became active during the season of puberty ceremonies and were driven by thirst. Only a few became more established and refined their aesthetics. But the low prestige of the half-mask among the Makonde implied that these groups would never rise to the level of renown of their helmet counterparts.

Two other eccentric inventions left some mark in the 1980s. The first was a grotesque soccer game played by twenty-two fully dressed mapiko, fumbling after the ball in their awkward armature. It was pioneered in the lowlands but soon imitated in the plateau. Soccer was becoming more and more popular among the youths, and this was indeed a juvenile game that elders did not approve of. The second was the mask of *shitamanga* or *galada* from the village of Shitunda, a reinvention of the old *chipalamoto* burning mask.[22] The dancer would set fire to his bark costume, sometimes coming out dramatically from within a mound of straw, leaving blazing trails after his dance steps. The invention did not manage to spread; the fire dance was prohibited after the skillful dancer burned himself to death.

The original neijale masks—*João Anabadula*, *Fátima*, and *Gong'o Gong'o*—would suffer a similar fate. In 1990, Renamo bands occupied the communal village of Mapate to use it as a base for incursions on the plateau. The village was burned; people fled, leaving behind everything, and with the thatched roofs went the old large-eared mask. The times were somber, and the drums lay still. On the occasion of a visit to Mueda in 1990, Cosme Nhussi Nantova "the immortal" carved an idiosyncratic and emblematic skull-mask (*shivanga*), conceived as a meditation on the colonial massacre and the present ruin.[23]

5. *Mang'anyamu* came in the aftermath of war as a resurgence and an explosion. Martins Jackson Mwanjigula—the carver who imagined and cut the wondrous animal masks—connects it to a euphoria of peace and free movement similar to the one that followed the abolition of slavery: "The country now is well. And we people, we are going around without problems. And there is rejoicing (*kufurai*). Because we were becoming thin, at that time, and many drums were not danced; but now, play must just be there."

The process of invention itself was, however, haphazard and by far not a mere reflection of the enthusiasm for peace.[24] It started with a neighborhood friendship among a group of youths in the small communal village of Matambalale in the mid-1980s. Together, the boys had organized mapiko soccer matches; sung in bwarabwà groups at funerary ceremonies; and danced mashalagwesha during initiation season hoping to make some money from the families of the initiates. Right after the war, in the rainy season of 1993, they patched up one of these *lishalagwesha*. Martins had left for Tanzania in 1989. Lacking a carver, the others bought a cheap and ugly mask, which danced to the sound of old hoe blades. "We are just partying (*kutamba*), with irons. We know: the rituals are coming out. And we party. We are in the middle of the rituals and we eat some money." The mask was a depiction of an unfashionable poor boy rejected by women:

| Vashingwita nangu | They used to reject me |
| Angwona miwani | I don't see through sunglasses |

One day in late December, as the boys were partying around, destiny stared from the corner of a village street, in the shape of an abandoned antelope horn. Someone from the group picked up the horn and played with it. Someone thought, "Let's put it on our mask. Let's use an old skin to cover the holes." The mask already "looked like a pig"; with the horn protruding from the skin cover, "it didn't look like anything." The mask with the skins and the horn became the group's asset for the initiation season. Some called it *Tina*, because of a song dedicated to a village girl:

| Tina nagwalia inguvo | Tina doesn't wear a cloth |
| Madalena nagwalia ishupi | Madalena doesn't wear panties |

Some called it *Ntojo*, the name of the dancer:

| | |
|---|---|
| Ntojo kwiva dinyedi | Ntojo steals snails |
| Shinjili' mumpuku | He slips them into his pocket |

The group's means were minimal. "There was no pelvis-cloth. There was no drum. We relied only on the irons. And he danced as he wished, now, just following the songs. And we: 'Give us a drink!' We split [the money], a thousand each, and there we go." The horn made the mask heavy. "You would wear it for thirty minutes and you had wounds all over." But ugly and weird as it was, *Tina* became a local success. "People see it: '*Ba!* How's that? The horns are dressed only in skins?' Well, this thing is worthy. And people want it."

Martins returned from Tanzania in the midst of the initiation season, and he met his friends as they were partying around with the weird lishalagwesha. Martins is a master of the knife. Carving is a talent that flows in his blood, for he is the nephew of the great Nampyopyo. "This thing is like luck (*ibati*). Luck, because I didn't learn it anywhere." From the old master he inherited the innate ability of doing shining things: carving masks, sculptures, and stamps; constructing and playing electric guitars; repairing radios (fig. 19). "Some people in the family call me Nampyopyo. And I answer that name." As he saw the mask that didn't look like anything, he said, "I'm going to arrange something different for you guys."

In Tanzania, Martins had acquired a passion for glossy brochures of game reserves and got his hand in drawing animal figures. He eventually became almost obsessed with the topic, which he dreamt about recurrently, as Makonde blackwood artists often do.[25] The mask of the "horn covered in skins" tapped into Martins's animal fantasy. Martins devised a technique of attaching strips of animal skins to mapiko masks with tiny wooden nails, in such a way as to appear seamless. In a few weeks of tireless work, he produced six headpieces: a lion, a leopard, a rhino, a monkey, a buffalo, and a crocodile.[26] The masks combined the naturalistic and fearful strands of Makonde carving aesthetics. On the one hand, they aimed to be realistic depictions of animals that people would recognize and admire for their verisimilitude. On the other hand, they aimed to achieve the same terrifying and puzzling effect as Shumu's old masks:

> Me, in the times from where I come, my friends would scare
> me, *mapiko, mapiko, mapiko.* And I would fear the masks. Some

FIGURE 19. Nampyopyo's nephew *(Rui Assubuji, Matambalale, 2009)*

were pranking masks (*mapiko adimbenje*). They scared me, and I ran away. This, before I had wits. Now that I have wits, I made mine to hit back at those who scared me. And people fear me; some people run away and hide in the houses, in the daytime.

As he uncovered the masks to the group members, he convinced them to transform *Tina* into something different, a dance in its own right that would "never be called a lishalagwesha again." Martin's uncle, nicknamed Calado ("silent"), composed the song that provided the name and the concept for the new dance:

| | |
|---|---|
| Wetu apa wetu mwanda | Us, here we go |
| Mang'anyamu wetu | We are scary wild animals |
| Vanemba kushema | Call the boys |
| Vanemba vaide | Let the boys come |
| Vaide twavele | Let them come, let's play |
| Tutambe likumbi | Let's party the ritual |
| Ushaka atutamwa | We refuse provocations |
| Tutambe likumbi | We party the ritual |
| Mang'anyamu wetu | We are scary wild animals |

*Mang'anyamu* was a neologism introduced by Calado, a modification of the word *linyanyamu*, itself derived from the word *nyama* ("meat, animal"). "*Linyanyamu*, it means something scary, which makes you tremble, you as a human being in your own body. If you see one of these beasts that wants to eat you, all the blood in your veins draws out and you look pale like earth. That's a *ling'anyamu*. That's Shimakonde." Calado's song conveyed another essential quality of the animals: they had to circulate, so as to be able to dance in different houses on the same day, thus earning more money than static groups. To such effect, the rhythmic section was composed of hoe blades; *shimbombo* shoulder drums—a vernacularization of European band drums pioneered in the militaristic *muganda* dance and then in the youth *shingenge* circular dance; and a light and loud *ntojo*, to command the mask.[27] The costume drew from mashalagwesha but was more structured: battered sneakers and long football socks completed the sporty feel of the sweater, and the *lutove* corset was ornamented with colorful cloth stripes or shiny biscuit envelopes (*korokosho*). As in neijale, the *ingonda* was made with an old used sack. The masks were thus easy and quick to prepare, while giving an impression of "a slovenly thing" (*kudabadabyanga*, from *kudoba*, "being tired"), of "hairy animals who wear tattered things without value, things that no one washes, the dirtiest possible."

During the summer months of 1994, the boys rehearsed the dance, introducing a variety of styles, most of which were nameless and not mimetic. While each mask was free to perform its own gimmick, imitating the movements of this or that animal, the sequences of synchronized dance consisted of abstract choreographies rich in foot stomping and concluding with the animals jumping in the air and landing on their bottoms. A dozen songs were composed in an original idiom, which drew on bwarabwà funerary singing, nshesho melodic choirs, and Tanzanian pop music.

The following initiation season, the group was ready to hit the villages. The scary wild animals became an instant sensation. As money flowed in to the group's cashiers, conflict arose. How should the money be divided? Should it be split after each performance or saved in order to build up the group? How much drinking should be allowed? Who would keep the masks, effectively resisting the temptation of selling them, now that they had become coveted commodities? In 1997, the boys sought counsel from Maurício Siminda, a local war veteran and former security guard of Eduardo Mondlane in Tanzania. "We were all youths (vanemba). And now, there was too much youthfulness (shinemba) and we didn't get along with each other. He brought commandment (malamulo)." Siminda had been passionate about the new dance since the moment he had first seen it:

> Because I am a playful man, I used to follow them. Wherever they go I followed them. Now, they themselves, they saw: "This elder doesn't leave us. He really likes this thing." And they put themselves all together and they chose me as leader of the group. [. . .] We kept the money we made in the initiations to buy skins; we sent people in Mueda to buy irons. The group went far. They even carved a song for me. "Chief Siminda is stingy with money," because I didn't want to throw money at everybody.

The fame of mang'anyamu grew quickly. The radio announcer Nandenga promoted it, by recording and broadcasting the group's songs. Siminda was elected village representative of culture, thus offering to the group a more solid institutional coverage. In the space of a few years, the dance was imitated all over Muidumbe, with groups being created in a dozen villages. Martins himself taught how to carve animal masks to new burgeoning groups in Mwambula, Lutete, and Namande.

Some of the acolytes were former neijale practitioners, who, like Malyamungu, quit the large-eared jester to embrace the disorderly hairy animals. Those who continued dancing neijale insisted in establishing a direct relationship between the two dances: "All of these, mang'anyamu and *naupanga*, they come from the place of neijale. That's where these people come from. Like somebody's father, or the owner of the dance (*mwene ing'oma*)."[28]


6. Nshesho practitioners rejected mang'anyamu much more radically than they had neijale. They associated its appearance with the demise of socialism and the coming of democracy, which was itself widely seen as the end of orderly society and a surrendering to Renamo through its legitimation as a political party. Just like the new political regime—and the neoliberal conditionality that had midwifed it—the animal masks were multiple, noisy, and disorderly; pervaded by bad speech and disrespect; performed by inexperienced youths; and ultimately driven by an appetite for money. Beasts were also connected to the unmentionable enemy, Renamo, which in songs and common speech was often referred to with unflattering euphemisms drawn from the animal realm: hyenas, worms, spiders, and partridges.

In 2002, nshesho practitioners from the village of Mwambula in Muidumbe demanded that the administrator ban mang'anyamu. The occasion for conflict came with the nationwide Second Festival of Popular Dance (II FNDP), organized by the government on the occasion of ten years of peace. The festival was constructed on the model of its 1978 predecessor but had a very different political agenda, on the one hand promoting "a culture of peace and national unity" and on the other serving as a covert platform to smooth a change of leadership within Frelimo. At the local phase in Mwambula, the loud hoe blades of the mang'anyamu group disrupted the rhythm of the nshesho drum orchestra. The latter quit the dance-field, complaining bitterly.

Mang'anyamu was defended on the grounds of pluralism by the administrator of Muidumbe. "We are in times of democracy and all are free to do what they want. Moreover, arts always evolve. This is an evolution and I must defend it."[29] Not only was mang'anyamu not prohibited; the original group from Matambalale unexpectedly showed up and won the district phase of the II FNDP in May 2002. Rallied under the patronage of Siminda, the group presented a shining performance that rendered homage to the Frelimo flag, while at the same time delighting the crowds with buffoonery and disorganized dance. The group defied the practitioners of nshesho on their own ground with an adaptation of a famous war-veteran song:

| | |
|---|---|
| Tutunduvenge Mang'anyamu | We have commenced mang'anyamu |
| Wetu tuvene | We are the owners |
| Antigo Mang'anyamu Muidumbe | The veterans of mang'anyamu, Muidumbe[30] |

Months later, the conflict worsened because of a crisis of sorcery. Wild lions attacked and devoured people in the area of Muidumbe, and the killings were widely attributed to lions "fabricated" through sorcery.[31] When a survivor said that he had been stabbed by a person wearing a lion mask on the face that looked "just like a mang'anyamu," the genre was associated with the worse kinds of sorcery—the sorcery of destruction (lwanongo) that was itself used as a popular political metaphor for the devouring appetites of politicians in times of neoliberal democracy.[32]

Ndeja-Ndeja from Mwambula—a master of mask-dressing, father of skillful dancers, animator, and fanatic—thus argued his contempt for disorderly money-mongering masquerades:

> They didn't manage to dance mapiko with dinjuga and they started neijale. Some people take them, cook food for them. And there he goes. To receive money. If the government supports them, like this: neijale, that's his work . . . But me, neijale, I don't want it. These are mapiko of envious speech (njeje). They are full of people that do like this. And the mapiko who wear mang'anyamu, like this . . . These ones, I really refuse them, really! I refuse them. Because they kill us, they grab us with provocations (ushaka). They do a training to capture us. That's why, the people that are destroying our district, that's them. If you want to support them, well, you go on. But me, those, I refuse them.[33]

Afraid of the consequences, the group from Matambalale renounced the victory. For the duration of the lion crisis, the animal masks lay prudently still, and they reemerged from it scared and shaken.

7. Passing through Maputo after fieldwork in October 2002, I showed a tape of the mang'anyamu performance at the post-phase of the II FNDP to Vicente Muanga (see chap. 2, sec. 4). It began with four animals—monkey, leopard, crocodile, and rhino—parading in military march and standing to attention in front of a flagpole under the podium of honor. As the monkey took hold of the drum, scratching its butt, the crocodile clumsily advanced toward the flagpole, manipulating the flag with little respect. In the background, the singers intoned:

| | |
|---|---|
| Frelimo aina mwisho | Frelimo is infinite |
| Ukabanga vandakuduma | If you are wicked, they will punish you |

This is arguably the most famous revolutionary anthem ever, which will move to tears urbanite struggle nostalgics. In the official song recording, performed by the Women's Detachment choir, the first verse is followed by a list of notable "reactionaries" (Simango, Nkavandame, and five others).[34] Omitted is the second verse that indexes the song's practical usage throughout the socialist era, as a soundtrack for the public flogging of scoundrels. In the communal villages, where many bear the scars of such punishments, the anthem is sung neither often nor lightly. To this ominous soundtrack, the crocodile fumbled with the flag and eventually raised a cloth with the image of President Chissano. After this political prelude, the group went on with the usual dancing styles and animal gimmicks. The monkey took a baby from the crowd and picked off his fleas. The four animals then walked out stylishly from the competition space, singing a puzzling multilingual song.

Like many other Makonde in Maputo, Vicente was disillusioned with Frelimo and somewhat irritated with village "fanaticism," "backwardness," and "ignorance." The performance delighted him; he laughed, satisfied: "Finally, the Makonde are mocking Frelimo!" As the tape circulated, promoting the little-known animal masks in Maputo and as far as Beira, the reactions were the same: bemused satisfaction for a daring political mockery.

But when I went back to Matambalale and asked the performers about their festival "provocation," they described it as a heartfelt homage to the heroic deeds of the liberation struggle. "We, the kids, we were taught by our elders. It was a historic day, the twenty-fifth of June [the anniversary of Independence], when the colonialist flag went down and we raised our flag, that of Frelimo."[35] Clearly, the bemused crowds and the festival jury, who awarded the victory, did not think much differently.

8. It is in terms of generational ambivalence—rather than concealed criticism or tactical praise—that the aesthetics of mang'anyamu can best be apprehended. Herein lies its family resemblance with the large-eared neijale. The majority of mang'anyamu dancers belong to the generation of the "sons of Samora"—young men born during the Ten Years' War, who did not know the world of hamlets, lineage, and colonial domination except in the stories told by their fathers; who did not fight the war but have at best the memory of running away from it (*kutukutila*) when they were kids; and who are separated from their fathers by a fundamental physical boundary, the lack of scarifications (*dinembo*) on the face and on the body. These young men witnessed the glory of the first years of the revolution and venerated the father figures of Independence:

| | |
|---|---|
| Kwaendile | Where he went |
| Kwaendile baba Machel kwaendile | Where papa Machel went, where he went |
| Ata kukalepa dashi | Even if it's far, then what? |
| Wetu mwanda | We go |
| Tummwoda baba Machel kwaendile kula | We follow papa Machel, there, where he went |
| Ata pakadingadinga dashi | It can be dark-dark there, then what? |
| Tundapaleta pele | We will slip in |
| Tummwoda baba Machel kwaendile akó | We follow papa Machel, there where he went |
| Mukaigwa kwaendile kushu kwannungu kulepa | And if you hear: he went far, at God's place, that's far |
| Tuvene tupaleta vila pele | Ourselves, we will just slip in |
| Kwannungu kulepa | God's place, that's far away[36] |

Unlike the most fortunate members of this generation—who benefitted from Frelimo's pioneering investments in education, went to excellent "pilot schools" in Cabo Delgado, and built careers in the public sector—these young men stayed in the village, nurturing the soil to which their peers would come back. While people in the cities experienced the lulling sound of rain on corrugated zinc (*kulala mabati*, "sleeping tins"), village youths continued to cut bamboos, carry stones, and thatch their roofs. While their fathers received war pensions—often squandered on women and alcohol—they continued to work the land. From the village, they saw the hopes of revolution crumbling, opportunities narrowing down, and the state taking on an ugly face:

| | |
|---|---|
| Ukapata madengo | If you receive a job |
| Bai tatako namanyoko lipambedye bwana | Take care of your mother and father, friend |
| Upate pakuwikila | So you'll have a place to land |
| Ntondo madengo kukumya | Tomorrow they fire you from the job |
| Undashang'apa kuwikila | You have no place to land |
| Shilikali lamina uji kuvili | The state is a two-edged blade[37] |

Bricolage was the most creative activity in store; alcohol the most tempting. The excursions to the *maringue* brought out an unnameable rage:

| | |
|---|---|
| Vadada vankutulapa nadimongo | Our sisters complain strongly |
| Muwakati watukumbila ugwalwa wetu | When we drink our drinks |
| Tunkushidi kwangaikanga mala jemba | We go around wretched and without objective |
| Tunkuka nankoma ndyavo | We go and beat our wives |
| Umanyie mwaa wanyamani | Go and tell why |
| Ukava na unkali | If you are full of rage |
| Ukava na unkali 'kakamanane na mashanga | If you are full of rage go and pick a fight with Renamo people |
| Vakongwe tuvakoma bila mwaa | The women, we beat them without reason |
| Ashinava shipato kunyambikanga | There is no profit from being in tatters[38] |

The other form of divertissement was amorous adventuring. With the transformation of puberty rituals in the aftermath of Independence, young girls would wait years before marrying, in which they were available as lovers for peers or married men. The intensity of such activities gave rise to bawdy accidents that songs treat in a flippant and self-congratulatory tone:

| Ishupi yangu yambone ndileka | My good underpants, I left them at |
|---|---|
| kwashove akó | that young one's place |
| She! Shinamadi sho! Porra! | She! You did it on purpose! Shit! |
| Ashinava shinamadi, wé | It wasn't on purpose |
| Ninjenu kungunagwela Teresa | Me, your friend, I like Teresa so much[39] |

The underpants forgotten at a lover's place are not a pledge of love (or a Freudian slip); they will be kept by the girl as a form of payment, to compensate for what the lover has not given. As the extreme poverty that the plateau suffered in the years of isolation—marked by the lack of commodities, high prices, and illegal smuggling (*candonga*)—was followed by glaring liberalization of the markets, sex became wholly monetized. Loving exchanges with unmarried *vali* were to be unfailingly remunerated in money or goods.[40] Courting would be preceded by ruthless negotiation:

| Kummwing'a shilingi moja | I give her one shilling [5,000 MTZ] |
|---|---|
| Kummwona lundunda | I see her head shaking |
| Kummwing'a shilingi mbili | I give her two shillings |
| (nnatu, nsheshe, tanu, sita, saba, nane, tisa) | [then three, four, five, six, seven, eight, nine . . . ] |
| Kushi kummwing'a shilingi kumi? | What about giving her ten shillings? |
| Kummwona dabwali dabwali dabwali | I see her head goes up and down, up and down |
| Alo! Mwali! | Hey! Girl! |
| Tuli' nshabwede! | Let's eat our enjoyment! |
| A-a-a, tuvé ndó! | A-*a-a*, we are full! |

Charged as it was with such licentious overtones, the language of love was nonetheless used to express political appreciation for the newly appointed secretary general of the Frelimo Party and candidate for presidential elections, Armando Emilio Guebuza:

| Guebuza nakupenda | Guebuza I love you |
|---|---|
| Uvé wangu wamaisha | You are mine for life |

Wholehearted political enthusiasm and a cynical outlook on the misadventures and miseries of village life in times of democracy might not seem to combine well. Under the cover of "sunglasses" (*miwani*)—alcohol and marijuana consumed before the dance to "take away the shame"—mang'anyamu dancers performed precisely such contradiction and ambivalence, treading in a space where serious nshesho had never dared. Challenging socialist realism, idioms of lamentation, and the prescription of monolingualism, they reverted to obscurity bordering on meaninglessness:

| | |
|---|---|
| Akuno kwashi, akuno kwashi? | Where are we? Where are we? |
| Kulipanda | In the initiation house |
| Kulipanda kwa-Nigore | In Nigore's initiation house |
| Mande mande | Mande mande |
| Naifu | Knife |
| Wani boxi | One box |
| Yes! | Yes! |
| Wani nshabwede! | One enjoyment! |

Recorded and broadcasted by the radio announcer Nandenga and then performed on the victorious occasion of the II FNDP, this had become the signature song of the Matambalale group, and of mang'anyamu more generally. No one could really figure out what it meant, not even the dancers. It was Calado's creation, and he had kept the meaning to himself. Most people assumed that it evoked a situation of danger and exhilaration. Nigore was a much-contested healer who rose to prominence in the post-Independence period: a saint for some, a cheat for others. The knife and the box (as in boxing) were assumed to refer to the brawls provoked by drinking in the years of maringue and democracy. A nuisance? No, "one enjoyment"! What an allegory of the disorderly explosion of enjoyment in the collapse of a totalitarian order.[41]

When Calado returned from Tanzania in 2004, I could finally inquire about the song. He smiled: stabbing? boxing? "No. The 'knife' is the knife with which we carve the masks, which are our main asset; 'one box' is the PO box number one, because we are the number one; and Mande was a friend of mine there in Tanzania . . ." Like nshindo's mosquitoes (see chap. 5, sec. 9), this stands as a warning to the historian's desire to achieve interpretive closure, to attribute definite meanings to aesthetic forms.


9. While carrying out research in the lowland village of M'Bau in 2002, a group of teenagers performed a dance that involved roughly carved animal masks, partially covered with skins, which they called kenge. They pretended not to have been influenced in any way by

mang'anyamu and that the dance was based on some local tradition. The dance looked so different from its plateau equivalent and so reminiscent of nshindo that I granted some credence to their claim. A few days after, a monkey mask, also covered in skins, appeared glamorously in the midst of a *shikelya* spectacle (see chap. 2, sec. 4). As the monkey vanished after the performance, I could not trace the dancer and talk to him. Whence did these animal masks come? A few headpieces in extant collections make use of animal skins, especially one of a hooded monkey. Nshindo included realistic representations of animals, such as the dog and the hare. Ancient Messalo traditions tell of masks covered with furs from head to toe, coming out howling in the thick of the night to terrify everybody.[42]

Neijale was the reinvention of a nshindo character into a genre in its own right. As it climbed the plateau (*kwamboka*) and conquered the heart of a generation, the large-eared mask reactivated the playful ambivalence encapsulated in nshindo, which had been stifled by socialist seriousness and monologism. The trajectory of mang'anyamu seems to be more complex. The animal mask stemmed from chance encounters with African wildlife—the physical remains of an antelope as well as images from game parks—shaped in such a way as to express a generational ambivalence toward the bittersweet fruits of democracy. It filled the space opened by its predecessor, neijale, pushing the aesthetic boundaries in the terms of polyphony and multilayeredness. Could it also be the unconscious reactivation of an ancient tradition of animal masks preserved in the liminal Messalo lowlands—the space from which dance novelties always arise?

# 11 ∽ Puppets and Machetes
## Boys in a Wild World

| Kulukume uvone | Grow up, so you see |
|---|---|
| Uvone vanu pavajagwidye | So you see how people are dangerous |

—Song heard in Mwambula, 2009

1. A FEW weeks before the beginning of the new millennium, a group of teenagers from the communal village of Mwatidi went for a bicycle ride down to the Messalo lowlands.[1] Their aim was to buy some dried catfish near the shores of Nguri Lake and maybe some tomatoes, then to bring the products home to the plateau and squeeze some money out of their venture. While walking around the village of Myangalewa—a small commercial hub on the N1 national road, known for fish, wet-land agricultural production, mangoes, malaria, and petty crime—the boys stumbled on an acquaintance, who proposed to sell them a more arcane commodity. They nodded: "Let's see." He let them into his house and took a sack from the space between the thatched roof and the bamboo ceiling, where house-rats thrive. He laid out the contents on the floor: a few mapiko masks. "My nshindo group is dead. And I am left to take care of this equipment." He smiled, to make them understand that he would eat up the money. Most of the masks were roughly carved. The boys picked the best one: an old man with a spirit-dark complexion, white hair, a gray beard, a small straight nose, and a prominent chin; it was somewhat modeled on the formal conventions of *Neijale* but without the large ears. They paid forty *contos*, wrapped it in an old sack, and stocked it together with the dried catfish on the back of their bicycles.[2]

Before leaving, the boys asked about the character that in nshindo corresponded to the mask. What was it called? How did it dance? It was named *Nalupanga*, the seller said, after the site of an old graveyard. Its song went: "*Nalupanga* will kill you / You won't go back home" (*Nalupanga andakubyaa* / *Ntapa kwenu auka*). On the dance floor, *Nalupanga* did not do much, as it was one of those nightly lesser masks open to the fancy and improvisation of the youngest and drunkest (see chap. 5, sec. 3). The lowland host called a neighbor to take a photo, as a remembrance of the moment and of the mask in which he had once danced. The plateau boys then disappeared in a cloud of dust, racing on their bicycles toward the steep and slippery slope of Namakande, where they knew they would have to push and sweat.

A few weeks later, the boys from Mwatidi set off on another journey, to dance at initiation rituals in the village of Nangade. The boys presented a mediocre *nantyaka*; they were outshone on the dance-field by other groups and were making little money. In the midst of this unsuccessful trip, someone came up with the idea of dancing with the mask bought in Myangalewa. The mask was dressed with a worn-out green sweater and a sack around the pelvis, like a *lishalagwesha*; irons were struck for it; and the rest was left to the improvisation of the dancer, a twelve-year-old boy known as Shanjolo. Playing with the original name of the mask, *Nalupanga*, Shanjolo grabbed a machete (*upanga*) and danced with it menacingly and sinuously. The experiment—dubbed on the spot *naupanga*, "with-a-machete"—made the boys' day:

> Our objective was to dance nantyaka. But nantyaka let us down; it was a complete flop. It made us go down so badly. So, we shat on nantyaka. And we started naupanga. It began as a play-play thing; then when we came back home we saw the dance blooming nicely. And so the dance of nantyaka, we killed it and naupanga was left. And everybody liked it. And nantyaka, we shat on it.

Coming back home, the boys set to refining the invention through rehearsal. They structured the dance in two movements: *lishesho* and *nshakasha*, just like the respectable nshesho. The base rhythm (*kukudula*) would be played on a long bar of iron raised slightly off the ground, which produced a deafening sound, even stronger than the *mashalagwesha*'s wandering irons. This instrument had been pioneered in *mashawona*, a dance marked by extravagant tattered clothing and a sequence of energetic loin shaking that had become fashionable among the very young in the past years. The loud *ntojo* drum commanded. In the first part, the mask performed mimetic styles. The signature style consisted of three short backward movements, in-between *kunung'unula* (traditional pelvis shaking) and Michael Jackson's signature "moonwalk," followed by a kung-fu backward kick shot blindly in the middle of the crowd. Other styles featured machete-swaying (fig. 20). The second part was no less original. The dancers and the mask positioned themselves at a long distance from the iron bar strikers. The drummer played the nshakasha call. Responding from afar, *Naupanga* jumped on a bicycle and rushed at breakneck speed toward the drummers; as it was about to reach them, it peeled out and turned, kicking away the bike and standing on its feet. Then more mimetic styles came. When the drum called the end of nshakasha, *Naupanga* jumped again on its bike and vanished in a cloud of dust and stupefaction.

A new song was composed for the adventurous character, which, drawing inspiration from the nshindo original song, underlined its dangerousness:

| | |
|---|---|
| Naupanga njope | Fear *Naupanga* |
| Andakubyaa upanga | He will slay you with his machete |
| Ukavina uwavi | If you dance witchcraft |
| Dindakulya dimbwe | Dust will swallow you |

FIGURE 20. Fear *naupanga* (Paolo Israel, Mwambula, 2003)

Like *Neijale*, *Naupanga* was close to being a character but was not quite one. On the one hand, it retained the open-ended abstraction of daytime mapiko: the partition into two movements, and the flexibility to expand its repertoire of dance styles and songs and even to incorporate the rhythms and movements of other dances. On the other, the mask, the song, the machete, the bicycle, and the kung-fu kick shaped some kind of character identity. No commentary or presentation accompanied him, for he needed no introduction.

When the dance was launched in public, this time in the village of Mwatidi, it was an instant hit. The group managed to do without patronage. An employee from the hospital in Mwatidi sought to take the boys under his protective wing, but the experiment was short-lived and they preferred to maintain their independence. The dancer Shanjolo and a stuttering boy called Doto led the ensemble. In the space of a year, naupanga spread as its predecessors neijale and mang'anyamu had done—first in the district of Muidumbe, then northward to Mueda and Nangade and eastward in Mocimboa.[3] With its pop references and bragging attitude, the dance was particularly attractive to youngsters. The children feared it and adored it; they played the signature naupanga style on jerry cans, kicking about in the village squares. The youths from Mwatidi explained their invention as a challenge to the elders' inertia:

> The elders nowadays, others are tired. And us, we thought— what? Elders nowadays are nowhere. And us, we must make this dance grow, so that it goes forward. So that it doesn't lie still, without playing-playing. Because, if you trust only the elders . . . Some others, it's even worse, they go and live in the wetlands, and the village is left all cold. And us kids, we thought it good to ignite the hamlets.

The elders' reception was as dismissive as possible. Most shunned the dance as just another lishalagwesha, possibly as an "improved lishalagwesha"—a joking reference to the government-sponsored "improved huts" (*palhota melhorada*) and "improved latrines" (*latrina melhorada*). For some reason, the new invention pleased older women, who crowded to and applauded its performances. In 2004, for instance, women from a Nangade *lingundumbwe* group thought it important to inform me: "There is another one that is called naupanga. That one is even worse. It's dangerous."[4]

2. But not all the elders in the wetlands were lying idle or think-ing only about hoes. One of them produced a counterpoint to the Mwatidi boys' experimentations with machetes and bicycles. Mustafa Mwana Bonde was born in the lowlands of Lipelwa, between today's village of Mwambula and Namakande; his mother's lineage was from the Messalo area, so he sometimes referred to himself as "a son of the lowlands" (*mwana bondi*). After having fought in the Ten Years' War as a soldier, Mustafa worked in Tanzania; then he moved to the town of Montepuez to work in an irrigation scheme set up by "white people" in a collective field.[5] When the civil war began to rage, in the late 1980s, he moved back to the plateau and went to live in Mwam-bula, the closest village to his native lowlands. He stayed there "as a man without work," living on food that he grew on borrowed land. As the war ended and the paths to the lowlands reopened, Mustafa set to work on the wetlands that he had inherited from his father. He cleared a large sloping plot and, building on his Montepuez experi-ence, dug an artisanal system of irrigation canals that turned the field into a paddy. In the space of a few years, he became one of the fore-most rice producers of the district. On top of this, his status as a war veteran was acknowledged with a generous pension. Now reasonably wealthy, Mustafa bought a plot on the central avenue of Mwambula, where he built a large house with a winged structure inspired by a construction that he had seen in Tanzania.

As a wealthy and established man, Mustafa thought that he should contribute something in the field of culture. As a young man he had danced nshesho in a lineage ensemble, but after Independence he had not joined any "unity" village group. Most of all, he had been impressed by the masks of Nampyopyo and Shumu that he had seen in his youth. Mustafa thought that "as these masters died and their talent was not car-ried over," the memories of their inventions would fade away. "As the years passed, I saw: each person has a dance. And now, those dances, nobody resurrected them. And I though of doing like a copy."

It was the spirit, not the letter, of Nampyopyo's and Shumu's masks that Mustafa set to resuscitate: the capacity to baffle and stupefy. Mustafa crafted two extravagant and ugly masks out of melted rubber tires and other recycled materials (fig. 21). Unlike all other mapiko, they covered the en-tirety of the head, so that the dancer could see from the mask's eyes. Then he carved two wooden puppets—one drummer and one dancer—which he set on top of long bamboo poles, maneuvered by a system of concealed

FIGURE 21. *Ill-in-the-Rainy-Season* (Paolo Israel, Mwambula, 2003)

strings so that their legs and arms could move independently. The masks and the puppets performed in coordination. They were introduced by a song that explicitly connected the invention to the master of yore:

| | |
|---|---|
| Wetu tunkulodya maimyo akala | We show ancient history |
| Kwaludeya Nang'unde | In the village of Nang'unde |
| Ashindapagwa Nampyopyo | Existed Nampyopyo |
| Wetu tunkulodya maimyo akala | We show ancient history[6] |

The masks were dressed and danced following the Messalo fashion, with cloths held together by horizontal vegetal ropes, *meeve* rattles, and sequences of foot stomping. The dance was named after the main character, *Shuku Nwele* ("Ill-in-the-Rainy-Season"), who held a long carbine to signify its status as a hunter. The masks were introduced by a moral commentary spelled out by Mustafa:

> Long live peasant culture! The meaning: everything must be told with its meaning. If you hear *Shuku Nwele*, it's this one. This is *Shuku Nwele*. His wife, *She-Bothers-the-Husband's-Mother* (*kunyatilika anyoke nnume*). This one, he is really lazy. His work is hunting, hunting, hunting. Water, nothing, *Shuku Nwele*, it's even worse. A field? No way. This elder here is lazy. During the dry season he feels better . . . But when the toads arrive, bye-bye, he becomes *Ill-in-the-Rainy-Season*. And his wife, *She-Bothers-the-Husband's-Mother*. Long live culture![7]

*Shuku nwele* was rehearsed by Mustafa in 1999 in Lipelwa with his closest associates and first presented in public in the year 2000. Two plaques nailed on the puppet poles commemorated the date and meaning of the invention: "Muidumbe seat. Peasant culture of Lipelwa. Chuku Nwele"; and "Muidumbe seat. Historical culture. Chuku Nwele, 2000."[8] The masks danced rarely—three or four times per year—but their fame quickly spread in the district and beyond. Unlike naupanga and its disorderly predecessors, shuku nwele did not become a genre. None could imitate it, as none managed to decipher the masks' and puppets' technical secrets. Some suspected that they were made of rubber, but no one could tell precisely, in the dust and confusion of the dance-field. Mustafa did everything possible to conceal these secrets, keeping the group small—within the close circle of friends and family—so that none would divulge them. Like Nampyopyo, defying imitation seemed to him the best strategy for a playful man:

A thing like this is complicated. And what makes it complicated
is: it is not something that comes all of a sudden, "Let's do this."
It's something that comes from the thinking of a man alone. [. . .]
Now, if someone wants to imitate me; there is no one that comes
near me; and those who come near do not manage me. Because
I am a playful person, and I began a long time ago; and the first
thing that a playful person knows is: you must be nasty!

3. Both naupanga and shuku nwele were run through with references
to global modernity in more visible ways than their predecessors. The
wild animals of mang'anyamu were inspired by glossy magazines of
Tanzanian game parks, but they still could be read as a regression to
a feral state caused by the civil war (see chap. 10, sec. 1). In the new
millennial mapiko, the push was much more radical: kung-fu and pop-
music dancing moves, the bicycle, and recycled materials made them
hip and self-consciously global. They might be considered alongside
the icons of African popular culture that have fascinated the world of
contemporary art over the past decades. Naupanga could ride together
with the syncretic Yorùbà sculpture of a *Man with a Bicycle* praised
by Anthony Appiah as an example of "the all-consuming vision of a
less-anxious creativity."[9] Shuku nwele echoes Romuald Hazoumé's
*masques bidon*—masks made out of recycled jerry cans, intended to
convey a critique of the ecological disaster wrought by Western capital-
ism, and then used as authentic objects in religious ceremonies.[10]

We have covered enough ground to steer away from the fallacy that
explains the syncretic appetite of African dance as a recent product
of urbanization and globalization. Sparked by schismogenetic competition, the incorporation of foreign elements into the dramatic texture
of mapiko goes back as far as the historical eye can see. Naupanga's
bicycle and kung-fu and shuku nwele's rubber are not different in
essence from the helicopter night-mask or the appropriation of the
coastal dance *chakacha*; from the masks of Queen Elizabeth the Second and the *Germans-in-the-Hamlet*; or from the "spicing-up" of songs
with Kiswahili words. Rural ritual dance is as extroverted—to use Jean
François Bayart's fortunate expression—as Congolese urban painting
or Tanzanian hip-hop.[11]

This extraversion goes so far back that exploring its meanings without giving in to sweeping assertions or all-too general abstractions is

difficult (chap. 2, sec. 8). We know that multilayered meanings were attached to these gestures of appropriation—ambivalent morality, realism, playful boasting—but we can no longer go and ask Nampyopyo. We are faced now with two recent and extreme examples of extraversion. What motivated them? What outlook did they express toward the foreign items that they played with? Was it really bereft of anxiety?

4. One can begin—quite unoriginally—with the influence of the new media. In the years after the civil war, owners of *maringue* drinking enclosures began acquiring video players, stereo systems, and fuel-powered generators, projecting films at night, when the drinking was to be suspended because of the increased risk of brawls. The entry fee was low—one *conto*—and *videwo*, as it was known, became a popular attraction and a site of interaction for youths. Those who could not afford the ticket peeped through the cracks of the bamboo fences. Each night two films would be projected, each falling into a specific genre: a fight film (*yamangumi*, "of blows"), mostly starring Bruce Lee or Chuck Norris; and a musical video, of Congolese *souk* or American pop.

Much has been written on the reception of media in the global periphery, mostly with the intent of demystifying the idea of passive reception—stressing, that is, the creative interpretations of audiovisual production by various audiences.[12] In the case of Muidumbe in the early 2000s, one should affirm, against all political correctness, that the great majority of viewers ignored the basic facts about filmmaking, thinking that films are shot live and that the actions correspond to real events.[13] Most viewers believed or confusedly imagined that Chuck Norris or Bruce Lee killed lots of people in front of the camera; that Arnold Schwarzenegger is endowed with superhuman strength; and that monsters such as Predator really roam the wild forests of the world (the latter closely resembled a sorcerer, with its invisibility and its appetite for meat).[14] The conditions of projection did not facilitate critical inquiry: the screen was small, the tapes quickly wore out, and the buzz of the generator overrode the already distorted sound coming from the loudspeakers. As each of the taken-for-real blows was struck, crowds of young children screamed in delight: *Toma!* "Take that!" Rules of genre were equally misunderstood. One of the video houses in Mwambula projected porn movies on specific nights (here the supposition of realism was justified), its loudspeakers blasting orgasmic screams, again to the delight of children.

It is a complete lack of coordinates—of what Fredrick Jameson called "cognitive mapping"—that guides the apprehension of these global images.[15] Some disbelieve or doubt what they see. Is it really possible? Is it truly for real? Others situate it in the blurred category of sorcery. The state, which once controlled the production and diffusion of sounds and images in the countryside, mostly of a documentary nature, has retreated and given up on the role of cognitive and moral guidance. Schoolteachers—who often lecture in the maringue as well—have little certainty to offer. The West features as a provider of mindless violence and moral corruption. Seen from the video house, the world appears in an uncertain and disquieting light.

5. The ingredients of naupanga's signature dance style mimicked the dual structure of video projections: Michael Jackson and Bruce Lee; music and blows. The machete was generally interpreted as a representation of violence, and the dance became famous on this account, as referring to the drunken brawls and thuggery that more and more characterized everyday life in postsocialist communal villages. The sugarcane *nipa* liquor characteristic of Muidumbe was indeed renamed naupanga, partly because the sugarcane was cut with a machete but also because of the liquor's consequences. New dance sketches added other dimensions to naupanga's depiction of village life. The lipiko acted as a barber, in a dance style vaguely remindful of Chaplin's *Great Dictator*, or played soccer with another mask. The bicycle in the dance also referred to the youths' ability in performing gimmicks with old made-in-China brakeless "wrecks" (*shikwata*). Mwatidi was among the largest communal villages of Muidumbe, a place in the bush that tried to self-style itself as a small city, with youngsters painting their houses in the Tanzanian fashion, wearing flashy secondhand clothes, and adopting whatever image came from afar.

Cosmopolitan in outlook, naupanga was the dance of a youth with an attitude, ready to push the boundaries of political irreverence. A sketch prepared for the district phase of the II FNDP (see chap. 10, sec. 6) was supposed to represent a census. The sketch was prudently introduced by the machete-wearing mask waving around a leaflet with the image of President Chissano. Afterward, all authorities in the crowd—policemen, village presidents, and myself—were interpelled with a pencil, as if to ask their name. Without waiting for an answer,

*Naupanga* jotted it down in a notebook. Once the authorities in the crowd were all accounted for, the mask began to count, and add to the list, its own body parts: head, nose, chin, and nape; arms and legs; finishing with the butt and the "family jewels." Another dance style represented the Christian Eucharist, a topic explored with dramatic results during colonialism (see chap. 3, sec. 5). The lipiko danced wildly, and when the call *Yesu Nkristu* was exclaimed by the singers, it fell to its knees and held out its hands.

The rise of Guebuza to the presidency of Frelimo—and foreseeably to the presidency of the country itself—was hailed in cheeky tones in a self-praise defiant song:

| | |
|---|---|
| Guebuza tundinkodya | Guebuza, we found him |
| Aikele mulukoma | Sitting in a porch |
| Wetu tunditwala | We took him |
| Alangalele Moshambiki | And put him to lead Mozambique |
| Kwalala kwalala | How beautiful, how beautiful |
| Kulamulila naupanga | Naupanga rules |
| Kwalala kwalala | How beautiful, how beautiful[16] |

The more the group became famous, the more it flirted with symbols of violence. The group incorporated into its song repertoire the anthem of the witch-lynchers who were killing people suspected of transforming into lions in the 2002–3 crisis—*vashikaji noma* ("young idiots," referring to the people lynched). They also sang about these lynchings, connecting them to the much-heralded death of Jonas Savimbi:

| | |
|---|---|
| Woya-woyana, woya-woyana | It's a chop-chop, chop-chop |
| Kubondi akó | There in the lowlands |
| Ukatauka mmudye Savimbi mwatutandalé | If you insist, ask Savimbi how we do |
| Ukatauka mmudye Dhlakhama mwatutandalé | If you insist, ask Dhlakhama how we do |

Explicit references to sex also featured in songs, if not in dance, especially in a piece that spoke of "grabbing" or "holding" oneself—meaning either grabbing the hips of one's partner in the height of pleasure or masturbating (or both):

| | |
|---|---|
| Likamulile | Grab/hold yourself |
| Ukwona kunogwa, likamulile | If it feels good, grab/hold yourself |

Some imitators pushed the boundaries even more. A group from the village of Nshongwe called Naing'ong'o ("with a cudgel") was banned by the local government because one of its songs referred to "snuff-tobacco in your mother's vagina." Others copied naupanga but toned down its most provocative aspects, substituting the more innocent cashew fruit (*nalibibu*) or clay (*naulongo*) for the iconic machete.

Naupanga stemmed from the imagination of the "sons of Chissano," born after the death of Samora Machel (1986), with only vague memories of "running away on their own legs" (*kutukuta nimwene*) from the bazooka fire of the civil war. It provided a poignant metaphor to think through the pervasive violence of the postsocialist era, which had the drinking enclosure as its gravitational center. If the youths were not able to cognitively map the sources and generic conventions of the global images that they appropriated in their dance, they could certainly seize—practically and emotionally—its results and vividly embody them in the new genre.

The dance's initiators, however, prudently (and slyly) denied that the machete had anything to do with violence. Instead they indexed its use as an agricultural tool and referred to the moral significance of cultivation work in a peasant society:

> —Because if you want to play, you have to cultivate. You must receive food, otherwise you won't eat. And we thought, "with-a-machete," and we thought the name *naupanga* and we called it *naupanga*.
>
> —But now, with the machete, does he want to cultivate or to kill people?
>
> —No, no, his work is to cultivate, not to kill people, no.
>
> —But now, the song, doesn't it say . . .
>
> —That song, we put it [so] because . . . If you arrive in a village, people must make room for you. They must make room so that you can dance properly. So, it's just to scare off people. He doesn't kill people, no. It's so that you make room. [. . .] Because if you molest him, he will hit you as he dances. You'd better back off, or else he will slay you with the machete, right there . . .[17]

6. *Shuku Nwele* was more explicitly moralistic, as it represented the classic character of the lazy person who does not want to work the land:

"When the rainy season comes, there are others who lose all strength for cultivating. 'So-and-So is ill,' 'So-and-So is ill.' But in the dry season, they are well. It is a form of pointing out [bad behavior]."[18]

Shuku nwele, however, gained its fame less on account of its morality and more from its ingenuity and the creative usage of unusual materials. On the dance-field very few people could clearly hear Mustafa's presentation, which was sometimes omitted from the performance. Most watched with admiration the puppets and the unfathomable rubber masks. This bafflement was precisely the aesthetic response that Mustafa wanted to achieve; it was generated in turn by Mustafa's own bafflement by and admiration for modern technology. Just as science is always inventing something new, so too "culture comes from always augmenting (*kwanjadyedya*), like the white people do."[19] This parallelism between masking creation and Western technology emerged in all the discussions that we had:

> These things now, I started them myself. Like the white people (*vajungu*) thought about the mines and the gloves. Now, I thought: If I do like this and like that, it will be good. And I built it. Then I called some people and I showed them. Each and every one went: "Bah! What is this thing?" Until they took it and watched it [closely].

Besides initiating shuku nwele, Mustafa learned to play the musical bow, a very uncommon instrument in northern Mozambique, which he constructed and mastered after having seen it on the occasion of a national festival. Mustafa composed a range of songs in a unique genre that he called *shilanga* as an homage to the art of the old masters (see chap. 6, sec. 4), despite the fact that the two were different both in music and in lyrical style.[20] Like his masks, Mustafa's *vilanga* were also characterized by the intertwining of morality and admiration for technological progress:

| | |
|---|---|
| Wetu kala atushimanya | Once upon a time we didn't know |
| Iradio tushishema mandandosha avanjungu | The radio, we called it the white man's undead |
| Shinema tushishema vanu vakumoka | The cinema, we called it ghost-people |
| Wetu kala atushimanya | Once upon a time we didn't know |
| Ishumana vandavalanga | That the weeks can be counted |

| Mwedi vandavalanga | That the months can be counted |
| Mwaka vandavalanga | That the years can be counted |
| Vinu avi vyó | These things |
| Tundimanya mwaa kushomya kutulangudya | We learned them because we studied and we were shown |

Admiration was mixed with the regret of someone who did not study, of an old man who understood that his time for truly getting to know what he desired to know was past. "You can't bend a catfish when it is already dry," only when it is fresh and supple. From this regretful position, Mustafa admonished the youth to come:

| Atunatango' vyoe | Let's not talk too much |
| Tukashamidye anatango' vyoe | Us who have not studied, let's not talk much |
| | |
| Tunkushi doni: | We say: |
| "Likambale avanampinda" ajumile | "You cannot bend a catfish when it's dried" |
| Vavetu vave' naibati | Our friends are lucky |
| Valinkushomya shikola | They are studying in school |
| Vakangapele valinkumanya kwandika | When they grow old they will know how to write |
| Kenga atumanya | Us, we don't know |
| Wetu tukashamidye kupata tabu | Us who have not studied, we suffer |
| Ibalugwa yakutumidya anamali' vyoe | The letters addressed to us, we don't go far |
| Kenga kwandika mwene | And writing is the same |
| Lipundishe tundamanya wé | Let's study so that we learn |

The song was concluded by an explanation and a moral appeal: "My son, don't leave school. So that you know what happens in the country (*vipita nshilambo*)." A staunch defender of modernist education, Mustafa maintained a solid moral outlook on the new mores of postsocialist communal villages:

| Kukumbila kwashinang'olo | The elders' drinking |
| Igwa manangu | Hear, my friends |
| Vitandeke ku-Maringue ku-Mwambula | What happened at the maringue in Mwambula |
| Ndya' njetu ku-Maringue | The wife of a friend of ours at the maringue |
| | |
| Andilodya shinema yó | She showed a film |

| | |
|---|---|
| Wetu atunshema lina | We don't call the name |
| Tunjopa ntwagwe andankamanga | We fear that her husband will beat her |
| Ndya' nyangu ku-Maringue | The wife of a friend of mine at the maringue |
| Andilodya shinema yó | Showed a cinema |
| Bila kugwala ishupi | Without wearing underwear |
| Kukwela muwa kulepa we | Climbing up, that's far |
| Lyamba ntandavala | The dawn is breaking |
| Mwenu makongwe | You, the women |
| Mwenda kukumbila | Who go to drinking |
| Gwala ishupi | Wear underwear |
| Nno' njenu vitandeke | Look what happened to your friend |
| Andilodya shinema | She showed a film |

This moral condemnation of drinking and misbehavior was also connected to a personal predicament. Mustafa's sons from both his wives turned to alcohol and laziness. The older one—significantly nicknamed Malyatabu ("rich in suffering")—was meant to take care of the father's rice fields but only managed to get drunk on sugarcane alcohol that he brewed in the lowlands. The younger ones benefited from the father's wealth, doing little for the family business and failing even to take school seriously. They hung out with "market boys"—village youths aspiring to move to the city, who spend their days in the shadows of the market without activity and prospect if not grabbing a drink, a girl, or a one-day job. The sight of this waste of opportunity saddened Mustafa, who did not even admit his sons into the shuku nwele group, fearing that they might be tempted to sell the masks.

Mustafa received another hard blow from the 2002–3 lion crisis. His effort to construct a new communal village in the lowlands of Lipelwa raised the jealously of the nearby leader of Mandava. When a boy was abducted and devoured by a lion, Mustafa was accused of being a "lion's master," together with seven other people who were at the forefront of the construction of the new village. Four people were killed by the popular militia of Mandava's president. Mustafa managed to survive the severe beating. He was the only one among all the lynched people to turn to justice, and he managed to have his persecutor arrested, if only briefly. The ordeal weakened Mustafa's body but not his morale or curiosity, nor his faith in progress. In one of our last conversations, the elder inquired about the ways in which technological innovation occurs. Does it stem from the genius of a single person? Or is it something that occurs cooperatively? How was the bicycle invented? And the radio? As I stumbled my way through a long answer, Mustafa, tired, dozed off.[21]

7. If the two millennial inventions naupanga and shuku nwele stemmed from a desire for the global, they were also the product of a much older local cultural dynamic, whereby innovations produced in the liminal Messalo lowlands "climb" the plateau and there acquire new fame, status, and resonance. Like neijale before it, shuku nwele was akin to a nshindo character, polished and transformed in a genre. Mustafa liked to stress his lowland roots: "I grew up where you have just been. In the wetlands. I was born there and I grew up there. I climbed [the plateau] only later. My life is there; my wetlands are my home." Shuku nwele's song referenced Nampyopyo because of his iconic status on the plateau, but Mustafa had seen Shumu's lowland masks and considered them superior: "In that family of mapiko, the best one was Shumu." Naupanga's connection to the lowlands were more substantial than the haphazard purchase of a mask in the village of Myangalewa: the elder with the machete closely resembled the old mask of *Nandulumbuka*, "the crazy one," who clears the funerary ceremony with cudgel blows and could come to the dance-field menacingly armed with a bow—or a machete.

While the lowlands were providing new inspiration for plateau masquerading, nshindo itself went through a revival and a new effervescence. After the glories of the late colonial years, the dance had been briefly resurrected in the late 1970s (see chap. 8, sec. 10) but the onslaught of Renamo in the lowlands blocked it once again. With the end of the war, a new generation of youth—some in their thirties, some in their mid-twenties—initiated new groups. They sought instruction and magical protection from their elders. The villages of Myangalewa and Litamanda emerged as the new centers of nshindo: in the former lived many of the players of Lipato's original ensemble who had moved there from Mbau; in the latter, Shalele Mawasha, inventor of the sorcerer's mask. Other groups emerged around Mbau, instructed and led by old players of Lipato's ensemble.

The youths who took over respected the fundamental rules and sequence of the old funerary masquerade, introducing, however, new characters and dancing styles. Their critical gaze turned on the elders, with the iconic mask of the overly proud war veteran who marries a young girl—a theme also widely exposed in feminine song (see chap. 9, sec. 6). Playful ambivalence did not spare the youths themselves, who identified with the characters of *Nampanga* and *Litunu*, "I-Will-Roll-It" and "Hyena," seasoned smokers of marijuana—a drug that, like alcohol, had escaped the old boundaries of consummation in connection with agricultural labor to become widespread among the youths. In the performance, the two smoking buddies consume the joints with propitiatory gestures, waving the joint around the head so as to make it "go down," and then blissfully laughing at each other's distorted features.

While the groups from the area of Mbau maintained the traditional nshindo attire, the ones from the Messalo introduced radical elements of novelty. The group from Myangalewa used Manchester United t-shirts as dancing outfits; one young artist introduced military belts with turtle shells decorated with a mixture of ancient *lagesha* beads and fake brand plaques. More significantly, the cross on the forehead of Shipindi the sorcerer was replaced with the Nike logo. Consumerism, not religion, was now seen as the strongest arcane power from which a sorcerer might want to draw.

The new nshindo enjoyed a renewed popularity in the lowlands, where it was danced mostly at funerary ceremonies but also on the occasion of state festivals. The groups from Myangalewa even ventured to dance on the plateau, defying the mistrust of conservative practitioners—but significantly omitting the final mask of the sorcerer. The cumbersome nature of nshindo, however, prevented it from traveling beyond local boundaries. The dance required heavy materials (sacks of masks); a relatively large number of performers; and most of all, the setting up of an enclosure "mined" against magical attacks, for even (or especially) in times of democracy none would dare reproduce the actions of sorcerers without protection.


8. It was precisely naupanga's portability and flexibility that earned it a fleeting passage in the limelight. After the district phase of the II FNDP, all of the three selected groups renounced the victory, refusing to mingle with other groups—as required by the festival rules—to form a single ensemble. Nshesho elders despised the animal masks who had arrived first; the mang'anyamu boys wanted to go en masse;

and Mustafa, who had also qualified, was worried about having to reveal the secrets of his puppets and rubber masks. The conflict became dangerous as the lion crisis unfolded. Elders crossed their arms, and the district culture representative, a school professor called Gerónimo Mussa Katembe, began to worry that Muidumbe—the heartland of Makonde dance—would not have a delegation to go to Pemba.

As a last resort, and with a little help from my side, Katembe turned to the youths. A few days before the departure date, we contacted the Naupanga boys, who accepted enthusiastically. "Six people is enough! One dancer, one drummer, one for calling, and another for answering . . ." Katembe insisted in summoning another iron-striking youth group, *mashawona,* that he loved: "It is strong and very healthy." Furthermore, the two groups would have no difficulty in merging. A selection of the district's *utamaduni* groups was formed, to stand in as a third dance and complement the masculinity and youthfulness of the others. The delegation that was constituted in such haste met with the one from Mueda, where yet another gender struggle had taken place over the participation of *lingundumbwe,* this time won by the men. The bus traveled the long, bumpy road to Pemba alternating between moments of elated singing and tiredness. It arrived well after dark, and the dancers were accommodated in old naval quarters. As the dawn broke, the Naupanga boys—dancers of the global dance of videos and violence—stared in silent stupefaction at the sea that they had never before seen in their lives. Then they gathered courage and swam until they were called back to the quarters.

Naupanga did not perform well on the festival stage, and not only because of the haste with which it had been summoned and the lack of rehearsals. The dance did not have the same look on the podium as it did in the village. Lost in the vastness of the open-air theatre, the machete seemed more childish than threatening; there was not room enough for complex tricks with the bicycle; and because the boys were unaware of the functioning of microphones, the songs were lost. Shanjolo's sinuous dance styles raised roars of applause, but the dance overall did not impress the conservative judges.

An all-mapiko ensemble from the district of Nangade brought home the prize. The group had been choreographed by the administrator. It consisted of a combination of nshesho and the "slave-masks" *nantyaka* and *lingoti.* The nshesho had been prepared in such a way as to flow seamlessly; the dancers had been instructed to stay close to the microphones. The show provided a spotless embodiment of socialist aesthetics, tempered in the second part by the more playful face-masks.

A party was organized to celebrate the end of the festival's provincial phase. Those who would go on to Maputo were electrified. Some of the losers were scornful—especially the mapiko dancers from Mueda, who had been defeated by the much younger Nangade ensemble. Most were happy anyhow about making it that far. Each and every one had been given a commemorative t-shirt and cap. It was a cool windy July night in Pemba, and the party was held in a luxurious house at the far end of the bay. As the night dragged on, no food appeared; there were only some cans of beer and soft drinks that were quickly drank or stored away to be sold for cash, back at the village. Sitting in a well-lit rondavel, the vice-minister of culture and the director of the National Company of Dance and Song—the main organizers of the event—shared a copious meal, encircled by the famished and shivering dancers. A trolley filled with whiskeys sat close to the table. As the leader's Mbembean dinner dragged on, someone screamed: "There, they are stealing the meat"![22] A crowd encircled a vehicle belonging to an officer of the provincial directorate of culture and intercepted some crates of meat and beer, which were ransacked and distributed. The meal for the artists came much later, and it was no different from what we had been eating throughout the festival: a plate of rice with a small piece of meat. When the prize-giving ceremony took place, toward midnight, the popular invocations to Frelimo elicited by the vice-minister came faintly and were blown away by the cold ocean breeze.


9. The end of the festival ushered in a new phase in Mozambican history, which marks the threshold where this book's narrative ends. Armando Emilio Guebuza was elected president of the Party and candidate for the presidency. There was little doubt that he would win the elections. In 2003, Chissano traveled throughout the country to bid farewell to the people whom he had led through thick and thin for twenty years. His journey started in Mueda and coincided with the first provincial festival of mapiko promoted by the ministry of culture. Unlike the II FNDP, in which variety and novelty were encouraged, here only mainstream nshesho groups were admitted. Naupanga showed up,

uninvited, but was not allowed to compete—only to dance as an extra group at the end of the festival. The first prize went to the local group of war veterans, the famous Niyere, unchallenged by the Nangade group, which had been delayed on the road and could not make it.

Guebuza won the elections in early 2005. One of the first acts of the presidency was to unify the Ministries of Education and Culture into a single entity called MEC—an explicit reference to the Department of Education and Culture (DEC) that Guebuza had presided over during the liberation struggle, indicating a return to the instrumentalist conception of culture as weapon of political control. Together with the Ministry of War Veterans, the MEC launched a program of memorialization of the history of the struggle, in a mode reminiscent of Zimbabwean "patriotic history."[23] Guebuza's government also institutionalized cultural festivals. A Festival of Popular Song was held in Pemba in 2006, and one took place every second year, focusing on a specific aspect of Mozambique's performative heritage. The provincial festival of mapiko was also institutionalized as a biannual event.

A major marker of Guebuza's presidency was the introduction of a new light currency, which dropped three zeros from the previous one, dubbed Nova Família Metical ("the New Family of Metical"). The old banknotes with the images of Frelimo's leaders—Mondlane, Samora, and Chissano—were replaced by the monolithic icon of Samora:

| | |
|---|---|
| Tunnambwalele Baba Guebuza | Let's thank papa Guebuza |
| Andikandyanga njuluku Nova Familia Metical | He arranged the money New Family of Metical |
| Mushu mwake kupagwa Samora | On the front there is Samora |
| Nashilangola ntandi | Our first leader[24] |

The currency was an icon of Guebuza's new course: a marriage of authoritarianism resting on struggle credentials and neoliberalism, which looked to China as a model. The neoliberal honeymoon that had characterized the years of Chissano's democratic rule was over, and soon popular protest would explode in Mozambique's cities. The government preempted possible malcontents among the Makonde by showering the plateau with war pensions. Everybody now became a veteran, even people who were too young to have fought the war. At the same time, foreign investment was called in. In 2009, provisions were made for the lands of the previous state farm of Nguri in the Messalo lowlands—a "sleeping giant," to use Guebuza's expression—to be leased to a Chinese company. In the communal villages of Muidumbe, three visible phenomena signaled this turn to neoliberal authoritarianism: the fencing of soccer fields so that people had to pay to watch; the appearance of permanent garbage mounds, signifying the final decline of the socialist duty of "collective cleaning" and the prospect of slummification; and a new style of cementing the outside of the huts (*kubuliziya*) in a rough way, so that people could not lean against the walls.

Mapiko wavered between commodification and political patronage. In the years before his death, Mustafa considered the idea of building a fenced dance hall to show his masks to a paying audience. Meanwhile, video owners were cashing in on the tapes that I produced, and dance groups asked me to make them DVDs that they would sell. On the other hand, the governmental promotion of nshesho through festivals generated a revival of this nationalist genre. Following the example set by the victorious Nangade ensemble, new youth groups emerged, in Chai, Litamanda, and Mocimboa; some of the old groups, such as the historical one from Nampanya, were revamped by youths. Reacting to the absence of state support and the preference for male ensembles, the lingundumbwe group from Mueda refused to partake in state festivals and began dancing at high prices for the occasional cultural tourists. An enterprising nshesho group from Chai managed to secure an NGO donation by participating in AIDS awareness campaigns, which unleashed the jealousy of the nonsponsored groups of the area.

Faced with the dilemmas of neoliberal authoritarianism, the youths turned to a double language. On the one hand, they enrolled in the new nshesho groups, composed and sang songs of political praise for Guebuza, and devised new dance styles that enacted the history of the liberation struggle. On the other hand, even while celebrating patriotic history with the elders, youths voiced their discontent in other genres. Such was the case of the *bwarabwà* group from Chai, which provocatively called itself Nova Família and whose corrosive songs enjoyed a tremendous popularity as they were broadcast on the radio by Nandenga and sold on pirated tapes in the villages. The most iconic piece addressed the governor of Cabo Delgado, asking whether the "new family" idiom was a masquerade for nepotism and reminding the leaders of the old struggle rhetorics against lineage (*shinalikola*):

| | |
|---|---|
| Baba Lázaro Mati ne' tundakudya | Papa Lázaro Mati today we ask you |
| Ukalota kungunga ungunga | If you want to arrest me, arrest me |
| Ukalota matola ng'anyola | If you want to flog me, flog me |
| Bai wetu tulambe' kumanya | Well, we want to know |
| Ishilikali yamaduvano | If the government of nowadays |
| Ikava kenga iwena shinalikola | It now functions like a family |
| Kudyanga ungwauli' shana apa | You'd better tell us clearly here |
| Tundamanyia mwenu mavetu | We tell you, my friends |
| Mwika' kudimesa kenga mashepi | Who sit on the chairs like chiefs |
| Mukashema nkutano wetu atupagwa | If you call a meeting, we are not there |
| Ata mukalailila limbesha wetu atupagwa | If you tell us to do the cleaning, we are not there |
| Kamana tunkwona tuvene | That's why we saw by ourselves |
| Shikapagwa shakujavananga | If there is something to share |
| Uti nshilambo mujava shinalikola jó! | In the whole country you share it within the family, jó! |
| Mujava shinalikola, njomba eh! | You share within the family, uncle! |
| Mujava shinalikola, mama eh! | You share within the family, mama! |
| Kuva kenga ushitenda ing'ondo shinalikola | It looks like you did the war within the family |
| Yakupukusha njungu nkaloni kuMoshambiki | To expel the white colonist from Mozambique[25] |

Naupanga, in contrast, drew on the metaphor of orphanhood—or pennilessness—to call itself out of the game:

| | |
|---|---|
| Jugwa shonde Guebuza | I plead forgiveness, Guebuza |
| Naupanga não tem família | Naupanga doesn't have a family |

# Resurrections

| | |
|---|---|
| Kunnaila wetu mwanda | We say goodbye, we're going |
| Tunakadyana 25 de Setembro | We'll meet on the 25th of September |
| Kuka kwetu lude' Mwalela | We go home to our village, Mwalela |
| Amunagambane navadyavenu | Don't fight with your wives |
| Tunakadyana 25 de Setembro | We'll meet on the 25th of September |
| Ta ta ta mavetu ta ta ta | Bye-bye, friends, bye-bye |
| Tunkuka kwetu ludeya Mwalela | We go home to our village, Mwalela |

—NMA/Nshesho/Mwalela/2004

THE HISTORY of mapiko was presented in these pages as a sequence of actors and events—individuals and their ideas, inventions and their fortunes, institutions and their transformations—articulated in a narrative that framed them according to their mutual relations and their imbrication in broader sets of events and forces. In other terms, this is a history of things-that-happened (*res gestae*; in Shimakonde, *vitandeke*), predominantly based on the living recollections of the people who were its protagonists (or sidekicks).

If one were to reverse this image—as in the negative of a photograph or the hollow of a bas relief—it would look like the snapshot of the collective memory of a people taken at a determinate moment of time. It would reveal how much, and what, people remember of mapiko and why, and how the memory of that practice is important for them as individuals and for their sense of collective belonging. My inquiries raised the curiosity of several local people, who accompanied me to do interviews or debated with elders. They also sparked heated discussions about matters of aesthetics and genealogy, always fueled by the playful rivalry so deeply woven into the fabric of mapiko. Who really invented *neijale*: the Litamandas or the Mapates? Did the Mwalela group really deserve to win the 2002 festival? However, the recollections elicited in the course of this project, over more than eleven years, were not rooted in any vernacular genre of storytelling. Our conversations were understood by elders and youths alike as belonging to a specific speech genre, interviewing, with which they were familiar because of the somewhat high incidence of visits by research brigades over the past thirty years. A degree of autonomous storytelling must have occurred from generation to generation, but by and large the memory of older mapiko was not entrusted to the oral medium. It was instead preserved in performance.

This study argues that dance competition, itself rooted in ritual rivalry, fueled invention and innovation throughout the history of mapiko. The desire for fame made talented innovators cast their gaze far away to find inspiration, so as to tower above others; imitation made their inventions spread, coalesce into genres, and acquire generational significance; rivalry between groups and between practitioners of different genres charged these dynamics with larger-than-life emotions. The vitality and momentousness of mapiko is tied to such rivalry—heritage practitioners interested in its preservation should take note.

If competition engendered rupture, attuning mapiko to the times that it was swiftly traversing, continuity was ensured by the practice of resurrection (*kutakatuwa*): the reinvention of older styles based on a degree of fidelity to the original. Through resurrection, the memory of older forms of mapiko was kept alive in the performative archive of contemporary genres. "Resurrecting is like history (*maimyo*). Because there is the history spoken through the mouth, that tells the deeds of our elders, and there is history through mapiko."[1] It is thanks to Nampyopyo's and Shumu's resurrection of *mileya* that we can have a glimpse into the precolonial rhythms of mapiko; together with *nshindo* they conserved a character-based modality that would have otherwise been lost. Likewise, the large-eared revolutionary jester *Neijale* revived an antique mask from the times of colonial conquest. More generally, the mimetic dance sequences embedded within *nshesho* and all subsequent genres allowed for the reproduction and incorporation of older, forgotten dances. The oral transmission of knowledge around masquerading is always prompted by performance-related questions: What is this style that we are playing? What was this dance? Who was this character that we are dancing?[2]

Transmission and reproduction also occur in less explicit ways, as sometimes apparently novel masquerades resurrect archetypical forms. *Mang'anyamu*, the masquerade seen by many as the expression of democratic disorder, reactivated an age-old tradition of animal masking, embedded in *shilo* and possibly in more arcane genres. *Naupanga*, the globalized mask of videos and violence, was not only a reinvention of a nshindo character but also is also deeply reminiscent of other machete-carrying masks danced in the region, possibly representing a recurring archetype.[3]

Each mapiko genre is thus a repository of temporally layered performative memory—of forms topical, ancient, and possibly both. Such memory is eminently embodied. It resides in the schemata of performance, as well as in the know-how connected to the materiality of the mask: in carving, painting, weaving, and building a frame; in dressing, tying up, attaching, and arranging; in tanning, stretching, and warming up . . . Each of these actions is traversed by multiple temporalities, by innovation and tradition alike.

This temporally layered nature of mapiko also provides a warning, a signpost intimating not to cross the line that separates historicizing from historicism. As this book abundantly demonstrates, the aesthetics and practice of mapiko would be opaque without the work of historical reconstruction. Considering all genres and forms as merely a product of their times would, however, be a mistake. Resurrection and anachronism provide points of resistance to this temptation, which is inherent in the endeavor of historicizing, always reminding us of the *longue-durée* historical dynamics at work in each mapiko genre. For Charles Baudelaire, the master thinker of modernity and modernism, this dualism is at the core of the work of art itself, made of "the ephemeral, the fugitive, the contingent, that half of art, whose other half is the eternal and the immutable."[4]

# Notes

## INTRODUCTION

1. *Ntene* is *Bombax rhodognaphalon*. Native to southeastern Africa, it is often confused in the literature with kapok itself, which is a separate species. In Kiswahili it is called *msufi wa porini*.

2. Prof. Sandro Bruschi, conversation, Maputo, April 2001.

3. On the etymology of the word *mask*, from the Latin *masca*, see Cesare Poppi, "Persona, Larva, Masca: Masks, Identity and Cognition in the Cultures of Europe," in *Mind, Man and Mask*, ed. Subhash Chandra Malik (New Delhi: Indira Gandhi National Centre for the Arts, 2001), 129–54.

4. The verb *kutamba* also means "play" in other languages of the region.

5. Fredric Jameson, *The Political Unconscious: Narrative as a Socially Symbolic Act* (New York: Cornell University Press, 1983), 9.

6. See, respectively, amongst others, Henry John Drewal and Margaret Thompson Drewal, *Gelede: Art and Female Power among the Yoruba* (Bloomington: Indiana University Press, 1983); Jean Comaroff, *Body of Power, Spirit of Resistance: The Culture and History of a South African People* (Chicago: University of Chicago Press, 1985); Corinne Kratz, *Affecting Performance: Meaning, Movement, and Experience in Okiek Women's Initiation* (Washington, DC: Smithsonian Institution Press, 1994); and Mary Jo Arnoldi, *Playing with Time: Art and Performance in Central Mali* (Bloomington: Indiana University Press, 1995).

7. Terence Ranger, *Dance and Society in Eastern Africa: The Beni Ngoma* (London: Heinemann, 1975).

8. Johannes Fabian, "Popular Culture in Africa: Findings and Conjectures," *Africa* 48, no. 4 (1978): 315.

9. The best critique of this aspect of British Marxist historiography has been articulated by the Subaltern Studies Collective. See Dipesh Chakrabarty, *Habitations of Modernity: Essays in the Wake of Subaltern Studies* (Chicago: University of Chicago Press, 2002), 3–20.

10. Karin Barber, "Popular Arts in Africa," *African Studies Review* 30, no. 3 (1987): 12–13. The partition of African art into traditional, popular, and elite was then taken up by Yves Valentin Mudimbe in *The Idea of Africa* (Bloomington: Indiana University Press, 1994), 154–208. Barber would later dilute her tripartition into a more complex rendering; Karin Barber, "Introduction," in *Readings in African Popular Culture*, ed. Karin Barber (London: International

African Institute, 1997), 1–12. It is striking that the scholars who most lucidly critiqued the modernist teleology—Fabian and Mudimbe—reinscribed it in the field of Africanism through their theories of popular culture.

11. For an incisive discussion, see Sidney Littlefield Kasfir, *African Art and the Colonial Encounter* (Bloomington: University of Indiana Press, 2007), ix–xii.

12. Zoë Strother, *Inventing Masks: Agency and History in the Art of the Central Pende* (Chicago: University of Chicago Press, 1998). See also Edna Bay, *Asen, Ancestors and Vodun: Tracing Change in African Art* (Champaign: University of Illinois Press, 2008).

13. Sidney Littlefield Kasfir, "One Tribe, One Style? Paradigms in the Historiography of African Art," *History in Africa* 2 (1984): 163–93.

14. Such criticism does not aim to belittle Strother's work, whose profound influence on my own endeavor I wish to explicitly acknowledge. It is precisely because I took her book as a model that I was led to probe, and try to overcome, what I came to perceive as its shortcomings.

15. Kelly Askew, "As Plato Duly Warned: Music, Politics and Social Change in Coastal East Africa," *Anthropological Quarterly* 76, no. 4 (2003): 617. See also Mary Jo Arnoldi, "Playing the Puppets: Innovation and Rivalry in Bamana Youth Theatre of Mali," *TDR* 32, no. 2 (1988): 65–82.

16. NMA/Mang'anyamu/Matambalale/2004. At least half of the two thousand songs that I recorded have some competitive element.

17. Gregory Bateson, *Naven: A Survey of the Problems Suggested by a Composite Picture of the Culture of a New Guinea Tribe Drawn from Three Points of View* (Cambridge: Cambridge University Press, 1936) and *Steps to an Ecology of Mind* (Chicago: University of Chicago Press, 2000), 64–71.

18. Johan Huizinga, *Homo Ludens: A Study of the Play-Element in Culture* (London: Routledge, 1980), 12–13. For a discussion of theories of play in African performance, see Kennedy Chinyowa, "Towards an Aesthetic Theory for African Popular Theatre," *South African Theatre Journal* 21, no. 1 (2007): 12–30.

19. Mikhail Bakhtin, *Rabelais and His World* (Bloomington: Indiana University Press, 1984).

20. Kasfir, "One Tribe."

21. Frank Gunderson and Gregory Barz, eds., *Mashindano! Competitive Music Performance in East Africa* (Dar Es Salaam, Tanzania: Mkuki Na Nyota, 2005); Rebecca Gearhart, "Ngoma Memories: A History of Competitive Music and Dance Performance on the Kenya Coast" (PhD diss., University of Florida, 1998).

22. It is surprising that the masking traditions of the region—*mapiko*, *nyau*, and *makishi*—have not been explicitly linked to the Swahili culture of competition. The one exception is Elise Johansen, "Makonde Mask Dance: Performing Identity," in Gunderson and Barz, *Mashindano*, 255–70, which is about mapiko in Dar Es Salaam.

23. Jeremy Presthold, "On the Global Repercussions of East African Consumerism," *American Historical Review* 109, no. 3 (2004): 755–81.

24. João Paulo Borges-Coelho, "Moçambique e a África Austral: Uma Leitura Histórica do Presente," paper presented at the V Congress of African Studies in the Iberic World, Covilhã, 4–6 May 2006.

25. Johannes Fabian, *Time and the Other* (New York: Columbia University Press, 1983).

26. See Carlos Fernandes, "Dinâmicas de Pesquisa em Ciências Sociais no Moçambique Pós-independente: O Caso do Centro de Estudos Africanos, 1975–1990" (PhD diss., Universidade Federal da Bahia 2011). For Christian Geffray's scathing critique of the center, see Geffray, "Fragments d'un Discours du Pouvoir (1975–1985)," *Politique Africaine* 29 (1988): 71–85.

27. Christian Geffray, *La Cause des Armes au Mozambique: Anthropologie d'une Guerre Civile* (Paris: Karthala, 1990). For a critique, see Alice Dinerman, *Revolution, Counter-revolution and Revisionism in Post-colonial Africa: The Case of Mozambique, 1975–1994* (London: Routledge, 2006).

28. Michel Cahen, "'Entrons dans la Nation': Notes pour Une Étude du Discours Politique de la Marginalité: Le Cas de la RENAMO du Mozambique," *Politique Africaine* 67 (1997): 70–88.

29. See, for example, Alcinda Honwana, *Espíritos Vivos, Tradições Modernas: Possessão de Espíritos e Reintegração Social Pós-guerra no Sul de Moçambique* (Maputo: Promedia, 2002); and Harry West, *Kupilikula: Governance and the Invisible Realm in Mozambique* (Chicago: University of Chicago Press, 2005). West's ethnography has been tremendously influential to my own endeavor, setting the stakes of ethnographic detail and creative writing; it also prompted me to offer a different reading of Makonde history and subjectivity

30. For an account of this Cold War polarization, see Yussuf Adam, *Escapar aos Dentes do Crocodilo e Cair na Boca do Leopardo: Trajectoria de Moçambique Pós-colonial, 1975–1990* (Maputo: Promedia, 2006).

31. This is a more general problem of African historiography, which tends to "see political identity as derivative of either market-based or cultural identities." Mamhood Mamdani, *When Victims Become Killers: Colonialism, Nativism, and the Genocide in Rwanda* (Princeton: Princeton University Press, 2002), 21.

32. Leroy Vail and Landeg White, *Power and the Praise Poem: Southern African Voices in History* (Charlottesville: University of Virginia Press, 1991).

33. Adelino Munguambe, *A Música Chope* (Maputo: Promedia, 2000); Viriato Tamele and João Vilanculo, *Algumas Danças Tradicionais da Zona Norte de Moçambique* (Maputo: Arquivo do Património Cultural, 2003). For the bibliography on mapiko, see further, chap. 1, sec. 10.

34. On oral performance, however, see Jeanne-Marie Penvenne and Bento Sitoe, "Power, Poets and the People: Mozambican Voices Interpreting History," *Social Dynamics* 26, no. 2 (2000): 58–86.

35. Kelly Askew, *Performing the Nation: Swahili Music and Cultural Politics in Tanzania* (Chicago: University of Chicago Press, 2002); Laura Edmonson, *Performance and Politics in Tanzania: The Nation on Stage* (Bloomington: Indiana University Press, 2007); Lisa Gillman, *The Dance of*

*Politics: Gender, Performance and Democratization in Malawi* (Philadelphia: Temple University Press, 2009).

36. "The unifying principle of all microhistorical research is the belief that microscopic observation will reveal factors previously unobserved" (101). Giovanni Levi, "On Microhistory," in *New Perspectives on Historical Writing*, ed. Peter Burke (Cambridge: Polity Press, 2001), 97–199.

37. My doubts about multisited ethnography were reinforced by a conversation with James Clifford, who expressed his skepticism about the depth and texture of recent multisited monographs, Ecole des Hautes Etudes en Sciences Sociales, Paris, 2002.

38. Paul Feyerabend, *Against Method: Outline of an Anarchist Theory of Knowledge* (New York: New Left Books, 1975).

39. I carried out eight months of fieldwork in 2002; four in 2003; ten in 2004/2005; two in 2006; one in 2008; and two in 2009. In 2009 and 2011 I invited mapiko performers in Cape Town, where I live.

40. How many? I have not counted, but the figure must be in the order of three hundred.

41. In late 2004 and early 2005, initiations and elections overlapped; I wrote about this entanglement in "Kummwangalela Guebuza: The Mozambican General Elections of 2004 in Muidumbe and the Roots of the Loyalty of Makonde People to Frelimo," *Lusotopie* 13, no. 2 (2006): 103–26.

42. This use of mimetic syllabic sequences to describe drumming is common throughout Africa. Sometimes this can be very precise, indicating the way in which the drum should be struck.

43. While I benefited from festivals, holidays, and rituals to watch and film performances, in some cases I solicited a specific dance, motivating a group to take part in this or that event through a financial reward. This is an established local practice: groups demand money when they dance, for instance, in funerary ceremonies or puberty rituals.

44. The usual suspicions against a foreign researcher were amplified by my involvement in a witchcraft crisis that hit the district of Muidumbe in 2002–3. See Paolo Israel, "The War of Lions: Witch-Hunts, Occult Idioms and Post-socialism in Northern Mozambique," *Journal of Southern African Studies* 35, no. 1 (March 2009): 155–74.

45. On questions of allegoresis, my mind was especially expanded by Jameson, *Political Unconscious*, 17–107.

46. Jacques Depelchin taught me the first lesson; Paul Veyne the second; see *Writing History: Essay on Epistemology* (Manchester: Manchester University Press, 1984).

47. Jacques Revel, ed., *Jeux d'Echelles: La Micro-analyse à l'Expérience* (Paris: Le Seuil, 1996).

48. The meditation on the epistemology of historical knowledge that is the centerpiece of Ricoeur's last work settles on *jeux d'échelles* as a methodological way out of the conundrums of historical in/determinism, as well as a solution to the vexed question of collective consciousness; see Paul Ricoeur,

*Memory, History, Forgetting* (Chicago: University of Chicago Press, 2005), 209–15, 274–80. See also Matti Peltonen, "Clues, Margins, and Monads: The Micro-Macro Link in Historical Research," *History and Theory* 40, no. 3 (2001): 347–59.

49. I learned a few practical lessons concerning parataxis and omission from Ernest Hemingway; see especially *A Moveable Feast: The Restored Edition* (New York: Scribner, 2009).

50. This is Chinua Achebe's version of it, cited in Nicolas Argenti, "Masks and Masquerades," *Journal of Material Culture* 2, no. 3 (1997): 370.

51. Patrick McNaughton, *A Bird Dance near Saturday City: Sidi Ballo and the Art of West African Masquerade* (Bloomington: Indiana University Press, 2008).

52. https://sites.google.com/site/anaikala/ and https://vimeo.com/mapiko.

53. Achille Mbembe, "Writing Africa," in *New South African Keywords*, ed. Nick Sheperd and Steven Robbins (Athens: Ohio University Press, 2008), 247.

## CHAPTER 1: THE WAR OF SEXES

1. See, in a vast literature, Eduardo Medeiros, *As Etapas da Escravatura no Norte de Moçambique* (Maputo: Arquivo Histórico de Moçambique, 1988); and Edward Alpers, *Ivory and Slaves in East Central Africa: Changing Patterns of International Trade to the Later Nineteenth Century* (London: Heinemann, 1975).

2. Malyn Newitt, *A History of Mozambique* (Bloomington: Indiana University Press, 1995), 176.

3. Joseph Thomson, "Notes on the Basin of the River Rovuma, East Africa," *Proceedings of the Royal Geographical Society* 4 (1882), 67; Chauncy Maples, "Masasi and the Rovuma District in East Africa," *Proceedings of the Royal Geographical Society* 2 (1880), 347; Henry O'Neill, "Journey in the District West of Cape Delgado Bay," *Proceedings of the Royal Geographical Society* 5 (1885): 398.

4. O'Neill, "Journey," 393.

5. Ibid., 399, 402.

6. The language of the Tanzanian Makonde is generally referred to as Chimakonde; the one of their Mozambican neighbors as Shimakonde. In the latter language, tonal pattern and vowel length make the difference between the name of the Tanzanian and the Mozambican Makonde people: respectively, *vàmàkóònde* and *vámákònde*.

7. The first volume of *Os Macondes de Moçambique* was on landscape, history, and economics:, Jorge António Dias, *Os Macondes de Moçambique*, Vol. I: *Aspectos Históricos e Economicos* (Lisbon: Junta de Investigação Ultramarina, 1964), with a second edition published by Instituto de Investigação Científica Tropical in 1998. The second volume was on material culture: Jorge António Dias and Margot Dias, *Os Macondes de Moçambique*, Vol. II: *Cultura Material* (Lisbon: Junta de Investigação Ultramarina, 1964).

The third was on kinship, mentality, and ritual life: Jorge António Dias and Margot Dias, *Os Macondes de Moçambique*, Vol. III: *Vita Social e Ritual* (Lisbon: Junta de Investigação Ultramarina, 1970). The fourth was on oral literature: Manuel Viegas Guerreiro, *Os Macondes de Moçambique*, Vol. IV: *Sabedoria, Língua, Literatura e Jogos* (Lisbon: Junta de Investigação Ultramarina, 1966). A fifth volume, on arts, was planned but never written. On the occasion of a trip to South Africa, Jorge António Dias published *Portuguese Contribution to Cultural Anthropology* (Johannesburg: Witwatersrand University Press, 1961).

8. João de Piña-Cabral, "Anthropologie et Identité Nationale au Portugal," *Gradhiva* 11 (1992): 31.

9. On the local history of the Companhia do Nyassa, see Eduardo Medeiros, *História de Cabo Delgado e do Niassa (c. 1836–1929)* (Maputo: Central Impressora, 1997).

10. The first mission was established in 1924, but massive conversion did not occur until later. For further discussion, see chap. 3, sec. 5.

11. Dias and Dias, *Os Macondes III*, 163–64.

12. Ibid., 393.

13. George Harley, *Masks as Agents of Social Control in Northeast Liberia*, Peabody Papers 32, no. 2 (Cambridge, MA: Peabody Museum, 1950). See also Roy Sieber, "Masks as Agents of Social Control," *African Studies Bulletin* 5, no. 2 (1962): 8–13.

14. A demonstration that women are not in power even in rigidly matrilineal and matrilocal societies—that women's symbolic power is ultimately mustered by the men to their own advantage—is provided by Christian Geffray in *Ni Père ni Mère: Critique de la Parenté; Le Cas Makhuwa* (Paris: Le Seuil, 1990). Geffray shows that in the Makua case the exploited victims of the system were the cadets obliged to serve in the wife's lineage.

15. The capacity of drawing a good description despite one's interpretive prejudices: this is what postcolonial criticism discounts a priori. Atanásio Nhussi commented on Dias's work with such a pragmatic attitude: "He might have been a crazy colonialist, but some things, he got right" (conversation, Cape Town, May 2009).

16. Dias and Dias, *Os Macondes III*, 203–4.

17. Ibid., 204. Max Gluckman observes the same kind of women's participation "as the singing and sometimes dancing chorus" in the Zambian *makishi* and remarks that going through "a large body of literature on the ceremonies and masks and dances of these and congener tribes nowhere did we find a similar stress on the participation of women." Gluckman, "The Philosophical Roots of Masked Dancers in Barotseland (Western Province), Zambia," in *In Memoriam Jorge Dias* (Lisbon: Junta de Investigação Ultramarina, 1974), 144.

18. Dias and Dias, *Os Macondes III*, 180, 204.

19. Ibid., 204. For a general discussion, see Fritz Kramer, *The Red Fez: Art and Spirit Possession in Africa* (London: Verso, 1993).

20. Dias's translation of the last verse does not correspond to the Shima-konde text. *Tuvana Maliya* means "We are the Maria lineage": the group is exclaiming the name of the matrilineage.

21. Dias and Dias, *Os Macondes III*, 205.

22. Manuel Simões Alberto, "O 'Mapico,' Dança dos Macondes," *Império* 4 (August 1951): 35.

23. Costa Freitas, "Notas para um Estudo sobre a Dança do Mapico," *Memórias do Instituto de Investigação Científica de Moçambique*, no. 5 (1963): 128, 131.

24. Dias and Dias, *Os Macondes III*, 163.

25. Robert Dick-Read, *Sanamu: Adventures in Search of African Art* (London: Rupert Hart-Davies, 1964), 58.

26. Ibid., 59.

27. Ibid., 54.

28. "The powerful enemy charges into the arena and at first terrifies the villagers; but finally he is vanquished and chased back into the bush." Ibid., 59.

29. Ibid., 60. A photograph of the mask features in Dias and Dias, *Os Macondes III*, plate 89.

30. Renato Rosaldo, "Imperialist Nostalgia," *Representations* 26 (1989): 108.

31. Jean Bazin, *Des Clous dans la Joconde* (Paris: Anacharsis, 2008), 477.

32. Dias, *Os Macondes III*, 209.

33. For Valéry, the poem was "cette hésitation prolongée entre le son et le sens." Valéry, *Tel Quel* (1943). On the alternative between meaning and function, see Marc Augé, "Vers un Refus de l'Alternative Sens-Fonction," *L'Homme* 18, no. 3 (1978): 139–54.

34. "[a] Entities of non-human domains (mainly bush-spirits), [b] the dead (mainly in their specification as ancestors) and [c] initiation (mainly but not exclusively for young men, and mainly—but not always—associated with the yearly cycle), form the vertices of a triangle within which, arguably, it is possible to articulate the ideology and the practice of masquerading south of the Sahara." Poppi, "Persona, Larva, Masca," 128.

35. For Nicolas Argenti, Cameroonian masks reflect the historical processes of the slave trade as forms of embodied symptomatic memory. See Argenti, *The Intestines of the State: Youth, Violence and Belated Histories in the Cameroon Grassfields* (Chicago: University of Chicago Press, 2007).

36. The narrative of decline is not the anthropologist's prerogative: "Whatever one says, the most widespread conceptions of time view it as neither cyclical [n]or linear but as decline." Paul Veyne, *Did the Greeks Believe in Their Myths? An Essay on the Historical Imagination* (Chicago: University of Chicago Press, 1998), 137.

37. "At the early stages of pre-class and pre-political social order it seems that the serious and the comic aspects of the world and of the deity were equally sacred, equally 'official.'" Bakhtin, *Rabelais and His World*, 6.

38. Ibid., 7. On Bakhtin's conception of the carnivalesque, see Dominik LaCapra, "Bakhtin, Marxism and the Carnivalesque," in *Rethinking Intellectual History* (New York: Cornell University Press, 1983).

39. Luc de Heusch, *Pourquoi l'Epouser? Et Autres Essais* (Paris: Gallimard, 1971), 236.

40. David Napier, *Masks, Transformation, and Paradox* (Berkeley: University of California Press, 1986), xxii. See also Ossie Onoura Enekwe, *Igbo Masks: The Oneness of Ritual and Theatre* (Lagos, Nigeria: Department of Culture, 1987). In fact, even Harley referred to *Ge* maskers as "minstrels and clowns"; see Harley, *Masks as Agents*, 40–41.

41. Dias and Dias, *Os Macondes III*, 180, 204.

42. On the history of these protonationalist organizations and their role in the Mueda massacre, see Michel Cahen, "The Mueda Case and Maconde Political Ethnicity: Some Notes on a Work in Progress," *Africana Studia* 2 (2000): 29–46; and Joel Tembe, "*Uhuru Na Kazi*: Recapturing MANU Nationalism through the Archive," in *The Liberation Script in Mozambican History*, ed. Rui Assubuji, Paolo Israel, and Rui Thompson, special issue, *Kronos: Southern African Histories* 39 (2013): 251–78.

43. On Dias's reports, see Harry West, "Inverting the Camel's Hump: Jorge Dias, His Wife, Their Interpreter, and I," in *Significant Others: Interpersonal and Professional Commitments in Anthropology*, ed. Richard Handler (Maryland: University of Wisconsin Press, 2004), 51–90; and Rui Pereira, "Antropologia Aplicada na Política Colonial Portuguesa do Estado Novo," *Revista Internacional de Estudos Africanos* 4–5 (1986): 191–235 and "Introdução à Reedição de 1998," in Dias, *Os Macondes I*.

44. In the age of socialism, fieldwork was collective and researchers operated in state-sponsored "brigades," the most famous of which were the ones from the History Workshop of the Centro de Estudos Africanos at the Universidade Eduardo Mondlane.

45. Anna Fresu and Mendes de Oliveira, *Pesquisas para um Teatro Popular em Moçambique* (Maputo: Cadernos "Tempo," 1982).

46. Ibid., 38.

47. Ibid., 32. The same conceptual scheme is applied to *Nyau* masquerades.

48. Ibid., 40.

49. "Message from the Central Committee to the Mozambican People," *Mozambique Revolution*, spec. issue (25 September 1967): 5.

50. For Eric Hobsbawm, "inarticulate rebels" are "pre-political people who have not yet found, or only begun to find, a specific language in which to express their aspirations about the world." Hobsbawm, *Primitive Rebels* (Manchester: University of Manchester Press, 1959), 2.

51. Frantz Fanon, *The Wretched of the Earth* (New York: Grove Press, 1964), 243–44. I have slightly altered the translation. The first scholarly interpretation of African mimicry as resistance to the colonial order is to be found in Georges Balandier, *Sens et Puissance: Les Dynamiques Sociales* (Paris: Presses Universitaires de France, 1971), 202–14.

52. Jean-Claude Schmitt, "Les Masques, le Diable, la Mort dans l'Occident Médieval," *Razo: Cahiers du Centre d'Études Médiévales de Nice* 6 (1986): 87–119.

53. Kramer, *Red Fez*, 127–37.

54. See Ricardo Texeira Duarte, *Escultura Maconde* (Maputo: Universidade Eduardo Mondlane, 1987); Edward Alpers, "Representation and Historical Consciousness in the Art of Modern Mozambique," *Canadian Journal of African Studies* 22, no. 1 (1989): 73–94; Michael Stephen, "Makonde Sculpture as Political Commentary," *Review of African Political Economy* 48 (1990): 106–15; and Miguel Mkaima, "Mapiko Masks, Yesterday and Today," in *Makonde: Mapiko*, ed. Kristian Fenzel (Linz, Austria: Neue Galerie der Stadt, 1997), 163–65.

55. John Wembah-Rashid, *The Ethno-history of the Matrilineal Peoples of Southeast Tanzania* (Vienna: Acta Ethnological et Linguistica, 1975); Zachary Kingdon, *A Host of Devils: The History and Context of the Making of Makonde Spirit Sculpture* (London: Routledge, 2002), esp. chap. 2.

56. With the exception of John Wembah-Rashid, "Le Masque et la Tradition de Danse Masquée," in MAAO, *Art Makondé: Tradition et Modernité* (Paris: Musée des Arts d'Afrique et d'Océanie, 1989), 34–43.

57. West, *Kupilikula*, 113, 133–34. One chapter of West's *Ethnographic Sorcery* (Chicago: University of Chicago Press, 2007), 49–54, briefly describes a *nshindo* performance (see further, chap. 5).

58. Ricardo Texeira Duarte and Machado da Graça, eds., *Máscaras: Masks* (Maputo: Museu Nacional de Arte, 1992).

59. Alexander Bortolot, "A Language for Change: Creativity and Power in Mozambican Makonde Masquerades" (PhD diss., Columbia University, 2004) and the exhibition catalogue *Revolutions: A Century of Makonde Masquerade in Mozambique* (New York: Wallach Art Gallery, 2007).

60. Jacques Depelchin, "Reconnecting the Disconnected," paper presented at conference at the District Six Museum, Cape Town, South Africa, 8 July 2009.

## CHAPTER 2: PASSAGE, SECRECY, RIVALRY

1. On Makonde initiation, see Lyndon Harries, *The Initiation Rites of the Makonde Tribe*, Communication from the Rhodes-Livingstone Institute 3 (Lusaka, Northern Rhodesia: Rhodes-Livingstone Institute, 1944); Wembah-Rashid, "Ethno-history"; and Severino Gabriel Ngole, "Ritos de Iniciação Masculinos e suas Transformações Sociais no Planalto de Mueda entre 1924–1994" (MA diss., Universidade Eduardo Mondlane, 1997). What I describe here draws on my own fieldwork and historical inquiry, esp. Anashaledye 2004, Nanelo 2004, Nanelo and Nshamoko 2008, and Nanelo 2009.

2. A popular etymology relates *midimu* to the verb *kuduma*, "to counsel." This is, however, incorrect: words similar to *ndimu* (*mizimu*, etc.) mean "spirit" or "ancestor" in the region. In some ethnographic literature, *mapiko* itself is known as *ndimu*. The etymology is interesting insofar as it testifies to the importance of teachings in the rituals.

3. Nshamoko 2005.

4. See Claude Lévi-Strauss, "Father Christmas Executed," in *Unwrapping Christmas*, ed. David Miller (Oxford: Oxford University Press, 1995), 38–51.

5. Carlo Ginzburg, *Ecstasies: Deciphering the Witches' Sabbath* (Chicago: University of Chicago Press, 2004), 182–205.

6. Michael Taussig, *Defacement: Public Secrecy and the Labor of the Negative* (Stanford: Stanford University Press, 1999), 163.

7. The best critique of the social control hypothesis features in Beryl Bellman, *The Language of Secrecy: Symbols and Metaphors in Poro Ritual* (New Brunswick, NJ: Rutgers University Press, 1984). See also Patrick McNaughton, "Social Control and the Elephants We Scholars Make," *African Arts* 24, no. 1 (1991): 10–18.

8. Taussig, *Defacement*, 5.

9. Lingumwalela 2004.

10. Rashidi et al. 2004. Wembah-Rashid also remarks that "initiated women know what is a *lipico*, independently from the official version. At least amongst the Makonde, we know this has been the case since the beginning." Wembah-Rashid, "Le Masque," 41.

11. The symmetry between many masculine and feminine ritual ordeals (vipito) also reveals cooperation and communication between the two sexes.

12. Mannoni's theory is insightfully discussed in Slavoj Žižek, *For They Know Not What They Do: Enjoyment as a Political Factor* (London: Verso, 1991), 246–47.

13. Bateson, *Naven*, 175.

14. Ibid., 176–77.

15. Ibid., 177–86.

16. The sentences refer to three different moments of my fieldwork, which all took place in the year of 2004, in Muidumbe, Maputo, and Litamanda, respectively.

17. Kenji Yoshida comes to a similar conclusion for the Nyau: "[M]asquerade is a means of creating differences rather than a mere representation or arbitrator of existing gender differences." Yoshida, "Masks and Secrecy among the Chewa," *African Arts* 26, no. 2 (1993): 45.

18. Vicente later served as a middleman for the low-price purchase of Makonde artifacts exhibited in Bortolot's *Revolutions*.

19. Lingumwalela 2004.

20. Paolo Israel, "This Is Our Contemporary: Mozambican Masks in Cape Town," *Art South Africa* 10, no. 2 (2011): 45. Atanásio's quotation refers to the politicians' promises as well as to the invisible domain.

21. The best reconstruction is Gerhard Liesegang, "Sur les Origines et l'Histoire des Makonde du Mozambique," in *Dominique Macondé* (Saint-Gilles-les-Hauts, La Réunion: Musée Historique de Villèle, 2007).

22. Dias, *Os Macondes I*, 66. On the formation of the Maravi empire, see especially Malyn Newitt, "The Early History of the Maravi," *Journal of African History* 23, no. 2 (1982): 145–62.

23. Deborah Kaspin, "Chewa Visions and Revision of Power: Transformation of the Nyau Dance in Central Malawi," in *Modernity and Its Malcontents: Ritual and Power in Post-colonial Africa*, ed. Jean Comaroff and John Comaroff (Chicago: University of Chicago Press, 1993), 34–57. On the *nyau*

*yolemba* (nighttime nyau), see also Yoshida, "Masks and Secrecy"; David Kerr, "Unmasking the Spirits: Theatre in Malawi," *Drama Review* 31, no. 2 (1987): 115–25; and Laurel Birch Aguilar, *Inscribing the Mask: Interpretation of Nyau Masks and Ritual Performance among the Chewa of Malawi* (Freiburg: Universitätsverlag Freiburg, 1996).

24. Jeremy Gray, "A Journey by Land from Tete to Kilwa in 1616," *Tanganyika Notes and Records* 25 (1948): 40–45.

25. Ibid., 45.

26. I owe this suggestion to Malyn Newitt, personal communication, London, October 2005.

27. This draws on personal observation and discussion with speakers. In Guthrie's and subsequent classification of Bantu languages, Makonde is categorized in group P, together with Makua—just another sign of how these classifications are at a remove from the users' perceptions. On Shimakonde, see Estevão Jaime Mpalume and Marcos Agostinho Mandumbwe, *Nashilangola wa Shitangodi sha Shimakonde* (Pemba, Mozambique: Núcleo de Associação dos Escritores Moçambicanos de Cabo Delgado, 1991); Marcelino Liphola, "Aspects of Phonology and Morphology of Shimakonde" (PhD diss., Ohio State University, 2001); Sophie Manus, "Morphologie et Tonologie du Simakoonde Parlé par les Communautés d'Origine Mozambicaine de Zanzibar et de Tanga (Tanzanie)" (PhD diss., Institute National des Langues et Civilisations Orientales, 2003); and Benjamin Leach, "Things Hold Together: Foundations for a Systemic Treatment of Verbal and Nominal Tone in Plateau Shimakonde" (PhD diss., University of Leiden, 2010).

28. Basil Davidson, *The Black Man's Burden: Africa and the Curse of the Nation-State* (London: James Currey, 2005), 90.

29. Ethnographies of southern Tanzania clearly show the signs of such circulation taking place. See especially Karl Weule, *Native Life in East Africa* (London: Pitman, 1909), translated into Portuguese as *Resultados Científicos da Minha Viagem de Pesquisas Etnográficas no Sudeste da África Oriental* (Maputo: Departamento de Museus, 2000); and Wembah-Rashid, *Ethno-history*.

30. Alpers, *Ivory and Slaves*.

31. On Makua masks in Mozambique, see Pierre Macaire, *L'héritage Makhuwa au Mozambique* (Paris: L'Harmattan, 1996); and Eduardo Medeiros, *Os Senhores da Floresta: Ritos de Iniciação dos Rapazes Macuas e Lómuès* (Porto: Campo das Letras, 2007), 189–91, 313–26.

32. In an 1810 document from the Ibo archives, quoted in Liesegang, "Sur les Origines," 30. Before this, there is evidence concerning conflict between the Portuguese and the Makonde king of Mongalo, an Islamized coastal town south of Kilwa, in the 1760s. See Alpers, *Ivory and Slaves*, 133–34.

33. Dias, *Os Macondes I*, 63–65.

34. The difference between *likonde* 'drylands' and *likonde* 'plant' is tonal.

35. Jonathon Glassman, *Feasts and Riot: Revelry, Rebellion, and Popular Consciousness on the Swahili Coast, 1856–1888* (Portsmouth, NH: Heinemann, 1995), 40–42.

36. Dias did not ignore the flexibility of the Makonde in accepting strangers in the social group; see Dias, *Os Macondes I*, 86. Disregarding linguistic evidence, Yussuf Adam suggested that the Makonde are a mere agglomerate of slave refugees; see Adam, "Mueda, 1917–1990: Resistência, Colonialismo, Libertação e Desenvolvimento," *Arquivo: Boletim do Arquivo Histórico de Moçambique* 14 (1993): 10.

37. Shuliki 2003.

38. Reinata Sadimba, unpublished cut from *Tattoo Hunter: Mozambique* (Discovery Channel, 2009).

39. Shuliki 2003.

40. This stereotype is particularly strong in Tanzania. See Askew, *Performing the Nation*, 213; Kingdon, *Host of Devils*, 32; and Jonathon Glassman, *War of Words, War of Stones: Racial Thought and Violence in Colonial Zanzibar* (Bloomington: Indiana University Press, 2011), 179–80, 184–86.

41. See the poignant description of the Rovuma as a wasteland in Weule, *Resultados Científicos*, 82.

42. Dias and Dias, *Os Macondes III*, 352; West, *Kupilikula*, 78.

43. Kramer, *Red Fez*.

44. Ibid., viii–ix.

45. Michael Taussig, *Mimesis and Alterity. A Particular History of the Senses* (London: Routledge, 1993).

46. René Girard, *Things Hidden since the Foundation of the World* (Stanford: Stanford University Press, 1978), 103ff. Girard is a keen reader of Bateson, whose work he reinterprets in the manner of French pessimism.

47. For Girard, the mimetic crisis is not a concept but an event that really occurred. See René Girard, *Violence and the Sacred* (Baltimore, MD: John Hopkins University Press, 1977), 174–78.

## CHAPTER 3: MEAT IS MEAT

1. In *Music from Tanzania and Zanzibar*. This is an old *kwaula ntumi* song from Muidumbe (Namande is the name of a hamlet there). I could record corrupted versions of it sung in Mueda and Muidumbe.

2. Or "flesh is flesh." Shimakonde, like Latin languages, does not distinguish between animal meat and human flesh, which are both called *nyama*.

3. Makai 2003.

4. Kanduru and Amuli 2004. When not specified, the historical reconstruction presented in this chapter is grounded on consensual information that emerged across various interviews, esp. Amissi 2004, Anashaledye 2004, Baltazar 2005, Lijama 2004, Makai 2003, Najopa et al. 2004, Nkalau 2004, Nkangala 2004, Paulo 2003, and Shukulu et al. 2002 and 2003. I therefore reference only individual quotations or elements on which there was no consensus.

5. I use the English word *hamlet* to translate the Shimakonde *likaja*, referring to the small matrilineal settlements existing before Independence, and the word *village* for the post-Independence *aldeias communais* (communal villages).

6. Jean Laude, *La Peinture Française et "l'Art Nègre" (1905–1914): Contribution à l'Etude des Sources du Fauvisme et du Cubisme* (Paris: Klincksieck, 2006).

7. Edward Said, *The World, the Text and the Critic* (Cambridge, MA: Harvard University Press, 1983), 18–26.

8. Bortolot provides an insightful formal reading of mapiko carving styles. See Bortolot, "Language for Change," 39–47, in which he calls the new 1930s style "geometric"—a term not used by local practitioners—and the previous one "sleepy-eyed."

9. Several of these masks are reproduced in Fenzel, *Makonde: Mapiko*, 48–123.

10. On the hare theme, see Wembah-Rashid, "Le Masque."

11. Lijama 2004, Najopa et al. 2004, Shukulu et al. 2003.

12. Kingdon, *Host of Devils*, 47. Kingdon's source is Chanuo Maundu, a Makonde immigrant in Tanzania born in the 1930s.

13. Dias and Dias, *Os Macondes III*, 201.

14. Nkangala 2004. Also, whenever I enquired about the dance of this mileya genre, I was answered, "It was danced like Nampyopyo" (*indivinika kenga Nampyopyo*), or "I saw these masks danced by the elder Shumu" (Shukulu et al. 2003). Atanásio Nhussi, who repeatedly carried out field research on matters of mapiko, concurred with this reconstruction (personal communication, April 2009).

15. John Wembah-Rashid, "Isinyago and Midimu: Masked Dancers of Tanzania and Mozambique," *African Arts* 4, no. 2 (1971): 42.

16. Weule, *Resultados Científicos*, 253–55; and the pictures of masks in MAAO, *Art Makondé*, 82–95.

17. Medeiros, *Os Senhores da Floresta*, 313–26.

18. For a performative analysis, see Tamara Guhrs, "Nyau Masquerade Performance: Shifting the Imperial Gaze" (MA diss., Rhodes University, 1999).

19. Manuel Jordán, *Makishi: Mask Characters of Zambia* (Los Angeles: Fowler Museum, 2006); Gluckman, "Philosophical Roots."

20. Gerhard Kubik, *Makisi, Nyau, Mapiko: Maskentraditionen in Bantu-Sprachigen Afrika* (Munich: Trickster, 1993).

21. Strother reminds us that Pende masks are "complex composites of multiple conditions of personalities." Strother, *Inventing Masks*, xvii.

22. Dias and Dias, *Os Macondes III*, 200.

23. MAAO, *Art Makondé*, 44, pl. 2.

24. Nkangala 2004. This rhythm is the same of Nampyopyo's and Shumu's masks, as remembered by others.

25. Shukulu et al. 2003.

26. Moses Lijama Mede (in Lijama 2003), the oldest *mmapiko* that I could interview, first saw dutu in the years following the construction of the colonial road to the plateau, between 1917 and 1921.

27. Joana Makai (in Makai 2003) remembers having seen for the first time *nshesho* in 1943, the year when he came out from puberty rituals; the genre might, however, have emerged a few years earlier.

28. Seguro 2003.

29. West, *Kupilikula*, 29–34.

30. Nshamoko 2005.

31. Kanduru and Amuli 2004.

32. NMA/Dutu/Myangalewa/2004. This kind of song was widespread at the time, but because these songs were later prohibited by Frelimo, very few groups dared to sing them for me.

33. NMA/Dutu/Myangalewa/2004.

34. NMA/Dutu/Nshinga/2004.

35. Mustafa 2003.

36. Boasting was Bateson's chief example of symmetrical schismogenesis. See Bateson, *Naven*, 176–77.

37. Nshamoko 2005.

38. Converts working for the missionaries were exempted from forced labor. See West, *Kupilikula*, 109–20.

39. On the two phases, see Terence Ranger, "Missionary Adaptation of African Religious Institutions: The Masasi Case," in *The Historical Study of African Religion*, ed. Terence Ranger and Isaria Kimambo (Berkeley: University of California Press, 1972), 221–52.

40. NMA/Dutu/Nampanya/2004.

41. Dias and Dias, *Os Macondes III*, 353.

42. I have interviewed three people who underwent puberty rituals in the Nangololo Mission in the 1950s: Mwakala 2005, Seguro 2004, and Shilavi 2009. See also West, *Kupilikula*, 109–19; and Ngole, "Ritos de Iniciação Masculinos."

43. West, *Kupilikula*, 115.

44. Mwakala 2004.

45. Seguro 2004 and Mwakala 2005. A short-lived attempt to resurrect initiations and mapiko was promoted in 2003 at Nangololo.

46. Pedro Seguro, personal communication, 13 December 2003. The incident is remembered widely.

47. One can gauge the church's scarce influence on mapiko from the quasi-total absence of religious themes in song repertoires: only one among five hundred mapiko songs in my archive (an invocation to the Virgin Mary from the Mwambula group, whose leader is a devout Christian). Apart from the unfortunate Jesus Christ colonial-time mask, Pope John Paul II was the object of a character in the Mbau *shikelya* group.

48. Lilende Miyani, in Shukulu et al. 2003.

49. Nanelo and Nshamoko 2008.

50. See Edward Alpers, "To Seek a Better Life: Implications of Migration from Mozambique to Tanganyika for Class Formation and Political Behaviour," *Canadian Journal of African Studies* 18, no. 2 (1984): 367–88.

51. Makai 2003.

52. I provided an erroneous etymology for this word in Paolo Israel, "Mapiko Masquerades of the Makonde: Performance and Historicity," in *Eastern African Contours: Reviewing Creativity and Visual Culture*, ed. Hassan Arero and Zachary

Kingdon (London: Horniman Museum, Critical Museology and Material Culture series, 2005), 101, which then made its way into Bortolot, *Revolutions*, 18.

53. With all probability, the bells themselves were imported from Tanganyika.

54. Catarina Alves Costa, *Guia Para os Filmes Realizados por Margot Dias em Moçambique, 1958/1961* (Lisbon: Museu Nacional de Etnologia, 1997).

55. Dias, *Os Macondes III*, 147.

56. "These rites permit the participants to play out all the roles performed by the ancestors during the original crisis. They are enemies first, engaging in mock combats and symmetrical dances; then they put on their masks and change into monstrous doubles." Girard, *Violence and the Sacred*, 177.

57. Amissi 2004 and Manupa 2012.

58. The chakacha is "a rhythm that took the entire coast by storm" (Askew, "As Plato Duly Warned," 619) as a form of popular music in the 1950s; its roots as a feminine initiation dance, probably originating among Mijikenda communities, is much older. See esp. Janet Topp Fargion, "Nyota Alfajiri, the Zanzibari *Chakacha*," *Afrikanistische Arbeitspapiere* 42 (1995): 125–31; and Carol Campbell and Carol Eastman, "Ngoma: Swahili Adult Song Performance in Context," *Ethnomusicology* 28, no. 3 (1984): 467–93.

59. Gearhart, "Ngoma Memories: A History," 158–203 and "Ngoma Memories: How Ritual Music and Dance Shaped the Northern Kenya Coast," *African Studies Review* 48, no. 3 (2005): 21–47. Various contributions in Gunderson and Barz's *Mashindano!* also point to this appropriation. Kaingu Tinga describes the appropriation of Wanyasa masquerades in the northern Kenya coast. See Tinga, "Secrets of Slaves: The Rise and Decline of *Vinyago* Masquerades on the Kenya Coast" (master's diss., University of the Western Cape, 2012). A similar phenomenon on the southern Somalian coast is traced by Francesca Declich in *I Bantu della Somalia: Etnogenesi e Rituali Mviko* (Milan: Franco Angeli, 2002).

60. "They would urge the regiments to display their *Vinyago*—ships, etc." Ranger, *Dance and Society*, 24.

61. Gerald Hartwig, "The Historical and Social Role of Kerebe Music," *Tanzania Notes and Records* 70 (1969): 53–56.

62. Ranger, *Dance and Society*, 111–15; and see Ellison's contribution in Gunderson and Barz, James Ellison, "Competitive Dance and Social Identity: Converging Histories in Southwestern Tanzania," in Gunderson and Barz, *Mashindano!*, 199–232.

63. Reinhard Koselleck calls "asymmetric counterconcepts" exclusional subdivisions of humanity in two halves—such as Hellene vs. barbarian, Christian vs. heathen, Man vs. *Untermensch* in Nazi Germany—as opposed to identifications in terms of nation or ethnicity, which are not asymmetrical. See Koselleck, *Futures Past: On the Semantics of Historical Time* (New York: Columbia University Press, 2004), 155–91. On the divide between slaves and freemen on the Swahili coast, see Glassman, *Feasts and Riot*, 79–115.

64. Ranger, *Dance and Society*, 64–69.

65. Lamartine, quoted in Koselleck, *Futures Past*, 270.

# CHAPTER 4: MASTERS OF PLAY

1. Dias and Dias, *Os Macondes III*, 211.

2. Where not explicitly noted, the reconstruction of Nampyopyo's history is based on interviews with his descendants (*vana vake*, sons and nephews): Najopa et al. 2004, Najopa and Nshegwa 2009 and 2012, and Nkondya et al. 2004, as well as Mustafa 2003 and 2005.

3. See Dias and Dias, *Os Macondes III*, 162.

4. All such experiences were common for the people of his generation.

5. On the *mwene shilambo*, see West, *Kupilikula*, 29–34.

6. Jorge Dias, "Mudança de Cultura entre os Macondes de Moçambique," *Universitas* 6/7 (1970): 264.

7. Najopa et al. 2004. The list was obtained after quite some work of recollection. It is perhaps worth mentioning that *Nampyopyo* is an ideophone referring to sexual penetration: *pyo!*

8. NMA/Mileya/Nang'unde/2004. All songs in this section come from this source.

9. The Germans are cast in noun-class 6 (*ma-*), as if they were things or spirits, rather than persons (*va-*).

10. In Portuguese, the word is generally rendered as *dono*.

11. Najopa et al. 2004.

12. Mustafa 2005.

13. Estevão Mpalume dates the arrival of German planters in Cabo Delgado to 1918. See Mpalume, *Vyaka Vyoe Vyamauvilo mu Moshambiki* (Maputo: Núcleo de Associação dos Escritores Moçambicanos de Cabo Delgado, 1990), 39; see also João Paulo Borges-Coelho, *O Olho de Herzog* (Lisbon: Caminho, 2010).

14. Najopa et al. 2004.

15. This paragraph draws on Kingdon's fine historical reconstruction. See Kingdon, *Host of Devils*, 65–77; and Duarte, *Escultura Maconde*, 100ff.

16. According to Kingdon, the (mythic) initiator of the tradition was one Nyekenya Nangundu, living in the village of Miula. See Kingdon, *Host of Devils*, 66.

17. Ibid., 70.

18. This paragraph is based on interviews quoted in Duarte, *Escultura Maconde*, 100–103 and on Najopa and Nshegwa 2012. See also Bortolot, "Language for Change," 152–58.

19. See MAAO, *Art Makondé*, 124–29.

20. Njelo Johanes Najopa and Ngonya Tumaini Nshegwa (in Najopa and Nshegwa 2012), who recognized the images in MAAO, *Art Makondé*, 130–31 and 133–34, as being similar to Nampyopyo's. Similar statuettes were produced in the Macomia and Macuana areas. See Alvaro de Castro, "Artes Plásticas do Norte de Moçambique," *Boletim do Museu de Nampula* 2 (1961): 115–29.

21. According to Nshegwa (in Najopa and Nshegwa 2012), it was common at the time for colonial agents to take local names "as a strategy to befriend the Makonde."

22. Paulo Soares, "Un Demi-siècle de Transition dans une Ecole de Sculpture Africaine," in MAAO, *Art Makondé*, 116.

23. I failed to interview Nshemo in 2004, as he was at the time living in a remote lowland hut. I came to regret sorely this single episode of walking laziness, as the sculptor passed away in early 2012.

24. The hamlet is referred to as Mboo. Nampyopyo's associates—one of whom danced the Elizabeth the Second mask—remembered his visit. See Najopa 2004.

25. Dick-Read, *Sanamu*, 57.

26. A scholar of African art also observed this dualism between naturalism and the grotesque in mapiko: "The mask Konde reproduces often, with a sensible naturalism, feminine faces adorned with geometric scarifications. . . . On the other hand, many masks exacerbate the features of the face, while others refine them and draw more schematically their outlines." Jacqueline Delange, *Arts et Peuples de l'Afrique Noire: Introduction à une Analyse des Créations Plastiques* (Paris: Gallimard, 1967), 184.

27. The dichotomy *beautiful/sublime* was formalized in Kant's *Critique of Judgment* but was operative in all late eighteenth-century aesthetic thought. For its inaugural statement, see Edmund Burke's *A Philosophical Enquiry into the Origin of Our Ideas of the Sublime and Beautiful* (1757).

28. Kingdon, *Host of Devils*, 79–82.

29. Valingue 2001. I also rely on personal observations, informal conversations with sculptors in Mueda, and research carried out in Maputo in 2000. See Paolo Israel, "Maconde é Maningue Cultural: Danse et Sculpture Makonde à Maputo" (DEA diss., Ecole des Hautes Etudes en Sciences Sociales, 2001).

30. I could hear such commentaries as I was traveling around with a shetani piece in the villages around Diaca (Mocimboa da Praia) in August 2002.

31. "He himself used to come out and teach us his songs," recalled his daughters; see Nkondya 2004.

32. Amissi 2004.

33. Makai 2003.

34. Juakali 2008.

35. Amissi, Makai, and Juakali all went to the same event without understanding who the "white elder" was.

36. NMA/Nshesho/Nampanya/2005. This is a post-Independence choir, but the kind of antagonism that it depicts and embodies is much older.

37. Amissi 2009.

38. Amissi 2004. These styles were played in the hamlet of kuna-Kamushuni, close to Myangalewa.

39. Nanelo and Nshamoko 2008, which I render in free indirect discourse.

40. Kanduru and Amuli 2004, Likwekwe 2004. The three were members of the Ashalela group. I never researched the group from Mandava, because at the time my involvement in witchcraft-related tensions with the village leader prevented me from visiting the village. See Israel, "War of Lions."

41. Najopa et al. 2004.

42. I first heard Shumu's name mentioned as a mileya performer in Shukulu 2003, but at the time I did not connect it to Nampyopyo's style.

43. Amissi 2004, 2008, and 2009; Anogwa 2004; Lijama 2004; Mawasha 2004; and Mustafa 2005.

44. Amissi 2009.

45. Anogwa 2004.

46. Mustafa 2005.

47. Mawasha 2004.

48. Anogwa 2004.

49. Amissi 2008. A large fish basket can contain about a dozen masks. Did Shumu have in his arsenal five hundred masks? People exaggerate, but even cut to a quarter the figure would still be impressive.

50. Anogwa 2004. To "get tired" also refers to a weakness that is generated magically or to scarce force in the invisible domain. For further details, see chap. 5, sec. 2.

51. Mawasha 2004. What dull questions one can make in an interview, and what surprising answers one sometimes gets in return!

52. Amissi 2009.

## CHAPTER 5: LOWLAND NIGHTS

1. Myth recorded by Pater Adams in 1902. See also Dias, *Os Macondes I*, 76–77; Weule, *Native Life*, 316.

2. Mpalume and Mandumbwe, *Nashilangola*, 25–27.

3. Paulo 2003. The other would be the coming out of puberty rituals.

4. Two elders did remember seeing mapiko dancing at matanga on the plateau: see Shuliki 2003 and Lijama 2004.

5. In Shimakonde, *uwavi* encompasses notions of "witchcraft" and "sorcery," as these terms are used by Evans-Pritchard, and also covers medicinal plants (*mitela*) and the innate magical power of individuals. It is translated in Portuguese with the historically dense word *feitiço*. I use here *witchcraft* and *sorcery* interchangeably to translate *uwavi*. A person who is dedicated to uwavi is called in Shimakonde *mwavi* (Port. *feiticeiro*), a genderless noun that I render here as either *witch* or *sorcerer*. See also West, *Kupilikula*, 77.

6. Such interpretation has been enabled by Rosalind Shaw, *Memories of the Slave Trade: Ritual and the Historical Imagination in Sierra Leone* (Chicago: University of Chicago Press, 2002).

7. See, for instance, Jean Allman and John Parker, *Tongnaab: The History of a West African God* (Bloomington: Indiana University Press, 2005).

8. I ground the following reconstruction of nshindo on Shukulu et al. 2002, Yangua 2002, Bulashi 2004, Amissi 2004, Lijama 2004, and Mawasha 2004.

9. The word is related to the Swahili epithet for Arab immigrants, *wamanga*. See Glassman, *War of Words*, 159.

10. This comes from the imaginative reconstruction provided by Amissi 2004.

11. The songs, in order, are *Ida munnole ng'aka; Ida munno' likopito, liwaka moto;* and *Manamwana amunatile, ida munnole ng'ondo.*

12. The former being the group of Mbau, the latter of Mwatide. Both were dwindling in the early 2000s and have ceased to dance in the second decade of the new millennium.

13. I worked with groups from the villages of Nakitenge (where I returned in December 2003); Litapata and Shitashi (July 2004); Myangalewa, which has two, in the Pacheco and Maputo neighborhoods (September 2004); Mbau (September 2004); and Litamanda (April 2009). I have seen the group Myangalewa Maputo perform four times and the group from Mbau twice.

14. The group Shikelya from Mbau invited me to a matanga in December 2003, and the group Myangalewa Maputo in September 2004. Meanwhile, I observed three Christian matanga, animated by song only: in Mandava (Muidumbe), June 2003; in Awassi (Mocimboa da Praia), December 2003; and in Matambalale (Muidumbe), June 2008.

15. They are all captured on tape. In this section, most examples of presentations are drawn from the performance of the Myangalewa Maputo group, at a matanga in Shitunda, September 2004.

16. Most of the character songs introduced in the 1950s were sung without alteration in the early 2000s. Only in a few cases were songs modified.

17. *Nango' Ndemba, wakulya inyushi muilanga.*

18. Basil Davidson speaks of "dramas of the spirit that were afterward rehearsed in ritual dance and song, celebrating human survival against every mystery of death" in *Black Man's Burden,* 79.

19. Bakhtin, *Rabelais and His World,* 11, 62.

20. Ibid., 52, 50.

21. Ibid., 152.

22. Mawasha 2002 and 2004, Nampindo and Pamange 2009.

23. Mawasha 2002.

24. Mawasha 2004. This was probably because of the spread of the reformed version of Islam. In Lamu, ngoma were under attack by the Mohamedan Reform League in the 1930s. See Ranger, *Dance and Society,* 87–88. Vinyago masquerades in Kenya went through two waves of Islamic repression: one in the 1950s and the other in the 1970s. See Tinga, "Secrets of Slaves," 108. Sufi Islam also exerted a powerful influence on heathen practices in Tanzania. See Gearhart, "Ngoma Memories: A History," 70–114. Daria Trentini makes a powerful argument for the influence of Sufism on hinterland Makua ritual. See Trentini, "On the Threshold of a Healer's Mosque: Spiritual Healing, Hazard and Power in Northern Mozambique" (PhD diss., School of Oriental and African Studies, University of London, 2012), 111–36.

25. Mawasha 2004.

26. Ibid.

27. A description can also be found in Tamele and Vilanculo, *Algumas Danças,* 45–50.

28. It is around this paradox that West discusses a *uwavi* performance that he saw. See West, *Ethnographic Sorcery,* 49–54. Oddly, the sorcerers danced

at night, something that is against all rules of nshindo. Was this an invention meant to impress a researcher interested in the theme?

29. Nampada 2003.

30. Dancing nshindo at matanga goes with financial remuneration. Besides food and beverages, a group gets a sum, which at the time of my fieldwork varied between 350 and 500 contos.

31. This paragraph is my own small festive homage to the art of the sorcery-related field sketch featuring the anthropologist as a character, perfected by West in *Kupilikula* and *Ethnographic Sorcery*.

32. See Israel, "War of Lions."

33. Shukulu et al. 2002, Alivémwako 2003.

34. Nampada 2003.

## CHAPTER 6: MIGRANT TUNES

1. NMA/Dutu/Nampanya/2005.

2. The Rádio Moçambique archive in Maputo and Pemba contains some 1970s and 1980s tapes. I received a copy from the Vienna Phonogrammarchiv of the 1962 recordings by Gerhard Kubik, done in the Makonde Plateau as part of a broader campaign in east-central Africa. I have listened to the published recordings by Margot Dias (1959–60) but not to the archival material, which at the time of my visit to Lisbon (2001) was unavailable.

3. For a discussion of the dynamics of composition in African oral arts, see Karin Barber, *The Anthropology of Texts, Persons and Publics: Oral and Written Culture in Africa and Beyond* (Cambridge: Cambridge University Press, 2007).

4. William Samarin observes about Bantu languages that "a masterful use of language is probably always related to a generous use of ideophones." Samarin, "Perspective on African Ideophones," *African Studies* 24, no. 2 (1967): 117. See also Alec Pongweni, *Figurative Language in Shona Discourse: A Study of the Analogical Imagination* (Gweru, Zimbabwe: Mambo, 1992).

5. See Barber, *Anthropology of Texts*, 79–86.

6. Jan Knappert, *Four Centuries of Swahili Verse: A Literary History and Anthology* (London: Heinemann, 1979), 50.

7. NMA/Dutu/Mbau/2003.

8. NMA/Dutu/Myangalewa/2004, NMA/Lingundumbwe/Mueda/2005, NMA/Dutu/Namakule/2009. The song is the soundtrack of Licinio de Azevedo, *Reinata Sadimba: Mãos de Barro* (Maputo: Ebano Multimedia, 2003).

9. Personal communication, Pemba, August 2006.

10. Kashiano is a recurring character in Rashidi's songs.

11. On this point, see Carlo Ginzburg, *History, Rhetoric and Proof* (Hanover, NH: University Press of New England for Brandeis University Press/ Historical Society of Israel, 1999), 1–37.

12. NMA/Dutu/Myangalewa/2004.

13. Amissi 2008, Juakali 2008. Namwalu's post-Independence recordings are kept at RM Pemba.

14. Juakali 2008.

15. Many persons fluent in Kiswahili, to whom I submitted these songs, were not able to decipher them.

16. NMA/Dutu/Nshinga/2004.

17. *Tundashonga* is an example of Makonde conjugation (*tunda-*) of a Kiswahili verb (*-shonga*).

18. Amissi 2008.

19. Juakali 2008.

20. All of Juakali's songs in this section were sung to me by himself (NMA/Dutu/Shitunda/2008, Juakali 2008). Rashidi's songs were sung by the dutu players of kuna-Nkalau, a hamlet associated with Rashidi. For this reason, some of the self-praises refer to Laishi and Kashiano, friends of Rashidi (NMA/Dutu/Myangalewa/2004).

21. In the official version, Diwane and Vanomba were leaders of MANU (Mozambique African National Union); see Alberto Joaquim Chipande, "The Massacre of Mueda," *Mozambique Revolution* 43 (1970): 12–14. This version has been challenged by Michel Cahen, who argues that Diwane and Vanomba belonged to MAA-SAM (Mozambique African Association / *Sociedade dos Africanos de Moçambique*); Cahen, "Mueda Case," 35–41. Thirteen years after publishing this provisional article, however, Cahen has not yet produced the evidence to support his statements. On the history of MANU, see also Tembe: "*Uhuru Na Kazi.*"

22. I have spoken to five people who were present on the day of the massacre, including Joana Makai (Makai 2003) and Bernardino Juakali Nnamba (Juakali 2008).

23. In the version told by Vanomba to West, China fires a shot and someone throws a stone at the administrator. See West, "Sorcery of Construction and Sorcery of Ruin: Power and Ambivalence on the Mueda Plateau, Mozambique (1882–1994)" (PhD diss., University of Wisconsin, 1997), 147–49 and *Kupilikula*, 136, 156.

24. Some parts of the song were clearly reworked by Juakali later on: Pemba was called Porto Amélia at the time.

25. Litembo 2009.

26. Kubik recordings, Vienna Phonogrammarchiv, 1962.

27. The recording is published on the cassette that accompanies Margot Dias, *Instrumentos Musicais de Moçambique* (Lisbon: Instituto de Investigação Científica Tropical, 1986).

28. Dias and Dias, *Os Macondes III*, 169.

29. The Makonde xylophones have represented a small mystery to scholars of African music, because of close structural similarities with Kru and Baule xylophones from Ivory Coast and Liberia; see Gerhard Kubik, *Theory of African Music*, vol. 1 (Chicago: University of Chicago Press, 2010), 15–16.

30. Kubik, in notes to field recordings, Phonogrammarchiv Vienna, 1962, observes a "very starch European influence" in Makonde mashesho choirs.

31. Atanásio Nhussi told me that singers in the Companhia Nacional de Canto e Dança consider Makonde music "ugly to the ear" because the

Makonde "intone off pitch." It is also interesting to find, in recent Makonde pop-music recordings, the intentional reproduction of flat thirds when "quoting" mapiko choirs.

32. See Henri Meschonnic, *Critique du Rhythme: Anthropologie Historique du Langage* (Paris: Verdier, 1984).

33. NMA/Neijale/Nshongwe/2004 and NMA/ShukuNwele/Mwambula /2004, among others. On Malapende, see West, *Kupilikula*, 87–97.

## CHAPTER 7: TEN YEARS OF WAR

1. On people's wars in Africa, see especially Basil Davidson, *The People's Cause: A History of Guerillas in Africa* (Harlow, UK: Longman, 1981).

2. "All radical revolutionary projects . . . rely on this same fantasy of a radical annihilation of tradition and of the creation *ex nihilo* of a new (sublime) Man, delivered from the corruption of previous history." Žižek, *For They Know Not*, 261.

3. See the pioneering Aquino de Bragança and Jacques Depelchin, "From the Idealization of Frelimo to the Understanding of the Recent History of Mozambique," *African Journal of Political Economy* 1 (1986): 168–80; and Rui Assubuji, Paolo Israel, and Drew Thompson, eds., *The Liberation Script in Mozambican History*, special issue of *Kronos: Southern African Histories* 39 (2013).

4. On the engagement of the Makonde with MANU and then Frelimo see Adam, "Mueda, 1917–1990"; and Yussuf Adam and Anna Maria Gentili, "O Movimento Liguilanilu no Planalto de Mueda, 1957–1962," *Estudos Moçambicanos* 4 (1983): 41–75.

5. Seguro 2004.

6. Lingumwalela 2004.

7. For details about ngoda, I rely on Nampindo et al. 2004, Mandia 2005 and 2008, and Nkangusa et al. 2009.

8. NMA/Ngoda/Myangalewa/2004.

9. In East Africa the instrument goes by the name of *kipango* (in Tanzania), *bangu, bancu,* and *iwaya* (in Mozambique), and *bangwe* (in Malawi). It is made of a wooden board on which a long wire is stretched, in such a way as to produce five, six, or seven strings, which are strummed or fingered. Gerhard Kubik, "Neo-traditional Popular Music in Africa since 1945," *Popular Music* 1 (1981): 88. Judging from Margot Dias's and Kubik's recordings, the instrument was rather uncommon among the Makonde in the 1950s.

10. A Kenyan genealogy has been suggested for the latter instrument and for its name. I base my reconstruction of *magalantoni* on Mandia 2008 and Liloko 2008.

11. The first sector ran from the Rovuma to the Mueda-Mocimboa road; the second until the Messalo River; the third until Montepuez; the fourth up to the Lurio River.

12. Mandia 2005.

13. NMA/Magita/Mueda/2005.

14. Nampindo 2004.

15. NMA/Ngoda/Namakule/2005. The directives against tribalism began to appear within Frelimo after the first year of war.

16. For a close reading of such lyrics, see Paolo Israel, "Utopia Live: Singing the Mozambican Struggle for National Liberation," *Kronos: Journal of Southern African Histories* 35 (2009): 98–141.

17. Giorgio Agamben, "What Is a People," in *Means without End: Notes on Politics* (Minneapolis: University of Minnesota Press, 2000), 29, 31.

18. Alberto Mario Cirese, *Cultura Egemonica e Culture Subalterne* (Palermo, Italy: Palumbo, 1997), 16–17.

19. This can be immediately perceived by a reading of official magazines such as *Voz da Revolução* and *Mozambique Revolution*, in which the word is ubiquitous. The signifier had an afterlife in Zimbabwean politics, where it is still used by Mugabe in speeches.

20. Patrick Chabal, "The End of Empire," in *A History of Postcolonial Lusophone Africa*, ed. Patrick Chabal (London: Hurst, 2002), 23–25.

21. Shilavi 2009; Augusto Shilavi participated in the Litapata council.

22. The word *clique* appears early on in anti-Frelimo pamphlets to describe Mondlane's group, and it is taken up as a leitmotif in Nkomo's revisionist book on Simango. See Barnabé Nkomo, *Uria Simango: Um Homem, uma Causa* (Maputo: Novafrica, 2004). The letter, titled "Gloomy Situation in Frelimo," can be perused there (399–416). For a recent reading of the crisis, see Georgi Derluguian, "The Social Origins of Good and Bad Governance: Re-interpreting the 1968 Schism in Frelimo," in *Sure Road? Nationalism in Angola, Guinea-Bissau and Mozambique*, ed. Eric Morier-Genoud (Leiden, The Netherlands: Brill, 2012), 79–101.

23. Amilcar Cabral's essay "National Liberation and Culture," pronounced as a eulogy to Mondlane at Syracuse University, may have alerted Frelimo leaders to the importance of culture. See Cabral, "National Liberation and Culture," in *Unity and Struggle: Speeches and Writings* (New York: Monthly Review Press, 1979), 138–54.

24. On Zimbabwe, see especially Alec Pongweni, *Songs That Won the Liberation War* (Harare, Zimbabwe: College Press, 1982); and Thomas Turino, *Nationalists, Cosmopolitans, and Popular Music in Zimbabwe* (Chicago: University of Chicago Press, 2000).

25. "Dicionário de Ideias Feitas," in Maria-Benedita Basto, *A Guerra das Escritas : Literatura, Nação e Teoria Pós-colonial em Moçambique* (Lisbon: Vendaval, 2006), 176–85. I am indebted to her insightful reading.

26. Zaaqueu 2005.

27. Carlos Siliya, *Ensaio Sobre a Cultura em Moçambique* (Maputo: Promedia, 1996), 130–31.

28. Ashipambele 2005.

29. Baltazar 2005.

30. See West, *Kupilikula*, 145–47.

31. Gondola 2008

32. Basto, *A Guerra das Escritas*, 125–35.

33. Ibid., 128–29.

34. Ibid., 130; see also "What Is the Mozambican Culture," *Mozambique Revolution* 50 (January–March 1972): 50.

35. "Shaping the Political Line," *Mozambique Revolution* 51 (April–June 1972): 22.

36. NMA/Nshesha/Mwambula/2005.

37. NMA/Nshesha/Omba/2005.

38. Formed by the apposition of a durative verbal extension [-*ang*-] and a causative [-*dya*-].

39. On Frelimo education, see especially Mariano Gomes, *Educação Moçambicana: História de Um Processo, 1962–1984* (Maputo: Livraria Universitária da Universidad Europea de Madrid, 1999); and Brazão Mazula, *Educação, Cultura e Ideologia em Moçambique, 1975–1985* (Porto, Portugal: Afrontamento, 1995).

40. The Luanda pilot center was established in 1968 but received a new purpose, in terms of programs and directives, in 1970–71, and Maguiguane was established in 1971, according to Marcelino Ashipambele (Ashipambele 2005) and Jorge Zaaqueu Nhassemu (Zaaqueu 2005), who worked in these centers.

41. Zaaqueu 2005.

42. Turino, *Nationalists*, 125.

43. Hundreds of tapes of *makwaela* songs were recorded in Frelimo pilot schools in a national campaign between 1976 and 1978; these are conserved in the Rádio Moçambique archive in Maputo.

44. The list of tropes here is based on the analysis of around four hundred political post-Independence songs in Shimakonde, on comparison with an equivalent number of pre-Independence songs of different genres, and from occasional listening to many more.

45. See João Salva-Rei and António Pedro Muiuane, *Datas e Documentos da História da Frelimo* (Maputo: Imprensa Nacional, 1975), 32. In the second and subsequent editions, the name of Bento Chipeda was removed. Pedro Justino Seguro alerted me to this inaccuracy. The name of Bento Pachihi Nalyambipano, a relative of the more famous Teodoro Salesio Nalyambipano, also appears in a list prepared by the provincial directorate of war veterans of Cabo Delgado. See also Marcelino Ding'ano and Pedro Walecaia, "Subsídios à Reconstituição da História do Chai, 1964–1975," mimeographed preliminary report (Pemba: Arquivo do Património Cultural, 2004), 22.

## CHAPTER 8: YOUTH POWER

1. Also in "Kwalala Kombatente," *Canções do II Festival Nacional, Pemba*, CD, Rádio Moçambique and NMA/Nshesho/Mueda/2004.

2. Makai 2003, Ndeja-Ndeja 2003, Milete 2008; and the collective Mwaela 2004, Nshileu and Anawandala 2009, Baltazar et al. 2009, Lingandingo et al. 2009, and Litembo 2009. This observation is also based on conversations with many other practitioners.

3. The word *village* (*ludeya*) is a loanword from Portuguese *aldeia. Pa* is a locative, but it also indicates a marker of time (*pankaloni*, "the colonial time"; *paing'ondo*, "the wartime"; *paludeya*, "the time of villages").

4. For the resistance to the construction of communal villages in Mueda, see the courageous CEA (Centro de Estudos Africanos), *Poder Popular e Desagregação nas Aldeias Comunais do Planalto de Mueda* (Maputo: Universidade Eduardo Mondlane, 1986); and Bertil Egero, *Mozambique: A Dream Undone* (Uppsala, Sweden: Nordiska Afrikainstitutet, 1987), 143–70.

5. Milete 2005.

6. See the propagandistic Raimundo Pachinuapa, *Do Rovuma ao Maputo: A Marcha Triunfal de Samora Machel* (Maputo, 2005).

7. Frelimo, *Programa do Primeiro Festival de Dança Popular* (Maputo: Gabinete do Primeiro Festival de Dança Popular, 1978), 7.

8. "E' no Processo da Luta que Forjamos a Nossa Ideologia," *Voz da Revolução* 61 (1978): 8; "Resolução sobre a Cultura," ibid., 26.

9. The National Institute for Cinema is slowly working at the digitalization of this treasure trove, giving priority to political films. The films that are not digitized cannot be consulted. The First Festival was filmed by private agents; I could not locate the films in Maputo. Some footage of postindependence *mapiko* can be seen in the recently reedited *O Mundo em Imagens: Filmes do Arquivo do Instituto Nacional de Audiovisual e Cinema* (DVD, Arcadia Filmproduktion, 2012).

10. Three reels of 1970s and 1980s Makonde materials are available in Pemba, including *mapiko, limbondo,* and *utamaduni;* a few more recent recordings are in Maputo.

11. See the six-part series in *Tempo,* 356–61 (1977) and Basto, *A Guerra das Escritas,* 112–15.

12. Ruy Guerra, *Mueda, Memoria e Massácre,* film (Instituto Nacional de Cinema, Maputo, Mozambique, 1979); "Mauvilo a ku Mweda: Sobreviventes e Participantes Historiam Massacre," *Tempo* 350 (1977): 42–43; Ruy Guerra, "Mueda é o Respeito pela Realidade Histórica," interview by Sol de Carvalho in *Tempo* 512 (1980): 49–53. The performance was discontinued in the late 1980s because of the civil war and lack of support.

13. Harry West, "Voices Twice Silenced: Betrayal and Mourning at Colonialism's End in Mozambique," *Anthropological Theory* 3, no. 3 (2003): 353.

14. Lars Buur, "Xiconhoca: Mozambique's Ubiquitous Post-Independence Traitor," in *Traitors: Suspicion, Intimacy and the Ethics of State-Building,* ed. Sharika Thirangama and Tobias Kelly (Philadelphia: University of Pennsylvania Press, 2010), 24–27.

15. "A Cultura," in Frelimo, *Programa,* 3.

16. Nshesho choir, "Musica Tradicionál de Moçambique," recording reel (Pemba: Rádio Moçambique, 1986).

17. Frelimo, *Programa,* 28.

18. James Scott, *Seeing Like a State: How Certain Schemes to Better the Human Condition Have Failed* (New Haven, CT: Yale University Press, 1999), 223–262. West follows this reading in *Kupilikula,* 175–76.

19. Geffray, *La Cause des Armes*.

20. Addressivity is an utterance's "quality of being directed to someone." Mikhail Bakhtin, *Speech Genres and Other Late Essays* (Austin: University of Texas Press, 1986), 85.

21. NMA/Nshesho/Mwalela/2004.

22. NMA/Nshesho/Nampanya/2004. The Nampanya group was by all accounts the most famous of the Muidumbe zone until the 1990s.

23. NMA/Nshesho/Mwambula/2005. *Kwigwana* means literally "mutual hearing."

24. NMA/Nshesho/Nampanya/2004.

25. NMA/Nshesho/Omba/2003L.

26. NMA/Nshesho/Mwambula/2005.

27. NMA/Nshesho/Omba/2003.

28. NMA/Nshesho/Mwambula/2004.

29. Frelimo's soldiers were called "brothers of the night" (*vakaka vashilo*). Mpalume, *Vyaka Vyoe*, 56.

30. On Rui Pinho, see Ding'ano and Walecaia, "Subsídios à Reconstituição," 16. Like the song about the first shot (see chap. 7, sec. 11), this style did not map any direct experience.

31. In Portuguese, *feijão macaco* (*mucunia pruriensis*).

32. Mwale et al. 2009.

33. This paragraph draws from unrecorded conversations with Nandenga and Akungondo in Pemba, January 2005.

34. NMA/Nshesho/Mueda/2004. This song was part of Nandenga's collection.

35. In Shimakonde, *kwambola*, "to liberate," can also be conjugated without an object.

36. Mbanguia 2009. Paulo Soares provides a description of the group's performance at the First Festival in "O Grupo Cultural Mapico-Moderno," *Tempo* 397 (1978): 30–35. The other group was Malapende, founded in the 1980s.

37. Nhussi 2009 and many informal conversations.

38. On this group, see Siliya, *Ensaio sobre a Cultura*, 130–36.

39. Nhussi 2009, Mwale et al. 2009, and Manupa 2012. João Lingwa was the group's leader; the drummer Valério Mwale took over after his death in 2008.

40. Lilende Miyani, in Shukulu et al. 2003.

41. NMA/Dutu/Mbau/2003.

42. Ibid.

43. NMA/Dutu/Shitunda/2008.

44. Ibid.

45. NMA/Nshindo/Myangalewa/2005.

46. Shawa 2004.

## CHAPTER 9: FACELESS SPIRITS

1. See the case of Rufina Nioyo documented by Bortolot in "Language for Change," 181–83.

2. *Madalaka* indicates "authority or power," as opposed to *uhuru*, which means "real independence."

3. The source of this story is Shamwilanga 2004. Vingambudi et al. 2004 also believed that the dance originated in Nangade. Lingundumbwe is indeed very widespread in the northern part of the district.

4. For this version, see Navina et al. 2009. The women dismissed as a lie the idea that the dance originated in Nangade.

5. Vingambudi et al. 2004. That people in Nangade remember dancing "in the year of authority" (1974) contradicts the version that has the dance as originating in Mueda in 1975. Both Ntonya and Rafael had passed away at the time of my research, so I could not verify either claim.

6. This is a *likumbi* secret song. The list is based on groups from Mbwidi and Mueda.

7. NMA/Lingundumbwe/Litamanda/2004.

8. Tomé 2004. On the history of the Women's Detachment (DF), see Isabel Casimiro, "La Lutte de Libération Nationale au Mozambique et l'Emancipation de la Femme," paper presented at the UNESCO workshop Histoire de la Contribution de la Femme à la Lutte de Libération Nationale, Guinea-Bissau, 3–7 September 1983; Allen Isaacman and Barbara Isaacman, "The Role of Women in the Liberation of Mozambique," *Ufahamu* 13 (1984): 128–85; Harry West, "Girls with Guns: Narrating the Experience of War of Frelimo's 'Female Detachment,'" *Anthropological Quarterly* 73, no. 4 (2000): 180–94; Maria-José Arthur, Estevão Jaime Mpalume, Júlio Aquimo, and Valeriano Labés, "O Estatuto da Mulher na Luta Armada" (mimeographed report, Pemba: Arquivo do Patrimonio Cultural, 1992); Organização da Mulher Moçambicana, *A Mulher Moçambicana na Luta de Libertação Nacional: Memórias do Destacamento Feminino* (Maputo: Centro de Pesquisa da História da Luta de Libertação Nacional, 2013).

9. Shamwilanga 2004. This story is corroborated by Maria Pachinuapa's testimony; see Ana Bouene Mussanhane, *Protagonistas da Luta de Libertação Nacional* (Maputo: Marimbique, 2012), 579.

10. Casimiro, "La Lutte" 13.

11. Ibid., 14.

12. Josina Machel, "The Role of Women in the Revolution," *Mozambique Revolution* 41 (1969): 24–28. On Josina Machel, see Renato Matusse and Josina Malique, *Josina Machel: Icone da Mulher Moçambicana* (Maputo: Arquivo do Patrimonio Cultural, 2007).

13. Vingambudi et al. 2004. The women referred specifically to her last speech at Itanda.

14. Shamwilanga 2004.

15. Dias and Dias, *Os Macondes III*, 261. The vinyala danced on a Sunday, not Monday.

16. This much, that *vitengamato* means "undulate the loins," is known also to outsiders.

17. Dias and Dias, *Os Macondes III*, 261.

18. Ibid.

19. In fact, the dance that they observed was performed outside of initiation—for a wedding—but they still felt the need to ascribe it to a specific ceremony.

20. Shamwilanga 2004.

21. Working in the context of Zambian feminine puberty ritual, Elisabeth Cameron observed that women consider themselves *makishi* (masks) and that this prompts a reconsideration of masquerading beyond the European fixation with the headpiece. See Cameron, "Women = Masks: Initiation Arts in North-Western Province, Zambia," *African Arts* 31, no. 2 (1998): 50–61, 93.

22. There is a broad literature on Swahili spirit possession. See esp. Linda Giles, "Sociocultural Change and Spirit Possession on the Swahili Coast," *Anthropological Quarterly* 68, no. 2 (1995): 89–106. Feminine spirit possession cults exist also in central Mozambique. See Bettina Holzhausen, "Youth Culture in Rural Mozambique: A Study of the Significance of Culture for Young People in Rural Areas, Based on Fieldwork in the Districts of Nangade (Cabo Delgado), Mossurize (Manica) and Chókwe (Gaza)," research report, Zurich, 16 January 2007, available at http://www.nestcepas.ch/_pdf/Youth _culture_in_rural_Moz.pdf.

23. Vail and White, *Power*, 231–71.

24. For the Makua, see Liazzat Bonate, "Traditions and Transitions: Islam and Chiefship in Northern Mozambique, ca. 1850–1974" (PhD diss., School of Oriental and African Studies, University of London, 2007), 63; and Trentini, "On the Threshold," 115–17.

25. Rashidi et al. 2004.

26. Ibid. The same connection between lingundumbwe and shinyala was pointed out by Maria Mmaka (see Mmaka et al. 2002).

27. NMA/Lingundumbwe/Mwalela/2004. Kumposha is the name of the village president.

28. For the case of Mapate, see Anapambula and Mmembe 2004; for Malangonya, see Liteka et al. 2004.

29. Navina et al. 2009.

30. "It is with a certain sadness that they remember the time of the struggle, when, despite all difficulties, their work and their contribution was regarded, appreciated and respected." Casimiro, "La Lutte," 24. The same feelings were conveyed by the DF members that I interviewed in Pemba (Galinha 2005, João 2005, and Tomé 2004) but less so in Mueda or Muidumbe (e.g., Naiva et al. 2004).

31. These two songs appear in various versions, of which I give the most complete: NMA/Lingundumbwe/Mwalela/2004, NMA/Utamaduni/Nshinga/2004, and NMA/Utamaduni/Nang'unde/2004. Maria Chipande died in the fatal Antonov crash of 31 March 1986.

32. Makai 2003. I comment extensively on this interview in "Utopia Live," 98–99.

33. NMA/Utamaduni/Mwalela/2004.

34. NMA/Utamaduni/Mbwidi/2004.

35. Ibid.

36. NMA/Utamaduni/Mapate/2004.

37. Machel, "Role of Women," 24.

38. David Robinson, "Curse on the Land: A History of the Mozambican Civil War" (PhD diss., University of Western Australia, 2006), 178.

39. Samora called hyenas the "Enemies of the People." See West, "Voices Twice Silenced," 363.

40. NMA/Utamaduni/Nshinga/2004. In 2005, an officer confessed projecting such films to me. Renamo war crimes were heinous, but they did not affect the Makonde Plateau as they did other parts of the country.

41. NMA/Likulutu/Nampanya/2004L. The partridge is Renamo's symbol.

42. See Israel, "Kummwangalela Guebuza," 111–12.

43. Seguro 2004 and Shikumene 2008. I was part of one of these "celebration" groups in 2005, without knowing precisely what I would encounter. It was only by a whisker that the vice-representative of Renamo was not lynched under my eyes.

44. Unrecorded conversation with the members of the group.

45. See Girard's insightful discussion of Freud's theory of ambivalence in *Things Hidden*, 352–62.

46. For Malawi, see Gillman, *Dance of Politics*; for Tanzania, see Edmonson, *Performance and Politics*.

## CHAPTER 10: DON'T GO ASTRAY

1. Skype videochat, August 2010.

2. Nhussi 2009.

3. CNCD (Companhia Nacional de Canto e Dança), *Ode a Paz* (Maputo: Companhia de Educação Civica e Eleitoral, 1993).

4. Makai 2003.

5. Nandodo and Pulumbamba 2009, Mawasha 2002.

6. Nandodo and Pulumbamba 2009.

7. Mambwembwe et al. 2004.

8. Nandodo 2002. The beekeeper was another nshindo character. Shalele Mawasha (see Mawasha 2002) commented, however, that "*Namwombe* was one beast; *Neijale* another."

9. Mambwembwe et al. 2004. Bortolot interestingly argues in *Revolutions* (21) that the iron-melting *shikuvo* was part of Frelimo's self-reliance campaign; however, this idea is anachronistic, as the style was introduced two or three years earlier.

10. Milan Kundera, *The Unbearable Lightness of Being*, translated by Michael Henry Heim (New York: Harper and Row, 1984).

11. Januário Cabeça "Nandodo" (see Nandodo and Pulumbamba 2009)

12. Nandodo and Pulumbamba 2009.

13. Only the group Kwanja Lyela from Nshongwe, which had been taught by the Mapates, remained faithful to the original inspiration. The three

characters remained; the dancing styles and songs were less parodic than Nandodo's; and the new name given to the dance maintained the original meaning (*kwanja lyela* means "eat beforehand," or otherwise you will forget about food and you will be ensnared by the drums). Mmadun'ga 2002.

14. On Mandushi, see Mpalume, *Vyaka Vyoe*, 45–47.

15. NMA/Neijale/Mapate/2004.

16. NMA/Neijale/Mapate/2004 and NMA/Ngoda/Nampanya/2005 (without the last verse).

17. NMA/Neijale/Mapate/2004.

18. Baltazar 2005.

19. NMA/Neijale/Mapate/2004.

20. Personal conversation, July 2004.

21. Pedro Seguro suggested that such a directive was an outcome of Frelimo's Fourth Congress (1983). Seguro, personal communication, November 2004.

22. Juakali 2008. On chipalamoto, see Wembah-Rashid, "Isinyago and Midimu," 38.

23. Nhussi 2009. Jaime Manupa Kanyanga (see Manupa 2012) then carved a single imitation of this piece. Nantova's mask was danced in 2011 in Cape Town by Atanásio Nhussi's troupe. See Israel, "This is Our Contemporary," 46.

24. The following invention story is based on three interviews: the first with Martins, the carver (Mwanjigula 2003); the second with many group members (Ntukwinye et al. 2004); and the third with Martins and the group patron (Mwanjigula and Siminda 2009).

25. This widespread discourse of dreaming has, of course, fueled the primitivist imaginaries: "It is the spirits who send them the messages. . . . The work of art is born without any previously studied plan, except from dreaming." Júlio Carrilho, "O Espirito da Arte ou a Arte dos Espiritos: A Propósito de Miguel Valingue, Reinata Sadimba e Matias Ntundo," in *Outras Plasticidades* (Lisbon: Camões Institute, 2000), 50.

26. Four of these belong to the safari category of the "big five" and are animals that Martins never saw except in pictures. The one missing is the elephant, which was introduced by other groups. The other two animals— monkey and crocodile—belong to everyday Makonde experience.

27. The *shimbombo* drum was already in use in 1962, as it features in Kubik's notes.

28. Nandodo and Pulumbamba 2009.

29. Pedro Seguro, personal communication, April 2002.

30. The original song, in Portuguese, went, "Let's go all the comrades / We are / The war-veterans from Mueda."

31. Israel, "War of Lions."

32. West, *Kupilikula*, 256–62.

33. Ndeja-Ndeja 2003.

34. Coral das Forças Populares de Libertação Moçambique, Destacamento Feminino, *Frelimo: Canções da Luta Armada de Libertação Nacional* (Maputo: Rádio Moçambique, undated).

35. Ntukwinye et al. 2004.

36. NMA/Mang'anyamu/Matambalale/2004.

37. Ibid.

38. Ibid.

39. NMA/Mang'anyamu/Mwambula/2004.

40. The price of a sexual relationship varied between 10 and 50 *contos* in the years between 2002 and 2006. Such commodification is widespread in Mozambique.

41. Žižek, *For They Know Not.*

42. Lijama 2004.

## CHAPTER 11: PUPPETS AND MACHETES

1. The following reconstruction is based on many conversations with Naupanga dancers; on Shanjolo and Doto 2008; and on an unrecorded interview with the seller of the mask (Myangalewa, September 2004).

2. 40.000 *meticais* [MT] was at the time the equivalent of 1.50 USD. Before 2005, in common parlance, 1,000 MT was the equivalent of 1 *conto.*

3. Bortolot discusses at length in "Language for Change" (81–83) the boastful claim of a Mbau group of having invented naupanga in 2001. This is impossible, as the group was beginning to imitatively "try out" (*kulingangila*) the dance when I visited the village in mid-2002.

4. Vingambudi et al. 2004.

5. Mustafa 2005. All following quotations come from this source.

6. NMA/ShukuNwele/Mwambula/2004.

7. Ibid.

8. I use the standard Shimakonde orthographic spelling *shuku* instead of Mustafa's *chuku.* Mustafa himself pronounced the word *suku.* The three sounds are realizations of the same phoneme.

9. Antony Appiah, "Is the Post- in Postmodernism the Post- in Postcolonial?" *Critical Inquiry* 17, no. 2 (1991): 357.

10. Romuald Hazoumé, *La Bouche du Roi* (Paris: Flammarion, 2006).

11. For an insightful discussion, see Ferdinand De Jong, *Masquerades of Modernity: Power and Secrecy in Casamance, Senegal* (Edinburgh: International African Library, 2007).

12. See a critical discussion in Partha Chatterjee, "A Critique of Popular Culture," *Public Culture* 20, no. 2 (2008): 321–45.

13. This is based on the frequentation of *videwo* and on numerous informal conversations, sparked by a chat with one of Seguro's nephews, a relatively well-off secondary school pupil. Fidel Mbalale has carried out a similar informal inquiry in Montepuez secondary schools in 2006, with similar results. The situation might have changed since then.

14. I assisted in the projection of *Predator* in Litamanda, noting the audience commentaries, in September 2004.

15. Fredric Jameson, "Cognitive Mapping," in *Marxism and the Interpretation of Culture,* ed. Cary Nelson and Lawrence Grossberg (Champaign: University of Illinois Press, 1988), 347–57.

16. NMA/Naupanga/Mwatidi/2004.

17. Shanjolo and Doto 2008. The boys explained the kicking style in similarly contradictory terms ("it is like when you fight with a friend" vs. "but it is to make room for the mask to dance").

18. Mustafa 2008.

19. Mustafa 2005.

20. See also the song below the title of chap. 6.

21. Mustafa passed away in March 2009.

22. The reference is to Achille Mbembe's "aesthetics of vulgarity." Mbembe, *On the Postcolony* (Berkeley: University of California Press, 2001), 137.

23. Terence Ranger, "Nationalist Historiography, Patriotic History and the History of the Nation: The Struggle over the Past in Zimbabwe," *Journal of Southern African Studies* 30, no. 2 (2004): 215–34.

24. NMA/Nshesho/Mocimboa/2009.

25. NMA/Bwarabwà/Chai/2008.

## EPILOGUE

1. Mustafa 2003.

2. The case of the resurrection of nshindo in the 1990s by groups of youths, instructed by knowledgeable elders, is emblematic. See Shawa 2004.

3. Such as the Luvale's Mupala, discussed in Jordán, *Makishi*, 27, and the Pende's Pumbu, discussed in Strother, *Inventing Masks*, 211–17.

4. Charles Baudelaire, "Le Peintre de la Vie Moderne" (1863), in *Œuvres Complètes* (Paris: Le Seuil, 1968), 553, §IV.

# Glossary of Shimakonde Terms

*dinembo* (sing. *inembo*): Scarifications.

*dinjuga* (sing. *injuga* but most often used in the plural): Metal bells that adorn the body of the lipiko dancer.

*ibondi* (pl. *dibondi*, locative *kubondi*): Lowland.

*indona* (pl. *dindona*): Wooden ornament inserted through the upper lip. When it includes a short metallic spike, it is called *nkalinga*.

*ing'oma* (pl. *ding'oma*): Feminine puberty ceremonies, dance.

*ing'ondo* (pl. *ding'ondo*): War.

*ing'ope* (pl. *ding'ope*): Face, mask (as euphemism).

*kububuwa*: To command the movements of a masked dancer through the rhythm of a lead drum.

*kujaluka*: The coming out of initiation rituals; by extension, celebrating the end of something. The causative form is *kujalula*.

*kujedya*: To imitate.

*kujela*: To shoot, to launch, to inaugurate.

*kujowa*: To be fearsome, dangerous.

*kukamadyanga*: To be complicated, to baffle.

*kukudula*: To strike a reiterative rhythm that forms the basis for a dance.

*kulingangila*: To rehearse, to try out.

*kunannua*: To warm up drums on a fire.

*kunema*: To brag, to show off.

*kunung'unula*: Pelvis shaking in dance (esp. in shinalombo and mapiko); euphemism for intercourse.

*kupanga*: To organize; also used metonymically for "to dance mapiko."

*kupika*: To transform something with the help of magic; to evoke a magical spirit or fabricated animal.

*kushalagwesha*: To make something delay.

*kushamalela*: To intone songs in a call-and-response modality (from *kushema*, "to call").

*kutakatuwa*: To make something rise; to resurrect.

*kuujia*: To repeat something over, esp. a song verse.

*kuumanga*: To be famous (lit. "to repeatedly go out").

*kwaula ntumi*: Lit. "telling the lion," announcing the coming out of initiation rituals.

*kwetu*: One's homestead, also used more generally as the equivalent of the French *chez nous*.

*likaja* (pl. *makaja*): Hamlet inhabited by people belonging to one matrilineage and placed under the authority of an elder (*likaja*).

*likola* (pl. *makola*): Matrilineage.

*likomba* (pl. *makomba*): Facial masks and related masquerades.

*likumbi* (pl. *makumbi*): Masculine puberty ceremonies.

*likuta* (pl. *makuta*): Hut, cabin, initiation hut.

*lingongo*: Wooden enclosure.

*linjonda* (pl. *manjonda*): Feather crown used especially on nantyaka and majoji face masks.

*liyoka* (pl. *maoka*): Ghost, spirit of the dead.

*lutove*, also *lutandove*: Raffia rope used to weave the traditional beds (*igoli*); also a corset made of such rope worn by the lipiko over the torso.

*lyeve* (pl. *meeve*): Small round fruits that grow in the Messalo and Rovuma lowlands; also foot rattles made with such fruits, when dried.

*maringue*: Drinking enclosure, from the name of Renamo's central base in Beira.

*mashindano*: Dance competition; loanword from Kiswahili.

*matanga* (from Kiswahili): Funerary ceremony held some time after death, when grief is abandoned.

*midimu* (sing. *ndimu*): Secret teachings imparted during puberty ceremonies, both masculine and feminine.

*mmapiko* (pl. *vamapiko*): Mapiko practitioner, including drummers, singers, and group participants.

*mpingo*: African blackwood (*Dalbergia melanoxylon*).

*mpolo* (pl. *mipolo*): Secret place where the masks are kept; metonymically, a masquerade ensemble.

*muti* (pl. *myuti*): Head, headpiece, unworn mask.

*muundu*: Faucet often used in the mapiko performance.

*mwene* (pl. *vene*): Owner, master, person responsible for something.

*nang'olo* (pl. *vanang'olo*, addressive *manang'olo*): Elder, knowledgeable or powerful man.

*ndagwa* (pl. *vadagwa*): A person without any grace or talent (see *udagwa*).

*nkulaula* (pl. *vakulaula*): Healer.

*nkungunyale* (pl. *mikungunyale*): Ceramic phallus used to instruct girls during puberty rituals.

*nnalombo* (pl. *vanalombo*): Ritual specialist of puberty ceremonies.

*nnanda* (pl. *valanda*): A talented person (see *ulanda*).

*nnemba* (pl. *vanemba*, addressive *manemba*): Young man, especially if unmarried.

*nneya* (pl. *mileya*): Elongated drum carved in hard wood with a harpoon.

*nshamoko*: Vegetal medicine that makes the wearer desirable or famous; typically consumed with honey, worn on one's person, or concealed in a drum.

*ntadala*: Highlands, plateau.

*ntela* (pl. *mitela*): Plant or root with medicinal properties; also medicine.

*ntene*: Wild kapok tree (*Bombax rhodognaphalon*).

*ntete* (pl. *mitete*): Hamlet of a different lineage than the speaker.

*nyama* (pl. *dinyama*): Meat, flesh.

*nyanyamala*: Precolonial times.

*shigwali* (pl. *vigwali*): Bits of wood used to secure the lipiko's arm and leg cloths, from the verb *kugwala* (to wear). Also *shigwadyo* (pl. *vigwadyo*) from the causative form *kugwadya* (to dress someone).

*shijela* (pl. *vijela*): Magical arrow or "rocket" (from the verb *kujela*).

*shikuvo* (pl. *vikuvo*): Style; also a rhythmical sequence connected to specific dance steps.

*shilo*: Night, nighttime masquerades.

*shimbili*: Fame.

*shinalombo*: Dance of the nnalombo.

*shinemba*: Youth, the quality of being young; also the name of a mapiko style that emerged in the late 1940s.

*shinganga* (pl. *vinganga*): Chalice-shaped drums used as a rhythmic basis in mapiko performance.

*shingula* (pl. *vyungula*): The hare, the boy selected as leader in the initiation camp activities.

*shipito* (pl. *vipito*): Ordeal, exam (from the verb *kupita*, "to pass").

*shitendo* (pl. *vitendo*): Actions, theatrical part of danced performances.

*shitengamatu* (pl. *vitengamatu*): Clay feminine masks (lit. "open your ears").

*shiwanja*: Public place, field (from Kiswahili *shiwanjani*).

*tapwito*: Twirl that concludes the nshakasha dance sequence.

*udagwa*: Ungainliness, inability to carry out a good life, badly dancing.

*ulanda*: Innate talent, artistry, gift (similar to Kiswahili *uwezo*).

*ushaka*: Deliberate provocation, affront, violent gesture.

*uwavi*: Sorcery, witchcraft, both malevolent and benevolent, innate and learned.

# Mapiko Genres and Other Dance Genres

## MAPIKO GENRES, CIRCA 1920–2010

*mileya* (pre-1920s–64): Preconquest form, presumably based on charactering, resurrected and expanded in the 1940s by Nampyopyo, Shumu, and others.

*shilo* (dates unknown): Mask of spiritual animals danced at night, during initiation rituals and for funerary ceremonies.

*dutu* (1920s–2008): Abstract genre, divided into two parts, also called *mapiko alikuti*, characterized by participation irrespective of lineage (*nyama ni nyama*, "meat-is-meat").

*nshesho* (1940s–): The most widely known genre of mapiko, divided into two parts, characterized by mimetic choreographies (*vikuvo*) and large choirs; also called *aligoma* or *ashinemba* (youth style).

*lishalagwesha* (pl. *mashalagwesha*, 1940s–): Juvenile mask that dances during initiation rituals to the sound of hoes; has danced for remuneration from the 1980s onward.

*nshindo* (1940s–64, 1976–83, 1994–): Parade of mask-characters dancing by night for funerary ceremonies; it is called *shikelya* in M'Bau and *timbwiri* in Nkoe.

*nantyaka* (1940s–): Face masks of Makua-Yao origin appropriated by the Makonde in the Messalo lowlands.

*lijoji* (pl. *majoji*, 1940s–): Face masks of Ngoni origin appropriated by the Makonde in the Messalo lowlands.

*machapila* (1940s–): Stilt face mask of Tanzanian Makonde origin, appropriated by the Makonde, especially in the area around Nangade.

*shinyala* (1940s–64): Feminine dance depicting a decayed Portuguese woman, identified as a form of mask despite the absence of headpiece.

*lingoti* (1950s–): Face mask from the Rovuma River area, characterized by capers and by loud striking of two likuti drums. It arrived on the Makonde Plateau in the mid-1990s as *ng'odo*.

*lingundumbwe* (1975–): Feminine masquerade in which the face is covered with a cloth; from the 1980s onward replaced by utamaduni, a maskless dance, in many villages.

*neijale* (1976–): Large-eared jester mask, based on the preconquest mask-character named *Mbangi*. It is called *kwanja lyela* in Nshongwe.

*shitamanga* (1980s): Mask that dances in fire, introduced in Shitunda and prohibited when its inventor caught fire and died.

*mang'anyamu* (1992–): Animal masquerade introduced by a group of youths in Matambalale.

*naupanga* (2000–): Juvenile dance representing a machete-carrying elder; it appears in many variations (called *naulongo, nalibibu, naing'ong'o*).

*shuku nwele* (2000–2010): Rubber masks accompanied by dancing puppets on poles.

## OTHER DANCE GENRES

*ligwalema* (1920–64): Funerary ceremony dance.

*nshaila* (1920s–): Women's circular dance.

*nkala* (1920s–): Women's circular dance.

*ngoda* (1964–74): Wartime dance, characterized by the sound of hand rattles.

*limbondo* (1969– ): Circular dance marked by tattered costumes and political lyrics.

*nnonje* (1970– ): Quasi-military dance in line, with political lyrics.

*likulutu* (1975– ): Demonstration of military activities carried out by women.

*bwarabwà* (1980s– ): Funerary ceremony dance, sung to the rhythm of hoes.

*utamaduni* (1980s– ): Women's dance; a maskless evolution of *lingundumbwe*.

*shingenge* (1980s– ): Juvenile circular dance invented by Makonde expatriates in Tanzania, marked by the shoulder-drum *shimbombo*.

*mashawona* (1990s–): Youth dance marked by loin movements and tattered garments.

# Makonde Drums and Other Musical Instruments

*dimbila:* Xylophone.

*iwaya:* Seven-string zither played inside a calabash or metal pot; when played inside a hand-carved resonance case similar to a guitar, it is called *ligita* (pl. *magita*) or *ligalantoni* (pl. *magalantoni*).

*ligoma* (pl. *magoma*): Cylindrical drum with openings at the bottom, struck with the hand, used to command the mask in the nshesho genre.

*likuti* (pl. *makuti*): Chalice-shaped drum. It comes in two forms: large (*likuti likumene*), as a leading drum of dutu, nshindo, and lingoti; and small (*likuti lidikidiki*), as a base drum of many dances (neijale, utamaduni, etc.) or as a complementary leading drum of nshesho.

*lipalapanda* (pl. *mapalapanda*): Antelope horn blown during performances.

*lishanjo* (pl. *mashanjo*): Hand rattles made with cans filled with seeds or grains.

*nneya* (pl. *mileya*): Elongated drum used solely in mapiko.

*ntoji* (pl. *mitoji*), also *ntojo*: Light drum carved in *ntene* wood, used as a lead drum in many dances, including youth mapiko and utamaduni.

*shimbombo* (pl. *vimbombo*): Shoulder drum imported from the militaristic dance *muganda* of the Yao, then used in the youth dance *shingenge*.

*shinganga* (pl. *vinganga*): Small chalice-shaped drum used in mapiko performance. It is covered with boa (*mbidi*) skin, is very light and high pitched, and readily catches fire when heated; or it can be covered with gazelle (*mmala*) skin. In the Messalo lowlands, it terminates with a long stick that is stuck in the ground.

*shitali* (pl. *vitali*): Lit. "irons"; refers to hoe blades or pipes struck with bicycle parts.

*shityatya:* Thumb piano with five or seven blades.

# Bibliography

Adam, Yussuf. *Escapar aos Dentes do Crocodilo e Cair na Boca do Leopardo: Trajectoria de Moçambique Pós-colonial, 1975–1990*. Maputo: Promedia, 2006.

———. "Mueda, 1917–1990: Resistência, Colonialismo, Libertação e Desenvolvimento." *Arquivo: Boletim do Arquivo Histórico de Moçambique* 14 (1993): 4–102.

Adam, Yussuf, and Anna Maria Gentili. "O Movimento Liguilanilu no Planalto de Mueda, 1957–1962." *Estudos Moçambicanos* 4 (1983): 41–75.

Agamben, Giorgio. *Means without End: Notes on Politics*. Minneapolis: University of Minnesota Press, 2000.

Aguilar, Laurel Birch. *Inscribing the Mask: Interpretation of Nyau Masks and Ritual Performance among the Chewa of Malawi*. Freiburg: Universitätsverlag Freiburg, 1996.

Alberto, Manuel Simões. "O 'Mapico,' Dança dos Macondes." *Império* 4 (August 1951): 35, 51.

Allman, Jean, and John Parker. *Tongnaab: The History of a West African God*. Bloomington: University of Indiana Press, 2005.

Alpers, Edward. *Ivory and Slaves in East Central Africa: Changing Patterns of International Trade to the Later Nineteenth Century*. London: Heinemann, 1975.

———. "Representation and Historical Consciousness in the Art of Modern Mozambique." *Canadian Journal of African Studies* 22, no. 1 (1989): 73–94.

———. "To Seek a Better Life: Implications of Migration from Mozambique to Tanganyika for Class Formation and Political Behaviour." *Canadian Journal of African Studies* 18, no. 2 (1984): 367–88.

Alves Costa, Catarina. *Guia Para os Filmes Realizados por Margot Dias em Moçambique, 1958/1961*. Lisbon: Museu de Etnologia, 1997.

Appiah, Anthony Kwame. "Is the Post- in Postmodernism the Post- in Postcolonial?" *Critical Inquiry* 17, no. 2 (1991): 336–57.

Argenti, Nicolas. *The Intestines of the State: Youth, Violence and Belated Histories in the Cameroon Grassfields*. Chicago: University of Chicago Press, 2007.

———. "Masks and Masquerades." *Journal of Material Culture* 2, no. 3 (1997): 361–81.

Arnoldi, Mary Jo. "Playing the Puppets: Innovation and Rivalry in Bamana Youth Theatre of Mali." *TDR* 32, no. 2 (1988): 65–82.

———. *Playing with Time: Art and Performance in Central Mali*. Bloomington: Indiana University Press, 1995.

Arthur, Maria-José, Estevão Jaime Mpalume, Júlio Aquimo, and Valeriano Labés. "O Estatuto da Mulher na Luta Armada." Mimeographed report. Pemba: Arquivo do Patrimonio Cultural, 1992.

Askew, Kelly. "As Plato Duly Warned: Music, Politics, and Social Change in Coastal East Africa." *Anthropological Quarterly* 76, no. 4 (2003): 609–37.

———. *Performing the Nation: Swahili Music and Cultural Politics in Tanzania*. Chicago: University of Chicago Press, 2002.

Assubuji, Rui, Paolo Israel, and Rui Thompson, eds. *The Liberation Script in Mozambican History*. Special issue of *Kronos: Southern African Histories*, no. 39 (2013).

Augé, Marc. "Vers un Refus de l'Alternative Sens-Fonction." *L'Homme* 18, no. 3 (1978): 139–54.

Azevedo, Licinio de. *Reinata Sadimba: Mãos de Barro*. Maputo: Ebano Multimedia, 2003.

Bakhtin, Mikhail. *Rabelais and His World*. Bloomington: Indiana University Press, 1984.

———. *Speech Genres and Other Late Essays*. Austin: University of Texas Press, 1986.

Balandier, Georges. *Sens et Puissance: Les Dynamiques Sociales*. Paris: Presses Universitaires de France, 1971.

Barber, Karin. *The Anthropology of Texts, Persons and Publics: Oral and Written Culture in Africa and Beyond*. Cambridge: Cambridge University Press, 2007.

———. "Introduction." In *Readings in African Popular Culture*, edited by Karin Barber, 1–12. London: International African Institute, 1997.

———. "Popular Arts in Africa." *African Studies Review* 30, no. 3 (1987): 1–78.

Basto, Maria-Benedita. *A Guerra das Escritas: Literatura, Nação e Teoria Pós-colonial em Moçambique*. Lisbon: Vendaval, 2006.

Bateson, Gregory. *Naven: A Survey of the Problems Suggested by a Composite Picture of the Culture of a New Guinea Tribe Drawn from Three Points of View*. Cambridge: Cambridge University Press, 1936.

———. *Steps to an Ecology of Mind*. Chicago: University of Chicago Press, 2000.

Baudelaire, Charles. "Le Peintre de la Vie Moderne." In *Œuvres Complètes*, 546–66. Paris: Le Seuil, 1968.

Bay, Edna. *Asen, Ancestors and Vodun: Tracing Change in African Art*. Champaign: University of Illinois Press, 2008.

Bazin, Jean. *Des Clous dans la Joconde*. Paris: Anacharsis, 2008.

Bellman, Beryl. *The Language of Secrecy: Symbols and Metaphors in Poro Ritual*. New Brunswick, NJ: Rutgers University Press, 1984.

Bonate, Liazzat. "Traditions and Transitions: Islam and Chiefship in Northern Mozambique, ca. 1850–1974." PhD diss., School of Oriental and African Studies, University of London, 2007.

Borges-Coelho, João Paulo. "Moçambique e a África Austral: Uma Leitura Histórica do Presente." Paper presented at the V Congress of African Studies in the Iberic World, Covilhã, 4–6 May 2006.

———. *O Olho de Herzog*. Lisbon: Caminho, 2010.

Bortolot, Alexander Yves. "A Language for Change: Creativity and Power in Mozambican Makonde Masquerades." PhD diss., Columbia University, 2004.

———. *Revolutions: A Century of Makonde Masquerade in Mozambique*. New York: Wallach Art Gallery, 2007.

Bouene Mussanhane, Ana. *Protagonistas da Luta de Libertação Nacional*. Maputo: Marimbique, 2012.

Bragança, Aquino de, and Jacques Depelchin. "From the Idealization of Frelimo to the Understanding of the Recent History of Mozambique." *African Journal of Political Economy* 1 (1986): 168–80.

Burke, Edmund. *A Philosophical Enquiry into the Origin of Our Ideas of the Sublime and Beautiful*. London, 1757.

Buur, Lars. "Xiconhoca: Mozambique's Ubiquitous Post-Independence Traitor." In *Traitors: Suspicion, Intimacy and the Ethics of State-Building*, edited by Sharika Thirangama and Tobias Kelly, 24–47. Philadelphia: University of Pennsylvania Press, 2010.

Cabral, Amílcar. "National Liberation and Culture." In *Unity and Struggle: Speeches and Writings*, 138–54. New York: Monthly Review Press, 1979.

Cahen, Michel. "'Entrons dans la Nation': Notes pour une Étude du Discours Politique de la Marginalité: Le Cas de la RENAMO du Mozambique." *Politique Africaine* 67 (1997): 70–88.

———. "The Mueda Case and Maconde Political Ethnicity: Some Notes on a Work in Progress." *Africana Studia* 2 (2000): 29–46.

Cameron, Elisabeth. "Women = Masks: Initiation Arts in North-Western Province, Zambia." *African Arts* 31, no. 2 (1998): 50–61, 93.

Campbell, Carol, and Carol Eastman. "Ngoma: Swahili Adult Song Performance in Context." *Ethnomusicology* 28, no. 3 (1984): 467–93.

Carrilho, Júlio. "O Espirito da Arte ou a Arte dos Espiritos: A Propósito de Miguel Valingue, Reinata Sadimba e Matias Ntundo." In *Outras Plasticidades*, 49–53. Lisbon: Camões Institute, 2000.

Casimiro, Isabel. "La Lutte de Libération Nationale au Mozambique et l'Emancipation de la Femme." Paper presented at the UNESCO workshop Histoire de la Contribution de la Femme à la Lutte de Libération Nationale, Guiné Bissau, 3–7 September 1983.

CEA (Centro de Estudos Africanos). *Poder Popular e Desagregação nas Aldeias Comunais do Planalto de Mueda*. Maputo: Universidade Eduardo Mondlane, 1986.

Chabal, Patrick. "The End of Empire." In *A History of Postcolonial Lusophone Africa*, edited by Patrick Chabal, 3–28. London: Hurst, 2002.

Chakrabarty, Dipesh. *Habitations of Modernity: Essays in the Wake of Subaltern Studies*. Chicago: University of Chicago Press, 2002.

Chatterjee, Partha. "A Critique of Popular Culture." *Public Culture* 20, no. 2 (2008): 321–45.

Chinyowa, Kennedy. "Towards an Aesthetic Theory for African Popular Theatre." *South African Theatre Journal* 21, no. 1 (2007): 12–30.

Chipande, Alberto Joaquim. "The Massacre of Mueda." *Mozambique Revolution* 43 (1970): 12–14.

Cirese, Alberto Mario. *Cultura Egemonica e Culture Subalterne*. Palermo, Italy: Palumbo, 1997.

CNCD (Companhia Nacional de Canto e Dança). *Ode a Paz*. Maputo: Companhia de Educação Civica e Eleitoral, 1993.

Comaroff, Jean. *Body of Power, Spirit of Resistance: The Culture and History of a South African People*. Chicago: University of Chicago Press, 1985.

Coral das FPLM (Forças Populares de Liertação de Moçambique), Destacamento Feminino. *Frelimo: Canções da Luta Armada de Libertação Nacional*. Maputo: Rádio Moçambique, undated.

Curran, David. "Nyau Masks and Ritual." *African Arts* 32, no. 3 (1999): 68–77.

Davidson, Basil. *The Black Man's Burden: Africa and the Curse of the Nation-State*. London: James Currey, 1992.

———. *The People's Cause: A History of Guerillas in Africa*. Harlow, UK: Longman, 1981.

De Castro, Alvaro. "Artes Plásticas do Norte de Moçambique." *Boletim do Museu de Nampula* 2 (1961): 115–29.

Declich, Francesca. *I Bantu della Somalia: Etnogenesi e Rituali Mviko*. Milan: Franco Angeli, 2002.

De Jong, Ferdinand. *Masquerades of Modernity: Power and Secrecy in Casamance, Senegal*. Edinburgh: International African Library, 2007.

Delange, Jacqueline. *Arts et Peuples de l'Afrique Noire: Introduction à une Analyse des Créations Plastiques*. Paris: Gallimard, 1967.

Depelchin, Jacques. "Reconnecting the Disconnected." Paper presented at the District Six Museum, Cape Town, South Africa, 8 July 2009.

Derluguian, Georgi. "The Social Origins of Good and Bad Governance: Reinterpreting the 1968 Schism in Frelimo." In *Sure Road? Nationalism in Angola, Guinea-Bissau and Mozambique*, edited by Eric Morier-Genoud, 79–101. Leiden, The Netherlands: Brill, 2012.

Dias, Jorge António. *Os Macondes de Moçambique*, Vol. I: *Aspectos Historícos e Economicos*. Lisbon: Junta de Investigação Ultramarina, 1964.

———. "Mudança de Cultura entre os Macondes de Moçambique." *Universitas* 6/7 (1970): 260–66.

———. *Portuguese Contribution to Cultural Anthropology*. Johannesburg, South Africa: Witwatersrand University Press, 1961.

Dias, Jorge António, and Margot Dias. *Os Macondes de Moçambique*, Vol. II: *Cultura Material*. Lisbon: Junta de Investigação Ultramarina, 1964.

———. *Os Macondes de Moçambique*, Vol. III: *Vita Social e Ritual*. Lisbon: Junta de Investigação Ultramarina, 1970.

Dias, Margot. *Instrumentos Musicais de Moçambique*. Lisbon: Instituto de Investigação Científica Tropical, 1986.

Dick-Read, Robert. *Sanamu: Adventures in Search of African Art*. London: Rupert Hart-Davies, 1964.

Dinerman, Alice. *Revolution, Counter-revolution and Revisionism in Post-colonial Africa: The Case of Mozambique, 1975–1994*. London: Routledge, 2006.

Ding'ano, Marcelino, and Pedro Walecaia. "Subsídios à Reconstituição da História do Chai, 1964–1975." Mimeograph, preliminary report. Pemba, Mozambique: Arquivo do Património Cultural, 2004.

Drewal, Henry John, and Margaret Thompson Drewal. *Gelede: Art and Female Power among the Yoruba*. Bloomington: Indiana University Press, 1983.

Duarte, Ricardo Teixeira. *Escultura Maconde*. Maputo: Universidade Eduardo Mondlane, 1987.

Duarte, Ricardo Teixeira, and Machado da Graça, eds. *Máscaras: Masks*. Maputo: Museu Nacional de Arte, 1992.

Edmonson, Laura. *Performance and Politics in Tanzania: The Nation on Stage*. Bloomington: Indiana University Press, 2007.

Egero, Bertil. *Mozambique: A Dream Undone*. Uppsala, Sweden: Nordiska Afrikainstitutet, 1987.

Ellison, James. "Competitive Dance and Social Identity: Converging Histories in Southwestern Tanzania." In Gunderson and Barz, *Mashindano!*, 199–232.

Enekwe, Ossie Onoura. *Igbo Masks: The Oneness of Ritual and Theatre*. Lagos, Portugal: Department of Culture, 1987.

Fabian, Johannes. "Popular Culture in Africa: Findings and Conjectures." *Africa: Journal of the International African Institute* 48, no. 4 (1978): 315–34.

———. *Time and the Other*. New York: Columbia University Press, 1983.

Fanon, Frantz. *The Wretched of the Earth*. New York: Grove Press, 1964.

Fenzel, Kristian, ed. *Makonde: Mapiko*. Linz, Austria: Neue Galerie der Stadt, 1997.

Fernandes, Carlos. "Dinâmicas de Pesquisa em Ciências Sociais no Moçambique Pós-independente: O Caso do Centro de Estudos Africanos, 1975–1990." PhD diss., Universidade Federal da Bahia, 2011.

Feyerabend, Paul. *Against Method: Outline of an Anarchist Theory of Knowledge*. New York: New Left Books, 1975.

Freitas, Costa. "Notas para um Estudo sobre a Dança do Mapico." *Memórias do Instituto de Investigação Científica de Moçambique* no. 5 (1963): 125–31.

Frelimo. *Programa do Primeiro Festival de Dança Popular*. Maputo: Gabinete do Primeiro Festival de Dança Popular, 1978.

Fresu, Anna, and Mendes de Oliveira. *Pesquisas para um Teatro Popular em Moçambique*. Maputo: Cadernos "Tempo," 1982.

Gearhart, Rebecca. "Ngoma Memories: A History of Competitive Music and Dance Performance on the Kenya Coast." PhD diss., University of Florida, 1998.

———. "Ngoma Memories: How Ritual Music and Dance Shaped the Northern Kenya Coast." *African Studies Review* 48, no. 3 (2005): 21–47.

Geffray, Christian. "Fragments d'un Discours du Pouvoir (1975–1985)." *Politique Africaine* 29 (1988): 71–85.

———. *La Cause des Armes au Mozambique: Anthropologie d'une Guerre Civile*. Paris: Karthala, 1990.

———. *Ni Père ni Mère: Critique de la Parenté; Le Cas Makhuwa*. Paris: Le Seuil, 1990.

Giles, Linda. "Sociocultural Change and Spirit Possession on the Swahili Coast." *Anthropological Quarterly* 68, no. 2 (1995): 89–106.

Gillman, Lisa. *The Dance of Politics: Gender, Performance and Democratization in Malawi*. Philadelphia: Temple University Press, 2009.

Ginzburg, Carlo. *Ecstasies: Deciphering the Witches' Sabbath*. Chicago: University of Chicago Press, 2004.

———. *History, Rhetoric and Proof*. Hanover, NH: University Press of New England for Brandeis University Press/Historical Society of Israel, 1999.

Girard, Réné. *Things Hidden since the Foundation of the World*. Stanford: Stanford University Press, 1987.

———. *Violence and the Sacred*. Baltimore, MD: John Hopkins University Press, 1977.

Glassman, Jonathon. *Feasts and Riot: Revelry, Rebellion, and Popular Consciousness on the Swahili Coast, 1856–1888*. Portsmouth, NH: Heinemann, 1995.

———. *War of Words, War of Stones: Racial Thought and Violence in Colonial Zanzibar*. Bloomington: Indiana University Press, 2011.

Gluckman, Max. "The Philosophical Roots of Masked Dancers in Barotseland (Western Province), Zambia." In *In Memoriam Jorge Dias*, 139–57. Lisbon: Junta de Investigação Ultramarina, 1974.

Gomes, Maria. *Educação Moçambicana: História de Um Processo, 1962–1984*. Maputo: Livraria Universitária da Universidad Europea de Madrid, 1999.

Gray, Jeremy. "A Journey by Land from Tete to Kilwa in 1616." *Tanganyika Notes and Records* 25 (1948): 40–45.

Guerra, Ruy. *Mueda, Memoria e Massácre*. Film. Instituto Nacional do Cinema, Maputo, Mozambique, 1979.

———. "Mueda é o Respeito pela Realidade Histórica." Interview by Sol de Carvalho. *Tempo* 512 (1980): 49–53.

Guerreiro, Manuel Viegas. *Os Macondes de Moçambique*, Vol. IV: *Sabedoria, Língua, Literatura e Jogos*. Lisbon: Junta de Investigação Ultramarina, 1966.

———. *Rudimentos de Lingua Maconde*. Lourenço Marques [Maputo], Mozambique: Instituto de Investigação de Moçambique, 1963.

Guhrs, Tamara. "Nyau Masquerade Performance: Shifting the Imperial Gaze." MA diss., Rhodes University, 1999.

Gunderson, Frank, and Gregory Barz, eds. *Mashindano! Competitive Music Performance in East Africa*. Dar Es Salaam, Tanzania: Mkuki Na Nyota, 2005.

Harley, George W. *Masks as Agents of Social Control in Northeast Liberia*. Peabody Papers 32, no. 2. Cambridge, MA: Peabody Museum, 1950.

Harries, Lyndon. *The Initiation Rites of the Makonde Tribe*. Communication from the Rhodes-Livingstone Institute 3. Lusaka, Northern Rhodesia: Rhodes-Livingstone Institute, 1944.

Hartwig, Gerald. "The Historical and Social Role of Kerebe Music." *Tanzania Notes and Records* 70 (1969): 41–56.

Hazoumé, Romuald. *La Bouche du Roi*. Paris: Flammarion, 2006.

Hemingway, Ernest. *A Moveable Feast: The Restored Edition*. New York: Scribner, 2009.

Heusch, Luc de. *Pourquoi l'Épouser? Et Autres Essays*. Paris: Gallimard, 1971.

Hobsbawm, Eric. *Primitive Rebels*. Manchester: University of Manchester Press, 1959.

Holzhausen, Bettina. "Youth Culture in Rural Mozambique: A Study of the Significance of Culture for Young People in Rural Areas, Based on Fieldwork in the Districts of Nangade (Cabo Delgado), Mossurize (Manica) and Chókwe (Gaza)." Research report, Zurich, 16 January 2007. Available at http://www.nestcepas.ch/_pdf/Youth_culture_in_rural_Moz.pdf.

Honwana, Alcinda. *Espíritos Vivos, Tradições Modernas: Possessão de Espíritos e Reintegração Social Pós-guerra no Sul de Moçambique*. Maputo: Promedia, 2002.

Huizinga, Johan. *Homo Ludens: A Study of the Play-Element in Culture*. London: Routledge, 1950.

Isaacman, Allen, and Barbara Isaacman. "The Role of Women in the Liberation of Mozambique." *Ufahamu* 13 (1984): 128–85.

Israel, Paolo. "Kummwangalela Guebuza: The Mozambican General Elections of 2004 in Muidumbe and the Roots of the Loyalty of Makonde People to Frelimo." *Lusotopie* 13, no. 2 (2006): 103–26.

——. "Maconde é Maningue Cultural: Danse et Sculpture Makonde à Maputo." DEA diss., Ecole des Hautes Etudes en Sciences Sociales, 2001.

——. "Mapiko Masquerades of the Makonde: Performance and Historicity." In *Eastern African Contours: Reviewing Creativity and Visual Culture*, edited by Hassan Arero and Zachary Kingdon, 99–121. London: Horniman Museum, Critical Museology and Material Culture series, 2005.

——. "This Is Our Contemporary: Mozambican Masks in Cape Town." *Art South Africa* 10, no. 2 (2011): 44–47.

——. "Utopia Live: Singing the Mozambican Struggle for National Liberation." *Kronos: Journal of Southern African Histories* 35 (2009): 98–141.

——. "The War of Lions: Witch-Hunts, Occult Idioms and Post-socialism in Northern Mozambique." *Journal of Southern African Studies* 35, no. 1 (March 2009): 155–74.

Jameson, Fredric. "Cognitive Mapping." In *Marxism and the Interpretation of Culture*, edited by Cary Nelson and Lawrence Grossberg, 347–57. Champaign: University of Illinois Press, 1988.

——. *The Political Unconscious: Narrative as a Socially Symbolic Act*. New York: Cornell University Press, 1983.

Johansen, Elise. "Makonde Mask Dance: Performing Identity." In Gunderson and Barz, *Mashindano!*, 255–70.

Jordán, Manuel. *Makishi: Mask Characters of Zambia*. Los Angeles: Fowler Museum, 2006.

Karlström, Mikael. "On the Aesthetics and Dialogics of Power in the Post-colony." *Africa* 73, no. 1 (2003): 57–76.

Kasfir, Sidney Littlefield. *African Art and the Colonial Encounter*. Bloomington: University of Indiana Press, 2007.

———. "One Tribe, One Style? Paradigms in the Historiography of African Art." *History in Africa* 2 (1984): 163–93.

Kaspin, Deborah. "Chewa Visions and Revision of Power: Transformation of the Nyau Dance in Central Malawi." In *Modernity and Its Malcontents: Ritual and Power in Post-colonial Africa,* edited by Jean Comaroff and John Comaroff, 34–57. Chicago: University of Chicago Press, 1993.

Kerr, David. "Unmasking the Spirits: Theatre in Malawi." *Drama Review* 31, no. 2 (1987): 115–25.

Kingdon, Zachary. *A Host of Devils: The History and Context of the Making of Makonde Spirit Sculpture*. London: Routledge, 2002.

Knappert, Jan. *Four Centuries of Swahili Verse: A Literary History and Anthology*. London: Heinemann, 1979.

Koselleck, Reinhardt. *Futures Past: On the Semantics of Historical Time*. New York: Columbia University Press, 2004.

Kramer, Fritz. *The Red Fez: Art and Spirit Possession in Africa*. London: Verso, 1993.

Kratz, Corinne. *Affecting Performance: Meaning, Movement, and Experience in Okiek Women's Initiation*. Washington, DC: Smithsonian Institution Press, 1994.

Kubik, Gerhard. *Makisi, Nyau, Mapiko: Maskentraditionen in Bantu-Sprachigen Afrika*. Munich: Trickster, 1993.

———. "Neo-traditional Popular Music in Africa since 1945." *Popular Music* 1 (1981): 83–104.

———. *Theory of African Music*. Vol. 1. Chicago: University of Chicago Press, 2010.

Kundera, Milan. *The Unbearable Lightness of Being*. Translated by Michael Henry Heim. New York: Harper and Row, 1984.

LaCapra, Dominik. *Rethinking Intellectual History*. New York: Cornell University Press, 1983.

Laude, Jean. *La Peinture Française et "l'Art Nègre" (1905–1914): Contribution à l'Etude des Sources du Fauvisme et du Cubisme*. Paris: Klincksieck, 2006.

Leach, Michael Benjamin. "Things Hold Together: Foundations for a Systemic Treatment of Verbal and Nominal Tone in Plateau Shimakonde." PhD diss., University of Leiden, 2010.

Levi, Giovanni. "On Microhistory." In *New Perspectives on Historical Writing,* edited by Peter Burke, 97–119. Cambridge, UK: Polity Press, 2001.

Lévi-Strauss, Claude. "Father Christmas Executed." In *Unwrapping Christmas,* edited by David Miller, 38–51. Oxford: Oxford University Press, 1995.

Liesegang, Gerhard. "Sur les Origines et l'Histoire de Makonde du Mozambique." In *Dominique Macondé,* 29–39. Saint-Gilles-les-Hauts, La Réunion: Musée Historique de Villèle, 2007.

Liphola, Marcelino. "Aspects of Phonology and Morphology of Shimakonde." PhD diss., Ohio State University, 2001.

MAAO (Musée des Arts d'Afrique et d'Océanie). *Art Makondé: Tradition et Modernité*. Paris: Association Française d'Action Artistique, 1989.

Macaire, Pierre. *L'héritage Makhuwa au Mozambique*. Paris: l'Harmattan, 1996.

Machel, Josina. "The Role of Women in the Revolution." *Mozambique Revolution* 41 (1969): 24–28.

Mamdani, Mamhood. *When Victims Become Killers: Colonialism, Nativism, and the Genocide in Rwanda*. Princeton: Princeton University Press, 2002.

Manus, Sophie. "Morphologie et Tonologie du Simakoonde Parlé par les Communautés d'Origine Mozambicaine de Zanzibar et de Tanga (Tanzanie)." PhD diss., Institute National des Langues et Civilisations Orientales, 2003.

Maples, Chauncy. "Masasi and the Rovuma District in East Africa." *Proceedings of the Royal Geographical Society* 2 (1880): 337–53.

Matusse, Renato, and Josina Malique. *Josina Machel: Icone da Mulher Moçambicana*. Maputo: Arquívo do Patrimonio Cultural, 2007.

Mazula, Brazão. *Educação, Cultura e Ideologia em Moçambique, 1975–1985*. Porto, Portugal: Afrontamento, 1995.

Mbembe, Achille. *On the Postcolony*. Berkeley: University of California Press, 2001.

———. "Writing Africa." In *New South African Keywords*, edited by Nick Sheperd and Steven Robbins, 247–54. Athens: Ohio University Press, 2008.

McNaughton, Patrick. *A Bird Dance near Saturday City: Sidi Ballo and the Art of West African Masquerade*. Bloomington: Indiana University Press, 2008.

———. "Social Control and the Elephants We Scholars Make." *African Arts* 24, no. 1 (1991): 10–18.

Medeiros, Eduardo. *As Etapas da Escravatura no Norte de Moçambique*. Maputo: Arquivo Histórico de Moçambique, 1988.

———. *História de Cabo Delgado e do Niassa (c. 1836–1929)*. Maputo: Central Impressora, 1997.

———. *Os Senhores da Floresta: Ritos de Iniciação dos Rapazes Macuas e Lómuès*. Porto, Portugal: Campo das Letras, 2007.

Meschonnic, Henri. *Critique du Rhythme: Anthropologie Historique du Langage*. Paris: Verdier, 1984.

Mkaima, Miguel. "Mapiko Masks, Yesterday and Today." In Fenzel, *Makonde: Mapiko*.

*Mozambique Revolution*. Special issue, 25 September 1967.

———. "Shaping the Political Line." Issue 51. April–June 1972.

———. "What Is the Mozambican Culture." Issue 50. January–March 1972.

Mpalume, Estevão Jaime. *Vyaka Vyoe Vyamauvilo mu Moshambiki*. Maputo: Núcleo de Associação dos Escritores Moçambicanos de Cabo Delgado, 1990.

Mpalume, Estevão Jaime, and Marcos Agostinho Mandumbwe. *Nashilangola wa Shitangodi sha Shimakonde*. Pemba, Mozambique: Núcleo de Associação dos Escritores Moçambicanos de Cabo Delgado, 1991.

Mudimbe, Yves Valentin. *The Idea of Africa*. Bloomington: Indiana University Press, 1993.

Munguambe, Adelino. *A Música Chope*. Maputo: Promedia, 2000.

*Music from Tanzania and Zanzibar*, CD, Caprice Records, 1997.

Napier, David. *Masks, Transformation, and Paradox*. Berkeley: University of California Press, 1986.

Neil-Tomlinson, Barry. "The Nyassa Charted Company: 1891–1929." *Journal of African History* 18, no. 1 (1977): 109–28.

Newitt, Malyn. "The Early History of the Maravi." *Journal of African History* 23, no. 2 (1982): 145–62.

———. *A History of Mozambique*. Bloomington: Indiana University Press, 1995.

Ngole, Severino Gabriel. "Ritos de Iniciação Masculinos e suas Transformações Sociais no Planalto de Mueda entre 1924–1994." MA diss., Universidade Eduardo Mondlane, 1997.

Nkomo, Barnabé Luis. *Uria Simango: Um Homem, uma Causa*. Maputo: Novafrica, 2004.

O'Neill, Henry. 1885. "Journey in the District West of Cape Delgado Bay." *Proceedings of the Royal Geographical Society* 5 (1885): 393–404.

Organização da Mulher Moçambicana. *A Mulher Moçambicana na Luta de Libertação Nacional: Memórias do Destacamento Feminino*. Maputo: Centro de Pesquisa da História da Luta de Libertação Nacional, 2013.

Pachinuapa, Raimundo. *Do Rovuma ao Maputo: A Marcha Triunfal de Samora Machel*. Maputo: Privately printed, 2005.

Peltonen, Matti. "Clues, Margins, and Monads: The Micro-Macro Link in Historical Research." *History and Theory* 40, no. 3 (2001): 347–59.

Penvenne, Jeanne-Marie, and Bento Sitoe. "Power, Poets and the People: Mozambican Voices Interpreting History." *Social Dynamics* 26, no. 2 (2000): 58–86.

Pereira, Rui M. "Antropologia Aplicada na Política Colonial Portuguesa do Estado Novo." *Revista Internacional de Estudos Africanos* 4–5 (1986): 191–235.

———. "Introdução à Reedição de 1998." In Dias, *Aspectos Historícos e Economicos*, v–lii.

Piña-Cabral, João. "Anthropologie et Identité Nationale au Portugal." *Gradhiva* 11 (1992): 31–46.

Pongweni, Alec. *Figurative Language in Shona Discourse: A Study of the Analogical Imagination*. Gweru, Zimbabwe: Mambo, 1992.

———. *Songs That Won the Liberation War*. Harare, Zimbabwe: College Press, 1982.

Poppi, Cesare. "Persona, Larva, Masca: Masks, Identity and Cognition in the Cultures of Europe." In *Mind, Man and Mask*, edited by Subhash Chandra Malik, 129–54. New Delhi: Indira Gandhi National Centre for the Arts, 2001.

Presthold, Jeremy. "On the Global Repercussions of East African Consumerism." *American Historical Review* 109, no. 3 (2004): 755–81.

Ranger, Terence. *Dance and Society in Eastern Africa: The Beni Ngoma.* London: Heinemann, 1975.

———. "Missionary Adaptation of African Religious Institutions: The Masasi Case." In *The Historical Study of African Religion,* edited by Terence Ranger and Isaria Kimambo, 221–52. Berkeley: University of California Press, 1972.

———. "Nationalist Historiography, Patriotic History and the History of the Nation: The Struggle over the Past in Zimbabwe." *Journal of Southern African Studies* 30, no. 2 (2004): 215–34.

Revel, Jacques, ed. *Jeux d'Echelles: La Micro-analyse à l'Expérience.* Paris: Le Seuil, 1996.

Ricoeur, Paul. *Memory, History, Forgetting.* Chicago: University of Chicago Press, 2005.

Robinson, David. "Curse on the Land: A History of the Mozambican Civil War." PhD diss., University of Western Australia, 2006.

Rosaldo, Renato. "Imperialist Nostalgia." *Representations* 26 (1989): 107–22.

Said, Edward W. *The World, the Text and the Critic.* Cambridge, MA: Harvard University Press, 1983.

Salva-Rei, João, and António Pedro Muiuane. *Datas e Documentos da História da Frelimo.* Maputo: Imprensa Nacional, 1975.

Samarin, William. "Perspective on African Ideophones." *African Studies* 24, no. 2 (1967): 117–21.

Schmitt, Jean Claude. "Les Masques, le Diable, la Mort dans l'Occident Médieval." *Razo: Cahiers du Centre d'Études Médiévales de Nice* 6 (1986): 87–119.

Scott, James. *Seeing Like a State: How Certain Schemes to Better the Human Condition Have Failed.* New Haven, CT: Yale University Press, 1999.

Shaw, Rosalind. *Memories of the Slave Trade: Ritual and the Historical Imagination in Sierra Leone.* Chicago: University of Chicago Press, 2002.

Sieber, Roy. "Masks as Agents of Social Control." *African Studies Bulletin* 5, no. 2 (1962): 8–13.

Siliya, Carlos. *Ensaio Sobre a Cultura em Moçambique.* Maputo: Promedia, 1986.

Soares, Paulo. "Un Demi-siècle de Transition dans une Ecole de Sculpture Africaine." In MAAO, *Art Makondé,* 113–21.

———. "O Grupo Cultural Mapico-Moderno." *Tempo* 397 (1978): 30–35.

Stephen, Michael. "Makonde Sculpture as Political Commentary." *Review of African Political Economy* 48 (1990): 106–15.

Strother, Zöe. *Inventing Masks: Agency and History in the Art of the Central Pende.* Chicago: University of Chicago Press, 1998.

Tamele, Viriato, and Vilanculo, João. *Algumas Danças Tradicionais da Zona Norte de Moçambique.* Maputo: Archivo do Património Cultural, 2003.

*Tattoo Hunter: Mozambique.* Film, Discovery Channel, 2009.

Taussig, Michael. *Defacement: Public Secrecy and the Labor of the Negative.* Stanford: Stanford University Press, 1999.

———. *Mimesis and Alterity: A Particular History of the Senses.* London: Routledge, 1993.

Teixeira Duarte, Ricardo. *Escultura Maconde.* Maputo: Universidad Europea de Madrid, 1987.

Tembe, Joel. "Uhuru Na Kazi: Recapturing MANU Nationalism through the Archive." In *The Liberation Script in Mozambican History,* edited by Rui Assubuji, Paolo Israel, and Rui Thompson, 251–78. Special issue of *Kronos: Southern African Histories* 39 (2013).

*Tempo.* "Mauvilo a ku Mweda: Sobreviventes e Participantes Historiam Massacre." Issue 350 (1977): 42–49.

Thomson, Joseph. "Notes on the Basin of the River Rovuma, East Africa." *Proceedings of the Royal Geographical Society* 4 (1882): 65–79.

Tinga, Kaingu. "Secrets of Slaves: The Rise and Decline of *Vinyago* Masquerades on the Kenya Coast." Master's diss., University of the Western Cape, 2012.

Topp Fargion, Janet. "Nyota Alfajiri, the Zanzibari *Chakacha.*" *Afrikanistische Arbeitspapiere* 42 (1995): 125–31.

Trentini, Daria. "On the Threshold of a Healer's Mosque: Spiritual Healing, Hazard and Power in Northern Mozambique." PhD diss., School of Oriental and African Studies, University of London, 2012.

Turino, Thomas. *Nationalists, Cosmopolitans, and Popular Music in Zimbabwe.* Chicago: University of Chicago Press, 2000.

Vail, Leroy, and Landeg White. *Power and the Praise Poem: Southern African Voices in History.* Charlottesville: University of Virginia Press, 1991.

Veyne, Paul. *Did the Greeks Believe in Their Myths? An Essay on the Historical Imagination.* Chicago: University of Chicago Press, 1998.

———. *Writing History: Essay on Epistemology.* Manchester: Manchester University Press, 1984.

Viegas Guerreiro, Manuel. *Os Macondes de Moçambique,* Vol. IV: *Sabedoria, Língua, Literatura e Jogos.* Lisbon: Junta de Investigaçoes do Ultramar, 1966.

*Voz da Revolução.* "E' no Processo da Luta que Forjamos a Nossa Ideologia." Vol. 61 (1978): 8.

———. "Resolução sobre a Cultura." Vol. 61 (1978): 26.

Wembah-Rashid, John A. R. *The Ethno-history of the Matrilineal Peoples of Southeast Tanzania.* Vienna: Acta Ethnological et Linguistica, 1975.

———. "Isinyago and Midumu: Masked Dancers of Tanzania and Mozambique." *African Arts* 4, no. 2 (1971): 38–44.

———. "Le Masque et la Tradition de Danse Masquée." In MAAO, *Art Makondé: Tradition et Modernité,* 34–43. Paris: Musée des Arts d'Afrique et d'Océanie, 1989.

West, Harry G. *Ethnographic Sorcery.* Chicago: University of Chicago Press, 2007.

———. "Girls with Guns: Narrating the Experience of War of Frelimo's 'Female Detachment.'" *Anthropological Quarterly* 73, no. 4 (2000): 180–94.

———. "Inverting the Camel's Hump: Jorge Dias, His Wife, Their Interpreter, and I." In *Significant Others: Interpersonal and Professional Commitments in Anthropology*, edited by Richard Handler, 51–90. Madison: University of Wisconsin Press, 2004.

———. *Kupilikula: Governance and the Invisible Realm in Mozambique*. Chicago: University of Chicago Press, 2005.

———. "Sorcery of Construction and Sorcery of Ruin: Power and Ambivalence on the Mueda Plateau, Mozambique (1882–1994)." PhD diss., University of Wisconsin, 1997.

———. "Voices Twice Silenced: Betrayal and Mourning at Colonialism's End in Mozambique." *Anthropological Theory* 3, no. 3 (2003): 343–65.

Weule, Karl. *Native Life in East Africa*. London: Pitman, 1909.

———. *Resultados Científicos da Minha Viagem de Pesquisas Etnográficas no Sudeste da África Oriental*. Maputo: Departamento de Museus, 2000. Portuguese translation of *Native Life in East Africa*.

White, Luise. *Speaking with Vampires: Rumor and History in Colonial Africa*. Berkeley: University of California Press, 2001.

Yoshida, Kenji. "Masks and Secrecy among the Chewa." *African Arts* 26, no. 2 (1993): 34–45, 92.

Žižek, Slavoj. *For They Know Not What They Do: Enjoyment as a Political Factor*. London: Verso, 2008.

## NMA FIELD RECORDINGS

NMA is an acronym for Namadodo Makonde Archive, a digital archive consisting (to date) of about 2,000 songs, 200 interviews, and 100 hours of video performance that I have recorded together with Evaristo "Angelina" Januário, Mario "Malyamungu" Matias, Fidel Suka Mbalale, and others in Cabo Delgado, Mozambique. Only material quoted in the book is referenced here.

## I. INTERVIEWS

Interviews are listed by name and date. Some people wished to be identified only by their "playing name" (*lina lyakupikitila*), others by their full name, still others by both. When available, the playing name is used for reference. For repeated interviews with the same person, the place is not mentioned unless it changed after the first interview.

Alivémwako 2003. Rec. int., healer, Mbau, December 2003.

Amissi 2004. Rec. int. with Amissi Luis Tomás, *dutu*, *nshindo*, and *mileya* player, Myangalewa, September 2004. Amissi 2008. Rec. int., June 2008. Amissi 2009. Film int., April 2009.

Anapambula and Mmembe 2004. Rec. int. with Rosalina Anapambula and Tomasina Mmembe, leaders of *utamaduni* and formerly *lingundumbwe*, Mapate, July 2004.

Anashaledye 2004. Rec. int. with Monero José Anashaledye, *nnalombo*, Mwalela, September 2004.

Anogwa 2004. Rec. int. with Albino Laja Anogwa, drummer and tattoo drawer in the Shumu ensemble 1 de Maio, Myangalewa, September 2004.

Ashipambele 2005. Rec. int. with Marcelino Ashipambele, DEC officer during the liberation struggle, Pemba, February 2005.

Baltazar 2005. Rec. int. with Eduardo Baltazar, leader of *nshesho* group, Mwambula, January 2005. Baltazar et al. 2009. Film int. with Baltazar and other members of *nshesho* group, April 2009.

Bissali 2004. Rec. int. with Sabina Bissali, *nkala* dancer and *nnalombo*, Mwatide, January 2004.

Bulashi et al. 2004. Rec. int. with Janja Bulashi and other members of *nshindo* group, Shitashi, July 2004.

Chababe et al. 2002. Int. with Martins Chababe, Januário Doglas, and Orlando Martins, members of *naupanga* group, Namakule, January 2002.

Dinema 2003. Int. with Ernestina Dinema, chief of *utamaduni* and *material* group 24 de Março, March 2003.

Galinha 2005. Rec. int. with Galinha, former DF member, Pemba, February 2005.

Gondola 2008. Int. with Manuel Gondola, composer of struggle music, Pemba, July 2008.

João 2005. Rec. int. with Enriqueta João, former DF, Pemba, February 2005.

Juakali 2008. Rec. int. with Bernardino Juakali Nnamba, *dutu* singer, carver, and dancer, Rwarwa, Shitunda, June 2008.

Kanduru and Amuli 2004. Rec. int. with Kanduru Paulo and Sauti Amuli, former players of Ashalela ensemble, Namakande, August 2004.

Kanteke 2004. Rec. int. with António Lazáro Kanteke, former *dutu* singer, along with his wife, Josephina Masheka, Nshinga, July 2004.

Lijama 2004. Rec. int. with Moses Lijama Mede, ultra-centenary *dutu* player, along with Feliz Jona Amadeus Nomwe, his nephew, Myangalewa, September 2004.

Likwekwe 2004. Rec. int. with Dominico Likwekwe, former *dutu* and *mileya* player, Namakande, August 2004.

Liloko 2008. Rec. int. with Fiel Liloko, *magita* player, Shinda, July 2008.

Limbesha et al. 2004. Rec. int. with Limbesha, Américo Vitor, Joana Vitor, and Elias Awashi, former *dutu* players, Nampanya, January 2005.

Lingandingo et al. 2009. Film int. with Lingandingo and other *nshesho* players, Nampanya, April 2009.

Lingumbo 2004. Rec. int. with Quénia Lingumbo, *nnalombo*, Nangade sede, July 2004.

Lingumwalela 2004. Rec. int. with three leaders of *lingundumbwe* group (the names are inaudible because of a technical problem), Mwalela, July 2004.

Lipato 2004. Rec. int. with Martin Lipato Mudua, descendant of the elder Lipato, *kuna*-Lipato, M'Bau, August 2004.

Liteka et al. 2004. Int. with Ernestina Liteka, Filomena Joana, Augusta Jaime, Samanina Mwalimu, and Rosa Valério, *utamaduni* players, Litapata, August 2004.

Litembo 2009. Collective film int. with *nshesho* group, Litembo, April 2009.

Maimba 2003. Rec. int. with Erique Eusébio Maimba, *nantyaka* leader, Namwembe, July 2003.

Makai 2003. Rec. int. with Joana Makai, *dutu* and *nshesha* player, Mueda sede, June 2003.

Makala and Joni 2004. Rec. int. with Simba Makala and Tomás Joni, leaders of *nshindo*, bairro Pacheco, Myangalewa, September 2004.

Mambwembwe et al. 2004. Rec. int. with Simoni Mambwembwe, Francisco Simão Amissi, and Armando Estevão Maukilo "Mangongo," initiators of *neijale*, Mapate, September 2004.

Mandia 2005. Rec. int. with Samuel Mandia, Mueda, January 2005.

Mandia 2008. Rec. int. with Samuel Mandia, *magita* singer, Mueda, June 2008.

Manupa 2012. Int. with Jaime Manupa Kanyanga, *mapiko* carver, Maputo, November 2012.

Mawasha 2002. Rec. int. with Shalele Mawasha, former *dutu* and *nshindo* player, Litamanda, September 2002. Mawasha 2004, rec. int., September 2004.

Mbambanda 2002. Int. with Mbambanda, dancer from the Mapate *neijale* group, Mwambula, September 2002.

Mbanguia 2009. Film int. with Luis Madal Mbanguia, founder of the Mapico Moderno group, April 2009.

Milete 2005. Rec. int. with Alberto Litinga Milete, leader of *nshesho* group, Mueda, June 2003. Milete 2008. Film int., Mueda, June 2008.

Milombo 2004. Rec. int. with Joaquim Cristovão Milombo, leader of *ng'odo* (*lingoti*) group, Nampanya, December 2004.

Mmadung'a 2002. Int. with Nalyoi Mmadung'a, leader of *kwanja lyela* group, Nshongwe, January 2002.

Mmaka et al. 2002. Int. with Maria Mmaka, Tereza Mashaka, and Consolata Lucas, leaders of *utamaduni* group, Mwambula, January 2002.

Mpwesa and Elias 2002. Int. with Ernesto Mpwesa Ntakwani and Simão Elias, leaders of *mang'anyamu* group, Lutete, January 2002.

Mustafa 2003. Rec. int. with Mustafa Mwana' Bonde, former *dutu* player and leader of *shuku nwele*, Mwambula (Muidumbe), July 2003. Mustafa 2005. Rec. int., February 2005. Mustafa 2008. Film int., June 2008.

Mwakala 2005. Int. with Pedro Rafael Mwakala, former informant of Jorge Dias, Pemba, February 2005.

Mwale et al. 2009. Film int. with Valério Mwale, Jito Kwimbantela, and Atanásio Cosme Nhussi, *nshesho* players, Maputo, May 2009.

Mwalela 2004. Collective film. int. with *nshesho* group, Mwalela, July 2004.

Mwanjigula 2003. Rec. int. with Martins Jackson Mwanjigula, *mang'anyamu* carver, Matambalale, December 2003. Mwanjigula and Siminda 2009.

Film int. with Mwanjigula and Mauricio Siminda Ngui, *mang'anyamu* leader, Matambalale, April 2009.

Naiva et al. 2004. Rec. int. with Verónica Naiva, Luis Mitema Nandimba, and Focas Ambrosio, commanders of the Frelimo central base historical site, Nang'unde, August 2004.

Najopa et al. 2004. Rec. int. with Njelo Johanes Najopa, Rado Misila Namakong'o, Ngonya Tumaini Nshegwa, and Bento Piushi Linolo, descendants of Nampyopyo, Nang'unde, August 2004. Najopa and Nshegwa 2009. Film int., April 2009. Najopa and Nshegwa 2012. Int., December 2012 (conducted by Fidel Mbalale).

Nampada 2003. Film int. with Americo Nampada, *nshindo* leader, Nakitenge, December 2003.

Nampindo et al. 2004. Rec. int. with Américo and Adriano Nampindo, Semente Serra, Zeinaba Mamadi, and Jorge Nanshinga, *ngoda* and *limbondo*, August 2004. Nampindo and Pamange 2009. Film int. with Nampindo and Jambo Shalowa Mpilibyao Pamange, former Ngoni-mask player, April 2012.

Nandimba et al. 2004. Rec. int. with Luis Mitema Nandimba, Focas Ambrósio, and Rashidi Shivenamyaka, former *mapiko* players and guerrillas, central base, Nang'unde, August 2004.

Nandodo 2002. Rec. int. with Januário Cabeça "Nandodo," leader of the 25 de Setembro group, Litamanda, September 2002.

Nandodo and Pulumbamba 2009. Film int. with Nandodo together with Janéiro Pulumbamba, Constancio Makopa, and Tomé Kavenje, *neijale* players, April 2009.

Nanelo 2004. Rec. int. with Lucas Njasi Nanelo, *nnalombo*, Mwambula, November 2004. Nanelo and Nshamoko 2008. Rec. int. with Nanelo and Nnambe Nshamoko, *vanalombo*, Mwambula, June 2008. Nanelo 2009. Film int., April 2009.

Navina et al. 2009. Rec. int. with Marieta Navina, Faustina Paulo Manjeda, and Dorotea, *lingundumbwe* players, Mueda, April 2009.

Ndeja-Ndeja 2003. Rec. int. with Januário Matias Ntumuke, prominent player of *mapiko* group from Mwambula. Ndeja-Ndeja 2009. Film int., April 2009.

Nhussi 2009. Film int. with Atanásio Cosme Nhussi, *mapiko* dancer, Cape Town, May 2009.

Nkalau et al. 2004. Rec. int. with Zacarias Nkalau, José Kavinga, and António Tomás, *dutu* singers, Myangalewa, August 2004.

Nkangala 2004. Rec. int. with Lucas Mateus Pedro Nkangala, former *dutu* player, Mwalela (Nangade), September 2004.

Nkangusa et al. 2009. Int. with Nkangusa, Juwana Vitoli Mmande, António Alame, and Pita Mbaluko Analimanga, *ngoda* and *dutu* singers, Nampanya, April 2009.

Nkondya et al. 2004. Rec. int. with Kwareta Nkondya, Paulina Tomás, and Anastásia Shivenamyaka, daughters of Nampyopyo and *utamaduni* players, Nangu'unde, August 2004.

Nshamoko 2005. Int. with Nnambe Nshamoko, *nnalombo*, Mwambula, January 2005.

Nshileu and Anawandala 2009. Film int. with Joanes Bilari Dimboko Nshileu and Bernardo Bento Anawandala, leaders of *nshesha* group, Namakule, April 2009.

Nshusha 2004. Rec. int. with Filomena Simão Nshusha, former student in a Frelimo school, Mwambula, December 2004.

Ntukwinye et al. 2004. Rec. int. with Oracio Rafaél Ntukwinye, Martins Jackson Mwanjigula, Maurício Siminda Ngui, Calado, Domingo João Manuel, Marcelino Mbogwa, Neshi Nopelé, Nkongwesii, Njudi, and Mashoto, *mang'anyamu* players, Matambalale, December 2004.

Paulo 2003. Film int. with Paulo, ultracentenary, Nakitenge (Mocimboa da Praia), December 2003.

Rashidi et al. 2004. Rec. int. with Bertina Rashidi, Lucas Mwida, and Rosa Majuli, *utamaduni* players, Nshinga (Muidumbe), August 2004.

Seguro 2003. Rec. int. with Pedro Justino Seguro, administrator of Muidumbe, Mwambula, September 2003. Seguro 2004. Rec. int., December 2004.

Shalima 2002. Int. with Marcos Shalima, leader of the Kwanja lyela, 24 de Março, January 2002.

Shamwilanga 2004. Int. with Bernadeta Mateus Shamwilanga, former DF member, Pemba, September 2004.

Shanjolo and Doto 2008. Film int. with Joaquim Lucas Mitene Shanjolo and Doto, dancer and leader of *naupanga*, Mwatidi, June 2008.

Shawa 2004. Rec. int. with Shawa, healer of *nshindo* group, Bairro Maputo, Myangalewa, September 2004.

Shikumene 2008. Rec. int. with António Shikumene, village president, Mwambula, June 2008.

Shilavi 2009. Film int. with Augusto Shilavi, former administrator of and participant on the council of Litapata, Mwambula, April 2009. Conducted by Rui Assubuji.

Shitungulu et al. 2002. Int. with Bernabè Shitungulu, Rei Julião, Pascoal Gaspar, Mario Matias Malyamungu, Remígio Julião, and Ernesto Gaspar Nampunde, *mang'anyamu* players, Mwambula, January 2002.

Shukulu et al. 2002. Int. with Nakashenga Shukulu, Lilende Miyani, Shinyenga Likambe, Njebwa Shamana, and Damião Matunu, *dutu* and *shikelya* players, M'Bau (Mocimboa da Praia), July 2002. Shukulu et al. 2003. Film int., August 2003.

Shuliki 2003. Rec. int. with Focas Domingos João Shuliki, leader of Nshaila group, master drummer of *nshaila*, Mwambula (Muidumbe), June 2003.

Simba and Afonso 2002. Int. with André Simba and Vinagre Alfonso, *machapila* players, Nshongwe, January 2002.

Tomé 2004. Rec. int. with Ernestina Cornelio Tomé, former DF member and secretary of Renamo's Women's Department, Miezi, September 2004.

Valingue 2001. Rec. int. with Miguel Valingue, blackwood sculptor, Maputo, April 2001.

Vingambudi et al. 2004. Rec. int. with Ernestina João Vingambudi, Regina Nkavandame, and Bendita João, leaders of a *lingundumbwe* group, Mbwidi (Nangade), September 2004.

Yangua 2002. Rec. int. with Yangua, brother of the deceased *régulo*, 1 de Maio (Myangalewa), September 2002.

Zaaqueu 2005. Rec. int. with Jorge Zaaqueu Nhassemu, poet and composer of struggle anthems, Pemba, February 2005.

## II. SOUND RECORDINGS

Recordings are referenced by archive/genre/place/date. Thus, for instance, NMA/Nshesho/Mwambula/2004 indicates a recording from the nshesho group of the Mwambula village carried out in 2004. The designation "L" indicates live performances recorded on the dance-field. All other performances were solicited for the purpose of research (i.e., recorded sitting in the courtyard of a group member), either a cappella or accompanied by rattles or minimal drumming.

# Index

abduction of women, 69, 172

abstraction: in African indigenous arts, 52; in carving, 59–60; Frelimo's rejection of, 154, 163; in *mapiko* performance, 1, 55, 64–65, 68, 80, 91–92, 95, 120, 122, 139, 176, 180, 194, 225, 237; in song lyrics, 127, 149. *See also* obscurity in song

Achebe, Chinua, 263n50

actions, in masking performance, 107, 114, 176

Adam, Yussuf, 270n36

aesthetics: African indigenous, 52; colonial, 90; diversification of, 55, 185; interpretation of, 4, 10–14, 33; of the law, 128; Makonde vernacular, 86, 88, 130; reconstruction of, 2, 58, 91, 256; romantic, 89; socialist, 143, 163–65, 174, 184, 188, 198, 202, 204, 252; of vulgarity, 252, 290n22

African art, study of, 5–7

African popular culture, 5–6, 241

airplane: dance style, 92–93; mask-character, 100

alcoholism, campaign against, 169, 219. *See also* drunkenness

allegorical interpretation, 14–15, 33–35, 232, 262n45

alterity. *See* mimesis: of otherness

ambivalence: in Bakhtin, 29; in *mapiko*, 15, 44, 56, 110, 114, 117, 119–21, 144, 174, 207, 213–17, 229, 232–33, 242; psychoanalytical interpretation of, 204, 287n45; and socialism, 176, 207, 214, 229, 232

Amissi, Luis, 137, 211

anachronism: in masking, 258; risk of, 14; in song, 138

ancestors, 1, 47, 50, 121, 265n34, 273n56

ancestral supplication, 47, 70–71, 130, 135; in masking, 94; in song, 71, 135

animals: in *mapiko*, 1, 27–28, 48, 59–60, 92, 100–101, 104, 107, 109–10, 120–21, 139, 175–76, 209–11, 221–28, 232–33, 241, 250, 258, 288n26; as political metaphor, 202, 216, 226–27, 287n39; transformation in, 2; wild, 20, 82, 109, 210. *See also names of individual animals*

antelope: hides, 16; horns, 2, 64, 221, 233; as mask-character, 104

anthems: national, 176; revolutionary, 152, 177, 228, 244. *See also* Frelimo: *aina mwisho*

appropriation, 6, 11, 87, 90, 141, 213, 242; of coastal dance culture, 11, 55, 76–77, 241, 273n59; of dance styles, 91–92; mimetic, 176; of slave-masks, 113, 220; of songs, 123; of temperate harmony, 141

Arab: as derogatory term, 45–46, 103, 276n9; as mask-character, 61, 64, 109

Arabic, 76, 148

Argenti, Nicolas, 265n35

Arquivo do Património Cultura (ARPAC), 10, 13

Arriaga, Kaulza, 152–53, 156

Ashalela (carver), 93–94, 275n40

Askew, Kelly, 6

*assimilado*: in carving, 87

authority: native, as mask-character, 112; traditional, 9–10, 80, 84, 90, 103, 112; year of, 199, 285n2

avarice, critique of, 85, 110, 213, 225

Bakhtin, Mikhail, 7, 29–30, 110, 112, 204, 214, 265n38

Banga, Guilherme, 183–84

baobab fruit. *See Malonje* (mask-character)

barbarism, 20, 50, 77, 103

Barber, Karin, 5, 259n10

Bateson, Gregory, xii, 7, 42, 47, 53, 270n46, 272n36
Baudelaire, Charles, 258
beasts. *See* animals
beauty: of masquerading, 16; of scarifications, 69; in song, 201, 161, 244; and truth, 128; vernacular concept, 86, 88, 89, 91, 121
bee hunter. See *Ndemba* (mask-character)
Beira, 228
Beira base, 186
belief: in ancestors, 10, 47; in the church, 134; in Hopi spirits, 41; in *mapiko* as ghost, 29, 39–40, 42, 47, 72; in the reality of fiction films, 242–43; in *shilo* as spirits, 27–28, 100–101
bells, iron. See *dinjuga*
*beni ngoma*, 5, 76–77
bicycles: in communal villages, 234–35, 243; in masking, 236–37, 241, 243, 251
boasting: in Bateson's work, 43, 272n36; of dance performers, 6, 13, 16, 44, 91, 127, 130, 141, 171, 173, 183, 198, 210, 214, 242, 289n3; masculine, 69, 72; of ritual masters, 46
Bocarro, António, 48
Bortolot, Alexander, 35, 268n18, 271n8, 273n52, 287n9, 289n3
bricolage, 230
buffalo: as mask-character, 1, 27–28, 95, 104, 209, 222
bushbaby, lesser: as mask-character, 109–10
*bwarabwà* (dance), 218, 254; influence on *mang'anyamu*, 221, 225

Cabo Delgado: cape, 19; commissioner of, 151; governor of, 181, 254; province, 31, 148, 151, 167, 190, 202, 209–10, 229
Cahen, Michel, 9, 279n21
car: as mask-character, 27, 104; in song, 181
carnivalesque, 7, 24, 29, 110
carving: blackwood sculpture, 34, 86–89, 130, 212, 222; and dreaming, 222, 288n25; of drums, 69; of *mapiko*, 6, 21–22, 58–59, 65, 80, 84, 130, 222, 258, 271n8; as metaphor for song composing, 126, 130, 131, 133–36, 225; and performance, 4, 28, 61; talent for, 65, 79, 80, 119, 215, 222, 238
centipede (mask-character), 61, 95

ceremonial, state, 89, 91, 157, 162, 168–69, 176–77, 179, 186, 203
Chai, 67, 108, 204, 215; attack of, 146, 158–59, 175, 218, 282n45
*chakacha* (dance), 76, 241, 273n58
characters: in East-Central African masquerades, 60–61; in *mapiko*, 1, 44, 56, 59–60, 65, 82–83, 85, 87, 91–93, 96–97, 103, 105–7, 110, 114, 120–22, 124, 176, 194–95, 207, 213–15, 219, 235–37, 240, 245, 249–50, 257–58, 272n47, 287n8, 287n13
Chewa: masks, 27, 48, 60, 268n17, 268n23; people, 27, 48, 60
Chipande, Alberto Joaquim: in songs, 158–59, 171, 199, 286
Chipande, Maria, 286n31; in song, 286
Chipeda, Bento, 159, 282n45
Chissano, Joaquim Alberto: on currency, 253; farewell to Mueda, 252; image of, 228, 243; in song, 200; sons of, generation, 245
choirs: musical influence of church, 64, 141, 279n30; in *nshesho*, 15, 24–25, 68, 139, 155, 165, 173, 174, 198, 225, 279n31; in *nshindo*, 106–10, 183; struggle, 228; in *utamaduni*, 199. See also *makwaela*
Chokwe masks. *See* Makishi masks
Christianity: in Cabo Delgado, 21; and funerary ceremonies, 102, 112, 277n14; influence on initiations, 71; influence on *mapiko*, 272n47; and laughter, 29
cinema: itinerant, 163; in songs, 246, 248. *See also* National Institute of Cinema (INC)
circulation: of dance styles, 78, 146, 148; of people, 73; of social practices, 49, 269n29; of songs, 124; of tapes, 228
civil war, 197, 207; interpretation of, 9; on the Makonde plateau, 183, 209, 219, 238, 241–42, 245, 283
clay: masks (see *shitengamatu*); phallus, 36; soils, 99
closure: interpretive, 120, 232; of performance movement, 174
cognitive mapping, 243, 245
cold war, 9, 261n30
collective memory. *See* memory
colonialism: and African art, 4–6, 35; agents of, 88; and the Church, 21, 70; epistemological legacy of, 13, 17, 22, 28, 72, 75, 264n15; Frelimo's

Foucault, Michel, 167–68

Frelimo: aesthetics, 165; *aina mwisho,* song, 228–29; camps and bases, 80, 100, 143, 145–46, 148, 153, 155; crisis of, 151, 154, 156, 189, 281n22; and culture, 11, 149, 151, 153–54, 157, 162–65, 170 272n32, 281n15; discourse, 8–9, 13, 17, 33–34, 59, 72, 159, 175, 186; disillusionment with, 204, 228, 253–55; and elections, 203–4, 226, 231, 244; flag, 227; formation of, 30–31, 55, 138; ideology, 9, 145, 150, 153, 157, 169; orphanages, 190; policies, 167, 172, 189; schools, 156–57, 229, 282n39, 282nn39–40

Fresu, Anna, 31–34

functionalism, 17, 21–22, 26–29, 31–35, 39, 75, 265n33

funerary ceremonies: and alcohol, 219; description of, 100, 110, 183; fieldwork on, 277n14; influence of missionaries on, 102; and *neijale,* 212–14, 217; and night-masks, 48, 100, 276n4; and *nshindo,* 56, 103–4, 106, 108, 114, 119, 249–50, 262n43, 278n30; singing for, 102, 218

gashing (mask-character), 95

Geffray, Christian, 9, 167

gender: differentiation, 4, 7, 42–43, 46–47, 52, 77, 149, 197, 268n17; struggle, 10, 17, 23, 32, 143–44, 157, 159, 169, 189, 198–200, 204–5, 251. *See also* schismogenesis

generation: ambivalence, generational, 229; antagonism between, 66, 68, 77, 125; born after Independence, 163, 207; difference of, 1, 8, 10, 28, 46, 52; of *dutu,* 44; of *mileya,* 89–91; transmission from, 257; of the war-makers, 143, 151, 163. *See also* Chissano, Joaquim Alberto: sons of; Mondlane, Eduardo: sons of; Machel, Samora: sons of

genres: diversification of, 55, 72, 185; interpretation of, 10, 14–15, 53, 106–7, 120, 122, 257; invention of, 44, 56, 64–65, 68, 74, 82, 89, 92, 102, 113–14, 143, 156, 188, 194, 207, 213, 215, 233, 240; spread of, 65, 77–78, 92, 156, 175, 188, 207, 210, 215, 240, 257; vocabulary for, 77–78

Germans: as mask-characters, 1, 79, 83–85, 121, 184, 241, 274n9, 274n13

ghost, *mapiko* as, 38–40

Girard, René, 52–53, 75, 270n46, 287n45

Gluckman, Max, 264n17

gluttony: in masking, 106, 109–10, 175

Gordian Knot, 153–54, 156

gourds: and Makonde carving, 87; in masking, 24, 109; medicinal, 103, 109

grief, 56, 100, 102, 110

grotesque realism. *See* realism, grotesque

Guebuza, Armando Emilio, 207, 244, 252–54; in song, 231, 255

guerrilla. *See* liberation struggle

guitars, electric, 148–49, 154, 222. *See also* zither

hamlet: circulation between, 73; colonial-era, 65, 80, 88, 93–95, 102, 132, 148, 184, 229, 270n1, 275n24, 275n38; definition of, 270n5; geography of, 98; and *mapiko* performance, 36, 58–60, 66, 69, 71–73, 82, 161, 163; ownership of, 84, 151; precolonial, 20, 80; in salutations, 128; in song, 68–69, 79, 82–83, 155, 172, 182, 241, 279n20

hare: in initiation rituals, 38, 60; as masking character, 60, 105

Harley, George W., 22–23, 266n40

Hauka, 33

head: euphemism, 4

healers: in *mapiko* performance, 109, 115, 198; from the Messalo lowlands, 118–19; sealing the *nshindo* enclosure, 113, 117; in song, 132, 180, 232

helicopter: as mask-character, 100–101, 104, 241, 277n11; of witchcraft, 118

helmet shape of *mapiko,* 2, 21, 49, 51, 59, 88, 113, 220

Hemingway, Ernst, 263n49

hernia: mask-character, 112; in song, 68

heroes: Heroes Day, 186; homage to, 228; monument to, 168; mythology of, 155; in song, 157–58

heteroglossia, 6, 44, 131, 148, 150, 152, 232

historicity: of *mapiko,* 31, 35, 49, 53, 58, 78, 86, 100, 120, 141, 207, 241; study of, 4–14, 17, 258

Hobsbawm, Eric, 33, 266n50

*homo ludens,* 7, 86

Huizinga, Johan, 7, 86

hunting: in the lowlands, 43, 99; in masking performance, 24, 52, 108–9, 175, 216, 240; taught during initiation, 36

huts: cemented, 254; during the Struggle, 146; improved, 254; initiation, 36–37; tax on, 87
hyena: as mask-character, 27, 250; as political metaphor, 202, 216, 226, 287n30

iconoclasm, 70–71, 92
identity. *See* subjectivity
ideology: Christian, 102; colonial, 70, 90; of masquerading, 101, 265n34. *See also* Frelimo: ideology
imitation: of church harmony, 141; gendered, 40, 196–97; of rival dances, 68, 92–94, 123–24, 129, 200, 220, 225, 240–41, 245, 257, 288n23, 289n3; in song, 196. *See also* mimesis
Independence, Mozambique, xi, 30, 130; anniversary of, 228; and authority, 285n2; rejoicing for, 188
Indian Ocean, 19, 47, 49, 89
*ing'oma. See* puberty rituals
*ingonda*, 66, 113, 146, 148, 183, 186, 195, 224; in song, 185
insult: in initiation, 43, 149; in songs, 68, 71, 149, 162
invention: histories of, 13–15; in *mapiko*, 1, 6–8, 68, 74, 77, 86, 92, 114, 121, 129, 180, 212, 220, 221, 240, 256–58; of the radio, 249; of *shetani*, 89. Also see *dutu; lingundumbwe; mang'anyamu; naupanga; neijale; nshesho; nshindo; utamaduni*
inversion: in initiation rituals, 70
irons: as musical instruments, 69, 218–19, 221–22, 225, 235
irony, 46, 112, 125
*ishima. See* respect
Islam: of coastal people, 44, 77, 269; conversion to, 50, 133; and masking, 49, 114, 194; reform, spread of, 277n24; in song, 132–33; and spirit possession, 194; and the Yao, 49

Jackson, Michael, 236, 243
Jameson, Fredric, 4
Januário, Angelina, 12, 44
Jesus: in masking, 72, 272; in song, 134, 182
John Paul II, Pope, 272n47
joking relationships, 7, 50–51, 77, 132
Juakali, Paulo, 129, 132–38, 181, 275n35, 279n20
judicial institutions, 128

Kabu, Faustino, 213–14
Kanteke, Rosário, 129
*Kanyembe. See* violin
kapok. *See* wild kapok
Kasfir, Sidney Littlefield, 6
Katembe, Gerónimo Mussa, 251
Kimwani language, 103, 131
kinship, 49, 130, 264n7. *See also* lineage
Kiswahili: conjugated in Makonde, xv, 130, 279n17; lexicon in *mapiko*, 74–77, 197; in Makonde singing, 6, 130–31, 137, 140–41, 210, 220, 241; poetry, 125; as prestige language, 130
kitsch, 214
Koselleck, Reinhard, 273n6
Kramer, Fritz, 52–53, 61
Kubik, Gerhard, 163
Kuxa Kanema, 163

labor: forced, 21, 70, 88, 272n38; migrant, 30, 73, 130, 157–58; peasant, 164–65, 250
laughter, 29, 40, 52, 110, 117, 214; and grief, 102, 119; and *mapiko*, 183, 112, 212; mask-character, 111
lead: drummers, 16, 62, 65, 174, 183; singers, 123; speakers, 107
leaders: of choirs, 157–59, 170, 181, 190, 199, 204, 244, 254; mythology of, 90, 155; revolutionary, 34, 138, 149–52, 164–65, 252–53, 281; visit of, 168, 170–71, 178–79, 203, 217. *See also* Chissano, Joaquim Alberto; Guebuza, Armando Emilio; Machel, Samora; Mondlane, Eduardo
Lee, Bruce, 242–43
leopards, 66; as mask-characters, 27, 66, 209, 222, 228
liberation struggle, 10–11, 30, 31, 33–34, 146, 148; first shot of, 146, 159, 204; myth of, 145, 168; represented in *mapiko*, 165, 174, 179, 216, 228, 254; in song, 139, 142–43, 145–47, 149, 156, 158–59, 174, 178, 216, 284n35; women's involvement in, 186, 188–92, 203, 285n8
*ligoma* (drum), 62, 64–65, 91–92, 122; in song, 79
*ligwalema* (dance), 123, 176
Likankoa, Samaki, 89
*likulutu. See* military training
*likumbi. See* puberty rituals
*likuti* (drum), 62, 64, 69, 91–92, 132, 136, 139, 180

*limbondo* (dance), 154, 283n10
lineage: abandoned as basis of *mapiko*,
55, 57–58, 77, 84; exalting of, 24, 74;
Frelimo's rejection of, 154, 162, 170,
254; Makua, 264n14; origins of, 50;
resettlement of, 99, 146, 149; rivalry
between, 24, 52, 66; in song, 137,
254–55; war between, 65, 128. *See also*
meat-is-meat
*lingoti* (genre), 220, 251
*lingundumbwe* (genre): fortune of, 195–98,
254; invention of, 186–92, 285n3; and
*naupanga*, 237; at the Second Festival,
251; and *shinyala*, 192–95, 286n26; in
song, 185; songs, 188, 196, 198–203
lions, 99; in initiation rituals, 27, 66, 203;
magical, 101, 118, 227, 244, 248, 251,
262n44, 275n40; as masks, 28, 209, 222;
in song, 131
*lipalapanda. See* antelope: horns
Lipato, 56, 102–6, 114, 119–21, 213; legacy
of, 184, 249
lip plug, 20, 49, 83, 193; in song, 68–69
Litamanda, 108, 114–15, 117–18, 129, 163, 214,
216, 217, 249, 256, 268n16, 277n13, 289n14
Litandakua, 118, 163
Litapata: council of, 151, 281n21; in song,
182
*longue durée*, 11, 258
lowlands: and alcohol production, 112,
219, 248; dance contests in, 95, 132; and
*dutu*, 180; of ku-Iyanga, 43; during the
liberation struggle, 146, 151, 161; and
Makonde ethnogenesis, 50, 98; of the
Messalo, 56, 92, 97, 136; movement of
dances from, 233, 249; and *naupanga*,
234–35; and *nshindo*, 44, 102, 117, 184,
213, 232–33, 250; people from, 80; and
Renamo, 209; scholarship on, 100, 106;
and secrecy, 45; and *shuku nwele*, 238;
and slave-masks, 184, 220; in song, 105,
244; travel to and from, 73, 80, 94, 113,
120, 249; and water, 99, 105; and witchcraft, 118–19, 217
love: in communal villages, 230–31;
during the liberation struggle, 192;
among the Makonde, 51; poems, 154;
songs, 139–40
lullabies, 141

*machapila* (genre), 220
Machel, Josina, 188–91, 196, 198–99, 201,
203–4

Machel, Samora, 31, 152, 162, 181, 186,
189, 202, 216, 229, 245; and counter-
revolutionaries, 164, 202, 216, 287n39;
on currency, 253 (*see also* Nova Família Metical); death of, 245; masks of,
166; in song, 188, 229; sons of, generation, 229; visit of, 218
machete: in East African masquerades,
258, 290n3; in *mapiko* competitions,
70; used by *nandulumbuka*, 70; used
by *naupanga*, 207, 235–38, 243, 245,
249, 251
*magalantoni. See* zither
*majoji* (genre), 113
Makai, Joana, 211–12, 275n35, 279n22
Makishi masks, 60, 286n21, 290n2
Makonde: elder, as mask, 61, 64, 83, 94,
106; ethnogenesis, 47–51, 269n29,
269n32; identity, 43–45, 50, 151, 157,
180, 270n36; literature on, 22, 34–35,
100, 261n29; salutations, 127–28; stereotype of, 20, 51, 270n40
Makonde Plateau, 6–8, 10–11, 20–22,
25–26, 30, 43–44, 47, 49–51, 55, 58, 83,
100, 102, 145, 151, 179, 183, 209, 212,
253, 278n2, 287n40
Makua: language, 48, 269n27; lineages,
264n14; as mask-characters, 83, 109,
120, 182; masking, 51, 60, 114, 118,
120, 269n31; ritual, 49–50, 277n24; in
songs, 57, 68–69; south of the Messalo, 99
*makuti. See likuti*
*makwaela* (dance), 31, 157, 160, 177, 197,
282n43
Malapende: chief, 142, 280n33; dance
group, 284n36
malaria, 98, 100, 234
*Malonje* (mask-character), 106, 112, 114.
See also *nnonje*
Malyamungu, Mario Matias: 12, 45,
210–11, 218, 226, 311
*mang'anyamu* (genre): aesthetics of, 228–
33; encounter with, 210; at the First
Mapiko Festival, 211; historicity of,
241, 258; invention of, 1, 212, 221–25;
and *neijale*, 225, 237; and *nshesho*,
250; songs, 209, 227, 229–32
Mannoni, Octave, 41
MANU. *See* Mozambique African National Union
Mapate, 209, 213, 215, 220, 256; in
song, 218

Nshemo Nampyopyo Nkondya, 88, 275n23

*nshesho* (genre): competition, 68; dance styles, 175–77; during colonialism, 71, 91–94, 238; during the liberation struggle, 153, 160; at Festivals, 250, 252, 254; historicity of, 122, 257; after Independence, 163–65, 180, 183, 210–11; invention of, 64–65, 271n27; and *lingundumbwe*, 188, 196–98; and *mang'anyamu*, 225–27, 232, 250; and Nampyopyo, 79; as national symbol, 178; and *naupanga*, 235; and *neijale*, 213, 216–17; parody of, 183–84; songs, 1, 19, 36, 79, 124, 139, 140–41, 145, 161, 170–74, 202, 256; taught to the Makua, 113

*nshindo* (genre): aesthetics of, 110–12, 114; costuming of, 113; encounter with, 44–45; fieldwork on, 107; fortune of, 106, 108, 204, 213, 290n2; historicity of, 120–21, 232–33, 257–58; invention of, 102–3; and *mashalagwesha*, 219; and *naupanga*, 233–36; and *neijale*, 214–15; and *shuku nwele*, 249–50; and sorcery, 117–19, 277n28; songs, 98, 104–5, 107–9, 114, 117, 119–20, 183, 235

*ntene. See* wild kapok

*ntoji* (drum), 62, 69, 213, 219, 224, 236

Ntonya, Filoména, 186, 192, 195, 285n5

*nyau* masquerading, 27, 48–49, 60, 268n17

Nyerere, Julius, 30, 189

obscurity in song, 15, 110, 124, 158, 194, 232

O'Neill, Henry, 20

oral history, 12–14, 17, 106, 257, 276n51

ordeal, 27, 36–39, 268n11

Organização da Juventude Moçambicana (OJM), 217

Organização da Mulher Moçambicana (OMM), 203

organizing the masks: idiom, 4, 58, 101, 193

orphanhood, metaphor of, 198–99, 255

ownership: of mask ensembles, 55, 58, 94, 104, 226–27; vernacular concept, 84, 151

Pachinuapa, Raimundo, 184

parataxis, 14–15, 263

patronage: of Makonde carving, 88–89, 93; of mask ensembles, 84, 103, 227, 237, 254

peasantry, 9–11, 31, 145, 150, 164, 176, 200

peasant society, 110, 112, 175, 213, 240, 245

pelvis cloth, 66, 222, 235

pelvis-shaking, 74–75, 101, 195, 215, 236

Pemba, 13, 79, 163, 165, 178–79, 251–53; in song, 138

Pende masks, 5–6, 271n21, 290n3

perambulation of masks, 69, 219, 224

performance: interpretive importance of, 59–60, 66, 95, 106; language of, 4; of *mapiko*, 4, 15, 25, 27–28, 44, 56, 58, 62, 65, 68, 72–73, 75, 80, 82–85, 103, 115, 119–20, 122–23, 130, 143, 176–77, 183–84, 186, 193–97, 204, 210–11, 213, 219, 220, 225–26, 228, 231, 233, 236–37, 240, 243, 246, 250–51, 257, 277n13; ritual, 17, 23, 41, 43, 77; study of, 5, 7, 10, 12–14, 42, 53, 261n34

people: signifier, 150–51, 165. *See also* "we, the People"

people's war, 143, 145–46

photography: as metaphor, 85; use of in fieldwork, 93, 106, 209

Picasso, Pablo, 58

pilot centers, Frelimo, 156–57, 229, 282

Pinho, Rui, 175, 284n30

play: Makonde vernacular concept, 4, 86, 90, 130, 225, 240–41; of scales, 14–15, 262n46; theory of, 7

playfulness of *mapiko*, 15, 24, 27, 29, 46, 64, 76, 80, 82, 85, 102, 105, 113–14, 130, 174, 176, 194, 216–17, 242, 250, 252, 256

political subjectivity. *See* subjectivity

polyrhythm, 15, 141

popular culture, 5–6

pornography, 242

possession. *See* spirit possession

postsocialism, 8, 10, 207, 243, 245, 247

praise: political, in song, 165, 170, 188, 216, 229, 254; self-praise, 173, 244, 279n20

primitivism, 4–6, 8, 17, 21, 27–29, 52–53, 58, 140, 266n50, 286n19

prostitute (mask-character), 1, 83, 108

provocation: gendered, 149, 159, 196; in initiation rituals, 43; of joking relationships, 7, 50; *mapiko* of, 95; against other lineages, 66, 128; songs of, 68, 71, 76, 91, 127, 133, 143, 162, 172–73, 198, 224, 228; youth, 70, 125

proximity, risk of, 106

puberty rituals, Iatmul, 42

puberty rituals, Makonde: after Independence, 162, 230; coming out of, 36, 276n3; description of, 36–39; in the Diases' work, 22, 25, 27; during the struggle, 148–49, 157, 189–90, 192; and elections, 203; emotions related to, 46; and ethnicity, 50–51; initiation hut, 37; interpretation of, 7, 39, 46–47; launching of, 36; major, 80; and *mapiko*, 93, 100, 132, 179, 197–98, 210; masters of, 32, 75; and missionaries, 71, 272n42; organization of, 58, 84, 219, 262n43; secrets of, 37–38, 43, 125, 285n6; in song, 149, 224; songs, 122; sources on, 167n1. See also *nkamangu*

puberty rituals, Makua, 50, 60

purity, 27, 88, 98–99, 117

Radio Moçambique (RM): archives, 163; creation of, 176; and dances, 176–78, 198, 202, 219, 225, 232; recording for, 13, 137; in song, 246

rage: against the political enemy, 144, 204; in songs, 141, 200; against women, 46, 230

Ranger, Terrence, 5–6

rattles: foot-, 113, 220, 240; hand-, 146, 154, 188, 213, 216–7; in song, 126, 196. See also *dinjuga*

realism: grotesque, 2, 29, 110, 112, 174, 184, 193, 212–14, 220, 275n26; in masking, 1, 52–53, 242; socialist, 1, 32, 163, 165, 175–76, 188, 199, 214, 232. See also naturalism

reconciliation, discourse of, 202

regeneration, utopian, 31–32, 35, 145, 150, 159

rehearsal, 78, 123, 136, 186, 194, 210, 225, 235, 240, 251, 289

Renamo (Resistencia Nacional Moçambicana): in Cabo Delgado, 202, 209; in the Makonde plateau, 201, 203, 207, 287n40, 287n43; in the Messalo lowlands, 100, 220, 249; in song, 202–3, 230, 244; support for, 9; surrendering to, 226

respect: vernacular concept, 4, 40–42, 45, 73, 76, 84, 86, 169, 185

resurrection: of dead sorcerers, 115; of *dutu*, 180; of the *mileya* genre, 59–60, 91, 93, 96; of mimetic styles, 176; of Nampyopyo's masks, 238; of *nshindo*, 249, 290n2; vernacular concept, 8, 78, 257–58

Revel, Jacques, 14

Ricoeur, Paul, 262n48

riddles in masking, 119

ritual. See funerary ceremonies; puberty rituals; rivalry

rivalry: as engine of creativity, 2, 6–8, 257; between lineages, 24–25, 66, 69; between *mapiko* groups, 55, 76, 84, 91, 123, 169, 171–73, 180, 182, 198, 200; between Nampyopyo and Shumu, 1, 56, 95–96; between Rashidi and Juakali, 132–36; resistance of, 11, 143, 176, 246; in Swahili culture, 6–8, 76–77; between women and men, 43–44

Rouch, Jean, 33

Rovuma River: language from, 220; masks from, 60; region, 19–20, 48, 50, 98–99, 148, 186, 270n41, 280n11; war across, 148

Rovuma to Maputo: journey, 162, 164, 186; trope, 158, 171, 176

rhythm: Congolese, 104, 148; of *mapiko*, 15, 23, 26, 45, 62, 114, 127, 163; rhythmic poetry, 75, 139, 173; sequences of, 12, 74, 92, 107. See also drumming

rubber, masks made of, 238, 240–41, 251

rumor. See sorcery

Salazar, António de Oliveira, 21

salt, mask carrying, 103–4, 120

Santimano, Sérgio, 209–10, 212

Savimbi, Jonas, 244

scarification, 20, 37, 50, 69, 229; on carvings, 87; drawn on masks, 44, 59, 61, 96, 275n26; and Islam, 49

schismogenesis: and the analysis of *mapiko*, 8, 10; in Bateson's thought, 7, 42–43, 53, 272n36; complementary, 72, 78, 90, 149, 197–98, 241; and Frelimo, 143, 159, 169, 171; and puberty rituals, 46–47, 69; and slavery, 51, 65–66; symmetrical, 53, 66, 70–71, 122, 128, 197

Schwarzenegger, Arnold, 242

Scott, James, 167

scoundrels, 160, 202, 216, 219; in song, 155, 165, 228. See also enemy: of the people

scrooge (mask-character), 107

sculpture. See carving

Second Festival of Popular Dance, 11, 106, 226–28, 232, 243, 250–53, 256

secrecy: during the struggle, 157; interpretation of, 33, 35; of *mapiko*, 4, 22–23, 38, 86, 90, 94, 113, 193, 196–98, 219, 240, 251; as obscurantism, 33, 143, 167, 169, 190; as play, 7, 185; of puberty rituals, 37–48, 52, 58, 71–73, 122, 125, 188, 195; public, 39, 73; in song, 36;

sublation, 41
supplication. *See* ancestral supplication
surrealism in masking, 95–96, 104, 106
Swahili: dance culture, 7–8, 74, 77, 124, 260n22; spirit possession, 89, 286n22. *See also* Kiswahili
sympathetic magic, 26, 29, 34, 53
synchrony in dance, 64, 74, 75, 225
syncretism, 5, 72, 241

talent, 58, 65–66, 73, 76, 79, 84–86, 91, 94, 96, 119, 129, 162, 183, 185, 222, 238, 257; lack of, 66, 68, 70, 73
Tanga, 57, 130
Tanganyika, 28, 30, 74, 77, 130, 136, 140, 273n53
Tanzania: communal villages, 148, 243; and Frelimo, 30, 138, 146, 148, 179, 189; masks from, 60, 210, 212; music from, 225; travel to, 221–22, 232, 238; wildlife, 241
Taussig, Michael, 39, 41, 52–53
teleology, 5, 34–35, 156
theatricality: in *mapiko*, 17, 27, 29, 104, 115, 139, 203; and Marxist interpretation, 33–34
theft. *See* stealing
tooth-chipping, 37, 49, 151
tragedy, lack of, 204
traitors, 155, 165, 216. *See also* enemy: of the people; scoundrels
traveling: as excuse for dancing *mapiko*, 73; with masks, 95–96; songs on, 83, 130–31
Trentini, Daria, 277n24
tropes in political singing, 158, 282n44
*tuvenentete. See* "we, the People"

*udagwa. See* talent: lack of
*ulanda. See* talent
unity: flambeau of, 175; parody of, 184; principle of, 1, 158–59, 162, 165, 172, 238; in song, 171
universalism, 76, 78
unmasking, 39, 41–42
*utamaduni* (genre): invention of, 197–200; and *lingundumbwe*, 195; in the RM archives, 283n10; at the Second Festival, 251; songs, 199–200, 202

Valéry, Paul, 28, 265n33
Vanomba, Faustino, 136–37, 279n21

vernacularization, 50, 76, 78, 130, 192, 224
Viegas Guerreiro, Manuel, 21
Vintani, Jerónimo, 192
*vinyago*, 76, 273n59
violence: colonial, 65, 137, 175; political, 204; postsocialist, 207, 245, 251, 258; scapegoating, 118, 244; spousal, 172, 196
violin bow, 123
visibility, in communal villages, 167, 182

war material, carrying of, 158, 189, 203
war veterans, 172, 179, 213, 225, 238, 253, 282n45; as mask-character, 183–84, 250; in song, 161, 177–78, 200–201, 227, 288n30
watchwords in songs, 1, 154, 156, 158–59, 164, 168, 171
"we, the People," 11, 143, 149, 158–59, 170–71; in song, 149, 155, 170, 181
wearers: in *mapiko* costuming, 66, 113; in song, 185, 196; used by women, 186, 195–6
West, Harry, 34, 261n29, 277n28, 278n31, 279n23
Weule, Karl, 60
wild kapok (*Bombax rhodognaphalon*), 2, 259
winnowing (dance style), 76, 175
witchcraft. *See* sorcery
worry wrinkles, 212

Xiconhoca, 165, 202, 219
xylophones, 123, 141, 215, 218, 279n29

Yao: ethnogenesis, 48–49; masks, 51, 60, 220
Yoshida, Kenji, 268n17
youth, 1, 80, 86, 143, 160, 207, 217, 238, 254; in communal villages, 220–21, 224–46, 230, 242, 245, 248–51; defiance of, 68–70, 237; in song, 133, 182, 185, 217, 247; talent of, 66, 219. *See also* *nshesho*

*xigubo* (dance), 31

Zimbabwe: independence of, 181; patriotic history, 253; struggle songs from, 152
zither, 123, 148–49, 154, 195, 219, 280nn9–10